BY JONATHAN DANIELS

Ordeal of Ambition

Ordeal of Ambition

JEFFERSON, HAMILTON, BURR

by Jonathan Daniels

DOUBLEDAY & COMPANY, INC.
Garden City, New York
1970

LIBRARY OF CONGRESS CATALOG CARD NUMBER 79–111155
COPYRIGHT © 1970 BY JONATHAN DANIELS
ALL RIGHTS RESERVED
PRINTED IN THE UNITED STATES OF AMERICA

To Lucy for patience, labor, love

Contents

I.
THE LAST WORD

Confiding in his dark, adoring daughter Theodosia, as he often did in flippant fashion, Aaron Burr wrote her a gay letter in June 1803. Vice-President of the United States, he was also then a widower still slim and handsome. Whimsically he described to Theo his uncertain courtship of a young Philadelphia lady named Celeste. Nothing came of the affair. Apparently the beauty was too coy to begin and too eager at the last. Only the name Celeste survives in history like a lingering perfume. But in Burr's letters about this romantic interlude, which he made tantalizing, charming, and amusing, he was instructive, too. Theo was not only his beloved child, as he was to the end her hero father. Also she was the glamorous proof of Burr's purpose from her childhood to show that behind her wide, very feminine eyes could be the intellect then expected only of a man.

There are, he told her, two ways of telling a story.

"One by beginning with the oldest event, and so traveling down to the close of the tale, and this is the mode commonly used by philosophers and historians. The other is by commencing with the most recent fact . . . which is the mode universally practiced by lovers, and, generally by poets. I could even quote Homer and Virgil as authorities in support of this latter method. Further, I may add, that this retroprogressive arrangement seems more congenial with the temper and feelings of the fair sex. Thus, you see, most ladies turn first to the last chapter of a novel or romance."

That inclination has not been restricted to ladies or to poets and lovers. Politicians like to look back from their last chapters with romantic attention to their earlier ones. Philosophers and historians, in dealing with Burr's own case, have generally preferred the "retroprogressive arrangement" which he ascribed to lovers and poets. That is an arrangement which can serve not only love and poetry but enduring enmity too. Wicked as Burr may have been, his story seems generally to have been told, not forward with the calendar, but backward from much late-shaped malign mythology. Some of it Burr could have dispelled but for his polished disdain for detractors. Much of it was made by the furtive agents of greater men who themselves were often victims in an age of slander. But some of the malevolent mischief directed at Burr was at least prepared with the connivance of such masters in the shaping of history as two men who hated each other and were also Burr's enemies: Alexander Hamilton and Thomas Jefferson.

Burr in his lifetime was convicted of no high crime or misdemeanor. Indeed, he was acquitted in every court and condemned only by a Presidential hue and cry. He confessed to nothing except peccadilloes in gallantry and desperate maneuvers in a pitiful exile. Too many of Burr's letters were destroyed or distributed for their souvenir value by his friend in life and literary executor, Matthew L. Davis. Burr left few documents in explanation of his life. Indeed, Allan McLane Hamilton, the grandson of his first enemy, said that "so far as is known Burr never openly wrote anything, and there are no literary remains except his diary, which is a curious and eccentric production. . . ." And that was only a journal of a proscribed and impecunious man in Europe. That is not quite true. His letters to his two Theodosias did not often solemnly report great events but they vividly portrayed a witty, headlong, and courageous man.

Alexander Hamilton wrote too much in confidential condemnation of enemies—in impulsive defense of himself and in attack on others. He produced great papers which mightily helped in the establishment of the nation. Also, to the delight of his enemies, he published a confession of tawdry private immorality to protect his reputation as a public servant. Mr. Jefferson left behind more documents, papers, letters, explanations than either of the other two. But only once, and in confidential correspondence, did he slightly crack the door on any possible moral lapses.

He undertook to combine the two ways of telling a story which Burr described to Theodosia. Writing forward with the calendar and backward in revision, he told in such fashion much of Burr's and Hamilton's stories as well as his own. The man, who in youth wrote the Declaration of Independence, in old age prepared a collection of his papers which he labeled his *Anas*. Shaped, as he said, for his future vindication, it was obviously intended for posthumous publication. Any ordinary person would have called it a diary, even though doctored in "retroprogressive arrangement." The dictionary defines "anas" as a collection of the memorable sayings of a person or of items of information relative to a subject of curious interest. Jefferson's *Anas* put his observations and opinions together, the first always colored by the last. He commenced making his record, he wrote, as a member of the Cabinet of George Washington. In it he questioned the first President's faith in republican government. He described Washington's sometimes violent temper. He considered his colleagues: Hamilton as a "monarchist and corruptionist"; Secretary of War Knox as a fat "blabber"; and his fellow Virginian and once disciple, Edmund Randolph, as a trimmer who gave "his principles to one party and his practice to the other, the oyster to one, the shell to the other. Unfortunately the shell was generally the lot of his friends, the French and republicans, the oyster of their antagonists." So, Jefferson said, he made his notes and began to collect his papers as he stood almost alone against "a system of corruption which defrauded the poor, debased the rich, & changed the morals of a nation."

In strange secretiveness, which he himself described, he began a quarter of a century or more later to put the papers into some order in three volumes bound in marbled paper. He employed for the task, he wrote, "a binder who came into my cabinet, did it under my own eye, and without the opportunity of seeing a single paper." Evidently in his old age Mr. Jefferson, who had seen much of spies in his lifetime and had employed some, would not even trust a craftsman with regard to these papers.

In the *Anas*, the great Virginian both disparaged the collection and stressed its supposed objectivity. He recalled that as Secretary of State he "began to make memorandums on loose scraps of paper, taken out of my pocket in the moment, and laid by to be copied fair at leisure, which, however, they hardly ever were. These scraps, therefore, ragged, rubbed and scribbled as they were, I had bound. . . ."

But: "At this day, after the lapse of twenty-five years, or more, I have given to the whole a calm revisal, when the passions of the time are passed away, and the reasons of the transactions act alone on the judgment. Some of the informations I had recorded, are now cut out from the rest, because I have seen that they are incorrect, or doubtful, or merely personal or private, with which we have nothing to do."

The retired statesman at Monticello was at least seventy-two when he began this "calm revisal." At that time he told a correspondent that writing was becoming laborious and irksome to him. Five years before he had written of his memory as "a faculty never strong in me, and now too impaired to be relied on." Still, as he indicated in his revisal, he picked and chose among the items. Evidently he did some rewriting. He made some marginal notes, in one of which he spoke of Hamilton as dead though at the time of the incident that brilliant man was to the Virginian offensively alive. Moreover, in the volumes he left much evident gossip, a good deal of it from his too-much-forgotten aide, defender and informer, John Beckley. Of one such report he wrote, "Beckley is a man of perfect truth as to what he affirms of his own knowledge, but too credulous as to what he hears from others."

In his own time many thought Jefferson gullible as to what he heard and noted. In his *Anas* he indicated an expectation that history might be credulous too. He was not much mistaken. Many writers have taken the *Anas* as a record of fact, not as a recital for vindication. Even some of his most laudatory biographers, however, have found in it alibis shaped after the events. When it was first published, it was greeted with astonishment and indignation by still living witnesses of the history he reported. Indeed, his early eulogistic biographer, Henry Stephens Randall, to whom the Jefferson papers, since scattered, were made available, felt it necessary to write a score of pages in defense of Jefferson's baleful bequest of the *Anas* to history.

It brought upon him, Randall wrote, "more bitter animadversion than any, than all, the other acts of his life put together." It had, the biographer said, "in thousands of bosoms converted what would have been mere partisan prejudice, into personal and vindictive hate." Finally, he reported, "The public have been eloquently told of hate and bitterness surviving the tomb—of profanations of the sanctuary of the grave, to 'shoot' from it 'poisoned arrows' at the dead and the living."

Randall seemed overwrought in this passage as he sometimes did in others. Partisanship has grown less sharp, at least about the long dead, since Randall wrote. Few will feel today that Jefferson, in his cabinet with the blinded binder, committed the crime of his career. Self-vindication which may require the vilification of others has become an autobiographical commonplace.

It is difficult, nevertheless, to understand Jefferson's feeling that his greatness needed this final footnote on his rectitude. Behind him was a career of such accomplishment in such a variety of fields as to justify the view that he is the intellectual giant of all the Presidents of the United States. His pedestal, already shaped beneath him then, could never be shaken. Indeed, he possessed at the end of his life such a vast treasure of accomplishments that he could dispense even with his Presidency in the listing on his monument of the things for which he wished to be remembered. He did not care to mention on his stone the continental expansion of the United States which was accomplished under his administration. By his direction engraved above him were only the facts of his authorship of the Declaration of Independence, the Statute of Virginia for religious freedom, and of his place as founder and father of the University of Virginia. He could spare in a sort of marble modesty enough evidence of eminence to make another giant.

Yet the old man working covertly with his papers was not satisfied to leave for the shaping of recollection only an abbreviated inscription on a stone. Whatever the faults in his memory, he had not forgotten the great hostilities of his life. In the preparation of his *Anas*, he felt it necessary to do more than explain and justify himself. He kept to the last the will to damn the two men to whom he gave a sort of black accolade of his aversion, the two somehow both opposite and identical gentlemen from New York—Alexander Hamilton and Aaron Burr. Also, oddly, the *Anas* seemed a sort of confession of concern for his own role. He seemed uneasy at the last that he might seem less the political saint than the kind of prince who, sometimes with more skill than scrupulousness, had seized and exercised the kind of power required to make the nation for which the Constitution only provided the frame. Some villains or victims had been required in that process. He left as a sort of testament his last words about them.

Of course, as Aaron Burr told Theodosia, there are more ways than one of telling a story. In a triangle of enmity there generally are three tales about it. And seldom has there been such a triangle of hostility in history as that involving Hamilton, Burr, and Jefferson. When Jefferson prepared his *Anas*, Hamilton was dead as a result of privately saying such things, while living, as Jefferson waited to say publicly from his grave.

No such things needed to be said then of Burr to accomplish the disgrace proposed for him in life and prepared for him in death. Certainly Burr had been an ambitious man, a bold gambler for wealth and fame. But possibly he chiefly sinned by getting in the way of a plutocrat and a philosopher. The three come down in the American story almost as cliché figures of the slightly soiled martyr, the luminous traitor, and the patrician sage of democracy. Jefferson, in the story of their enmity, may best have assured his role as the good, wise man because he spoke the last word in the tragedy of all three.

II.
THE ADVERSARIES

1.

The Golden Chain

For tall Jefferson his appointment in 1784 as Minister in Paris provided escape from bitter memories and personal tragedy. He was then and ever after aware that he had made an awkward exit from the abrasive politics of Virginia. In 1781 as Governor, he had so acted as to be long charged with ineptitude and cowardice in the face of a British invasion which put him to flight and overran the state. Then, though proposed investigation of his behavior was dropped, he felt, as he wrote his young friend and neighbor James Monroe, that he had "stood arraigned for treason of the heart and not merely the weakness of the head." Of political ambition, he declared, "every fibre of that passion was thoroughly eliminated." He wanted no office. In the pursuit of happiness he only wished for the life of a happily married, scholarly Virginia gentleman surrounded by his books, his lands, and his slaves, counting the change of seasons by bird cries and the blossoming and fading of plants. Such serenity did not last long.

His wife, Martha (Wayles) Skelton, who had borne him six children in ten years, languished and died at thirty-three in 1782. Little is known about their lives together. They read, as everyone else was reading, the works of Laurence Sterne, though they apparently paid more attention to his pathetic than his lively passages. From memories, romantic portraiture has been made of them as a couple happy in a beautiful house on a lofty hill where he, with the violin, and she, with the pianoforte, made gay music together. Their Monticello, said a perceptive historian, was a "château high above contact with man."

When she died in the house with its narrow, twisting staircases, her body had to be lowered from a window. In grief Jefferson rode heedlessly day after day over the hills. Yet, as a man who saved masses of papers in his lifetime, he destroyed all correspondence between himself and Martha and most other memorabilia about her. She was a "pretty lady" servants said. Little more is known. She remains only a wraith in history, a vague spirit in the complicated halls of Monticello. In love and hatred Jefferson generally hid his heart, though head and heart were often in juxtaposition in his mind and mouth.

In Paris he found release from both political bitterness and personal grief. The city was a sedative for unhappy memories. He was welcomed there as the Apostle of Liberty who had written the Declaration of Independence not only for America but for a restive world. As sandy-haired widower, for him the days extended one after another like a golden chain. He had had his share of the heat and the storm. The summer of stress was behind him. His life seemed to have come to that season which at home across the sea was called Indian summer. The ardent and the philosophical gathered at his table in his capacious Hotel de Langeac at the *grille de* Champs Élysées. It had been built for one of the mistresses of Louis XV by the same architect who designed the Arc de Triomphe. Still alterations had to be made to meet Jefferson's requirements.

In this great house he not only talked and listened with such an old Revolutionary friend as the Marquis de Lafayette who sometimes now seemed too radical to Jefferson. Others spoke much there of liberty, an enthusiastic subject which Jefferson only modified by writing in these years that to free those reared in the habits of slavery might be like abandoning children.

Yet, as the 1780s advanced, few of his guests quite realized that in France this was the autumn of the *ancien régime*. Certainly the restiveness of the people and the philosophers did not trouble Mr. Jefferson. Sometimes America in its new liberty seemed more explosive than France. In Massachusetts, where the liberty tree had first blossomed, poor farmers and others had risen in anger under a man named Daniel Shays. Shays's Revolutionary service had been such that Lafayette had presented him with a handsome sword. Now so poor that he had to sell the sword, he had taken up other arms to halt the dispossession of farmers by hard creditors in the courts. The well-to-do were appalled. Jefferson's friend and wife of his old companion in independence, John Adams, wrote him in such outrage that she was careless of her spelling and the legibility of her lines.

Abigail Adams told Jefferson, "Ignorant, wrestless desperadoes, without conscience or principals [sic] have led a deluded multitude to follow their standard, under pretense of grievances which have no existence but in their imaginations." Jefferson was not so disturbed. It was then that he wrote lines long remembered. To James Madison he commented that "a little rebellion now and then is a good thing." And to Abigail's son-in-law, William Stephens Smith, he made the dramatic declaration that "the tree of liberty must be refreshed from time to time with the blood of patriots and tyrants. It is its natural manure."

Paris seemed pleasant, in 1786, in comparison with the overwrought reports from Massachusetts. In France the poor muttered and sometimes dared to spit after carriages which rolled by them choking them with dust or spattering them with mire. Yet, the Bastille still stood. Ladies and gentlemen at Versailles played as shepherds and shepherdesses in plush pastoral pretense. Even some among them thought of America as an Arcadia for all—some on the basis of Mr. Jefferson's very interesting conversations and his much admired *Notes on Virginia*. He deplored the extravagances of the court and the condition of the multiplying poor already pouring to America in a stream none thought could be interrupted. He insisted to such a visiting American as the beautiful, young Mrs. William Bingham, whose elaborate entertainments were to make her America's most famous hostess, that the simple domestic pleasures of America were much preferable to the superficial society of Europe.

He did not find that society entirely superficial. He searched the bookstalls. He visited the studios of artists. As architect by avocation, he admired the monuments of antiquity. With explorers he discussed the vast American West with which he was early concerned but was never to see —or to see only at a distance in credulity and confusion and at the last in public outrage and private dismay. He enjoyed the gay, gifted, or merely decorative international set which gathered in his mansion. The music of lute and pianoforte, of song sounded in his household over his choice wines. He dressed in fashion. He powdered his hair. A maître d'hôtel managed his establishment. The epicurean dishes he began to serve then later led Patrick Henry to cry that he had abjured his native victuals. Also, they caused another American to say that he wished his French politics was as good as his French food. As epicurean democrat, he presided over a kind of court of his own which he called his "charming coterie."

Two young men who helped gather this company indicated its complexity. To it William Short, Jefferson's secretary and almost adopted son, brought visitors from lofty Parisian society with a member of which he was already hopelessly in love. Doomed to disappointment in diplomacy as well as love, Short was to remain Jefferson's friend, ready to lend him money to the last. In addition, artistic persons were brought by the Minister's protégé and houseguest John Trumbull. Trumbull, who was to become one of Jefferson's bitterest critics, was then also receiving patronage and easy loans from John Barker Church, rich, rough, and not too scrupulous English businessman. Church had married pretty, flighty, flirty Angelica Schuyler, sister-in-law of Jefferson's New York acquaintance Alexander Hamilton, already being heard about as a luminary rising on the American scene. Angelica herself was often in the "coterie." And to it, in 1786, was added Maria Louisa Catherine Cecelia Hatfield Cosway.

An artist of many gifts, this glamorous Maria had been born in Italy of English parents who kept a boardinghouse for tourists. Left an orphan, but a very pretty one, she had gone to England where she married Richard Cosway, a highly successful miniaturist years older than herself. In 1786 the Cosways came to Paris where he was commissioned by the Duke of Orleans to do miniatures of his lady and children. The Duke afterwards was to lose his head on the guillotine. Now Jefferson all but lost his head over Maria. In addition to her painting, Maria composed music. She played the harp and the pianoforte. She sang. In a self-portrait she is shown with a mass of golden curls, wide blue eyes, slightly pouting, very kissable mouth. She was definitely the sort of blonde gentlemen were said later to prefer.

Certainly Jefferson had a precipitate preference for her. Immediately after he met her, as he himself wrote, he lied out of other important engagements to be much with her. The forty-three-year-old Minister flamed in infatuation for the twenty-seven-year-old married Maria. In this golden September, Jefferson, as he afterwards put it himself, was caught in a difficult but delicious struggle between the Head and the Heart. This time he described the conflict of these symbolic items of anatomy in an amazing dialogue which he wrote and sent to Maria. There were many reasons why the head should triumph. Not only was Maria married and

Jefferson middle-aged, but also, at the time of this interlude of excitement, he had received a gloomy report from the manager of his plantations at home. From his palatial Hotel de Langeac he wrote, "I am miserable till I owe not a shilling: the moment that shall be the case I shall feel myself at liberty to do something for the comfort of my slaves."

Still his Head won over his Heart only after an accident. Exhibiting his exuberance by attempting to jump over a large decorative kettle in his courtyard, he fell and broke his wrist. Then Maria was gone, never to be forgotten. And not long after her departure and after Shays's ragged rebellion in America had been put down by troops financed by Boston merchants, he suffered a sort of second fracture. This time it was in his judgment, not his wrist. It came from his enthusiastic introduction to America of two other coterie companions of this dazzling autumnal interlude. They were the Count de Moustier and his sister-in-law, the Marchioness de Bréhan.

Count de Moustier was well known in the social and diplomatic circles of Europe. A half a dozen years before, young Edmond Charles Genet, whose antics in America were both to hurt and help Jefferson later, made a note of seeing the Count, then the French Minister at Cologne. The diplomat was in a box at the theater "screened because he is afraid to show his wife who is ugly and crazy." Next day the Count had solemnly warned young Genet of a danger of youth—that the lady he had accompanied to the theater had a very bad reputation.

Now from Paris, Jefferson gave the Count and his definitely not ugly sister-in-law the very best reputation as they prepared to sail together for America where the Count had been assigned as French Minister. He wrote to John Jay, then handling the foreign affairs of the confederated states, that the Count should give "the most perfect satisfaction to America." In letters to his friend and Virginia neighbor James Madison, already becoming one of the first founding fathers, he described the Count as "a great enemy to formality, etiquette, ostentation and luxury." Jefferson regarded himself and the Count, as he told that personage, in their two diplomatic positions as "the two end links" in the chain of Franco-American friendship. Still, as the American link and as head-ruled diplomat, he informed Madison that de Moustier was "remarkably communicative."

"With adroitness he may be pumped of anything," he wrote.

But of the Marchioness, an artist like Maria, he had no reservations:

"She is goodness itself. . . . The way to please her is to receive her as an acquaintance of a thousand years standing. She speaks little English. You must teach her more and learn French from her. She hopes by accompanying Monsieur de Moustier, to improve her health, which is very feeble, and still more, to improve her son in his education, and to remove him a distance from the seductions of this country. . . . The husband of Madame de Bréhan is an officer, and obliged by the times to remain with the army." Trumbull wrote that she was separated from her husband because of his brutality.

Whatever may have been the lady's situation, Jefferson's farewell to the Marchioness, to whom he had given ideas of an Arcadian America, was in such language as he might have addressed Maria: "Heaven bless you, madame, and guard you under all circumstances; give you smoothe waters, gentle breezes and clear skies, hushing all its elements into peace, and leading with its own hand the favored bark, till it shall have safely landed its precious charges on the shores of our new world."

Across the wide sea Jefferson's French friends received the attentions he requested for them. Soon the Count and the Marchioness held an "exalted opinion" of the small, prim Madison, later described as a man looking like a schoolmaster dressed for a funeral. Cyrus Griffin wrote to his Congressional colleague at his Virginia plantation, Montpelier, of the French couple's constant inquiries about him. Griffin, who was seeing much of the Minister and his lady, was then the president of the Continental Congress. Despite high positions he held, Griffin has seemed an obscure man in the society and the history of his times. He has been passed almost unnoticed as one who later helped preside over two great trials about which Jefferson and Madison were to be much concerned: those of the journalist James Thomson Callender under the Alien and Sedition Laws; and of Aaron Burr for treason. Now evidently, however, Griffin was enjoying the international company clustering about the capital of the Confederation. He described the Marchioness as a sweet companion. He reported her curiosity about the American Indians. Her health was much improved. She was walking five miles a day. Also he passed on to Madison, who was eager to please Jefferson's friend, a request she made.

"The lady has procured a Negro girl," he told Madison, "and only wants a boy in order that they may breed to use her language."

Evidently Griffin was a little startled by the lady's language. Madison was ready to oblige. When he returned from Montpelier to Congress, he wrote home to his father:

"Tell my brother Ambrose if you please that he must draw on Mr. Shepherd for the price of the Negro boy for the Marchioness."

If the lady's interest in genetics did not seem eccentric at the time, other aspects of the de Moustier ménage did. The Count, who was listed in the press as Ambassador of His Most Christian Majesty, was described at one dinner party as a gentleman wearing "red-heeled shoes and earrings." At others, guests were appalled when he declined the delicacies provided and had his own cook bring in his food. Furthermore, gossip mounted that the Minister and his sister-in-law "neglect the most obvious precautions for veiling their intimacy." At his serene post in Paris, late in 1788, Jefferson received an outburst in cipher from an evidently disillusioned Madison. In his pleasant Hotel de Langeac the Minister read the conclusions of his Virginia friend about his French ones.

"He is unsocial, proud and niggardly and betrays a sort of fastidiousness toward this country. He suffers also from his illicit connection with Madame de Bréhan which is universally known and offensive to American manners. She is perfectly soured toward this country. The ladies of New York (a few within the official circle excepted) have for some time withdrawn their attentions from her. She knows the cause, is deeply stung by it, views everything through the medium of rancor and conveys her impressions to her paramour over whom she exercises despotic sway."

Finally and officially the couple's enthusiastic sponsor in Paris received word about the embarrassing situation from Jay as chief of American foreign affairs. Possibly Jay was prodded by his own notoriously domineering wife. In November 1788 he wrote Jefferson that "appearances (whether well or ill founded is not important) have created and diffused an opinion that an improper Connection subsists between [Moustier] and the Marchioness. You can easily conceive the Influence of such an opinion on the minds and feelings of such a People as ours— For my part I regret it—she seems to be an amiable woman."

Evidently it was time for another triumph of Mr. Jefferson's head over his heart, his self-saving sagacity over his impulsive credulousness. As a diplomat he necessarily moved deviously. Nobody was ready to make formal charges of immorality against the Count and his lady. There was no vacant post to which he could be satisfactorily transferred. Jefferson avoided dealing with the French Foreign Ministry. He got his friend

Lafayette, now ascending to power in restless France, to intervene in the matter. It was arranged to give Moustier a leave of absence which could extend into absence altogether.

At this time Jefferson was preparing for a leave of absence for himself which he definitely did not mean to be permanent. And while he made his arrangements in February 1789, he wrote to Jay of the "politically and morally offensive conduct" of the Count. Yet a month later he was writing in warmth to the Marchioness. As a man almost womanly sensitive to the cold, he told her of the terrible winter in Paris with the Seine frozen and the poor warming themselves only by fires in the streets. He hoped, he said, though he knew otherwise, that he could see her the next summer in New York. Indeed, when that summer came he was writing of the then absent Count as one who had meddled in the great and growing problem of the Mississippi West where swarming American settlers were concerned about free movement of their goods down the river to the sea. Then three months later he expressed his regret to the Count that when he was "crossing over to America you were crossing back to France."

"Fortune seems to have arranged among her destinies," he told the Frenchman, "that I should never continue for any time with a person whose manners and principles had excited my warm attachment. . . . Of all this Fortune is the mistress; but she cannot change my affection, nor lessen the regrets I feel at their personal disappointment."

He did not expect then that Fortune had another destiny in store for him. His own crossing came in golden autumn weather, in 1789. Favorable winds filled the sails of his ship but they were mild enough soon to allay the seasickness he always feared. He headed to Virginia, "my country" as he always called it, on a holiday. There he planned to settle his two motherless daughters, inspect his estates and try to arrange better his troubled financial affairs. Then he proposed to go back to Paris and his charming coterie.

The "beautiful revolution" in France, which stirred his fervor for natural rights and his zeal for reformation, had begun the summer before he sailed in the attack on the Bastille. But logistics as much as liberty concerned him now. His return was no simple matter. Certainly as he sailed his equipage made him seem hardly the plain representative of liberty and equality. Though he was bringing home only part of his possessions, he had a whole shipload. The remainder, which would follow him next year, seemed at that time so monumental that a revolutionary mob insisted upon examining it as the probable property of a fleeing French aristocrat.

Still this load, which he was taking home only on a holiday, contained statues, cases of wine, boxes of books, muskets for the War Department of the new nation which had just come into being this year. Also he brought presents for President Washington, Jay, and the dying Benjamin Franklin. In addition on his way to sailing, in his incessant acquisitiveness, he purchased a Normandy shepherd bitch, big with puppies.

He needed the *Clermont,* vessel of two hundred and thirty tons, which he had engaged for his small party alone. His daughters, seventeen-year-old Martha called Patsy and eleven-year-old Mary called Polly, were with him. With them were two slaves: Sally Hemings, pretty sixteen-year-old octoroon, who had come to France with Polly as her only attendant two years before; and Sally's brother Jim, whom Jefferson had had taught the art of French cooking. So in the fairest weather, as the great Virginian's biographer Dumas Malone wrote, the diplomat and his daughters came home with "slaves, bitch and baggage." Also tenaciously held slave tradition said that, like the dog, young bright-skinned Sally was pregnant too.

The weather held in perfection to the Virginia capes. Then impenetrable mist settled down upon the *Clermont.* Without a pilot, the ship's captain made it safely to the wharf. But after the passengers disembarked, fire broke out in the vessel which came perilously close to destroying the Minister's papers and the mass of his baggage. This passage from serenity to fog and fire seemed almost symbolic of the change in plans which awaited Jefferson.

Though looking forward to return to Paris, he was happy in Virginia. All weather there seemed fair to him, beautiful even when storms capped the Albemarle hills about his Monticello. That great house with its graceful dome, thirty-five rooms, hidden stairways, and many ingenious devices for the convenience of its master, was forever home. Its fields were precious even when mortgaged and eroded. Now there he met tumultuous greeting from his slaves. When he reached his home hill two days before Christmas in 1789, his daughter reported, the black folk gave evidence that they were happy in the bondage upon which Jefferson depended though he deplored it. The day's scene became part of the Southern plantation panegyric. The Negroes insisted upon showing their delight by taking the horses from the shafts of his carriage and themselves pulling

him, as in a chariot, up the steep road to the house. To and through its
doors, the happy slaves carried him in their arms, laughing and weeping
for joy, kissing his hands and feet, the ground beneath him. He was
home.

Now Fortune proposed the separation from the persons and places
he preferred. In Virginia was Washington's invitation to join his government as Secretary of State. There was also Madison to urge its acceptance.
Jefferson himself had not been sure as to how his mind matched America's
mood. Before he left Paris he had written to a friend expressing fears that
he might have become an out-of-touch expatriate. As one reason for his
visit home, he wrote, he wished to "possess myself, by conversations with
my countrymen, of their spirits & their ideas. I know only the Americans
of 1784. They tell me this is to be much a stranger to those of 1789."

Whatever were his fears, the head triumphed over the heart again.
He accepted the appointment. He saw with approval the marriage of Patsy
to her cousin Thomas Mann Randolph. He was untroubled by such in-
breeding which resulted in some eccentricities and worse—particularly in
his aristocratic Randolph line. In his immediate family his sister Elizabeth
had wandered off to die in derangement. His brother Randolph was dull
if not retarded. Isaac, long one of the slaves at Monticello, remembered
that Randolph "was a mighty simple man; used to come out among the
black people, play the fiddle and dance half the night." His sisters were
caught in no such clowning. Mary was now married to an alcoholic.
Lucy, married to her first cousin Charles Lilburn Lewis, was already bearing sons who would turn out to be monsters in the West which Jefferson
was never to see.

With Martha married, he settled Polly with well-loved kin. She had
cousins aplenty and had gained closer kinship to many more in Martha's
marriage to young Randolph. Thomas was the eldest son in his family
which contained six girls and two other boys. Soon after her father went
north, Polly was visiting the eldest of her new sisters-in-law, Mary (or
Molly), who in the Randolph pattern had married her cousin David
Meade Randolph. This gentleman was to play an unhappy role in the
Jefferson story. In the early 1790s, however, when David was appointed
U. S. Marshal in Virginia, he and Jefferson were on very friendly terms
with David carrying packets and messages between Philadelphia and
Monticello. On his Presqu'ile plantation near Richmond, David was al-
ready gaining a reputation as one of the best farmers in the state.

Jefferson was content about his daughters. His financial affairs, however, were in disarray. From his dead wife Martha, he had inherited lands but debts too. Now he tried to arrange his affairs with Dutch bankers and English creditors. He possessed ten thousand acres and about two hundred slaves. In addition he owed money, which always seemed scarcer than lands or Negroes in Virginia. When he set out for New York, as a careful student of his finances wrote, "he must have wondered if a thoroughly realistic balance sheet would have shown him to be solvent."

Yet he was already planning for an establishment in New York which, though an inconsiderable house in comparison with his palace in Paris, he would remodel for his convenience during a few months at the cost of more than a year's rent. Moreover, in it he would feel the need for his Parisian maître d'hôtel. Some noted that the returned diplomat was "conspicuous in red waistcoat and red breeches, the fashion of Versailles." Senator William Maclay, doughty democrat from back-country Pennsylvania, wrote in his diary that he "had been long enough abroad to catch the tone of European folly." And in Philadelphia, where he stopped on his way to his new post, the rich Quakeress Deborah Logan reported that he wore "a suit of silk, ruffles and an elegant topaz ring."

He made no such patrician impression on his old friend Dr. Benjamin Rush in the Pennsylvania city. That complex and combative physician-politician-reformer, then at the height of his controversial fame, found his old colleague in the cause of American independence unchanged in his strong republican sentiments. Rush would have had no reason to express his faith in Jefferson's republicanism if he had not already been doubting that of other men. He was ready and eager to tell Jefferson about disturbing differences between the Americans of 1784 and some of those of 1789 and 1790. Indeed, a year before, Rush's favorite pupil and protégé David Ramsay, had vainly tried at the opening of the first Congress to prevent the seating of Congressman William Loughton Smith, of South Carolina, on the grounds that he was more a Tory stranger than an American citizen. If Rush and Jefferson did not mention Smith at this meeting, they would have reasons to note his actions later. But in 1790 rich, young Smith, who had sat out the Revolution abroad, was only one strutting individual among too many like him whom Jefferson reported he found in what his friends were already describing as the "court" around Washington in New York.

There Jefferson was warmly welcomed and by none more so than his

old friends John and Abigail Adams. Certainly, as he arrived, the Secretary of State gave no impression that he had begun to distrust the republican sentiments of even his long-time colleague, now Vice-President.
Two weeks later, Abigail, in a letter to her sister, wrote that Jefferson
added much to the society of the capital. One fanciful reminiscer pictured
him almost as a Parisian fashion plate at an elaborate Adams dinner party
in the great house, Richmond Hill, which they occupied then. There he
must have seemed like the center of another charming coterie.

Unfortunately for historical accuracy, this reporter placed at the same
party the Count de Moustier who with his lady had long since departed.
With greater possibility, one modern historian suggested that at such dinners Jefferson may have gossiped with the handsome, dominant Mrs. Jay
about the Moustier affair. That would seem very doubtful. Mr. Jefferson
would hardly have relished this matter in which he had so demonstrated
his credulity. He did not like to think of himself as gullible. What he reported later in his *Anas* was his "wonder and mortification" at other talk
at tables. The conversation, he said, was much about politics "and a preference of kingly over republican government was evidently the favorite
sentiment."

"An apostate I could not be," he recalled, "nor yet a hypocrite; and I
found myself for the most part, the advocate of the republican side of the
question, unless among the guests there chanced to be some member of
that party from the legislative houses."

Though historians have dated the rise of party division as coming
later, evidently Jefferson recognized party existence then. There were already "a republican side" and, as he put it, a "kingly one." Party labels
were developing. Among those who helped create the Federal union
there were differences. Some were already calling themselves republicans,
in loud insinuation that the Federalists wanted no republic but a monarchy
or at least a government in the hands of the powerful few. And Federalists
regarded the republicans as those who favored rule by the rabble.

Yet now, despite Mr. Jefferson's dinner party concern, there was
politeness and ceremony in government. Also, depending upon the point
of view, there was defense and derision of the rigid forms and resounding
titles proposed in the little nation which had cast aside royal authority
and presumably royal ways. But on the surface, at least, President Washington still had the government free from faction—a condition which he

felt to be essential. In most respects his Cabinet seemed a congenial company.

Early in the summer Jefferson only dreaded a sailing party with the President and others because of his fear of seasickness. A more ceremonial voyage to Rhode Island with the President later in the season he described as "a very pleasant sail," and this despite the fact that one of his companions was Congressman Smith who was already showing his supercilious aristocratic views.

Perhaps such company, which he too often found, and the pile of tasks, awaiting him when he came late and as "a stranger," contributed to the recurrence of the debilitating headaches he suffered. He described his life in the city as "triste enough." Also, sadly, in a letter to his daughter Martha he spoke of the "Discourses of Davila" then appearing in the *Gazette of the United States* which its editor, John Fenno, fancied as the "court" journal. In these "Discourses," Jefferson felt that his old friend, John Adams, was expressing sentiments indicating an anti-republican spirit and a preference for the British system of government.

Immediate concerns, however, occupied him. His hopes were still high as to France. He watched warily the British who were reported to have three frigates off the coast. He prepared reports on fisheries and on weights and measures. As an amateur scientist he must have taken pleasure in the last even if later his sailing companion, caustic Congressman Smith, described it as a "pedantic and plagiary compilation."

One small item of his work which must have relieved him has been much forgotten. In a fashion it marked his final personal farewell to France and his charming coterie there. As Secretary of State he drafted a letter to the beset King of France for President Washington's signature. This official message expressed the President's "entire approbation" of the conduct of the Count de Moustier while in the United States. Jefferson followed it with a letter of his own to the Count, now, with or without the company of the Marchioness de Bréhan, French Minister in Berlin. In it he echoed his chief's approval. Also he added that "as a testimony of these sentiments, we ask your acceptance of a medal and chain of gold."

Some think Jefferson in this matter acted reluctantly. Certainly in it the medal and the chain for the Count served as a cover for Jefferson's own credulity. He did not care to be exposed to wonder and mortification.

Yet, sometimes he wore a supposed credulity like a protective cloak. Indeed, in almost a cry of anguish and animosity, he pled his innocence in explanation for his part in a deal with his young, brilliant Cabinet colleague, Alexander Hamilton. This young Secretary of the Treasury was less a man of 1784 than almost *the* man of 1790. Behind Hamilton, already new men like William Smith and some older ones too were taking their places almost as gentlemen on parade. Against them, as Jefferson reported later, with special reference to himself, apparently only the guileless were on guard.

2.

Path to Glory

"The Clintons had the *power;* the Livingstons had the *numbers;* and the Schuylers had *Hamilton.*"

This often quoted sentence about the politics of New York in the early days of the republic may have oversimplified the sinuous and ruthless contentions in that state then. The statement did not overemphasize the position of the blond, brilliant newcomer who had aligned himself with the colony's old, entrenched Schuylers. Alexander Hamilton came from the West Indies looking like a ruddy young Scotsman. His deep blue eyes were sometimes steel gray but below them his mouth was kindly and appealing save when he spoke in anger or scorn. He took his place by marriage in the rich Schuyler heritage with confident grace. And he moved into the shaping of the republic with magnetism, imagination, an occasionally too quick pride, and the addition of endless energy to genius.

Yet, his story was improbable from its beginning. John Adams put the facts into crude terms when in anger later he called Hamilton "the bastard brat of a Scotch peddler." Alexander's birth was legally illegitimate because of the difficulties of divorce which could only be secured from the British Parliament far away from the West Indies. His mother, born Rachel Fawcett, of Huguenot descent, had herself been the child of a tempestuous broken marriage. And her own marriage as a much younger woman to an elderly, rich, possibly brutal Danish-Jewish planter named Levine was a failure. (Hamilton always spelled the name Lavine.)

So Rachel, unable to secure her legal freedom, made an open alliance, hardly frowned upon, with James Hamilton. He was not a peddler but the no-good son of a lordly Scottish family. Though he assumed the

moral, if not legal, obligations of marriage, this James added desertion of
Rachel to his record of irresponsibility. And though Alexander clung to
his wastrel paternity, others later, as is common in the case of prodigies,
suggested that some better man may have been his father. One tale even
supposed that he was the child of George Washington, who, as a young
man of twenty-four, was visiting in the Barbados while Rachel was there.
What Washington got there was the smallpox, not a son.

Whatever were Hamilton's origins, his brilliance was early clear. Left
an orphan at eleven by the desertion of his father and the death of his
mother, at fifteen he was in many ways the actual manager of a prosperous
counting house in St. Croix. In the same year he wrote for the chief English paper in the islands such a remarkable account of a hurricane that
relatives, friends, and neighbors all agreed he should have special educa-
tional advantages in America.

He came as no rewarded waif. Armed with letters from Dr. Hugh
Knox, his Presbyterian teacher on the island, he was headed toward
Princeton from which Knox had graduated. He was apparently already
imperious at sixteen. At the New Jersey college, from which Aaron Burr
had recently received his degree, he made such demands, for place in an
advanced class and for a promise that he might proceed at the pace of his
abilities, that he was denied admission. Less austere in its requirements,
King's College (later patriotically renamed Columbia) in New York City
accepted the young man.

Though he applied himself diligently to his studies, those were times
when more exciting things filled men's minds. The Bostonians had
dumped the tea in the harbor. Rough Sons of Liberty were elsewhere
roaring up from the waterfront, out of the shops, in from the farms. Jefferson later recorded as a note in his *Anas* the gossip that Hamilton wrote
a Tory pamphlet which men like the Sons of Liberty prevented from publication in New York. Yet some of Hamilton's distaste for the mob was
shown in his defiance of one. He helped protect the staunch Loyalist
president of King's College from a hooting crew which had come to his
residence with feathers and tar. But the clearest evidence is that he was
the author of such a powerful pamphlet in defense of the Colonial cause
that its many readers thought it must have been prepared by some such
"experienced practitioner" as Jay. Certainly, at a great liberty meeting in
the "Fields" which later became City Hall Park, he won the equal applause of both Sons of Liberty and well-to-do, more fastidious fashioners

of Independence. Early he left the campus for the camp. On March 14, 1776, aged nineteen, he was named captain of the New York Provincial Company of artillery. He spent his last remittance from the Danish islands to equip it.

He had dreamed of military glory as a boy. Now he was on the path to glory. With a good deal of early difficulty he disciplined his more ardent than orderly men. Soon he came perilously into the thick of action. He was one of a bewildered battalion in the rout of the American forces in New York in the summer of 1776. There and then he met another young man on the path to glory. In the confusion of this defeat, young Major Burr probably saved the life he later took. Insubordinately countermanding the orders of Hamilton's commander, General Henry Knox, who proposed a suicidal defense of a small fort against the British tide, Burr led the battalion to escape by back roads he knew well. Others remembered the incident longer and better than Hamilton.

Young Hamilton's literary ability rather than his prowess in arms brought him to the staff of General Washington. There in his fair hand and with his fine phrases he helped bring order to Washington's cluttered desk. His service at the desk and in the field also brought him into association with the best and bravest men in the service of the colonies—and some of the worst. But his work with the pen did not satisfy his desire for the sword. He also chaffed to the breaking point under Washington's imperious austerity. Outraged by an undeserved reprimand he bluntly resigned—and was one of the few to defy Washington and keep his regard. Indeed, in this case the young man's quick pride was matched by a patience and humility the great commander seldom showed. At the last of the war, the General gave his impulsive aide the chance to distinguish himself as fighting man again in the assaults which brought about the surrender of Cornwallis at Yorktown.

Yet, the most important event of Hamilton's war years occurred in November 1777. Then, in one of the parade and polish interludes which contrasted like a garden party with the grimness of Valley Forge, he met Elizabeth Schuyler (variously called Eliza, Betsy, or Betty). She was, of course, the daughter of General Philip Schuyler of New York. Apparently, however, Alexander was still fancy free just before Christmas in 1779, when he wrote to his friend John Laurens. This gay and gallant South Carolina aristocrat, doomed to death in an almost irrelevant skirmish later, was a man shaped for Hamilton's affections. As soldier he was brave to rashness. On a brief wartime mission to France, for which his friend Hamilton was considered, he was one of Jefferson's predecessors in Paris. Benjamin Franklin thought Laurens "brusqu'd the Ministers too much." But he had the esteem of Franklin and generals under whom he fought. Hamilton and Laurens were not always impatiently pushing war plans or storming redoubts. In the Christmas season of 1779 Alexander wrote Laurens "upon the subject of wife."

He described the ideal lady: ". . . she must be young, handsome (I lay most stress upon a good shape), sensible (a little learning will do), well-bred (but she must have an aversion to the word *ton*), chaste and tender (I am an enthusiast in my notions of fidelity and fondness), of some good nature, a great deal of generosity (she must neither love money nor scolding, for I dislike equally a termigant and an economist). In politics I am indifferent what side she may be of. I think I have arguments that will easily convert her to mine. As to religion a moderate stock will satisfy me. She must believe in God and hate a saint.

"But to fortune, the larger stock of that the better. . . ."

In many ways this was a description of Eliza Schuyler, though she was more pious than he suggested and she would have to be an "economist" to make their budget meet his elegant requirements. Possibly, however, this was a better description of Alexander than of Eliza. Though fidelity was not to be his forte and he had a good deal more than a little learning, he possessed youth, good looks and an amiable disposition. He was no saint. And the larger stock of fortune he wanted meant more than money.

Yet at the outset he might have seemed to have fallen short of the pattern the Schuylers preferred. General Schuyler had been furious when his eldest daughter, the Angelica of Jefferson's choice coterie, had eloped in 1779 with an unknown Englishman, then calling himself John Carter, who had come to America and made much money. Schuyler then complained, "Unacquainted with his family connections and situation in life the matter was extremely disagreeable and I signified it to them."

This John Carter, of course, was actually John Barker Church, the brusque Britisher who shared with Jefferson aid to the artist Trumbull. He had adopted the pseudonym because of trouble in England involving a duel. Now moving back and forth between London and New York, he chose Hamilton to invest his funds in America. They were associated in the establishment of the Bank of New York, set up as a conservative enterprise which would buttress the commercial interests against democratic pressures. It was said that everything that Church touched turned to gold. He shrewdly moved for profit to Hamilton at whose touch everything turned to power. No later gossip that there was more than a brother-sister relationship between Angelica and Alexander disturbed Church.

Possibly Schuyler's ultimate satisfaction in his son-in-law Church made him readier to accept son-in-law Hamilton at his face value. That was high at the headquarters of Washington where the young man moved in easy equality with aristocratic young Americans and such an ideal European as Lafayette. Certainly Schuyler showed no qualms about his daughter Eliza's choice of the young soldier whose family connections were obscure at best and whose situation in life was at the time uncertain. Of this admirable young man, whose manners were polished and whose self-assurance was complete, the old landed aristocrat had no doubt and apparently made no inquiries. Alexander and Eliza were married on December 14, 1780, in Albany. A great reception in the stately Schuyler mansion indicated Schuyler satisfaction.

Now Hamilton had the Schuylers. The General's vast properties and political influence were ready behind him. But it was not long before the importance of the fact that the Schuylers had Hamilton began to appear. His known abilities as well as Schuyler influence sent him, in 1782, to the moribund Continental Congress in Philadelphia. There he saw how unpaid Continental soldiers were so ready to turn their arms on the moneyless Congress that it had to flee to Princeton. Schuyler influence also brought him business when he acquired his license as lawyer. The time was a field day for patriots in the law since all Tory lawyers had been disbarred. Hamilton joined others, including his amiable acquaintance Colonel Burr, in reaping the harvest after the British army grudgingly departed from New York. His Schuyler connection naturally made him a member of the gentry—many of whom had been openly or covertly Tories during the war. Indeed, there had been ugly rumors about the loyalty of General Schuyler even when he led patriot forces.

More than in other states, in New York known and suspected Tories needed protection from the wrathful retribution proposed for them by many of the triumphant patriots. The vengeful spirit of their opponents even in peace was expressed by Governor George Clinton when he declared himself ready to roast in hell before he would "show mercy to a damned Tory." Tories needed protection—and justice. And in the courts, where they faced confiscations and imprisonment, young Hamilton was a leader among the lawyers who came to their defense. That enriched him with the fees not only of the Tories who had dared to remain but also those of conservative patriots who had wanted only separation from England. It brought him, too, the resentment of poorer artisans, men in the city like Shays's angry farmers, whom conservatives of all colors feared meant to make liberty a radical threat to the propertied classes.

Even as a soldier handling military correspondence and making lively inquiries "upon the subject of wife," Hamilton had been thinking and writing about a dependable government and financial supports for it. The need for such a government was increasingly evident now in economic confusion, growing fears of disorders, some senseless state rivalries. In this situation Hamilton was a steady, if not as yet forceful, voice for a constitution creating a nation with authority. He got, however, only silence in the Constitutional Convention when, as a delegate, he proposed a constitution shaped after the aristocratic British model. Under it, he said, "the rich and the well-born" would "check the unsteadiness" of the "turbulent and changing" mass of the people.

As a man preferring half a loaf rather than none, he gave his full support to the Constitution finally drafted. Indeed, in the *Federalist Papers*, which he wrote with Madison and Jay, he shaped the most persuasive arguments for ratification by the states. And possibly even more important was his fight for the Constitution in crucial New York. There crusty democratic Governor Clinton opposed any relinquishment of state power and sovereignty. Clinton was a tough adversary. Hamilton preferred a cover of velvet to a show of iron. And it was fortunate in this great contest that the Federalist Schuylers did have Hamilton to lead in alliance with the Livingstons who had numbers. Together they won a surprising victory over the roaring opposition of the Clintons who supposedly had the power.

Hamilton certainly had power now. In the new government of George Washington he became Secretary of the Treasury on September 11, 1789. That post was foremost in Washington's Cabinet since Jefferson was then only preparing to come home on a holiday. Also, in New York Hamilton had the aid again of the Livingstons both to win a Federalist majority in the legislature and to scare Clinton who only squeaked by in re-election as Governor. The alliance of the two old families was natural. When Clinton was first elected Governor during the Revolution

in a surprising victory over the old ruling families, Jay, who had no democratic inclinations, said that "Clinton's family and connections do not
entitle him to so distinguished a pre-eminence." Now, in 1789, the Livingstons had strong ideas about their entitlements.

They expected honors from the victories they had helped secure. The
patriarch of the family, Chancellor Robert Livingston, hoped to be Chief
Justice of the Supreme Court. As allies in carrying the legislature it was
thought that a Schuyler and a Livingston would be sent to the Senate.
Hamilton had other ideas. The Chancellor did not become Chief Justice.
Furthermore, not only was Hamilton's father-in-law chosen for the Senate.
Also, the great young Alexander so managed—or intrigued to use a word
popular on bitter lips in those days—that the other seat went to his close
friend Rufus King. That gentleman, whose mind Hamilton said he had
"revolutionized," was then only a newcomer to the State of New York
where he had married the daughter of a rich merchant. The Livingstons
got nothing.

Hamilton, at thirty-two, was riding high, and, as some of the chagrined felt, booted and spurred. Any resentments, however, could be disregarded in the society of Washington's "court," which seemed to
republicans to ape the manners and fashions of monarchy. Even John
Adams, Jefferson believed, had been so fascinated by the glare of royalty
and nobility, during his mission in Europe, that he regarded British
forms and fashions a necessary ingredient of government. Young Alexander and his Eliza moved in official circles like leading figures in a cotillion.
His conservatism was fashionable. Considering his war record only the
ultra-suspicious could think of him then, as Jefferson dourly noted in his
Anas later, as "bewitched and perverted by the British example." Yet, one
who entered that society like a welcome dancing partner, though an old
enemy, helped make him seem so.

Major George Beckwith, who had been stationed in New York for
at least three years before the end of the war, returned with shadowy
status as British representative, intelligence agent, or gentleman visiting
a familiar, pleasant scene. His social position was impeccable. Member of
a distinguished military family of Yorkshire, he was to become a lieutenant
general, colonial governor, and a Knight of the Bath. Now he talked to
important people, many of whom still looked back in nostalgia to the
empire or looked around them at the unruly possibilities of liberty. Naturally one of them was Hamilton, who, as lawyer, had been so helpful to

persons proscribed as Loyalists. Beckwith was only two years older than
the Treasury chief. They were congenial. Soon they were more than social
companions as men confidentially discussing British-American policies and
problems. In their discussions and informal dealings Hamilton strayed far
from his own departmental concerns.

Since there was no Secretary of State when Beckwith arrived, the expansive Hamilton, in his discussions with the unaccredited Britisher, felt
that he filled a vacuum. Evidently, however, he filled it secretly without
the knowledge of President Washington or John Jay who was still acting
as Secretary for Foreign Affairs. Beckwith designated the cooperative
Hamilton as "No. 7" in the cryptic secret code of his reports to his government. That did not brand Hamilton as a secret British informer. Such
cipher designations were commonly used in this time and not only by
diplomats and spies. Others who were not government officials were designated by numbers in Beckwith's reports.

Possibly Hamilton did not know the background of Beckwith which
in history makes him seem a sinister figure. Beckwith, as intelligence agent,
had handled much of the detail in the plot which culminated in the treason of Benedict Arnold. A secret service agent then he once was called
G[eorge] B[eckwith] Ring from the fact that two rings were used, one
kept by Beckwith and the other sent to Arnold to prove the authenticity
of messages between them. And when the young British officer's superior,
Major John André, lost his life in this treasonable transaction, Beckwith
continued in the secret service under Major Oliver De Lancey, who was
the most hated Loyalist officer in America. Ties with the Tory De Lancey,
however, did not seem damning to all in official society in New York in
1789. Senator Ralph Izard, of South Carolina, had married the niece of
Oliver De Lancey. Izard's daughter was the wife of the Treasury Secretary's good friend in the House of Representatives, William Loughton
Smith.

Beckwith's status was confusing. Even his fellow countryman, the
pompous but observant British Consul Sir John Temple, was exasperated
by his equivocal position. In one of his reports home he exclaimed that
the agent was considered as "a petty spy." Hamilton evidently regarded
him as a man of acumen and discretion with a clear if secret line to British
officialdom. Moreover, as an admirer of the British system, evidently he
felt that he and Beckwith might make arrangements which would lead
to better feeling and closer ties between Britain and its old colonies. As

lawyer, Hamilton had been aware of American failure to provide the protections assured British subjects under the peace treaty. He certainly knew his government's concern over the failure of England to yield posts in the Northwest and to grant commercial privileges to the new nation.

Evidently the relations of the two men were not only secret but intimate. Beckwith was a friend of the Schuylers—at least of the charming Angelica Church. That lovely lady evidently saw Major Beckwith on a visit he made to London. She wrote to her sister, Eliza Hamilton, gaily promoting the British officer, "Colonel Beckwith tells me that 'our dear Hamilton' writes too much and takes no exercise and grows too fat."

The report of fat on the supple frame of the young Secretary was a playful exaggeration. But, in addition to straying into diplomatic matters which were not his official business, he was working at a terrific pace. His great main task was to produce his plan for the fiscal policies of the United States, including the national assumption of the public debts, not only of the Confederation but those of the thirteen states as well. Certainly the credit of the country needed repair. Public securities had fallen to a fraction of their supposed initial value. But in the process Hamilton planned not only to establish the nation's credit. Also, he honestly believed that it was necessary to give the propertied and commercial classes a special interest in the government to bind them to the support of the precarious union and, not merely incidentally, to the purposes of its Secretary of the Treasury.

There was nothing new about speculation in the country's depreciated securities. The rich who could take a chance had long been buying them up from those who had to take what they could get. But just before Hamilton's report on assumption was made public there was notable activity in the market for the paper. Rumors ran through the Congressional lobbies and the taverns that some, including members of the Congress, were particularly active in the speculation on the basis of some sort of inside information. Some were dispatching relays of fast riders and pilot ships at full sail to distant places to buy up the paper from remote folk ignorant of plans in the Treasury. Agents of speculators were buying for a few shillings on the pound from veterans and others the securities they had sacrificed to buy when the cause of the colonies seemed doubtful at best. One who was charged with such activities was Congressman William Loughton Smith.

Smith was a man to attract attention, not all of it favorable. Born rich in Charleston, he had been sent to England for education in an exclusive school at twelve. He had remained abroad for a dozen years, only returning in 1783 with a British legal education and little sympathy for ideas of liberty and equality which Jefferson had put into the Declaration of Independence. An impeccably dressed young grandee with a long, readily lifted nose and a smug mouth, he was much at home in New York, where the De Lancey family of his wife's mother had been noted and hated Tories. From the beginning he vigorously supported Hamilton's assumption plans. Jefferson stated in his *Anas* that Smith was one of the "principal gamblers" who were dispatching fast ships and relays of horses to distant places to buy up securities at a certain profit. Records indicate that Smith's speculations only began later, but his caustic, vitriolic language to opponents of assumption made him particularly offensive to them. He stoutly defended slavery and hated Quakers who opposed it. As a leading Episcopal layman, he was even arrogant in arguments with the clergy. Washington and Hamilton, who had a high regard for his abilities, regretted the unpopularity for which he almost seemed to ask. He received unasked the early revulsion of Jefferson's aide and agent, John Beckley, who watched him from his desk as Clerk of the House of Representatives.

No similarity of names should serve to confuse this Clerk Beckley with Major Beckwith. The two men were as dissimilar as the suave royal agent and the republican keeper of the legislative records would be expected to be. As different also were their relations with the two chief Cabinet officers. In Hamilton, Beckwith found a sympathetic source of information and line of influence into the American government. To Jefferson, Beckley, as a strategically placed American politician, was a source of information about Hamilton and Beckwith, too. Indeed, an action by Beckley later was to bring a protest from Beckwith against Jefferson.

Beckley, little remembered and often incorrectly described, was a British-born Virginia radical. He was not, as has been said, the son of a knight, nor was he ever a student at Eton. Even his father's first name is unknown. He came to Virginia in 1769 as an eleven-year-old boy, obviously precocious, as the indentured scribe of the famous early Virginia botanist, John Clayton. Evidently Beckley learned more than botany from Clayton who was also Clerk of Gloucester County. Clayton died four years after the boy arrived. But somehow the youngster found means to attend William and Mary College, where he was a member of the Phi Beta Kappa, some said one of its founders.

Certainly early he began to keep the records—not of *flora* but those of *fauna*, known as politicians—in Virginia political and legislative meetings. He grew up in exciting times though no records of any war service seem available. He became Mayor of Richmond. And in 1789, aged thirty-one, Madison secured his election as Clerk of the national House of Representatives, the first chosen of the staff of the new Congress.

Jefferson in understatement called him the best clerk in the United States. Certainly, so far as keeping the records was concerned, he met the satisfaction of all. But early, it is clear, he became about the most energetic reporter and one of the most effective agents Jefferson was to have. Then the Secretary of State began to make notes of information or merely gossip which Beckley brought him. It has been said that the House Clerk had the biggest ears in the early republic. His mouth was often close to Jefferson's ear. He was, however, no mere gossip and clerk. Albert Gallatin later described him as belonging to the hotheaded faction of the republicans. He could write, speak, organize, and strike a blow that hurt. He was both henchman and bookman. As one who appreciated both his literacy and his political brass knucks, Jefferson was to make him the first Librarian of Congress.

As Clerk he was strategically placed to use his ears. Early he heard about the activities of speculators. He reported what he heard to Madison who lived, as he did, at Mrs. Elsworth's boardinghouse—a favorite shelter of republicans. One thing he heard would be increasingly significant later. It seemed possibly related to a bigger man than Congressman Smith. It was about a New Yorker named James Reynolds. This man had secured from the Treasury Department a list of Virginia veterans who held government paper for their services. Reynolds was said to have been able to buy a good many of their warrants at three shillings on the pound.

Gossip was growing. There was talk even about Hamilton's Assistant Secretary William Duer who, said one who enjoyed his hospitality, "lived in the style of a nobleman." With him at his elaborate parties presided his wife, still called in republican New York "Lady Kitty." She was Catherine, daughter of Major General William Alexander, who had fought as an American commander under his claimed British title of Lord Stirling. Lord Stirling may have been as bibulous in arms as some of his critics, including Aaron Burr, reported him to have been. But Duer's marriage to his daughter connected him with the Schuylers and so with Hamilton. Duer had other important ties. During the Revolution his vote as a member of the Continental Congress had been crucial to Washington when his enemies sought to remove him from command. Gossip was rising high when it touched Duer.

Hamilton, however, appeared both immaculate and invincible. He brushed aside protests from Madison, his old collaborator in arguments for ratification. That small, grave Virginian had become increasingly disturbed by what he heard from Beckley and what he saw with his own eyes. In the House he became articulately insistent that some compromise plan be devised to assure what he and others regarded as justice for the original holders and not merely spoils for the speculators.

But Hamilton's power held, as members of Congress voted for his plan and profited by it at the same time. So far as the continental debt was concerned, Hamilton won over Madison thirty-six to thirteen, while Jefferson was at Monticello celebrating the eve of his daughter's marriage. Now the Secretary of the Treasury pushed the second part of his plan, the assumption also of the debts of the states. Not all the states were eager to be relieved. Some had big debts, some none. And the same sort of speculation would be extended to provide more millions for the sure-thing gamblers in and out of Congress. Furthermore, rumors of corruption were reaching more ears than Beckley's. Behind the closed doors of the secretive Senate the bill was in trouble. The crusty democratic diarist, Senator Maclay, reported of Hamilton's two Senators that "King looked like a boy that had been whipped, and General Schuyler's hair stood on end as if the Indians had fired at him." But the real blow to Hamilton and the speculators came in the House, on April 12, 1790, when this assumption plan was defeated thirty-one to twenty-nine.

Then, after weeks of maneuvering, Hamilton made his own great speculation. He turned to his colleague Jefferson who had arrived in New York on March 21. The tall Virginian had been in the city three weeks before the adverse vote came against the assumption plan. His ears were big also and only amplified by Beckley's. He certainly had talked to Madison as the leader in this anti-assumption fight. Indeed, before he left Monticello, Madison had written him that speculators were "still exploring the interior and distant parts of the Union in order to take advantage of the ignorance of holders." At this time also, Mr. Jefferson must have been hearing of Hamilton's dealing with Beckwith about matters which were not his responsibility, though that was only brought into the open in July. Hamilton's meddling in State Department matters would not end then.

However, the relations of the two Cabinet officers, as Mr. Jefferson said later, were amiable. And very possibly knowing the two great questions before Congress then, the Virginian was not surprised when Hamilton came to him seeking two votes necessary to save assumption. Their value was high. Only Jefferson reported Hamilton's approach to him. And afterwards he tried to make himself out almost as bumpkin ignorant as any of the poor rural holders of securities from whom speculators had been buying.

Hamilton met him, the Secretary of State wrote later, at the door of the President's house. Apparently this was the same great house which Jefferson's surprising friends, the Count de Moustier and his lady, had occupied during their sojourn in New York. Jefferson did not mention that episode of delusion in the report he left of his meeting with his Cabinet colleague.

Hamilton was "in despair." As evidence of it, "his look was somber, haggard and dejected beyond description, even his dress uncouth and neglected." In this reported lapse from impeccability and poise, Hamilton walked Jefferson up and down on the street. Certainly the imperturbable Virginian and the reportedly despondent and disarranged New Yorker pacing the sidewalk before the Presidential mansion must have made a spectacle in the little city where there were then as now gawking tourists as well as statesmen.

Hamilton painted "pathetically" the situation as he saw it. The union was threatened. The creditor states would secede without assumption. The members of the administration should stand together for the administration's plans. Jefferson listened, as his report suggested, to his colleague's panic with patience and politeness. But he hedged, pleading ignorance. He had, he reported afterwards, arrived in the midst of the fight and "but a stranger to the ground, a stranger to the actors on it, so long absent as to have lost all familiarity with the subject, and as yet unaware of its object, I took no concern in it."

He agreed, however, to have one of his small, elegant dinners at which Hamilton could make his case to the holders of Virginia votes he needed. At the dinner Jefferson reported that it was observed in the talk at his table, over his walnuts and wines, that Hamilton's present plan would be a pill "peculiarly bitter to the Southern States." To sweeten it a little, it was proposed to fix the capital for ten years at Philadelphia and then permanently in a new city on the Potomac.

Jefferson did not say who proposed this sweetening. Actually Hamilton had earlier been ready to peddle the permanent capital to Philadelphia for Pennsylvania votes. Jefferson had been earlier hoping for the more southern location. Now, Jefferson said the capital by Virginia would be "an anodyne." The deal was made. Virginia got the capital and Hamilton got his votes. Both sides kept the bargain. Fixed opponents of the assumption were amazed. Even some speculators, like Andrew Craigie of Boston, who thought he had a direct line into the Treasury through Assistant Secretary Duer, were surprised. Craigie mourned, in the mounting market for securities, that he had sold some for less than he could have got after the deal.

Secretary Hamilton certainly did not now look dejected and disheveled. He moved with the true air of premier in Washington's Cabinet. The House of Hamilton, at this time only incidentally the house of Schuyler, was the seat of polished power. General Schuyler, who had an investment of sixty thousand dollars in the assumed securities, could, beside his son-in-law, more than ever indulge the air of superiority which did not endear him to all. The luminous younger man was more than ever "our dear Hamilton" to Angelica Church whose husband had made even more out of assumption than her father. However, pretty, patient, often-pregnant Eliza Hamilton, evidently not enriched, still had to perform miracles of household finance in maintaining the establishment Hamilton's prestige required. But her eyes shone with love and pride. Other ladies welcomed the light in Hamilton's own dancing eyes. Most men, including the British Colonel Beckwith and American speculators, fawned on the superb Secretary of the Treasury.

It is not clear when Jefferson in anguish and animosity repented of the deal. He lavished loving attention on plans for the capital on the Potomac which he had secured in the bargain. Apparently it was long after the event that he set down in his *Anas* his after-the-fact outrage about what Hamilton had got.

"I was most ignorantly and innocently made to hold the candle," he said of the trade made by the light of his own tapers.

Possibly he was early disturbed by news from back home in Virginia. There Patrick Henry, whose tongue could be sharp as well as golden, introduced a resolution denouncing assumption as "repugnant to the Constitution of the United States, as it goes to the exercise of power not expressly granted to the general government." His resolution was overwhelmingly passed. And to it was added a Protest and Remonstrance which bluntly stated that the Assumption Act was a plan to "erect and concentrate and perpetuate a large monied interest in opposition to the landed interests" which would put "agriculture at the feet of commerce" or bring about a "change in the present form of Federal Government, fatal to the existence of American liberty."

This language later might have been that of Jefferson. Indeed, the Remonstrance provided a precedent he followed later when laws were passed which he abhorred and which he thought—or seemed to think—states might nullify. It became a pattern for threatened secession at least from national law if not from the national union. Henry's Protest and Remonstrance might have been the model for the Virginia and Kentucky resolutions Jefferson fostered in his opposition to the Alien and Sedition Laws. Now in 1790, however, Henry's resolutions had no effect on the assumption law. Evidently, they had an almost panic effect on Jefferson, as a man who never failed to look behind him to his own constituency. They stated sharply the "strict constructionist" philosophy to which he sternly adhered after this lapse in bargaining by candlelight.

Possibly after the deal his claim that he had been duped was made a more bitter one because of his other discovery as friend of France—how much Hamilton had been operating in pro-British bias with Major Beckwith in connection with matters which were none of his business. That was basis for more than pique. Jefferson soon put the Beckwith business together with the assumption speculation in his insistence that his mounting feud with Hamilton was based purely on principles.

"Hamilton was not only a monarchist," he insisted, "but for a monarchy bottomed on corruption."

The friends of Hamilton, who never repented of his deal or felt any need to explain it, had other ideas about the basis of the differences between the two men. Years later when Jefferson was binding in his *Anas* this description of Hamilton, one who served Hamilton and hated his rival saw something less than high principles in Jefferson's role in the conflict.

"Jefferson soon discovered the force of Hamilton's superior genius," wrote Timothy Pickering, "and envy filled his breast. He perceived the weight of his opinions in the Councils of Washington and believed that Hamilton stood in the way of his ambition."

That, of course, was possibly venomous contradiction of Jefferson's constant plaints about his preference for Paris over politics and Monti-

cello above all the honors of the world. Worse things were to be said about
Jefferson. Congressman Smith was already building up the steam of his
resentment for future publication. In the conflict of ideas there was confusion of loyalties, too. That was true not only among the Americans but
also among the representatives of the British system which Hamilton so
much admired. Sometimes Hamilton's irregular relations with Major Beckwith and later with the officially accredited British Minister George Hammond were almost matched by Jefferson's contacts, via Beckley, with the
British Consul Sir John Temple. Sir John has been described by Julian
Boyd, the definitive editor of the Jefferson papers, as vain, garrulous, indiscreet, and lavish with exclamation points. He was also rich and evidently
resentful of the operations of both Beckwith and Hammond who apparently showed him less deference than he required. Jefferson described
Temple, though His Majesty's Consul, as "strong republican." He did this
on the basis of reports from Beckley who, the Secretary of State said, he
knew was intimate with this irascible British official. From Sir John by way
of Beckley, Jefferson got and duly recorded in his *Anas* an amazing report
about Hamilton and his chief aides. It was contained in a letter supposedly
come to Temple from the highest level of the British government.

It was, Jefferson wrote, "of the following purport: that the Government was well apprised of the predominancy of the British interest in the
United States; that they considered Colonel Hamilton, Mr. King, and Mr.
W. Smith of South Carolina, as the main supports of that interest; that
particularly, they considered Colonel Hamilton, and not Mr. Hammond,
as their effective Minister here; that if the anti-federal interest (that was
his term), at the head of which they considered Mr. Jefferson to be, should
prevail, these gentlemen *had secured* an asylum to themselves in England."

So, Jefferson wrote no longer quoting, these gentlemen understood
that they could go on boldly in their machinations to change the government. And "if they should be overset and choose to withdraw" they could
count on such protection and pension as had been given Benedict Arnold.
Some time after he wrote this apparently not even Mr. Jefferson could entirely swallow such a tale. In the margin beside what he had first written,
at some other time he made a note: "Impossible as to Hamilton; he was far
above that." He made no such marginal reservation as to Senator King and
Congressman Smith.

His own tale of his innocence in the bargain with Hamilton was at
least as incredible. He tangled himself up in after-the-fact insistence that

he was duped as an innocent in the assumption bargain. Even his most idolatrous biographer, Claude Bowers, wrote that his explanation of this matter was an alibi shaped after the crime. Indeed, he magnified his fault by the indignation with which he described the assumption to which he had agreed. As a result of it, he wrote, "immense sums were filched from the poor and ignorant, and fortunes accumulated by those who had been poor enough before. Men thus enriched by the dexterity of a leader would follow, of course, the chief who was leading them to fortune, and become the zealous instruments of all his enterprises."

The affairs of Secretary Hamilton, now looking his confident best, allowed little time for any such recrimination if he had cared to make any. He was already planning for the creation, with the support of his "mercenary phalanx," of a Bank of the United States which would, his great adversary believed, further enrich and corruptly bind important persons to his "monarchial" purposes. Both of the Secretaries were, however, concerned about arrangements for the move of the government to Philadelphia for a ten-year residence before its move to the Potomac place which had served as such an "anodyne."

Hamilton wanted a house near his office. Also, he wanted as low a rent as possible for a proper house for himself, Eliza, and their four charming children. He added of the move South: "A cool situation & exposure will of course be a very material point to a New Yorker. The house must have at least six rooms. Good dining and drawing rooms are material articles. I like elbow room in a yard."

He needed elbow room in his expansive life. Apparently it did not occur to him as he moved in power from New York that he had already prepared humiliation for himself and his Schuylers behind his back at home.

3.

Young Man in a Hurry

"O my Aaron! . . . Dearest of husbands. Best of fathers."

So almost sang Theodosia Prevost Burr in her love letters to young Colonel Burr who, in the 1780s as rising attorney, was constantly moving across New York State, and down beyond Jersey into Pennsylvania. From his happy household on Maiden Lane, he hurried on horseback, by sloop, canoe, and wagon to courts in Albany and smaller towns and to open lands which stretched back forever into an almost trackless but richly promising West. And Burr's letters came back to Theo filled with the same ardor, the same bitterness at separations. The correspondence between the small, dark, driving man and the frail, brilliant woman tells the story of a faithful love which only the most austere historians and venomous critics have questioned. Few such exchanges in conjugal adoration exist in American history. That is the more remarkable because from first to last Burr's true biography must be disentangled as much as possible from such a mass of legend about his lapses with the ladies that one generous biographer found much of his story shaped in venomous retrospect.

Theo tended to his business in his absences. She guarded his household containing their lovely younger Theo and her sons by an earlier marriage, now his sons, too. She read and discussed the many books he suggested. But, though she missed him desperately and feared for his health and her own, she tried to put only one stipulation upon him.

"I will only put an injunction on your riding so fast, or in the heat, or dew."

That was only a wish. Both knew that he was a man born to the relentless pursuit of a destiny he never doubted. Occasionally he did seem in his letters to prefer tranquillity to the chase and the challenge of his career. Once he wrote her of a scene of serenity from lands in upstate New York to which speculators including himself were turning gleaming eyes. It was, he told her, "formed for the residence of the loves and the graces, and is therefore yours by the best titles." He reported in admiration of the lands stretching forever west: "Here you behold the stately Mohawk roll his majestic waves along the lofty Appalachians. . . . What there was tenderness, here swells to rapture."

And again, halting to rest on a hard riding day, he wrote to her in wonder as to "why all animated nature enjoyed its being but man?" He went on in moralizing lament, "Why man alone is discontented, anxious—sacrificing the present to idle expectations;—expectations which, if answered, are in like manner sacrificed. Never enjoying, always hoping? Answer, *tu mihi, magna Apollo.*"

He interrupted his letter then because, he said, his companions were coming in. Men and tasks and time seemed always pressing in on Burr. He hurled himself headlong into life. Possibly that was strange. His father, another Aaron, and his grandfather, the great New England divine Jonathan Edwards, had both been contemplative men. Both, however, had been energetically engaged as austere Calvinists in driving the devil back into hell, from which some were to suggest the younger Aaron emerged panoplied. He inherited great gifts and complex traits. There never seemed any sign in him of the vague mysticism of his grandmother Sarah Pierpont Edwards, whose husband reported that from childhood she had privileged communion with God. She was "always full of joy and pleasure and no one knows for what." She enjoyed solitude in which she seemed "to have someone invisible always conversing with her." Charles Burr Todd, historian of the Burr family, spoke more bluntly of the Edwards line. He wrote, "The grandmother of Jonathan Edwards was insane . . . and several of her family were victims of the same malady."

Such intensity and eccentricity were not evident in Burr. From his mother, Esther Edwards, Burr inherited a saving sense of humor which she preserved in the Puritan intensity which he rejected. Something of his inheritance as a small man was foreshadowed in his aunt Mary Edwards. Her big husband, Major Timothy Dwight, it was said, could hold her at arm's length on the palm of his hand. Though only five feet six, nobody would ever try that with Aaron Burr. But the Dwight connection may have turned Burr's mind early toward the West.

Left an orphan in infancy, he was apparently quite a handful for the bluestocking uncle who became his guardian. Evidently, however, there were no lapses in the discipline of his mind. As a precocious boy in a hurry he presented himself at age eleven for entrance to Princeton which both his father and grandfather had served as president. But because he was "little Burr" then as always, he was forced to wait until he was thirteen when he was admitted to the sophomore class. Later he was described as an adolescent delinquent in the little college town in the woods. A lonely tombstone was pointed out there as a monument to his profligacy. Under it, solemn scandal said, lay the body of a young woman whom he had seduced and basely deserted. The Burr of this foul deed would have been under sixteen. Actually, the girl only came to Princeton years after Burr left and she died of tuberculosis, not a broken heart.

Burr was no saint and he had no plans to become one. It took him little time to discover that the ministerial career expected of him was not his role. He turned to law. But when the first guns of the Revolution sounded, in 1775, he hastened to the embattled Boston area with a letter of introduction to George Washington. The war seemed made for Burr and Burr for war. Frail but wiry he was impatient with the lack of action in Washington's enthusiastic but undisciplined forces. So to the distress of his relatives, the nineteen-year-old soldier volunteered for the daring dash, under Benedict Arnold, through the winter wilderness in an effort to win Canada to the Revolutionary cause. Young Aaron won his greatest glory on the heights of Quebec in the charge in which General Richard Montgomery fell. But even this passage of hardship and heroism was footnoted by a later report that he found an Indian squaw to share his blankets. The recorded certainty is that he became Captain Burr aged nineteen. Also on this campaign he served with comrades who would play important roles in his story later—including Captain James Wilkinson, also nineteen, who had abandoned medical studies to enter the army.

Very briefly, Burr served at Washington's headquarters in New York. Some historians—or chroniclers—have packed into a stay between assignments of little more than a week an amazing array of alleged misdeeds by him: he showed a carelessness about military decorum and was occasionally impertinent, they said. Also, in almost standard procedure, it was suggested that Washington learned that he had engaged in an unseemly amorous adventure. Burr would have had to have worked overtime in misbehavior to have established this record to which some attribute Washington's postwar antipathy toward him. Certainly he met Hamilton there, who afterwards was reckless with Burr's reputation, sometimes at Washington's ear. And the great Richmond Hill house in which Washington was quartered became a sort of symbol of the place Burr hoped to make for himself in an exciting world.

Far more significant than his brief duty with Washington was Burr's service as a boyish major on the staff of General Israel Putnam. This doughty Yankee had become almost a legend as Indian fighter and explorer before the Revolution began. He had been a leader in the Sons of Liberty and was credited with the long-remembered command at Bunker Hill: "Don't shoot, boys, till you see the whites of their eyes." Some of the fastidious were amused by his quaint language and awkward letters. To Burr, who was happy in his household, he was always "my good old General."

The younger man and the older one had prewar ties. Putnam had made the long voyage around Florida and a journey up the Mississippi to explore the Natchez region where Timothy Dwight, who had married Burr's diminutive Aunt Mary, and Dwight's brother-in-law, Phineas Lyman, shared a British land grant. Having taken an oath to the crown, Dwight, as the Revolution began, had scruples about joining the patriots and good reason to fear that the Sons of Liberty might not respect those scruples. So, leaving his wife behind, he set out for Mississippi. After many difficulties and hardships he died there on June 10, 1777, while Burr was serving with Putnam. The West was so far off then that Aaron's Aunt Mary did not get the news until a year after he died.

Some reports about Burr on Putnam's staff were not made until years later when in England the lurid memoirs of a famous courtesan, Mrs. Margaret Coghlan, were published. Along her primrose path she had been the mistress of the Duke of York. But she recalled with most tenderness the American "Colonel" who "subdued my virgin heart." Though the lady gave her subduer no name, Major Burr was tagged with her seduction when as fourteen-year-old Margaret Moncrieffe, daughter of a British officer, she was a sort of petted prisoner in Putnam's household. Certainly as credible was another version of the story that Burr spotted the girl as a precocious British spy. Old bluff Putnam, who had stout views about virtue, apparently never suspected Burr of any misbehavior in his house. The certain thing is that in service with Putnam, Burr had opportunity to learn to respect the plain, little-schooled, but sturdy men who had led the Sons of

Liberty. Many such men, feeling frustrated in freedom, would in Burr's time reassemble as the Society of St. Tammany.

The fortunes of war, however, brought him into the company of others as different as possible from the household of the plain, indomitable Putnam. As the actual commander of a regiment, which bore the name of a rich merchant who had equipped it, Burr came under the command of Lord Stirling. In the Battle of Monmouth, while others fumbled Burr's conduct was praiseworthy, though his health was injured by fatigue in the heat of that blistering June day. Also, his criticism of Washington's generalship at the time later helped with the aid of Hamilton to build the resentment and distrust of the first President. He was, indeed, perilously close to some of Washington's enemies. More important to Burr's own happiness, however, his service in New Jersey in battle and in secret service brought him to Paramus where lived Theodosia Bartow Prevost, wife of a British colonel absent in His Majesty's forces.

In her large, red sandstone house there Theodosia Prevost was a woman in a difficult position. As the wife of a British officer, Colonel Jacques Marc Prevost, whom she had married when she was seventeen, she was suspect. Many stern patriots wanted to expropriate her property. But she was a popular member of a society which found time for gaiety even in wartime. She was liked and defended by the ladies of Lord Stirling and his brother-in-law Governor Livingston of New Jersey. Like some others, Burr thought that Lord Stirling turned too often to the bottle. Later he was to say that a young Virginian named James Monroe, who was Stirling's aide, had as his chief duty keeping his general's glass filled. However, this young Virginian, in a facetious letter to Mrs. Prevost as his confidant in a love affair, best gave the spirit of the society in which Mrs. Prevost was accepted and defended and in which Burr found himself apparently hopelessly in love with a married woman. Holding her up as an example to the demanding young lady about whom he wrote, Monroe described the charming but beset Mrs. Prevost.

"I painted a lady," Monroe wrote to and of Theodosia, "full of affection, of tenderness, and sensibility, separated from her husband, for a series of time, by the cruelty of war—her uncertainty respecting his health; the pain and anxiety which must naturally arise from it. I represented, in the most pathetic terms, the disquietude which, from the nature of her connexion, might possibly intrude on her domestic retreat. I then raised to her view fortitude under distress, cheerfulness, life, and gayety, in the midst of affliction."

Certainly this lady was no such empty-headed beauty as it was suggested Burr so often pursued. Though a social favorite, she was such a woman as met the young Colonel's lasting faith in the intellectual equality of women. Her contemporaries did not regard her as beautiful. A scar from a burn marked her forehead. Yet hardly any lovelier and loving lady could be drawn than the picture she left of herself in her letters. She was not rich. She was ten years older than Burr and before he met her had borne her first husband five children—two of whom were old enough to be serving with their father in the British army. And, even when Burr met her, her health was frail. But her house was well stocked with the latest books from France and England. She could talk about them with spirit and understanding. She was at ease in discussion of the works of Voltaire, Rousseau, Lord Chesterfield, though as a pious person she expressed dislike of Chesterfield's cynical advice to his son. Above all she was, as her letters showed, a woman ready to bring eagerness and ardor to one she loved.

Not only in his love for her but in her house, Burr showed an understanding of women. Apparently he was present there on the night when Peggy Shippen Arnold, wife of the General just discovered in treason, came by in a state of hysterics which completely convinced Washington and Hamilton of her innocence. Burr had known Peggy as a playmate in childhood. He seemed unsympathetic to womanhood when he dismissed Peggy's tears as dissimulation. But archives opened later indicated not only her guilt with her husband but perhaps her incitement of his treason.

The news came that Colonel Prevost had died in the West Indies. Burr was now free to pay his court. His health was still impaired by his military service. He was hard up, having spent his never very large inheritance in almost reckless generosity to his men and others. Such sometimes indiscriminate charity was to mark him all his life. He still had to acquire his license to practice law. In Albany, where he pushed hard at his studies, he wrote Mrs. Prevost on December 6, 1781: "An old weather-beaten lady, Miss Depeyster, has given the whole history of Burr and much of Theo, but nothing unfavorable." In recognition of gossip, Theo had written him, "Our being the subject of much inquiry, conjecture, and calumny is no more than we ought to expect. . . . When I am sensible I can make you happy, I will readily join you to suppress their malice."

Difficulties lay in their way. Under the law a license as a lawyer could only be granted after an applicant had studied at least three years. In a hurry Burr effectually argued that special dispensation should be granted those whose studies had been interrupted by service to their country. He was allowed to take the examination, and to the surprise of his lawyer examiners, who had opposed his right to take it, his answers were so clear and cogent that they were reluctantly compelled to admit him to the bar. He long remembered the aid in this crisis of Judge Robert Yates.

His license was granted on January 19, 1782. He hung up his shingle in the little town of Albany. And on July 2, 1782, in Paramus he was married to Theodosia—he twenty-six, she in the middle thirties. Only afterwards did gossip stain those months of struggle and romance. Then it was reported that in the period between his examination and his marriage, he slept with the wife of a rural innkeeper who, on December 5, 1782, bore his son. The child's name was Martin Van Buren.

Certainly there seemed no stain on the Albany household over which the young lawyer presided. His name meant much. John Adams later thought it most served to help his advance. But he brought to his profession such an attractive personality and devotion to his causes that clients soon crowded to his door. With Tory lawyers disbarred, it was, as Hamilton had found, a good time for young lawyers who had been good Patriots. And Burr, though doing well in Albany, planned to move to the metropolis down the river. By November 1783, as the English troops marched out and the triumphant Americans took over, the young Colonel arranged for home and office in the Verplanck house "in Wall Street, next door but one to the City Hall."

Years later he told Jefferson that he came to the city as a stranger. With some he and Theo may at first have seemed unwelcome newcomers. In the same year in which they arrived, Theo's first cousin's husband, the Reverend Benjamin Moore, who had been Loyalist in sympathy during the war, was forced by Patriot members of Trinity Church to withdraw as new rector of the parish because of his "avowed sympathies with the British cause and his dislike of the new government." There were bristling divisions in the small city which still had a Dutch look though it had acquired English manners—and now some British antipathies.

Burr quickly made his Whig position, backed by his war record, clear. He had no great New York families behind him. If he wanted one he had to create a following of his own. That could not have been easy where old ties were strong and, even in 1790, only thirteen hundred of the city's thirty-five thousand people could vote under required property qualifications. Apparently only as a young man of evident promise, not eager for a place in politics, was he sent to the State Assembly of 1784–85. In it he attracted some attention by his effective opposition to a law which would have given a monopoly, directed by politicians, to existing tradesmen and mechanics. He also proposed early abolition of slavery in the state. He took so little part in the great debate over the adoption of the Constitution in New York, in 1788, that Hamilton was afterwards able to say that his position was "equivocal," which would be mild criticism coming from his equally diminutive rival.

Burr's really significant entry into politics came with a defeat in this same year of the ratification fight. He was put forward then by the Sons of Liberty "who are again called upon to contend with the sheltered aliens [Tories] who have, by the courtesy of our country, been permitted to remain among us." Indeed, some whose sentiments in the war had been doubtful were voting while Patriots were disfranchised. This ticket on which he was listed fourth was composed of William Denning, Melancton Smith, Marinus Willett, and himself.

Denning may or may not have been the "artificer" by that name who made wrought-iron cannon for the Revolutionary armies. About his political opinions little is known. But Smith, who had been effective in the detection and control of Tories during the war, was one of the few important landowners and merchants with strong democratic ideas. Willett had been a leading member of the Sons of Liberty and was a leader of radical Patriots in New York. Congress had given him an "elegant sword" for his services in arms. Later he was to be one of those who endorsed the notes of Burr in complicated financial transactions. Such men, in 1788, were too early in their feeling that the time had come to contend with Tories and other entrenched conservatives. They indicated a restlessness in a very limited liberty for most men.

Yet, a year after the defeat of this Sons of Liberty ticket, Burr seemed to provide basis for later charges of political inconsistency. Then he served with such strange companions as Hamilton and rich William Duer on a committee supporting Judge Yates, a mild Federalist, for governor. Important to Burr, Yates had been the chief man who helped him get his law license without long delay. The Judge was defeated but old perennial Governor Clinton barely squeaked through to re-election. Tough, shrewd Clinton set about rebuilding his almost shattered fences. He eliminated

Yates as a future opponent by making him chief justice of the state. And to Burr, then thirty-three, he offered the position of Attorney General. That indicated at least rueful respect for the young man. On September 25, 1789, Burr reluctantly accepted. Most of his work would be in New York which would reduce the too many separations from Theodosia.

Aaron and Theodosia moved little in the New York society to which, by every right, they belonged. That—or Jefferson's poor memory—may have been responsible for the Virginian's statement years later that in the high social circle of the city, said to contain only three hundred persons, he never met Burr. Theodosia quietly entertained Burr's friends— one a Randolph of Jefferson's Virginia tribe. Yet she seemed a more and more delicate recluse. She went out rarely, she wrote, and was one who never dressed "beyond a decent style at home." Both she and Aaron were much concerned about the education of little Theo—just six years old when Burr became Attorney General. Behind the flippancy with which he often wrote her later, Burr had a passionate purpose for the child. To her mother, he declared dramatically, "If I could foresee, that Theo would become a mere fashionable woman, with all the attendant frivolity and vacuity of mind, adorned with whatever grace and allurement, I would earnestly pray God to take her forthwith hence. But I yet hope by her to convince the world what neither sex appears to believe—that women have souls." Some thought that Burr was not sure that he had a soul. But with a variety of tutors and insistence on her instruction in matters of the mind as well as the graces, both her parents were pressing a regime which would make young Theodosia with dark auburn hair and large dark eyes both a paragon and an enigma in the years ahead.

Whatever may have been his contempt for mere ladies of fashion, Burr certainly did not scorn the fashionable world. As his income grew as attorney, he moved to large and larger houses. He was living now at the corner of Nassau Street and Maiden Lane in a residence with a large garden and grapery beside it. And now already he must have been dreaming of the possession of the great house Richmond Hill which had been Washington's headquarters and which Abigail Adams recalled, after her brief term in it, as "majestic and sublime." That mansion would match his aspiration. His spirit would fit its halls.

In 1790 he still traveled more than he and Theo wished with his saddlebags as briefcases. He moved with soldierly bearing and political appeal into 1791 when he was to be made in history to seem a little dark man who was the first American political dark horse. Not much advance excitement attended the meeting of the assembly which was expected to re-elect General Schuyler to the United States Senate. Off in Philadelphia, Secretary Hamilton was confidently moving forward with his financial plans. On December 14, 1790, he had formally proposed his plan for a Bank of the United States. The price of public securities soared at once. Sir John Temple used two exclamation marks in reporting the rise to his government. Soon, despite the also rising contention of Jefferson and Madison that the plan was unconstitutional, it would be approved. Then the democratic diarist Maclay would write in dismay and disgust: "The Congress may go home. Mr. Hamilton is all powerful, and fails in nothing he attempts."

It was no winter of unalloyed triumph for Hamilton. It was, indeed, a cold winter for everybody. On December 7 Jefferson noted that there had already been three snows in Philadelphia. On December 23 he wrote home that the Schuylkill River was frozen so that no vessel could get out. In New York the Hudson had frozen so early that the price of fuel rose to uncommon heights. But there was a special chill for Hamilton beyond the weather.

While he arrayed his forces behind his bank plan in Philadelphia, the state assembly met in New York. There had been no evident opposition to General Schuyler, who had drawn the short Senate term in 1789. His name was the only one presented. Amazingly, as it seemed to his friends, he was rejected. Then Burr's name was put in nomination on January 19, 1791. He was promptly elected in both houses. If there was dismayed surprise in the house of Hamilton-Schuyler then, there has been much political explanation since. Generally Burr has been pictured as merely a pawn to serve resentment. It was simply a case, one able historian has said, of "Get Hamilton" by defeating his father-in-law. The Secretary of the Treasury was Clinton's clear adversary in New York. The Livingstons had not forgotten Hamilton's disregard of them two years before. Yet neither alone could have defeated Schuyler despite that gentleman's gifts for unpopularity. So Burr.

Schuyler did not regard Burr as any mere stand-in for his enemies. Neither did Hamilton, whose implacable, though concealed, hatred can be dated from this humiliating event. Schuyler disdained any public comment but in bitterness he wrote his son-in-law a year after his defeat.

"As no good could possibly result from evincing any resentment to

Mr. Burr for the part he took last winter, I have on every occasion behaved toward him as if he had not been the principal in the business."

So did Hamilton. On every public and private occasion he met Burr with a smiling face but his grudge grew in his confidential letters. He did not give the honor of his enmity to an empty-handed pawn. He realized in politics the adroitness which he had often met in Burr in the court-room. What he called "intrigue," when others succeeded, was the politics played then, before and since.

Samuel H. Wandell and Meade Minnigerode state as a fact in their biography of Burr that his election was "unsolicited" and that "he had not been approached on the subject before hand." Nathan Schachner in his life says that any conjecture that Burr had intrigued and insinuated himself into the graces of the individual members of the legislature is unwarranted.

Yet it remains incredible that an election, so arranged that on the first ballot after the rejection of Schuyler Burr was promptly chosen, took place without his having any foreknowledge of what was going on. The possibility of a deal has been suggested. His elevation to the United States Senate made vacant his post as Attorney General which was soon filled by the appointment of Morgan Lewis, a Livingston connection who was later to be Burr's opponent in a critical election. A historian of New York politics has suggested that this may have been "foreseen" or prearranged.

The newspapers of the time expressed no surprise at Burr's election. His chosen biographer, Davis, saw no need to explain it. The young Colonel was, with competition only from Hamilton, the best orator in the state and the ablest lawyer at the New York bar. He was entangled in no feud of the families. He was an educated man of the best lineage with a war record of distinction. Only vindictive retrospect has put any taint on his character up to this time. And he possessed power with people and appeal to them which even stiff aristocrats realized could not be disre-garded. He was, as was only slowly understood, one of the first Americans to understand the value of compact political organization. Possibly that understanding was thrust upon him by his needs as a man with no great family behind him in New York.

Two years before Burr's election to the Senate the Society of St. Tammany, or the Columbian Order, had been founded to resist the domi-nating aristocrats in the Society of the Cincinnati. Many, including Jef-ferson, suspected that the Cincinnati, open only to those who had been officers in the Revolution, was designed to create a hereditary aristocracy. But the resentments which brought the Tammany society into being preceded its organization among many who had been Sons of Liberty and were now often disfranchised small merchants and artisans. Its founder and first grand sachem, William Mooney, was an upholsterer and dealer in wallpaper. Many of its members were those urban artisans whom Jefferson, who condemned cities, considered "as the panders of vice, and the instruments by which the liberties of a country are generally overturned." Not all were such. John Pintard was one of New York's most successful merchants at the time. He was not only the first sagamore of the society and later its grand sachem, but also a chief founder of the New York and Massachusetts Historical Societies as well as a historical museum connected with Tammany itself.

The fastidious, who are often also the fearful, greeted the rising Tammany with disdain and derision. The elite called its meeting place the Pig Pen. Later, after Burr was out of politics, the scorn for the society was fortified when Tammany founder Mooney, as superintendent of the arms house, spent public funds which he entered in his books as "trifles for Mrs. Mooney." But even as Tammany was forming, such a statesman as General Schuyler was, under laws he helped enact, grabbing richer baubles for Mrs. Schuyler. There would be jewels for Mrs. Church.

Burr recognized the rising tide of democratic resentment. In the New York legislature, as elsewhere, suspicions were aroused by the secrecy of the U. S. Senate sessions. In them Senators voted on legislation by which they enriched themselves. Schuyler as Senator, so Burr's early biographer James Parton put it, wished to exclude "the vulgar public from the deliberations of a body that felt itself to be the American House of Lords." Burr was then and afterwards in favor of opening its doors. That issue was symbolic to many who felt that they were shut out. Some of those who elected him, not quite the puppets of a Clinton-Livingston combination for revenge, must have felt that it was time to let a new man in.

Obviously this made inevitable changes, some painful, in the Burr household. There was no secrecy or mystery about the ascending position he prepared for himself in private life. In the year in which he was elected he took over the remainder of a ninety-nine-year lease from Trinity Church of the great mansion Richmond Hill. That loaded him with greater financial burdens. In the summer, as Senator-elect, he was driving hard again as lawyer. He wrote Theodosia that he had undertaken "a laborious piece of business" for "wages."

Once again in the mood of his earlier melancholy meditations by the Mohawk, he complained: "What sacrifices of time and pleasure do I make to this paltry object—contemptible indeed in itself, but truly important and attractive as the means of gratifying those I love."

His health, he wrote, was not good. The least fatigue brought on a fever. Theo, whose own health was far more precarious, answered calmly that he must "establish your health before you commence politician.

"When once you get engaged, your industry will exceed your strength; your pride cause you to forget yourself. But remember, you are not your own; there are those who have stronger claims than ambition ought to have, or the public can have."

She was not willing, however, to take the blame for his pursuit of paltry, contemptible money.

"Why did you undertake that very laborious task you mention? 'Tis certain I have a great pleasure in spending money, but not when it is accompanied with the unpleasant reflection of sacrificing your health to the pursuit."

By now she understood that pursuit and the endlessness of it. She sent her love in long letters. She wrote him in detail about the problems of young Theo's education. She told him of the endless small tasks, and such innumerable trifling interruptions "that my head feels as if I had been a twelvemonth at sea." She wished that they could be together more before he went off to be a Senator in Philadelphia. And once before he set off for the new capital she wondered about the long scrawls she sent him.

"God knows the quality of this epistle; but the quantity I am certain you won't complain of. 'Tis like throwing the dice—a mere game at hazard; like all gamblers, I am always in hopes the last will prove a lucky cast."

Her Aaron went off to Philadelphia never doubting his luck.

III.
BOTANY
TO BLACKMAIL

1.

Delenda Est Carthago

Pious and conservative Robert Troup, of New York, wrote a prophetic letter to Hamilton on the day of Burr's election to the Senate in January 1791. This wealthy New York lawyer and land speculator had been the close friend of both Hamilton and Burr in youth. His opinions and possibly his financial interests brought him almost to idolatry of the Secretary of the Treasury and to bitter political opposition to the new Senator. Now he told Hamilton that "we are going headlessly into the bitterest opposition to the Genl Government—I pity you most sincerely—for I know that you have not a wish but what is combined with the solid honor & interests of America."

Clearly what he meant by the general government were its policies as shaped by Hamilton. That was emphasized in the optimistic prophecy which he added: "The time will come when your enemies will blush they are in opposition to you."

His optimism was still holding, though modified, five months later. Then he wrote of a leisurely summer tour being made through New York and New England by Jefferson and Madison. Evidently Troup regarded this as no innocent excursion.

"There was," he told Hamilton in June, "every appearance of a passionate courtship between the Chancellor [Livingston], Burr, Jeffersen (sic) & Madison when the two latter were in town. Delenda est Carthago I suppose is the maxim adopted with respect to you. They had better be quiet, for if they succeed they will tumble the fabric of the government in ruins to the ground. Upon this subject, however, I cannot say that I have the smallest uneasiness. You are too well seated in the hearts of the citizens of the northern & middle states to be hunted down by them."

Mr. Hamilton seemed an unlikely quarry for anybody then. It was already certain that the stock of his Bank of the United States would be oversubscribed. Members of Congress as well as private investors were eager for shares. Even Jefferson, who vigorously opposed the bank, quietly advised his young friend Short in Paris to invest in its shares. Hamilton's friends and supporters like Congressman Smith were appointed to its directorate. Already moneyed men, headed by his friend William Duer who had resigned as Assistant Secretary the year before, were planning a privately financed million-dollar Society for Useful Manufactures based on the Treasury Secretary's great Report on Manufactures. Troup, who had chided Hamilton about neglecting his private fortunes for public service, was one of those investing. Moreover, on the same day that he wrote Hamilton warning about the Jefferson-Madison tour, he lent the Secretary two hundred dollars which he apparently urgently needed. Troup told him he could take his time about repaying. And in this year, while Hamilton was making plans involving millions of dollars, the Treasury chief had to write another friend asking for a loan of twenty dollars "for a few days." The friend sent him fifty dollars.

Curiosity, however, was not directed at Hamilton's small loans, which, of course, were made confidentially. It followed Jefferson and Madison. Despite all suspicions then and later, the two Virginians told their friends, families, and history that they were just two middle-aged gentlemen on a holiday. Their exploration of this northern area, they insisted, was only an interlude devoted to sight-seeing and the study of nature or, as Madison said, to "health, recreation & curiosity." Some color was given both to their contentions and to the suspicions of others. This arose from the presence at the beginning and at the end of their "botanical expedition" of their man Beckley. If now he was the many-faceted aide to the two traveling politicians, he was still the boy who had been aide to the botanist Clayton.

In the months between Troup's two 1791 reports to Hamilton, Jefferson had certainly given evidence of his predilection for natural science. While he was opposing Hamilton's bank plan and aware also that the Secretary of the Treasury was working with Beckwith to counter his insistence upon a more stern attitude toward Britain, he was speaking of his "detestable" duties. He would rather be free, he told his son-in-law, to study the "process of gestation & parturition" of the opossum.

As vice-president of the American Philosophical Society, he was also much interested in a study of the life habits and ravages on grain crops of the Hessian fly. This pest took its name from the belief that it had been introduced into America in the straw bedding of Hessian mercenary soldiers whom Britain had arrayed against the Patriots. Possibly to Jefferson the fly seemed an item among many lingering evils which the British had left in America.

In Philadelphia while the load of his tasks made him apologetic about delay in answering his letters, he wrote about the awakening year. Ice in the rivers delayed the delivery of some of his fine furniture. Snows came and melted. Then he reported the first croaking of the frogs in those swampy places about the city which his friend Dr. Rush strongly condemned. He noted first bird cries, first leaves, first blossoms. He corresponded with an old Virginia friend, who would soon be suspected of taking part in Spanish conspiracy in the Mississippi West, about prehistoric fortifications there. And he told this man, Harry Innes, that politics was a duty with him, but the pursuit of natural history was a passion. Certainly he was a man fitted by every inclination for a botanical expedition.

Still, in the winter and spring of 1791, he clearly had not put politics aside. In this period he wrote home that he was "laboring without pleasure to myself, or profit to others." As Hamilton pushed forward his domestic plans and frustrated Jefferson in his foreign policies, sometimes it must have seemed that all Jefferson had left after his famous deal with Hamilton was the capital on the Potomac. Some Hamiltonians even said that the reason he opposed the Bank of the United States, which would be located in Philadelphia, was that placing it there might mean that the capital would stay there, too. Sometimes it seemed that he could only be sure of the President's full backing in connection with the new national city which he and Washington created by proclamation on January 24.

Hamilton's power seemed at its brilliant solstice in the Congress. Burr's election was almost the first sign of a crevice in his power in the country. And with most of the newspapers in the hands of Federalists, such traveling companions as Jefferson and Madison had no nationally audible voice. The Gazette of the United States, edited by John Fenno, had acquired a semiofficial status as the organ of the government. Certainly it was the organ of Hamilton who had begun to make loans to Fenno before it moved from New York to Philadelphia. It was, Jefferson said, "a paper of pure Toryism, disseminating the doctrines of monarchy, aristocracy, & the exclusion of the influence of the people."

Apparently Jefferson took his first step to remedy the situation on February 28, 1791. Then he offered the post of translating clerk in the State Department to Philip Freneau. A Princeton man like Burr and Madison, Freneau had had rough British prison ship experience in the Revolution which perhaps made his patriotic poetry and his republicanism the more ardent. The job Jefferson offered him paid only two hundred and fifty dollars a year, but, as the Secretary pointed out, its limited duties would "not interfere with any other calling" its occupant might choose. Evidently "another calling" might be the use of Freneau's sharp, satirical pen in journalism.

If this was an offer of political subsidy with the government's money, as was later charged, it certainly was not lavish. However, Hamilton's loans to Fenno were generally no more than a hundred dollars. Some of Jefferson's gifts or loans later to amenable journalists were smaller. On this occasion, however, Freneau, then writing for *The New York Daily Advertiser*, turned the offer down. Then the Secretary of State tried to persuade the equally republican Benjamin Franklin Bache, grandson of his old great friend, to make a national paper out of *The Philadelphia General Advertiser* which later became famous as the *Aurora*. Bache shared Jefferson's opinions but he did not think his distribution ideas were practical.

Then suddenly Jefferson by accident, as he always insisted, made himself the voice his republicanism required. As orator, he was so softspoken that he could hardly be heard across a room. Then and forever after, he declared that he never wrote anything for the press. But abruptly, unintentionally he said, to his embarrassment he declared, his voice resounded through the land. The vigilant and vicarious Beckley perhaps inadvertently brought about the event, and Jefferson was insistently innocent in the matter. It was always an interesting combination, however, when Jefferson's innocence was combined with Beckley's operations.

In this incident, as in others, Beckley has received only the barest mention from historians. Indeed, Randall as the first important biographer of Jefferson blandly passed Beckley by. Malone, who recognized that from a political point of view the clerk was probably more important than many members of the Virginia Congressional delegation, erred in his description of Beckley's background. Nathan Schachner referred to him as "a Pennsylvania politician." Though he was the first clerk of the House of Representatives and first librarian of the Library of Congress, the *Dictionary of American Biography* does not contain a sketch of him.

As botanist to begin with, Beckley, in 1791, certainly was not merely concerned with the flowers. In England Edmund Burke, in mounting opposition to English approval of the French Revolution, had published his *Reflections on the Revolution in France* in 1790. And soon thereafter that old, stentorian publicist for revolution in America, Thomas Paine, answered it in England with blazing language in the *Rights of Man*. His was a voice familiar to America. No publication had so encouraged the troops of Washington as his *Common Sense* published in Philadelphia in 1776. This exhortation beginning with the ringing words, "These are times that try men's souls," had been produced, so Dr. Rush said, with his aid and inspiration. Certainly it was read to every corporal's guard with the blessing of Washington. Estimates of its sales run up to a half million copies. Many who had been stirred by its language would listen to its author again. But this new clarion cry stirred wrath as well as enthusiasm. In it Paine not only defended the French Revolution, under the nose of the British monarchy, he extolled the virtues of republicanism. With a quick charge of treason behind him, Paine escaped to more hospitable France.

Soon after the publication of the *Rights of Man*, Beckley got a copy. Regarding it as a good antidote to John Adams' "Discourses on Davila," which he and Jefferson condemned, the House clerk decided to have it reprinted in America. He made arrangements with John (or Jonathan) Bayard Smith, a printer. But before sending it to Smith he loaned it to Madison, who passed it on to Jefferson with the request that, after reading, he give it to Smith. When he passed the book on to the printer, Jefferson added a note:

"Th. Jefferson presents his compliments to Mr. Jonathan B. Smith, . . . he is extremely pleased to find that it will be reprinted here, and that something is at length to be publicly said against the political heresies which have sprung up amongst us. He has no doubt our citizens will rally a second time round the standard of Common Sense. He begs leave to engage three or four copies of the republication."

Smith promptly used his letter on the flyleaf as a blurb. This may have been, as Jefferson quickly told President Washington early in May, only "the indiscretion of a printer." He was, he said, "an utter stranger to J. B. Smith, both by sight and character.

"I certainly never made a secret of my being anti-monarchial, and anti-aristocratical," he added, "but I am sincerely mortified to be thus brought forward on the public stage, where to remain, to advance, or to retire, will be equally against my love of silence and quiet, and my abhorrence of dispute."

On the same May day, as a lover of quietness, he wrote his daughter Mary that in the week before "the gelderrose, Dogwood, Redbud and Azalea were in blossom." The lilac had blossomed eight days before. These signs of spring brought in no season of silence for him. Angers were exploding as flowers bloomed. Not only did Adams' son, John Quincy Adams, cry out in angry reply in the press under the signature of *Publicola.* Also, Jefferson found Hamilton and Major Beckwith "open-mouthed" against him. Beckwith even expressed his pained surprise to Tobias Lear, Washington's secretary, about this publication of treasonable sentiments about the British monarchy. More significant, the protests were met by a roar of approval in the republican papers and among the masses of the people. If Jefferson was embarrassed, he was also suddenly acclaimed as the great leader of those who wanted no aristocratical ideas in the government of their country. His popular reputation was made not only in the cities but in the back places where worn copies of the book were passed eagerly from hand to hand.

The tumult was growing as he planned for the "botanizing tour." If he wanted to get away from the explosion he had set off, his natural history interests provided excuse. While the protest and applause mounted, he called a meeting of his Philosophical Society committee on the Hessian fly. That bug was pertinent since his projected journey would take him through regions where the pest was raging. He made arrangements early in May with Madison, who was in New York with the ubiquitous Beckley. There is no doubt that Madison talked politics in that city, but, as a prim man with a predilection for peacock ladies, he had other interests in New York. He was an ardent admirer of the beautiful and charming widow Henrietta Maria Colden. This lady was said to have also "inspired in Jefferson a momentary flash." As one connected with a great Tory and

Federalist family, however, she could hardly have been in their political confidences or discussions.

Beckley, it was agreed, would make a trip of his own up the coast of New England to Boston while his two great patrons would proceed up the Hudson. Jefferson set out from Philadelphia to meet Madison at Mrs. Elsworth's boardinghouse in New York. There he did have a talk with Freneau—though, as one historian said, not in private. Then off the two statesmen went on their botanical sight-seeing tour.

They had been gone by carriage and sloop from New York to Albany less than a week before Sir John Temple, this time not sounding like the republican Beckley reported him to be, was reporting suspicions about their trip and its purposes.

"I am sorry to inform Your Grace," he told the Duke of Leeds, "that the Secretary of State's Party and Politicks gains ground here, and I fear will have influence enough to cause acts and resolves which may be unfriendly to Great Britain, to be passed early in the next session of Congress. The Secretary of State, together with Mr. Madison . . . are now . . . gone to the Eastern States, there to proselyte as far as they are able to a commercial war with Great Britain."

At this time Temple and Beckwith were in agreement. The latter wrote home that he thought the trip was designed to promote anti-British policies but that he had countered their purposes by a trip of his own. Others were traveling and watching. Beckley reported that even around Boston the sentiment was pro-Jefferson and anti-Adams in the debate aroused by the Paine book. He also said the *Publicola* diatribe was thought to be the work of John Quincy Adams using material furnished by his father. Beckley made no botanical pretenses about the purposes of his travels.

With the exception of Troup's letter, most of the American suspicions about this trip were written later. The standard version written by Hamilton's grandson and biographer was that "after frequent interviews with Chancellor Livingston and Burr, they made a visit to Clinton under the pretext of a botanical excursion to Albany, thence extended their journey to Vermont; and, having sown a few tares in Connecticut, returned to the seat of government." A more contemporary report sent to Hamilton after the tour was ended ridiculed the excursion of the two Virginians, "in which they scouted silently through the country, shunning the gentry, communing with and pitying the Shaysites. . . ."

Mr. Jefferson did not mention any meetings with the gentry in his letters home about this trip—or any meetings with Shaysites either. He told his children of the beauty of Lake George and added that there was "as much fever and ague and other bilious complaints on L. Champlain as on the swamps of Carolina." Like any other tourist he sent home a letter written on birch bark. He rediscovered his preference for the climate of Virginia which needed, he said, to envy no other part of the world. Certainly not New England!

"Here they are locked up in ice and snow for 6. months. Spring and autumn which make a paradise of our country are rigorous winter with them, and a tropical summer breaks on them all at once. When we consider how much climate contributes to the happiness of our condn [condition], by the fine sensation it excites, and the productions it is the parent of, we have reason to value highly the accident of birth in such a one as that of Virginia. . . ."

Still, almost as if it had been planned for that purpose, the excursion included a tour through the Massachusetts country in which Daniel Shays and other embattled farmers had engaged in bootless revolt. Theirs was, however, a more significant rebellion than it has generally been regarded in history. It emphasized the lean quality of liberty for many Americans. This was revolt against interest rates which ran to as high as forty per cent a year. It was war against a situation in which there were twenty times as many men in jail for debt in the area as for all other offenses combined. But it scared the well-to-do who heard that the creed of the Shaysites was: "That the property of the United States has been protected from confiscation of Britain by the joint exertions of *all*, and therefore ought to be the *common property* of all."

This pre-Marxian idea may have had its origins only in the fears of the rich. Its circulation made propertied people more anxious for the strong central government for which the Constitution was designed. Also, though repressed in Massachusetts, a multitude of people like Shays's rebels remained in America. They looked in suspicion at a strong government the powers of which might be used not merely to suppress disorder but to prevent protest. Shaysites were specimens in the natural history of politics with which Jefferson and Madison were to be much concerned. Now, however, Mr. Jefferson, emphasizing nature, headed the trip homeward by way of Long Island, where the Hessian flies were eating up the grain, in order that he might make inquiries as a basis for a philosophical report.

Suspicions about the trip were and are still only suspicions. If the two travelers were seeking alliances in the strategic big middle state, Jefferson bluntly denied that he saw Burr on this trip or that he had ever met him before it.

"I had never seen Colonel Burr," he wrote in his *Anas,* "until he came . . . as a member of the Senate. His conduct very soon inspired me with distrust. I habitually cautioned Mr. Madison against trusting him too much."

This was a strange statement. Jefferson wrote it in 1804, if not later. Obviously then he was undertaking to limit strictly his relationship with the Colonel. But when he passed through New York in the summer of 1791, he was very much aware of the increasing significance of Burr on the political scene. Indeed, shortly after Burr's election, the Secretary of State had received a perceptive report on the newly elected Senator from the decorative Mrs. Colden.

"The attention of the Good Folks of this City," she told him, "was lately engrossed by the Choice of a new Senator to Congress. The Gentleman brought in by Governor Clinton's party, *as they say,* 'Not to Oppose, but to keep a Sharp look out on the Measures of the Government' is a man of too considerable abilities, for the side he has taken. If he moves on Antifederal Ground, he may do *harm.*"

"Antifederal" then meant anti-Hamilton, or republican—even Jeffersonian. Despite her reputed brilliance, Mrs. Colden may have been a political innocent or, as some suspect, her letter may have been inspired by Hamilton still hoping to appease Jefferson's opposition. Hamilton always had time for little maneuvers even when he was as busy as he was that summer. Indeed, as he himself reported later, he had time for what seemed at first only a small misstep. It was during this summer of the "botanizing expedition" that in Philadelphia, as he reported later, he received a call from a lady in distress. Her name was Maria Reynolds and, she said, she was a stranger in the city, come to endeavor "to reclaim a prodigal husband." One of Hamilton's biographers described her as a woman of "coarsely handsome features." But one who saw her at the time declared that "her innocent Countenance appeared to show an innocent Heart." Neither then nor in history has there been any certain agreement as to whether she was vixen or victim. Certainly that summer she seemed a very small item in the American story.

Small items could be serious. Mr. Jefferson had rejoiced in the election of his political protégé Monroe to the Senate in 1790. Yet, Monroe's choice revived whispers of an old scandal involving the Secretary of State. In coming to the Senate Monroe had replaced John Walker, one of Jefferson's closest boyhood friends and the son of his guardian, Dr. Thomas Walker. Walker had held his seat as appointed successor to a deceased senator. Malone wrote that Walker was resentful of Monroe's election, though his biography in the *Dictionary of the U. S. Congress* states that he had never run for re-election. Whatever were the facts, the occasion was marked by revival of the long-whispered story that, when years before Walker had left his wife under his friend's protection in his absence, Jefferson had made improper advances upon her. In a limited degree, Jefferson admitted the charges. Now he heard that Hamilton knew about the affair and in extremity might use it against him.

No such incident of misstep or fear marked the summertime of 1791 for Aaron Burr. His days were crowded with preparations for office and with efforts to make the money he required. Already he was planning the backdrop for his ascent in life by the acquisition of the great mansion Richmond Hill. He moved much at laborious tasks but apparently he was in New York City when Jefferson and Madison passed through. No letters between him and Theo indicate his absence at the time. Yet he was much away. Indeed, his absences saved him from much blame in a hue and cry which arose this year over the sale by a state commission, of which as Attorney General he was an ex-officio member, of 5,542,173 acres of state lands at an average price of less than twenty cents an acre.

On one of his absences Theo wrote that the heat and drought exceeded all recollections. She was "not so sick as when I wrote you last, nor so well as when you left me." She wanted him to have a holiday with her at Pelham on Long Island. Apparently they were much together during the last months before he took his seat as Senator. No letters indicated his absence between July 31 and late October when he wrote from Philadelphia.

He had been welcomed there. He had received many civilities and attentions, he told her: "Many invitations to dine &c. All of which I have declined, and have not eaten a meal except at my own quarters." Three days later he was permanently settled as the only boarder in the house of two widows, one of whom was so deaf that she asked him not to try to speak to her for fear of injuring his lungs.

Communications were not so difficult with others. He had, of course, known many of the members of Congress, if not the Secretary of State, while the capital was located in New York. His surprise election had created curiosity about him. His abilities were quickly clear. Though the youngest senator he was given important committee assignments. Very soon he was enjoying Mr. Jefferson's acquaintance and conversation.

"I enclose you a news paper of this evening," he wrote Theo in mid-November, "containing a report by Mr. Jefferson about vacant lands. When you have perused it, send it to Melancton Smith. Take care, however, to get it back and preserve it, as it is one of Freneau's. I send you also three of Freneau's papers, which, with that sent this morning, are all he has published. I wish them to be preserved. If you find them amusing, you may command them regularly."

With the urging of Jefferson and Madison and with the approval of Burr, Freneau had begun his *National Gazette* on October 31, 1791. Already good republicans were rejoicing in his caustic wit and invective. And Burr at home and elsewhere was promoting the organ Jefferson had long wanted. Soon he and the Virginian became more than official acquaintances. During this first winter of Burr's Senate service, James Parton, who wrote the first objective biography of him, described Jefferson as "his friend." Burr, said Parton, "having deliberately turned politician," was eager to acquire knowledge concerning statecraft. Also, one of his projects was to write a history of the American Revolution. So, with Jefferson's permission and as an early riser, Burr went to the State Department at five every morning. He employed a messenger to make a fire, and a confidential clerk to assist him in searching and copying. With a servant bringing him his breakfast, he worked from dawn to ten o'clock. This practice, said Parton, was continued "until nearly the end of the session" which was May 8, 1792.

Wishing to know more about the western posts, to which the British had clung with some assists to Beckwith from Hamilton, he asked Jefferson for permission to make this particular examination. To his surprise the Secretary of State replied that "it had been *concluded* to be improper to communicate the correspondence of existing ministers." Burr regarded this, said Parton, as an "uncalled for and arbitrary proceeding." He might have better understood if he could have read a passage Jefferson put in his *Anas.*

Just a month before the end of the session, on April 2, Jefferson wrote of a Cabinet discussion about the right of Congress to see departmental papers. He quoted Hamilton as saying that members "might demand secrets of a very mischievous nature." The Virginian added a note in brackets: "Here I thought he began to fear they would go on to examining how far their own members and other persons in the government had dabbled in stocks, banks, &c., and that he probably would choose in this case to deny their power. . . ."

Mr. Hamilton would not want Aaron Burr rooting in his papers. Evidently, however, Burr was barred by a general rule based upon what Jefferson thought were Hamilton's fears. Burr was not rebuffed by Jefferson. In effect both were balked by Hamilton. Then and afterwards Burr enjoyed Jefferson's hospitality in the fine house he had remodeled for his occupancy. He wrote home a letter indicating this. He told Theo: "I despair of getting genuine Trent wine in this city. There never was a bottle of real unadulterated Trent imported here for sale. Mr. Jefferson, who had some for his own use, has left town."

Over such wine Burr found Jefferson's company and conversation "fascinating." So the New Yorker told the Virginian later. The talk in the tall Secretary's house always ranged over a wide field. The urban Burr could have contributed little to any conversation about the "gestation & parturition" of the opossum or the ravages of the Hessian fly. But he knew politics with which Jefferson was concerned even if he found it distasteful. And as a man who had felt the majesty and mystery of the West as he looked from the Mohawk up the sweeping Appalachians, Burr would have been enthusiastic about Jefferson's revival of his proposal for an exploration of the lands beyond the mountains.

This year, 1792, Meriwether Lewis, an eighteen-year-old boy from Virginia, begged his neighbor the Secretary of State to let him lead such an expedition beyond the Mississippi into regions of confused geography and of conflicting American, foreign, and Indian claims. Jefferson—perhaps Burr—listened to the importunities of the boy. There were enough problems in Philadelphia. The adventure, it was decided, was premature even though two hundred thousand Americans had already settled on the wide watershed of the Mississippi and were restless about their rights on that stream.

2.

Work of Art

"Mr. Trumbull is good enough to deliver this," Senator Burr wrote his much-missed Theodosia from Philadelphia in 1792. "You have long known and admired the brilliance of his genius and wit. I wish you also to know the amiable qualities of his heart."

Because of the uncertainty of the mails Burr often entrusted his letters home to traveling friends. Over the bad roads it was sometimes a three-day journey between New York and Philadelphia. As a busy member of Congress he seldom had three days to spare. The whole journey would have been arduous for delicate Theodosia. On several occasions, to cut the travel at both ends, he begged her to meet him in Princeton or Trenton. Steadily, however, their affectionate letters went back and forth. This particular Mr. Trumbull seemed a special messenger.

Connecticut Trumbulls were numerous in public affairs then. Almost certainly this was John Trumbull, the painter. Reference in the letter to Trumbull's wit could suggest that he might have been another John Trumbull, whose satirical poetry was popular at the time, but he seems to have been busy at home as a Connecticut state official in this year. Burr's friend could have been Jonathan Trumbull, who had been a successor to Hamilton as the military secretary of Washington. Certainly at this time he was in Philadelphia as a staunch Federalist member of Congress who was finding the policies of Jefferson and his friends repugnant. Nothing about him, however, suggested wit or genius. John, the artist, seems the likely messenger. This John, "the painter of the Revolution," who had been a member of Jefferson's choice coterie in Paris, was traveling much between New York and Philadelphia at the time.

Now at the height of his powers at thirty-six and as handsome as the portrait of him by his fellow artist Gilbert Stuart shows him to be, Trumbull had come home with his easel to paint the portraits of the great or the merely affluent in America. To the glamour of his life in the art circles of Europe where he had been Jefferson's guide as well as his protégé, he added a courtly bearing and a high-strung temperament. In the temporary capital on the Schuylkill, statesmen, already conscious of themselves as Founding Fathers, came to his studio to sit for him. And though political differences were already sharpening in the diverse company he painted, John Trumbull could count as his acquaintances such different personages as Jefferson, Hamilton—and Burr.

His painting was the artistic fashion in 1792. None of the gentlemen and ladies who came to admire his work apparently noted one defect which the great Stuart saw. That great portraitist, examining one of Trumbull's pictures, stood back puzzled.

"This looks," he said, "as if it was drawn by a man with but one eye."

It had been. As a child in Connecticut, the wellborn Trumbull had severely injured his left eye. That did not mar his appearance or, save in the penetrating two eyes of such a genius as Stuart, the quality of his work. Washington sat for him several times. One portrait of the President was especially admired by many. It was a large painting commissioned by Congressman Smith for the city of Charleston, South Carolina. Trumbull called it "Washington before the Battle of Princeton." But Smith politely turned it down. He did not think its "military character" would be acceptable to the people of Charleston. They remembered Washington as they had seen him on his recent tour of the South. So they would, Smith said, "be better satisfied with a more matter-of-fact likeness, such as they had recently seen him—calm, tranquil, peaceful." Apparently Trumbull, who was quick to take offense, accepted this criticism with grace. He painted another "Trumbull Washington" for Charleston. Smith may have been right. Subsequent South Carolinians regarded the portrait as one of the President's best likenesses showing him "without wig or false teeth."

Trumbull's easy indignation was turned on Smith's opposite in politics but his counterpart in political ruthlessness and audacity, William Branch Giles of Virginia. As Smith had become Hamilton's most arrogant floor agent, so Giles was ready with rough tongue and bold maneuver to serve Jefferson in the mounting antagonism between the Secretary of the Treasury and the Secretary of State. Giles had come to Congress, in 1790, before he was thirty years old. At Princeton his position in the Virginia plantation gentry was indicated by the slave body servant he required there. He had well learned his law at William and Mary but as lawyer and legislator he often operated with a bludgeon. He was unprepossessing in person. Possibly that made him more readily pugnacious with good-looking Trumbull who regarded him with one hostile eye and in a word portrait left a flat, repulsive image of him at Jefferson's epicurean table.

Naturally Trumbull, whom Jefferson had regarded as a member of his family and to whom he had offered a place as his secretary, was welcome in the great Virginian's house. In a sense the Secretary of State was eager for a sort of coterie in Philadelphia where he had rented and remodeled a house belonging to Thomas Leiper, who was to help him as both politician and tobacco dealer. The house had rooms aplenty. There was place for six horses and their equipage in its adjoining stables. Jefferson had urged both Madison and Monroe to come and live with him. Though they declined, they were often there. He had hoped that Maria Cosway, whom Trumbull had introduced to him, might also come to paint in Philadelphia.

There had been an unfortunate prelude to one dinner to which the Secretary had invited both Trumbull and Giles. At another party a few days before, so Trumbull wrote, he had made the young Virginian "ridiculous in the eyes of a lady to whose favorable opinion he aspired." Now Giles was ready for revenge. He began to "rally" the painter about "the puritanical character and ancestry" of his New England. From raillery Giles went on to what Trumbull called the most "broad and unqualified avowal of atheism." But what Trumbull remembered best and recorded most bitterly was that while Giles roared his scorn of religion, Jefferson sat "smiling and nodding approbation." He related the incident in his memoirs, he said, "as helping to elucidate the character of Mr. Jefferson." Certainly also, he melodramatically elucidated his own character as noble, faithful defender of the faith.

"Mr. Giles," the artist said he at last told the Congressman, "I admire your frankness, and it is but just that I should be equally frank in avowing my sentiments. Sir, in my opinion, the man who can with sincerity make the declaration which you have just made, is perfectly prepared for the commission of every atrocious action, by which he can promise himself the advancement of his own interest, or the gratification of his impure passions, provided he can commit it secretly, and with a reasonable probability

of escaping detection by his fellow man. Sir, I would not trust such a man
with the honor of a wife, a sister or a daughter—with my own purse or
reputation, or with anything which I thought valuable. Our acquaintance,
sir, is at an end."

After that speech, he said, he never spoke to Giles again and his acquaintance with Jefferson was "distant and cold." Still this recollection
written years later also sounds both distant and extravagant. Certainly it
reports a remarkable break with Jefferson by the young man to whom, a
few years before, the great Virginian had sent such messages as, "Kneel
to Mrs. Cosway for me, and lay my soul in her lap." Philadelphia was not
Paris nor was Jefferson the contented minister by the Seine. Trumbull
himself wrote that, "as the French Revolution advanced, my whole soul re-
volted from the atrocities of France, while he approved or apologized for
all." And already when Trumbull exploded in Philadelphia mobs in Paris
had begun the massacre of nobles and clergy. Still, when the artist described his outrage in his memoirs later, his speech resembled sermons already made by New England Federalists, like Burr's cousin, a younger
Timothy Dwight, who regarded democracy and infidelity as synonymous.

Furthermore, despite the golden interlude in Paris with Jefferson,
Trumbull had ties likely to put him on the Hamiltonian side in the feud
developing in the Cabinet. Indeed, before he joined the Jefferson coterie,
the artist had been the friend of John Barker Church. Undoubtedly it was
Trumbull who introduced Angelica Church as well as Maria Cosway into
Jefferson's charming coterie in France.

After meeting Church in America at the end of the war, Trumbull
had renewed his acquaintanceship in London where Church lived "in
great elegance . . . rich, honored and associated with the great." Even before he joined Jefferson's household Trumbull was receiving loans from
Church which came to "a considerable amount." Without Church's aid,
he wrote, "my subsequent success would have been checked by pecuniary
embarrassment." In Philadelphia he was still in debt to Church who had
come to America to join in the speculations under Hamilton's fiscal plans
at which Jefferson was now looking in outrage and suspicion.

More Hamiltonians than Church were well disposed toward Trumbull. This was emphasized in artistic fashion in March 1792. Hamilton was
at the high tide of his career. The powerful business community idolized
him. Leading New Yorkers arranged to have his portrait painted for a
public display of honor. And, of course, Trumbull was the artist chosen to

paint it. This undertaking required some travel by the artist between Philadelphia and New York on which he gladly carried messages for friends.

Though not by a drooping eyelash did the portrait show it, in this March Hamilton's position was shaken by the financial failure of Duer, his close friend and former chief assistant in the Treasury. The Secretary came serenely through the panic which followed. His resentment grew, however, over the wit, the slur, and the satire Freneau was aiming at him in the *National Gazette*. Obviously he was furious in July when Trumbull's portrait of him was hung in the old city hall of New York. He was not appeased by praise of his picture and its artist. Said the *Philadelphia Advertiser*: the work was "the best that ever came from his pencil." Its subject in this same month struck out in outrage at Jefferson. Using fictitious initials which fooled nobody, he published the fact that the Jeffersonian editor who was attacking administrative measures was getting a salary from the public funds of the State Department. And he put a dagger point on the charge: "In common life it is thought ungrateful for a man to bite the hand that puts bread in his mouth; but if the man is hired to do it, the case is altered."

Both the Jeffersonian and Hamiltonian gazettes were filled with virulent communications signed with a rich variety of Latin names. Hamilton wrote with industrious venom. Jefferson said he never did any such writing. But his supporters like Beckley were evidently busy bringing him materials. And even Madison took directions from Jefferson in writing. On both sides it mounted in virulence. Perhaps Congressman Smith, in language which some at first thought was Hamilton's, was most extreme in his bitter rhetoric.

Hamilton, as *Catullus*, had written that Jefferson's true character would be revealed "when the visor of stoicism is plucked from the brow of the epicurean; when the plain garb of Quaker simplicity is stripped from the concealed voluptuary; when Caesar *coyly refusing* the proffered diadem, is seen to be Caesar rejecting the trappings but grasping the substance of imperial domination. . . ." Almost like an echo, Smith wrote that Jefferson's pretenses had "long ago excited the derision of the many, who know that under the assumed cloak of humility lurks the most ambitious spirit, the most overweening pride and hauteur, and that the *externals* of pure Democracy afford but a flimsy veil to the *internal* evidences of aristocratic splendor, sensuality and Epicureanism."

This was certainly no time when a "calm, tranquil, peaceful" portrait could be painted of President Washington, harassed by the mounting warfare of his chief ministers and getting some sideswipes of criticism himself. Reluctantly he would agree to take a second term. But in this Presidential election year, out of the furies true political parties were formally organizing for the contest to fill or refill the Vice-Presidential place held by John Adams.

This was no time for any real or pretended botanizing. The situation had changed and sharpened since Jefferson and Madison had made their tour of New York and New England the summer before. Now a direct call for aid was sent to Burr by Beckley from Jefferson's ardent republican friend Dr. Rush.

"This letter will be handed to you by Mr. Beckley," Rush wrote from Philadelphia on September 24, 1792. "He possesses a fund of information about men and things. The republican ferment continues to work in our state; and the time, I think, is approaching very fast when we shall universally reprobate the maxim of sacrificing public justice and national gratitude to the interested ideas of stock-jobbers and brokers, whether in or out of the legislature of the United States."

Then he added a clarion call:

"Your friends everywhere look to you to take an active part in removing the monarchial rubbish of our government. It is time to speak out, or we are undone."

From this letter, it is evident that whoever Jefferson and Madison saw on their tour the year before, Beckley had not met Burr. He could not have found a better man to introduce him. The Senator not only admired the famous Philadelphia physician. Also, on personal grounds he had reasons for feelings of gratitude and affection for the doctor. Mrs. Burr's failing health was increasingly on his mind. In New York she had the attention of the almost-as-famous Dr. Samuel Bard, who, though a Loyalist, Washington had chosen as his physician. But in Philadelphia, Burr constantly sought the advice of Dr. Rush as to her treatment. On his part Rush knew that much hope for the "republican ferment" he desired lay in the debonair Senator from New York.

Burr was at this time not merely a rising young man just old enough to qualify as a senator. He was a soaring figure in the United States. His colleagues in the Congress recognized his brilliance, his industry and his eloquence. Also in Philadelphia there was appreciation of his popular ap-

peal in the country. There was then little question about his popularity in
the nationally strategic state of New York.

Governor Clinton's fifth term as Governor was ending in 1792. Some
thought he would not run again, having only squeaked through at the
election before. Many republicans and some Federalists proposed the election of Burr. Hamilton, still smarting from Burr's defeat of his father-in-
law the year before, was enraged by the feeling of many of his own friends
that the Colonel as an independent and moderate man might be most acceptable as a candidate. As sentiment showed itself the Senator seemed not
only a threat to republican Clinton but to Hamilton's leadership of the
Federalists as well. Burr let the demand for his candidacy grow. Then
when his strength was shown he announced that he would not be a
candidate.

Hamilton, who had persuaded Chief Justice of the United States
John Jay to run as the Federalist candidate, was relieved. Jay, he believed,
had a much better chance of beating Clinton than beating Burr, who
might pull many Federalist as well as republican votes. The idea of defeat
at the hands of the Senator was intolerable to the Secretary. He certainly
did not share the feeling of "real personal friendship" which one of his
henchmen assured him Burr felt for him.

Clinton grabbed the republican nomination which he had never
meant to relinquish. He certainly owed Burr the amiability which Hamilton displayed to him everywhere except in his confidential letters and
conversations. Not only was the Senator now removing himself from the
aging Governor's path. Also after the election he played an effective part
in what has been generally described as a process by which Clinton was
permitted to steal the election from Jay.

The returns showed more votes for Jay. But Clinton charging irregularities contested the result. Senator King and Burr were asked to judge
the matter. King agreed and Burr, as he said, reluctantly followed suit.
King's opinion would have seated Hamilton's Jay. Burr, however, made
the case by which enough Jay votes were ruled irregular to give the victory to Clinton. Both King and Burr arrayed other lawyers behind their
opinions. Burr's group was by far the most distinguished—including U. S.
Attorney General Randolph. Those who upheld his opinion, however,
included some staunch Federalists. Some measure of the validity of Burr's
position may be drawn from the fact that of the nine lawyers who supported his view all but two were of such eminence that their biographies

appear in the *Dictionary of American Biography*. King arrayed ten only
two of whom have been deemed worthy of such historical recollection—
and one of those was Hamilton's friend and Burr's opponent Troup. Under such circumstances it is difficult to understand the acceptance of
the Hamiltonian suggestion that Burr in this case engaged in sharp practice for partisan politics.

Burr acted from no love of Clinton, though his skill as attorney
served him. Indeed, he wrote soon afterward that he was aware that Clinton regarded him with "jealousy and malevolence." Certainly that was
true later. At this time such feelings were curiously shown. Later in the
year, perhaps once again seeking to annex Burr or shelve him, the Governor offered Burr a place on the State Supreme Court bench. Burr declined it. He had other ideas in mind.

In the long Congressional recess Burr was happily at home more of
the time. Mrs. Burr's health was apparently better though once while off
in Albany he chided little Theo for saying "not a word of your mamma's
health." More and more this child occupied his heart and mind. As the
fall came on, he wrote her during another absence—this time in West-
chester. He had been perplexed as to what book to buy her. In his letter
to her he wrote as though he addressed another person: "She reads so
much and so rapidly that it is not easy to find proper and amusing French
books for her; and yet I am so flattered with her progress in that language,
that I am resolved she shall, at all events, be gratified. Indeed, I owe it to
her."

Young Theo must have been gratified by such language from "the
best of papas." He went along in playful flattery.

"I went into one bookseller's shop after another. I found plenty of
fairy tales and such nonsense, fit for the generality of children of nine
or ten years old. 'These,' said I, 'will never do. Her understanding begins
to be above such things.'; but I could see nothing that I would offer with
pleasure to *an intelligent, well-informed* girl of nine years old."

Of course, he found the book he wanted. Unfortunately he did not
name it. He only described it as a work contained in two octavo volumes,
handsomely bound, and with prints and registers. He added: "It is a work
of fancy, but replete with instruction and amusement."

For him in early autumn a strange story was developing which might
be replete with instruction. Much mystery still attends it. One week before Rush invited him to republican battle, others regarded him as already

deeply involved as the possible chief opponent of the Federalists. On September 17 Senator King wrote Hamilton in warning:

"If the enemies of the government are secret and united," he said, "we shall lose Mr. Adams. Burr is industrious in his canvass, and his object is well understood by our Antis. Mr. Edwards is to make the interest for him in Connecticut, and Mr. Dallas, who is here and quite in the circle of the Governor and the party, informs us that Mr. Burr will be supported as Vice-President in Pennsylvania. Should Jefferson and his friends unite in the project, the votes of Mr. A. may be so reduced, that though more numerous than those of any other person, he may decline the office."

Of course, "the enemies of government" in King's letter and in his and Hamilton's eyes were those who disagreed with the policies of the Secretary of the Treasury. But to Hamilton, Burr constituted not only a national threat but a home danger as well. By heritage, like Jefferson, Burr was one of the aristocrats. Many Federalists found him personally and politically congenial. But he was an aristocrat with appeal to the people, and had easy contact with them which Jefferson lacked even when he led them. Brilliant and attractive, he was born to a position which Hamilton had had to make for himself by merit and marriage. Hamilton had reason to fear him as both a republican and one who might sap his strength as Federalist leader, too.

To resentment Hamilton added fear to make a concealed hatred which Nathan Schachner in his Burr biography concluded was "definitely pathologic in nature." Four days after he received King's letter of warning he began in "confidential" letters his secret incessant vilification of Burr. To a fellow Federalist he wrote in fury about the Vice-Presidential contest:

"Mr. Clinton's success I should think very unfortunate; I am not for trusting the government too much in the hands of its enemies. But still, Mr. C. is a man of property, and in private life, as far as I know of probity. I fear the other gentleman [Burr] is unprincipled, both as a public and a private man. . . . He is determined, as I conceive, to make his way to the head of the popular party, and to climb *per fas aut nefas* to the highest honors of the State, and as much higher as circumstances may permit. Embarrassed, as I understand, in his circumstances, with an extravagant family, bold enterprising, and intriguing, I am mistaken if it be not his object to play a game of confusion, and I feel it a religious duty to oppose his career."

Two days later he sent a copy of King's letter to President Washington, who was awaiting a visit from Jefferson at Monticello. To this he added the report of his spies that Burr had been in Philadelphia ten days before. Obviously, Hamilton was suggesting that in the recess his New York rival was up to some skulduggery there. Then, on September 27, in another confidential letter to a friend he promoted Burr in infamy: "In a word, if we have an embryo-Caesar in the United States, 'tis Burr."

Others, with misgivings of their own, heard reports of Burr's candidacy. Down in Virginia, Monroe, who by one year had deprived Burr of his position as the youngest Senator, wrote to Madison on September 18. "My opinion is briefly this: that if Mr. Burr was in every respect inexceptionable it would be impossible to have him elected. He is too young, if not in point of age, yet upon the public theatre, to admit the possibility of an union in his favor." Furthermore, he indicated that he was not certain as to exactly where Burr stood in the growing conflict of political principles.

Monroe's view, with which Madison agreed, was not universally shared by other prominent republicans. On October 11 these two figures, in what would become the Virginia Dynasty, received letters brought by a special messenger from Melancton Smith and Marinus Willett in New York and from John Nicholson in Philadelphia. All urged that Burr be substituted for Clinton as the republican candidate for Vice-President. Such support could not easily be disregarded.

These two wealthy republicans who in a real sense had brought Burr into politics as a Sons of Liberty candidate in 1788, now were both influential in New York politics. Nicholson's position was similar in Pennsylvania though his republicanism was less clear. He was a partner of Robert Morris, the financier of the Revolution, and with him was engaged in vast land speculations. They had huge holdings which they hoped to fill with the stream of refugees from San Domingo and France. Also they acquired seven thousand lots in the permanent capital-to-be on the Potomac. They would build a third of the structures standing when the government moved there. Nicholson was not only Burr's friend. Also, the New York Senator owned one hundred of the twenty-five hundred shares in Nicholson's Pennsylvania Population Company.

Leaving the answers to the letters of these gentlemen to Madison, Monroe suggested that Burr be given the most soothing assurances of esteem and confidence and that opposition to his nomination be placed, as Madison's biographer put it, "solely on his youth and late arrival on the national scene." Burr, indeed, was only thirty-six. Clinton was fifty-three. In retrospect it has been suggested that Madison, at forty-two, and Monroe, at thirty-five, then recognized that time would take care of Clinton as a Presidential competitor with the Virginians, but that if Burr were put forward Old Dominion hopes or expectations might be dashed by a formidable adversary. They adhered to Clinton as a candidate better known and "warmly supported by sundry influential characters."

The third and greatest of the three Virginians, Jefferson, had also been mentioned as a candidate. He was practically disqualified, however, by the Constitutional provision prohibiting any state from casting votes for two of its own citizens in the election of President and Vice-President. With Washington as the unanimous choice for re-election as President there would be sentiment, too, against one state having both offices. Jefferson had been one of those who persuaded Washington to accept a second term.

Now on September 27, before his colleagues had received the letters supporting Burr, Jefferson left Monticello for Philadelphia where the candidate would be chosen. On the way he stopped for a long morning's conversation with Washington. The two Virginians again expressed their mutual preference for their plantations over public office. In the course of their talk, Washington spoke his concern about the differences between Jefferson and Hamilton. He dismissed as nonsense Jefferson's fears of a monarchy. There were not, he told his minister, "ten men in the United States whose opinions were worth anything, who entertained such a thought." There were many more than he imagined, Jefferson insisted, mentioning specifically Hamilton and Schuyler. Tired old Washington ended the discussion with "another exhortation" that Jefferson not decide too positively on early retirement.

Jefferson reached Philadelphia on October 5. Evidently there was much discussion and maneuvering there. In a sense a party was being formed as well as its first candidate chosen. Possibly, as Jefferson wrote later, he distrusted Burr then. He had spoken of Clinton as "dishonorable" in the manner in which he took the election from Jay. Possibly he felt that Clinton and Burr in this matter were tarred with the same stick. Evidently, however, he was the chief of those who met to nominate. In terms of present visibility they acted in a smoke-filled room.

The best report of what happened came from the little-remembered Beckley who attended the meeting. (It was in this instance that he was described by Schachner as "a Pennsylvania politician.") The decision was made before the anti-Burr advice of Monroe and Madison reached Philadelphia. Writing on October 17, Beckley reported to Madison about "a meeting which was had last evening between Melancton Smith on the part of the republican interest of N.Y. (specially deputed) and the principal movers of the same interest here [Pennsylvania], to conclude *finally and definitively* as to the choice of a V.P.—the result of which was, unanimously, to exert every endeavor for Mr. Clinton, & to drop all thought of Mr. Burr." And, Beckley added, Colonel Burr had assured him "that he would cheerfully support the measure of removing Mr. A[dams] & lend every aid in his power to C[linton]'s election."

Some students of Jefferson feel that he was not much concerned about this Vice-Presidential nomination. In letters he suggested that he hoped Adams might be rebuked for his monarchial views by the loss of some votes but not enough to defeat him. Certainly, however, attended by his Beckley, he participated in the caucus which picked Clinton and put Burr aside. Evidently some sort of bargain was made which brought about both unanimous agreement and the assurance of Burr that he would cheerfully support Clinton of whose malevolence toward him he was aware. Burr claimed after the Presidential election of 1796 that such a deal had been made and that the Virginians violated the agreement.

Now Burr stood by his pledge. Washington was unanimously re-elected. But Adams was rebuked with only seventy-seven votes out of a possible hundred and thirty-two. And the alliance of New York and Virginia held firm contributing their full share to the fifty votes for Clinton. Jefferson got four votes. Burr received one vote from a friend in South Carolina.

Burr certainly was never a man willing to ride behind. And in this year he almost paraded his ambition by his occupancy of the great mansion of Richmond Hill. It was a sort of city man's Monticello. Splendid as it had been when Abigail Adams was delighted as its occupant, Burr set about to make it grander still. He bought costly furnishings, hung its walls with paintings. Its library was filled with more and more books like those he and Theodosia so often discussed in their letters. He improved the landscaping of the grounds. He dammed a brook to make a pond. In every fashion he prepared the house for hospitality to eminent American and foreign visitors and as a background for himself.

Yet it was the house of a dying woman. More and more when he was in Philadelphia, he would be consulting Dr. Rush on medication which might help her. Also from Philadelphia he corresponded with Dr. Bard. He reported a variety of recommended remedies: hemlock, laudanum, mercury. Yet even in his worries he kept up his instruction of ten-year-old Theodosia, correcting her misspelling of laudanum and urging her to learn the difference between "infusion" and "decoction."

Most revealing as to Burr's worries was one sentence in a letter to him from young Theo: "Ma begs you will omit the thoughts of leaving Congress." Yet in his reply, her father carefully told her that "omit" was wrongly used in this sentence. He told her, "You mean *'abandon, relinquish, or abjure the thoughts.'*" Obviously in concern and anxiety the driving politician was ready to relinquish, abandon or abjure his place in the Senate.

When he returned to Philadelphia early in November, the Colonel did not look like a man who had been bargained out of the candidacy for the Vice-Presidency. Pompous, honest John Adams, whom the artist Trumbull had thought beautiful when he had the powder combed out of his curly hair, presided over the Senate in which Burr sat. Adams would not decline to serve, as King had feared, because of the reduced vote for his continuance in office. He had accepted Jefferson's explanations that he meant no attack on him while approving Paine's evident strictures on his "Discourses." The election battle was over but the war was only begun. Mr. Jefferson, agreeing reluctantly to stay longer in his post, was prepared to believe anything bad about Hamilton. On November 19, 1792, he noted in his *Anas:* "Beckley brings me the pamphlet written by Hamilton, before the war, in answer to Common Sense. It is entitled 'Plain Truth'. Melancthon (sic) Smith sends it to Beckley, and in his letter says, it was not printed in New York by Loudon, because prevented by a mob, and was printed in Philadelphia, and that he has these facts from Loudon." Samuel Loudon, the printer, had had such an experience with a radical Committee of Mechanics in March 1776, but before this Hamilton had already written his pamphlet defending the Patriot cause and in the month of Loudon's troubles took up arms in its defense.

Beckley was industriously gathering other information about Hamil-

ton. Some of it was being compiled as the basis for resolutions charging
Hamilton with violations of the law and derelictions of duty as Secretary
of the Treasury. Drafted by Jefferson and Madison, who stayed in the
background, these would be introduced soon after the new year by Congressman Giles. Burr's connection with this business, if any, was nebulous.
Indeed, it has been scarcely noticed that he accompanied House Speaker
John P. C. Muhlenberg to see Hamilton on behalf of Jacob Clingman,
a former clerk in Muhlenberg's office, who had been arrested with one
James Reynolds of New York. These men were charged with suborning
a witness to commit perjury in an attempt at petty corruption in the
Treasury. Burr then apparently knew little about the business. He seemed
to be engaged only in helping Muhlenberg's clerk who was his New
York constituent. Certainly he could not have known then the extent of
Hamilton's secretly spread antipathy toward him. And Hamilton did not
know how much Burr or Muhlenberg knew about this seemingly small
messy matter. Evidently Hamilton was as amiable as usual. He promised
to do all he could for Muhlenberg's ex-employee. But then certainly his
smile must have been a work of art. It hid not only his hatred of Burr but
fears as well. Trumbull could not have done better with his one eye and
his facile brush. The Secretary was going to need the strong, handsome,
serene face the artist had painted in his portrait.

Antagonisms now were as harsh and strident as those aroused at
Jefferson's table when the harangue of Giles had been met by the haughty
rebuke of Trumbull. The scene was wider now and more than candlelit.
Men were ready not only to rebuke but to destroy each other. Perhaps
this was a good time for an artist to pack up his brushes and move away.
Trumbull did that. But this time he did not swing away in anger from a
repugnant dinner partner and a nodding and smiling host. He went in
congenial company to diplomacy which had long interested him almost as
much as his art, sometimes to his injury as artist. He accepted the position
of private secretary to Jay. That dignified patrician, who had not given
up his position as Chief Justice when he ran as Hamilton's candidate and
was not giving it up now, had been made envoy extraordinary to Great
Britain. There would have been no such job for Trumbull if Burr had
had his way. The Senator, though personally friendly to Jay, opposed his
confirmation as a pro-British reactionary. The Chief Justice was approved
for this extra job by a vote of eighteen to eight. Jay noted in a letter to his
wife that "Mr. Burr was among the few who opposed it."

The post to which the dignified patrician envoy called Trumbull was similar to the one Jefferson had offered him in Paris. In his place with Jay, Trumbull assisted in negotiating a treaty with England for the defense of which Hamilton would be stoned at a meeting before City Hall in New York.

3.

From Vine Street to Bizarre

The name of no arriving guest was more proudly shouted by liveried flunkies across the sidewalk, up the staircase, into the salon of beautiful Anne Willing Bingham in Philadelphia than that of Secretary of the Treasury Alexander Hamilton. With money of her own and that of her husband the banker, William Bingham, she provided not only social leadership for herself but the perfect setting for the small blond financial genius of the government.

Anne Bingham had not exactly taken the advice given her by Jefferson when she was in Paris for presentation at the court of Louis XVI. She had listened with her large eyes smiling then when the American Minister told her that she would be happier in the domestic pleasures of America than in the sophisticated society of Europe. She had come home. And she was having a remarkably good time spending her money, her wit and her vivacity in her domestic establishment, Mansion House, modeled on the residence of the Duke of Manchester, "the dimensions of the original being somewhat enlarged in the copy."

Hamilton seemed made for the society over which she presided. Anne, being no Puritan and no democrat, found the Secretary politically and personally congenial. Some were shocked by the lady's vocabulary and her taste for risqué jokes. Hamilton matched her wit and joined in her laughter. No one at her extravagant parties appeared to be so much the confident, gallant, sophisticated man of the world as he.

Not even the rich Robert Morris, who would have Pierre Charles L'Enfant design a marble palace for him, could compete with Mrs. Bing-.am's parties. Few others tried. Still, there were other parties in plenty.

Both Abigail Adams and Aaron Burr complained of the number of invitations they received. Abigail was no austere Puritan. Both she and the Vice-President, some felt, had been seduced by the social pomp and ceremony of England. Burr certainly was no Puritan despite—or because of —his dour Calvinistic ancestry. Still he found his way often into the quiet homes of Quakers, as did Jefferson. It was from Philadelphia that, in making plans for the education of his young Theodosia, Burr spoke contemptuously of mere ladies of fashion.

Others regarded Anne Bingham's entertainments with envy. Some attempted emulation. It was an extravagant time among many more than the rich and the supposedly wise. There were some gaps in the prosperity Hamilton was being praised for producing and upon which prodigality was supposedly based. Jefferson's editor, Freneau, published a verse about that at the time, ending with the lines:

> And, Sir, 'tis true
> (Twixt me and you)
> That some have grown prodigious fat,
> And some prodigious lean,

More preferred to be prodigious fat than prodigious lean and some grasped at the first or pretended to it. An admirer and defender of Hamilton wrote of two of the Secretary's acquaintances outside the Bingham guest list, Mr. and Mrs. James Reynolds, as grasping pretenders. Richard Folwell wrote of going by invitation to see this couple who "lived in stile in a large house in Vine Street next to the corner of Fifth." He went in December 1792, he said, "to see if possible how People supported Grandeur, without apparently Friends, Money or Industry."

Others were interested for more reasons than curiosity in such a spectacle—notably John Beckley. He was competent at his desk as clerk of the House. He was congenial in the lobbies, the boardinghouses, and the taverns. Perhaps he was sometimes credulous as Jefferson said. But, as he carried news to the Secretary of State and to his chief aides, Madison and Monroe, others brought interesting information to him. Not far from his desk was the office of Speaker Muhlenberg with whom Burr had gone to intercede with the amiable Hamilton for the Speaker's former clerk, Jacob Clingman. Either from Muhlenberg or Clingman, Beckley learned early of the supposed intimacy of the Secretary of the Treasury with Reynolds and his wife Maria.

Behind a bland clerk's face Beckley hid his resentment of Hamilton's attacks on Jefferson. Still, while handling his legislative papers, he wrote twice in the fall of 1792 to Madison about the Treasury chief's animosity toward him. He told his Virginia sponsor in the House that Hamilton considered him his "personal & political enemy." Beckley warned: "It would be wise to be watchful, there is no inferior degree of sagacity in the combinations of this *extraordinary* man. With a comprehensive eye, a subtle and contriving mind, and a soul devoted to his object, all his measures are promptly and aptly designed, and like the links of a chain, dependent on each other, acquired additional strength by their union & concert."

Beckley believed he had come upon an astoundingly fragile link in the Hamiltonian chain. He had already been as watchful as he urged Madison to be and some time between the middle of October and early in December, he secured, probably from Clingman with whom he had been associated in the small legislative bureaucracy, information which he believed proved Hamilton guilty of criminal conduct in speculation in the government securities over which he presided. Clingman told Beckley of a Treasury clerk named Andrew G. Fraunces, who he said had been the confidential go-between in speculations Hamilton had made with the now bankrupt Duer. Hamilton was supposed to have made thirty thousand dollars in this business. Fraunces was now apparently ready to squeal because Hamilton or his close friend and assistant comptroller, Oliver Wolcott, had turned him down in a small deal of his own. Fraunces was now said to be boasting that "he could, if he pleased, hang Hamilton." If Beckley's report of Fraunces as a man with a well-known love of money and drink was correct, the Secretary would have been careless in his agent. Apparently there was nothing to this tale, or somebody besides Beckley's friends met his needs in money and liquor. At any rate Fraunces disappeared from history.

Beckley seemed on a warmer trail in a different case Clingman told him about. He poured into Beckley's big ears a story about other friends: the Reynolds of grandeur at Fifth and Vine. He had been even closer than Fraunces to the Secretary in speculations. Apparently Clingman had become talkative after his arrest with Reynolds. He told Beckley he had been shown by Maria Reynolds letters signed by Hamilton in connection with payments of eleven hundred dollars he had made to her husband.

THOMAS JEFFERSON
By Jean Antoine Houdon.

ABIGAIL ADAMS
By Gilbert Stuart.

JOHN ADAMS
By C.B.J. Fevret de Saint-Mémin.

ALEXANDER HAMILTON
By John Trumbull.

ELIZABETH SCHUYLER HAMILTON
By Ralph Earl.

AARON BURR, AS VICE-PRESIDENT
By John Vanderlyn.

JAMES MADISON
After an original portrait by Gilbert Stuart.

DOLLEY MADISON
By Gilbert Stuart.

It is not clear whether Muhlenberg and Burr had this information when they interceded with Hamilton for Clingman. Certainly soon afterward Muhlenberg and Monroe, already briefed by Beckley, heard more when they called on Reynolds in the jail. There, they stated later, he strongly intimated that he could implicate Hamilton but that he was not going to talk until he was released. Adding Congressman Abraham Venable to their informal corps, the fat Pennsylvania Congressman and the humorless Monroe continued their detective work in a call on Mrs. Reynolds.

Though apparently reluctant, she was more talkative. She admitted burning at Hamilton's request many letters from Hamilton to her husband. Also, she showed them several anonymous notes which she believed to be from Hamilton and were so labeled by Reynolds. She told them that Hamilton had offered her husband "something clever" to leave Philadelphia and not return. She said that she thought this was not just a benevolent offer on the Secretary's part but was made because Reynolds "could tell something that would make some of the heads of departments tremble."

On December 13 the self-appointed committee interviewed Clingman. In a statement which he duly signed he said that he had first met Reynolds in September 1791. Evidently he became a frequent caller at the Reynolds' house. In January he met Hamilton there. The Secretary gave Mrs. Reynolds a paper, which he, Hamilton, said "he was ordered to give Mr. Reynolds." This phrase seemed curious to Clingman.

"Who," he reported that he wondered, "could order the Secretary of the Treasury of the United States to give that?"

The half answer that he found was that "in the course of the conversation Mrs. Reynolds said that Colonel Hamilton had helped her husband from time to time, once giving him $1,100."

The evidence grew stronger as the days passed and obviously several days did pass after the beginning of the committee's interrogations before they confronted Hamilton with their information on December 15. They came into the Secretary's office, grim and formal men. Hamilton later described them as the Jacobin Scandal Club. This time he was very polite. They told him what they had learned. An imaginative historian wrote that the luminous Colonel was "thunderstruck." Another described his furious indignation and astonishment. Possibly the usually imperturbable Secretary gave that impression of indignant surprise. Yet it seems hardly likely that he was completely astounded. Gossip moved swiftly in the small circles of the government. And nothing is so clear as that there were Beckleys on both sides. Hamilton was no exception to the rule that conscience makes cowards of us all, but he was not a man to show it. Whatever the facts, "the Reynolds affair" had been hanging heavily over his head for a year. By coincidence this call of the Congressmen came just a year to the day from the time when, according to Hamilton's version of the story, he began to be bled for his folly.

Once calmed, no cowardice shook his composure. He asked his three accusers to meet him at his residence that evening when he would present them with documentary evidence of his innocence of any misconduct in office. It is a safe presumption to say that he bowed them to the door. They gathered that evening at the Pemberton house where Hamilton, as he wished, had elbow room and from which, fortunately, Eliza and the children had gone on a visit to Albany. With Hamilton was Oliver Wolcott, his devoted aide and friend. Now evidently the Secretary was the picture of self-assurance. He greeted his visitors with aplomb as the able lawyer for the defense in his own case.

Obviously he had prepared his case with the same care he put into his great reports. But now he presented no brilliant array of arguments and statistics. Calmly he began a sleazy tale of private misconduct as proof of his probity as public servant.

"Some time in the summer of 1791," he began to his grim accusers, "a woman called at my house in the city of Philadelphia, and asked to speak with me in private." She requested help in getting back to her home in New York to escape a cruel husband. Hamilton was impressed, he said, with her "seeming air of affliction." He had no money with him at the time but promised to get aid to her later in the day. In the evening he put a bank bill in his pocket and went to the address she had given him. Possibly, as one writer has said without benefit of documentation, he furtively made "his way through the dimly lighted streets, away from the fashionable quarter into the section of cheap boarding houses." This was a few months before the time when Folwell reported the Reynolds residence as one of grandeur in a good residential neighborhood. Evidently Hamilton's destination now was a boardinghouse. (Perhaps a hostelry called In-Skeep's.)

"I enquired for Mrs. Reynolds, and was shown upstairs, at the head of which she met me and conducted me into a bedroom. I took the bill out of my pocket and gave it to her. Some conversation ensued from which it was quickly apparent that other than pecuniary consolation would be acceptable."

Frequent meetings followed, "most of them at my own house; Mrs. Hamilton with her children being absent on a visit to her father." Then, as he told it, he wearied of the relationship but found himself entangled. He presented letters which he said he had received from Maria Reynolds which made her seem an illiterate baggage and himself a not very fastidious fool. She sent a succession of notes by Negro messengers.

"I have kept my Bed these two days and now rise from My pillow wich your Neglect has filled with the shorpest thorns." And again, "I have woes to relate wich I never expected to know accept by the name Come therefore tomorrow sometime or Els in the Evening do I beg you to come gracious God had I the world I would lay It at your feet." Also, "I only do it to Ease a heart wich is ready Burst with Greef."

Listening to Hamilton's unrestrained recital of the amorous affair, Hamilton's accusers were embarrassed. They asked him to stop. But he insisted on being allowed to read on. That brought him closer to the reports they had heard of his public misconduct. Maria talked to him of more things than love and grief. She told him that her husband could give him information with regard to malfeasance in his department. Hamilton saw Reynolds who confessed that he had obtained a list of claims from Hamilton's friend and former assistant Duer, now in prison for debt. Evidently Hamilton regarded that as water over the dam. Also, Reynolds sought an office in the Treasury. Hamilton calmly told his uncomfortable listeners that Maria informed him her husband was seeking a reconciliation with her. He advised her to agree to it. He was, he said, becoming suspicious that Maria and her husband might be working together.

"Yet," he said, "her conduct made it extremely difficult to disentangle myself. All the appearances of violent attachment, and of agonizing distress at the idea of a relinquishment, were played with a most imposing art. This, though it did not make me entirely the dupe of the plot, yet kept me in a state of resolution."

The matter was not resolved by him. On December 15, 1791, the day after the House received his able report calling for the creation of a national bank, he received two letters. Maria wildly warned him: "I have not tim to tell you the cause of my present troubles only that Mr. has rote you this morning . . . and he has swore that If you do not answer It or If he dose not se or hear from you to day he will write Mrs. Hamilton he has just Gone oute and I am a Lone I think you had better come here one moment that you May know the Cause then you will the better know how to act. . . ."

Swiftly behind this letter came Reynolds' message of outrage: "I am very sorry to find out that I have been so Cruelly treated by a person that I took to be my best friend instead of that my greatest Enimy. You have deprived me of every thing thats near and dear to me . . . Sir you took advantage [of] a poor Broken harted woman. instead of being a Friend you have acted the part of the most Cruelist man in existence. you have made a whole family miserable . . . . now I am determined to have satis-faction. it shant be onely one family thats miserable."

Hamilton said he tried to deal with Reynolds who was by turns im-ploring and threatening. Then the complaining husband was crudely specific: "I have this proposal to make to you. give me the Sum Of thousand dollars and I will leve the town and take my daughter with me and go where my Friend Shant here from me and leve her to Yourself to do to her as you thing proper."

So, Hamilton reported, the blackmailing process began. On Decem-ber 22, 1791, he gave Reynolds $600, then $400 on January 3. He had receipts marked "in full of all demands." That was wishful thinking. In dribbles he paid $165 more. Maria begged him to come to see her. Reyn-olds asked more money. Hamilton sent him $50 and again $200.

This was unusual bookkeeping for Hamilton who devised great fi-nancial schemes but was often less than precise in his own accounts. His brother-in-law Church once wrote Jeremiah Wadsworth, who was one of those early aware of the secret Reynolds story, "I will thank you as soon as you can to send me our Account Current, for our Friend Hamilton not being very accurate in his Accounts is not clear that he has not made some Mistakes respecting the Monies you have paid him on my Account."

This time Hamilton not only made this recital of his payments but also presented to his three callers a collection of letters and documents relating to the whole affair. His man and witness, Wolcott, wrote that Monroe, Muhlenberg, Venable "severally acknowledged their entire satis-faction, that the affair had no relation to Official duties." Actually they—and especially Monroe—were far from satisfied. In their report of the inter-view they stated: "Last night we waited on Colonel Hamilton when he informed us of a particular Connection with Mrs. Reynolds; the period of its Commencement & Circumstances attending it—His visiting her at In Skeep's; the frequent supplies of Money to her & her Husband, on that Account; his duress by them, from fear of a disclosure, and his anxiety to be relieved from it and them. To support this he shewed a great number of letters from Reynolds & herself commencing early in 1791. He acknowledged all the letters in a disguised Hand in our possession to be his—We left him under the impression our suspicions were removed—He acknowledged our Conduct toward him had been fair and liberal—He could not complain of it—We brought back all the papers even his own Notes, nor did he ask their Destruction."

Hamilton did ask for copies. And: "It was decided to approach Beckley, who would be able to supply a truly discreet clerk." Beckley, of course, was obliging. He gave the task to one Bernard Webb. How many copies he made is not known. Webb took a copy to Hamilton who asked him who beside him knew of the affair. Webb said that Beckley did. The Secretary told him to tell Beckley that "he considered him bound to it." Beckley sent Webb back again with the message that he "considered himself under no injunction whatever." Such a reply did not endear Beckley to Hamilton and his friends.

Monroe, however, asked Beckley to keep it secret. The "secret" was certainly shared with Jefferson. Two days after Hamilton told his amazing tale the tall Virginian noted: "The affair of Reynolds and his wife—Clingman Muhlenb's clerk testified F. A. Muhlenb; Monroe, Venable—also Wolcott and Wadsworth—known to James Monroe, E. Randolph, Beckley and Webb."

Wolcott and Wadsworth, who as speculator had been blessed by Hamilton's policies, might be expected to keep quiet. So might be Attorney General Randolph. But at least a dozen others were in on the secret. Certainly soon the story must have been whispered with smirks not only in the lobbies of Congress but in the salons of Robert Morris and Anne Bingham.

Monroe put a revealing footnote on this melodrama or mystery on January 2, 1793. He noted: "Clingman called on me this Evening and mentioned that he had been apprised of Mr. Hamilton's Vindication by Mr. Wolcott a Day or two after our Interview with him—He further observed to me that he had communicated the same to Mrs. Reynolds, who appeared much shocked at it and wept immoderately. That she denied the

Imputation and declared that it had been a fabrication of Colonel Hamilton, and that her husband had joined in it, who had told her so, and that he had given him a receipt for Money and written Letters so as to give countenance to the Pretense—That he was with Colonel Hamilton the Day after he left the Jail when we suppsed he was in Jersey—He was of Opinion she was innocent and that the Defense was an Imposition."

Some others doubted Hamilton's "confession." Jefferson sneered at it. His feeling at this time was apparently the same as that he expressed later when he wrote that "his willingness to plead guilty as to the adultery seems rather to have strengthened than weakened the suspicions that he was in truth guilty of the speculations."

Hardly any sympathetic word has been spoken in history for Maria Reynolds. Perhaps she deserves none. Indeed, all the descriptions of her which have come down are from those eager to make a soiled doll of her for their purposes. But Hamilton attested as much to her fascination as to his own folly, even while showing her as a semi-illiterate, easily possessed bawd. He apparently accepted her statement that she came of respectable folk in New York, "a daughter of a Mr. Lewis, sister to a Mr. G. Livingston." He described her as a woman of "most imposing art."

The best description of her extant was one written to buttress Hamilton's description of her as bait in blackmail by Richard Folwell. Little is known of him. He was described only as a publisher but he was possibly a relative of Samuel Folwell, the miniature painter and engraver, living in Philadelphia at this time. He wrote for Hamilton's information a long statement about her, which is reprinted in the book about Hamilton's personal life written by his grandson. Folwell spoke of her "innocent Countenance" which "appeared to show an innocent Heart." When she came to Philadelphia seeking her husband, she was lodged at the house of Folwell's mother at the request of a relative of hers. Maria was an unhappy woman, he said, "far from being tranquil or consistent." At one moment she would express respect and affection for her husband. Then "levity would succeed with bitter Execrations" on him.

"In one or other of these Paroxysms," he wrote, "she told me, so infamous was the Perfidy of Reynolds, that he had frequently enjoined and insisted that she should insinuate herself on certain high and influential Characters—endeavor to make Assignations with them, and actually prostitute herself to gull money from them."

When she made up with her husband, Folwell wrote, his family de-

clined to have such an "infamous character" as Reynolds in their house,
so the couple moved to "a reputable Quaker Lady's" on North Grant
Street. The pious publisher, however, continued his acquaintance though
he heard that "letters were frequently found in the Entry inviting her
Abroad;—and that at Night she would fly off, as was supposed to *answer*
their *Contents*." She talked of speculations. Reynolds invited Folwell to
join in some. Then it was that they "lived in stile in a large House in
Vine Street."

This brought Folwell's story to the December of Hamilton's "confession." At the time of the publisher's visit Reynolds was in jail and pulling all possible strings in order to get out. Clingman was a caller at the
Vine Street establishment while Folwell was there. He seemed to Folwell
to "wish to darken instead of throwing light" on the situation. Maria apparently was babbling. Clingman questioned her.

"He asked her what Luck she had had in her Application for Reynolds' Liberation. She said she had called on the Governor, Mr. Mifflin,
and that he felt for her: Referred her to Mr. Dallas and that he felt also.
She said she called on Mr. Hamilton, and several other Gentlemen; and
that they had all felt."

Monroe had, he hoped, had enough of this case when Clingman
came to him early in January to tell him that he believed Hamilton and
Reynolds had lied. The two others in the great Virginia trio, Jefferson
and Madison, now moved into direct parliamentary attack on Hamilton
in a fashion not to be confused by artifice or adultery. In it they worked
with information furnished by backstage Beckley and with the aid as belligerent front man of swashbuckling Giles. Hamilton had conducted the affairs of the Treasury in lofty fashion, paying little attention to the
meddlesome Congress. In a cavalier allocation of public funds, he seemed
to be favoring his bank while holding back on debts due to France.

This was no Reynolds affair which could be dismissed in the flickering light of Mr. Hamilton's candles. The probe into the Reynolds affair
was conducted as an aspect of proper Congressional vigilance. However
righteous his adversaries may have felt, their next moves can hardly be
regarded as free from vindictiveness. Evidently they were planned while
Hamilton was being confronted with the Reynolds affair. While some
facts are obscure, it seems certain that in December and January, Jefferson, Madison, and Giles planned a House fight on the Treasury Secretary
in which they hoped to catch him off guard and trap him without elbow

room for defense. Their first move was like a zephyr. Then Giles was to loose the lightning.

Rather blandly for him, on January 23, 1793, Giles proposed that a general accounting be required of the Treasury. To such an apparently simple proposal the House acquiesced without debate or record vote. This time Hamilton was not to be gulled. He saw the trick in the introduction of the resolution at this date when only a little more than five weeks remained in the session in which vast data could be compiled and the report could be made to Congress. If no report was forthcoming within that time, republicans could use the failure to stir suspicions about Hamilton's conduct in the long Congressional recess. The Secretary of the Treasury was dealing with financial affairs he understood now, not femininity. Working under pressure himself and driving his staff day and night, he met the challenge. Within twelve days he began to pour in the reports. Within twenty-four days the House got all Giles had asked in four thick volumes filled with tables, charts, analyses of revenue and expenditures, explanations. Federalists rejoiced. Giles was surprised. But he had only played his first card from what seemed a stacked deck.

On February 27, less than a week before adjournment, Giles rose again. He introduced a series of resolutions. There was nothing mild about them. They accused Hamilton of playing high, wide, and handsome with public funds in disregard of the instructions of the Congress and the directions of the President. As a final fillip an accusation was added that he had been "guilty of an indecorum to the House." Apparently Jefferson had wanted to add another resolution calling upon the President to dismiss Hamilton—a sort of impeachment by indirection—but that seemed too much even to the pugnacious Giles. These constituted a second step in the maneuver of malediction. If allowed to hang over unmet in the long recess just ahead, they could be industriously used to rouse alarms among the people.

Jefferson, of course, did not appear in the situation. Madison only spoke primly as to the law in the case without any attack on Hamilton. But the gamecocks met in Giles and Smith of South Carolina. Giles wanted the delaying procedure of first consideration in the committee of the whole. Smith demanded immediate debate and decision.

"The question was," he declared, "had the Secretary violated a law? If so, let it be shown; every member was competent to decide so plain a question."

Others joined him in protest against postponement. So the deadly serious, last-minute debate began. Giles spoke in violent attack for what amounted to the prosecution. He added a pious plea that the Congress help the President get rid of this guilty Secretary of the Treasury. Smith's colleague, Robert Barnwell of South Carolina, ridiculed the idea of help for the President who had made no complaints. Then Smith denounced the animus behind the resolutions. He showed such knowledge of the affairs of the Treasury that many felt that while he voiced them the words in his speech were Hamilton's. He was sorry that the resolutions had been flung into the House in the last days of the session. Yet he was happy that "the vague charges of mismanagement with which the public had long been alarmed, were at length cast into a shape susceptible of investigation and decision." The decision was not much in doubt after he finished his speech. But republicans and others who had knowledge of the Reynolds affair must have grinned when Smith declared that "the Secretary would in the issue rise above every calumny, as fair as the purest angel in heaven."

Giles—or Jefferson—was routed. On the day before Congress adjourned, every resolution was defeated. On not a single one of them did the foes of Hamilton secure as much as a third of the votes of the House. Mr. Jefferson, whose role in the whole matter was kept behind the scenes as was Hamilton's part in the preparation of Smith's speech, wrote a note for his *Anas* as if he had had nothing to do with the matter in the beginning and was remote from the result.

Giles "and one or two others"—evidently not himself and Madison—he wrote, "were sanguine enough to believe that the palpableness of these resolutions rendered it impossible that the House could reject them." He had never been so innocent, he suggested.

"Those who know the composition of the House, 1, of bank directors; 2, holders of bank stock; 3, stock jobbers; 4, blind devotees; 5, ignorant persons who did not comprehend them; 6, lazy and good-humored persons, who comprehended and acknowledged them, yet were too lazy to examine, or unwilling to pronounce censure; the persons who knew these characters, foresaw that the first three descriptions making one-third of the House, the three latter would make one-half of the residue; and, of course, that they would be rejected by a majority of two to one. But they thought that even this rejection would do good, by showing the public the desperate and abandoned dispositions with which their affairs were being conducted."

Somewhere along the line in this matter, Hamilton tried to get a statement from the Secretary of State about a Cabinet discussion regarding European loans the handling of which was a main part of the proposed censure. Jefferson blandly told his adversary and associate that the matter had gone "out of my mind altogether, till the late enquiries brought it forward again." Also, he had told the President while the Giles maneuvers went on that he had kept himself aloof from "all cabal and correspondence on the subject of the government."

Now clearly Jefferson initiated the third step in the maneuver which was to convince the people that what amounted to Hamilton's acquittal had been accomplished by the votes of those whom he had corrupted in his financial policies. From Beckley he secured a list of the "paper men" or financial beneficiaries of the Hamilton policies in the Congress who had voted to uphold Hamilton. Evidently he also had a part in prompting his friend the Virginia Senator John Taylor of Caroline to write a pamphlet containing an even longer list. The vote for Hamilton's innocence, it was boldly stated, only proved his greater guilt.

While this maneuvering was going on, much-troubled Washington again almost plaintively expressed his wish to Jefferson that "Hamilton and myself could coalesce in the measures of the government." Hamilton was ready for such a truce, Washington told his Secretary of State. Yet, the fact was that at this time the two Cabinet antagonists were arrayed against each other in a world struggle which came to a climax on February 1, 1793, when France declared war on England.

Hamilton was confidentially giving the British Minister Hammond assurances that the United States would not support French arms. Three days before the Giles resolutions were introduced, Jefferson was telling Washington of the antipathy of the revolutionary French government to the American Minister in Paris, gay, shrewd, aristocratic Gouverneur Morris. Later in the spring he wrote to Monroe that "H[amilton] is panic-struck if we refuse our breach to every kick which Gr. Brit. may chuse to give it." However, to Washington's suggestion that, when he did finally retire as Secretary of State, he become Minister to France he demurred. He was bent on retirement. He "could never again cross the Atlantic." Nevertheless, he agreed to remain in office for a while longer.

In this season of scandal, charges, and chances of greater conflict,

Jefferson was disturbed about an ugly scandal back home in Virginia. It involved his Randolph connections. Also, it touched even more closely his daughter, Martha, who had married her cousin Thomas Mann Randolph, Jr. Randolph's seventeen-year-old unmarried sister Anne Cary Randolph, called Nancy, unhappy at home to which her father had brought a young second wife, went to live with her sister Judith. In the complex maze of Randolph intermarriages, Judith was the wife of Richard Randolph, brother of John Randolph of Roanoke, who had not yet begun his eccentric career in Congress. Richard's plantation was, as afterwards seemed, aptly named Bizarre.

Early in the fall of 1792 Richard, Judith, and Nancy went to visit at another fancifully named estate, Glynlyvar in Cumberland County, the plantation of the Randolph Harrisons. There Nancy was delivered of a child or had a miscarriage. Richard, believed to be the child's father, was charged with infanticide. Excitement surged about the courthouse where he and Nancy, as accessory, were held without bond. Richard's apprehension may be measured by the counsel he arrayed for the defense which included John Marshall, later Chief Justice of the United States, and Patrick Henry. The frail and aging Henry had declined to join the defense until the fee offered him was raised from two hundred fifty to five hundred guineas. At the trial, however, he showed no waning powers.

The principal witness against Randolph and Nancy was her aunt, Mrs. Carter Page, whose mother was also a Randolph. She testified that she had become suspicious that Nancy was pregnant and to satisfy her curiosity had peeped through a crack in the door to Nancy's room while she was undressing. Henry took the witness for cross-examination.

"Which eye did you peep with?"

The animosity of the courtroom dissolved in loud Virginia laughter. Richard and Nancy were acquitted. Jefferson, learning of the case through newspaper accounts, was not amused. Quickly he sent his sympathy to his daughter and son-in-law but he urged Martha not to fear any reflection on herself or her husband because of this scandal in the family. At such a time, he told her, she must more than ever show her affection for her sister-in-law and cousin. Martha had done her duty by her sister-in-law. She had appeared as witness for her, imperturbable even when the prosecution tried to show that she had given Nancy a medicine which might bring on an abortion. But she spilled her true feelings to her father.

"As for the poor deluded victim," she said, "I believe all feel much more for her than she does for herself. The villain having been no less successful in corrupting her mind than he was in destroying her reputation. Amidst the distress of her family she alone is tranquil and seems proof against every other misfortune on earth but that of a separation from a vile seducer."

Apparently Jefferson wrote no more about this case involving his mother's people, whose coat of arms bore the motto *Nil admirari,* "Wonder at nothing." Actually the story was to continue beside his career. There were conflicting intrafamily charges that either Judith or Nancy poisoned Richard in 1796. Judith later accused Nancy of sexual intercourse with a slave.

Burr seemed little concerned with feminine frailty, Reynolds or Randolph, in the winter and spring of 1793. True, he did as attorney secure a divorce for Maria Reynolds. She promptly—almost too promptly, she told Folwell—married Clingman. This could not have been with the advice or counsel of Lawyer Burr. Maria said that the only fault in the change was that she "got married to Clingman one half hour before she obtained the divorce." That fault was not fatal. She and her new husband moved to England where apparently Clingman had a successful career and they a happy marriage.

Except in the courts, however, Burr at this time was most interested, so far as his letters show, in proving the equality of "female intellectual powers" to those of men. He had found the basis for that faith, he told Theodosia, in her. Now on February 15, as the Jefferson-Madison-Giles explosion was about to be detonated, he enlarged upon the subject in his letters. As a man who apparently read everything, he had come upon the writings of Mary Wollstonecraft. He read with avidity, he wrote, this early feminist's *Vindication of the Rights of Woman.* It was not strange that Burr found a "coldness" in Philadelphia among the few aware of her work. Miss Wollstonecraft (in a sense she was a sort of early Lucy Stoner) was to become the wife of the radical philosopher William Godwin, friend of Thomas Paine, and mother of the wife of Percy Bysshe Shelley. She represented the radicalism which troubled many in Anne Bingham's salon. When Burr read her book with enthusiasm, she was in Paris sympathetically watching the French Revolution.

This series of letters on the equality of women, which Burr wrote early in 1793, apparently coincided with encouragement about the health of Theodosia. Something of her old liveliness seemed to have returned. He wrote her, "Your plan and embellishment of my mode of life are fanciful, are flattering, and inviting." Work then was going on in the embellishment of Richmond Hill. At this time he also spoke of the progress of her "cure." With evident elation, he said, "I bless Sir J., who, with the assistance of Heaven, has thus far restored you."

Mr. Jefferson, who had no such notions as Burr's about the equality of women, did not let their frailty long disturb him. As philosopher he quickly put aside such things as the scandal in his family in Virginia. In the spring of that trial, he was writing home from a small house he had taken in the country, on the Schuylkill near Gray's Ferry. The end of the Congressional session was a joyful event, he reported. And very simple and dignified was the second inauguration of Washington. It was quiet in the country where the Secretary of State in good weather worked outdoors in the sun. There seemed to be at least a little interlude in animosities at home despite war in a bristling world. He thought war between France and England might well serve America, producing in peace while greater nations wasted in war.

Some of the proscribed abroad, including both radicals and aristocrats, were bringing both talents and troubles to the United States and, as some feared, monarchial or mob dangers, too. Titled Frenchmen were often seen in the company at Mrs. Bingham's. One of them noted that "the English influence prevails in the first circles and prevails with great intolerance." Though Jefferson liked Mrs. Bingham's cuisine and was later to try to steal her chef, he was less welcome in such circles now. He was still strong in his affection for France and in his faith in the beneficial outcome of its revolution. This spring, indeed, when he heard that aristocrats were being sent in exile from Santo Domingo—four hundred of them to the United States—he came close to joke about it.

"I wish we could distribute our 400 among the Indians, who would teach them lessons of liberty and equality."

Still, in the middle of March, he wrote an old friend in Virginia that there had been no news of France since the beginning of the King's trial. When he wrote, the King had been guillotined seven weeks before.

IV.
ROAD
TO RETIREMENT

1.

Fever Season

Senator Burr had ways of finding out information about important matters before it was generally known. Often he could hear a whisper through a clamor. That seemed so in the tumultuous summer of 1793. Then republicans roared their affection for France and Federalist friends of England spoke in anger and disdain of the crowds which cheered the young, exuberant, and sometimes indiscreet French Minister Genet.

"We have a rumor here (very grateful to the Tories)," Burr wrote indicating he was not one of them, "that Genet has come to an open rupture with the President—that he has publicly threatened to appeal to the people, that as preparatory to this step he goes about visiting the Mechanics and the lower orders of the people, leaving cards at their houses when they are not at home! And the rumors add that it is in Contemplation of the President and his Ministers to dismiss the French Plenipo."

When the Senator sent this letter to his friend Nicholson in Philadelphia on July 16, though angers and irritations had been stirred and voiced in the Cabinet, no final decision in the matter had been made. The young, handsome Genet had soared over the American scene almost like his countryman Jean Pierre Blanchard. This pioneer balloonist, on January 9, 1793, made the first real air voyage in America to the applause of all persons in Philadelphia from the President down to the gamins in the streets. Genet had come more like a meteor than a balloon, though some felt he was puffed up with hot air. Many, when Burr wrote, were not certain whether his course would end in darkness or conflagration. Certainly his activities and his revolutionary rhetoric had illuminated or inflamed this troubled year when the frail young republic faced danger of involvement in the wars of the great powers.

The French diplomat is chiefly remembered in terms of impertinence in Philadelphia. Largely forgotten are his purposes in the American West which had so long fascinated Jefferson as philosopher. The Secretary of State's public and private curiosity about it had not abated. Before Genet's arrival, Jefferson in January, as vice-president of the American Philosophical Society, made arrangements to satisfy it as both private citizen and public official. Just the year before he had told young Meriwether Lewis that an exploration of the West would be premature. Now he completed plans for one. Despite the burden of his official duties and his involvement in the political attacks on Hamilton, he found time to raise money and write elaborate instructions for the project. He was sure he had found the right man for the job in André Michaux, famous French botanist. His projected journey, however, was definitely not to be such a botanizing journey as Jefferson and Madison had made two years before.

Michaux was no ordinary itinerant student of the *flora*. For generations his family had managed the royal parks at Versailles. He had worked and studied in the Jardin des Plantes. Then restless, he had studied plant life in England, the Auvergne, the Pyrenees, and along the Tigris and Euphrates rivers. In 1785 the French royal government sent him to study the forest trees of North America. He visited the Southern Appalachians. In 1792, the botanist, no longer a royal servant but an exponent of the republican cause, had botanized in Canada—even to Hudson Bay.

Jefferson's instructions to him were carefully prepared. "Sundry persons having subscribed certain funds for your encouragement," he wrote the botanist in January 1793, he was "to explore the country along the Missouri to the Pacific Ocean. . . ." He was to go above the Spanish settlements "that you may avoid the risk of being stopped." Spain, holding the mouth of the Mississippi which Jefferson felt inevitably must be part of the United States, was especially truculent at the moment. Similarly, though he was not specific about it in his instructions, he undoubtedly presumed that the botanist would go below the Northwest posts. Britain, still holding them despite the treaty, was sullen toward the United States and certainly would not be hospitable to a citizen of revolutionary France with which it was at war.

Within the next month Jefferson heard news about other plans for operation in the West from Colonel W. S. Smith, John Adams' son-in-

law, whom Jefferson had known well in Europe. Smith had had a gallant
record as Revolutionary soldier. Then after serving as American diplomat,
he had toured Europe with Francisco de Miranda, the fascinating and
inflammable Venezuelan advocate of South American independence. On
this tour Smith had learned much and enjoyed himself, though it was
Miranda upon whom Catherine the Great showered her favors. Now
Smith was full of information from the French government. The moderate ministry of the Girondists there had come to the end of its patience
with the aristocratic and antirevolutionary U. S. Minister Gouverneur
Morris. Smith mentioned apparently with approval the coming of Genet
as the new French Minister to the United States. Also he told Jefferson
of French plans to strike in the Americas against Spain which in monarchial fervor was about to join Britain in the war with France. The
French proposed to send forty-five ships of the line, under the command
of the Venezuelan revolutionist Miranda, against Spain in the Americas.
They meant, Smith reported, "to begin their attack at the mouth of the
Mississippi, and to sweep along the Bay of Mexico southwardly," and he
added, "they would have no objection to our incorporating into our Government the two Floridas."

This certainly was no botanizing expedition. Actually, Genet's instructions included "the emancipation of Spanish America, the opening
up to the inhabitants of Kentucky of the navigation of the Mississippi,
the deliverance of our ancient brothers of Louisiana from the tyrannical
yoke of Spain, and the addition, possibly, of the beautiful star of Canada
to the American constellation." With or without the help of the American
government, Genet was to "take all the steps compatible with his position
in order to foster the growth of the principles of liberty and independence
in Louisiana and in the other American provinces bordering on the
United States." This was quite an assignment for the thirty-year-old
Minister.

Even so sanguine a man as he was, he might have had misgivings
about his American mission if he had known the advance information
about him sent to America. Minister Morris from Paris wrote Washington, "I have seen Mr. Genet and he has dined with me. . . . He has, I
think, more genius than ability, and you will see in him at first blush the
manner and look of an upstart." Also: "He chose America as being the
best harbor during the storm, and . . . he will not put to sea again until
it is fair weather, let what will happen."

Despite Morris' sour comment there was nothing of the coward and certainly nothing of the upstart in Edmond Genet. He was, however, strangely cast as a revolutionary. His father had been an official in the office of foreign affairs of the King. His four brilliant sisters had held posts in the household of Marie Antoinette, the eldest of them being first lady to the Queen. Her loyalty to the Queen would not be shaken, even when she was torn from her by rough hands. And later, as Madame Jeanne Louise Henriette Campan, she was made by Napoleon superintendent of the school for the education of the daughters and sisters of the members of the Legion of Honor.

Edmond himself, as a precocious young man and remarkable linguist (English was only one of many languages he spoke fluently), had had a distinguished career as a young diplomat. He had served in Vienna, Geneva, St. Petersburg, and London. In London he had been secretary to Jefferson's disappointing friend the Count de Moustier. He had been expelled from St. Petersburg by Catherine the Great as representative of the revolutionary French regime. Yet his moderation was indicated by the fact that one of the reasons for his appointment to the American post was his part in a plan to save Louis XVI by carrying him into exile in America. The ship waiting to bring Genet was to bring the King too. This secret plan leaked to the terrorists. Louis' head fell while Edmond's carriage, with postilions mounted, was waiting to carry him away. The mischance was lucky for Genet. The carriage in which the King would have been hidden was stopped and searched by grim agents of the Commune. Then, finding nothing, they waved Genet on to America.

While he was at sea on March 30, Hamilton raised the question as to whether, as representative of a radical regime, he should be received. Washington, however, agreed with Jefferson that certainly he should be but, as the President felt, "not with too much warmth and cordiality." The young Frenchman found plenty of both when he landed in Charleston, South Carolina, on April 8. There began a season in which he was so toasted and dined by American friends of France that some were to say that his head was quickly turned.

But in Charleston where he received ardent welcome he might have taken warning, too. Senator Izard, in whose house the young Minister visited, spoke to him in "exalted terms" of Washington and Hamilton, but, so Genet said later, he described Jefferson as an "ambitious and intriguing demagogue" who was anxious to secure the reins of the government.

Genet demurred at this description of the friend of France. Then the Federalist Senator told him, "I see that you are going to fall into the snares of Mr. Jefferson and his party, and very probably will become their victim." The blond Frenchman did not know then, of course, that Izard's son-in-law Congressman Smith had said that the welcome given him was "a foolish thing."

If so, there was folly aplenty. Genet lingered in Charleston fitting out privateers to prey upon British shipping. He began arrangements with the French Consul there for expeditions to descend on Spanish Florida and Louisiana. There, too, his plans and instructions about activity in the American South and West were given dazzling encouragement by Alexander Moultrie, half brother of the Governor. He spoke in excitement of the Mississippi country and its promise. He compared the mouths of the Mobile and the Mississippi to "two keys which open the doors of a new and great world." On the Atlantic seaboard, Moultrie told him, "we find the soil degenerating fast, the country depopulating and mostly a foreign interest & mercantile aristocracy of the most poisonous kind prevailing there."

A man with his feet more firmly planted on the earth of the New World than Genet's were might have been dazzled by such a prospect and an early part in it for freedom and France. Certainly the welcome that he received as he moved in a procession of acclaim to Philadelphia seemed to many afterwards almost calculated to flatter him into foolishness about his popularity and his prospects. It could not be said then that the cheers came only from the mob. The most distinguished citizens feted him. And when he arrived in Philadelphia, deliberately not courting an extravagant welcome, he was met in jubilation not only by the discontented and dissatisfied, roughnecks and rowdies, as the Federalists suggested.

Also, leading in the welcome were members of the same American Philosophical Society which had supported Mr. Jefferson's plan for the exploration of the West. Hamilton called them "enemies and disturbers" but they included the mathematician David Rittenhouse, whom Jefferson would succeed as president of the society; Rittenhouse's son-in-law, the prominent lawyer Jonathan Dickinson Sergeant who had aided Burr in the Jay-Clinton election contest; the able and popular physician Dr. James Hutchinson; and Alexander James Dallas, secretary of the Commonwealth of Pennsylvania. In the enthusiastic company was also the ardent Freneau, whom Jefferson and friends had brought to Philadelphia to give republicans a newspaper voice. To the tune of "God Save the King," he provided a substitute song, "God Save the Rights of Man."

In July members of this same group, using a word coming to be synonymous with "republican," formed the Democratic Society of Pennsylvania, copies of which in other cities and states were to be called Jacobin clubs by the Federalists. Genet was not a Jacobin but a Girondist. Moreover though such clubs sprang up in other cities in this tumultuous season, their origin was more related to such earlier organizations as the Sons of Liberty than to anything foreign or strange. As a similar organization Tammany, containing many of Burr's supporters, kept its own name. Among members of the Philadelphia club were Rittenhouse, Dr. Hutchinson, and other such Jefferson friends as Dr. George Logan and the prominent merchant Charles Biddle. The last was Burr's close friend and the cousin-in-law of General James Wilkinson then back in military service in the West.

Later these clubs were to become the nucleus of the Jefferson political organization. As they seemed to line up behind Genet's flying coattails in the late spring and early summer of 1793, however, the Secretary of State was troubled by them and by the bombastic behavior of Genet. The Frenchman's ebullient confidence was encouraged by those who sang the "Marseillaise" and "Ça Ira," wore Liberty Caps, waved the tricolor and seemed not only ready but eager to follow the French Minister into war. Washington was increasingly made to seem as the father of neutrality also the enemy of liberty. Jefferson, as the pre-Genet American embodiment of the Rights of Man, seemed, in the eyes of Hamiltonians, the embodiment of possible anarchy. At this season Washington said that he feared this vastly more than the monarchy which appeared to be almost an obsession of the Secretary of State.

While questioning the wording of the Neutrality Proclamation adopted while Genet was on his way to Philadelphia and criticizing it in private conversations later, Jefferson had joined in the unanimous Cabinet decision to issue it. Others were not quiet in their criticism. Freneau's paper, generally regarded as Jefferson's organ, sometimes seemed to lead the hue and cry for France and against a neutrality which seemed to serve Britain. In the month in which Genet arrived in Philadelphia, the President, in a conversation with Jefferson, launched a tirade against Freneau and his *National Gazette*. He told his Secretary of State that he despised all such attacks on him personally, but that there never had been an act of the government which that paper had not abused.

"He was evidently sore and warm," Jefferson noted in the *Anas* on May 23, "and I took his intention to be, that I should interpose in some way with Freneau, perhaps withdraw his appointment of translating clerk to my office. But I will not do it."

And he added, "His paper has saved our Constitution, which was galloping fast into monarchy, and has been checked by no one means so powerfully as by that paper."

Two weeks later Jefferson wrote Madison of Washington's continuing irritation. "Little lingering fevers have been hanging about him for a week or ten days. . . . He is also extremely affected by the attacks made & kept up on him in the public papers. I think he feels those things more than any person I ever yet met with. . . ."

Feelings against Britain and neutrality were sharpened after June 8, when Britain announced it would seize all ships under any flag which were carrying foodstuffs to France. By a coincidence not evident in that day of slow news travel, that was a month to the day before the Cabinet had been discussing another of Genet's acts of defiance against neutrality. He had purchased cannon in Philadelphia for a privateer called the *Little Sarah*, then rechristened *Little Democrat*. The Frenchman did some furious quibbling about this matter even to Jefferson. Hamilton and Secretary of War Knox proposed artillery action against the ship to prevent its sailing. Jefferson wrote a long dissent in which he dramatically showed his antimonarchial colors.

". . . I would not gratify the combination of kings with the spectacle of the two only republics on earth destroying each other for two cannon; nor would I, for infinitely greater cause, add this country to that combination, turn the scale of contest, and let it be from our hands that the hopes of man received their last stab."

This contest threw Jefferson into what one biographer has diagnosed as a "psychosomatic fever." He was uncomfortable in the company of Hamilton, who was closer to the British Minister Hammond than Jefferson ever was to Genet. Indeed, Hamilton's intimacy with the British Minister grew while Jefferson's confidence in the French Minister cooled. His words in this period fell from fair weather relationship like a barometer before a storm.

On April 28 the Secretary of State was sure that Genet's arrival in

Philadelphia "would furnish occasion for the *people* to testify their affections [to France] without respect to the cold caution of their government."
After Genet's arrival he wrote on May 19, "It is impossible for anything
to be more affectionate, more magnanimous than the purport of his
[Genet's] mission." As late as June 4, in the matter of the arming of privateers by the belligerent nations, he wrote Monroe, ". . . France has
explained herself generously. She does not mean to interrupt our prosperity by calling for our guarantee [of the West Indies in the treaty]. On the
contrary she wishes to promote it by giving us in all her possessions all
the rights of her native citizens & to receive our vessels as her vessels. This
the language of her new minister. Great Britain holds back with the most
sullen silence and reserve." Yet it was at this time that Malone believes
that some republicans, who had ardently embraced Genet, began to be
embarrassed.

This was definitely not true of all republicans. Freneau's enthusiasm
was mounting. And on June 10 Madison reflected much republican impatience with neutrality as conducted by Washington. Such feelings were
shared by Monroe. Neither he nor Madison, however, were dealing with
Genet whose disagreement with American policy toward his country
mounted from petulance to insult. Jefferson told Monroe, "I fear he will
enlarge the circle of those disaffected to his country. I am doing everything in my power to moderate the impetuosity of his movements, and to
destroy the dangerous opinion that has been excited in him, that the people of the U.S., will disavow the acts of their government, and that he
has an appeal from the Executive to Congress, and from both to the
people."

There was no doubt about the Secretary of State's opinion of the
French Minister on July 7. Then he told Madison: "Never in my opinion
was so calamitous an appointment made, as that of the present Minister
of France here. Hot headed, all imagination, no judgment, passionate,
disrespectful and even indecent toward the P. in his written as well as his
verbal communications. . . . He renders my position immensely difficult."

Yet, two days before, the Secretary of State had made a calm entry
in his *Anas* about a continental American operation which Genet was
preparing to make. Late in June the Minister had taken on Jefferson's
Western explorer Michaux as his own for much more serious business
than natural history. Now on July 5 he called on Jefferson to outline to
him the militant mission on which he planned to send Michaux. Genet

said he was communicating these matters not to the Secretary of State, but to "Mr. Jefferson." Apparently the American Minister listened as such. Evidently as excuse for himself Jefferson wrote that Genet read "very rapidly" the instructions he had prepared for Michaux. They differed substantially from the instructions Jefferson himself had written for Michaux in January. Also, presumably still speaking rapidly, Genet read an address to the inhabitants of Louisiana which he had written and another to the people of Canada. No botanical matters were referred to.

"In these papers," Jefferson recorded, "it appears that, besides encouraging those inhabitants to insurrection, he speaks of two generals in Kentucky who have proposed to him to go and take New Orleans, if he will furnish the expense, about £3,000 sterling. He declines advancing it, but promises that sum ultimately for their expenses; proposes that officers shall be commissioned by himself in Kentucky and Louisiana; that they shall rendezvous *out of the territories of the United States*, suppose in Louisiana, and there making up a batallion to be called the ———— ———— of inhabitants of Louisiana and Kentucky, and getting what Indians they could, to undertake the expedition against New Orleans, and then Louisiana to be established into an independent State, connected in commerce with the United States and France; that two frigates shall go into the river Mississippi, and cooperate against New Orleans. The address to Canada was to encourage them to shake off English yoke, to call Indians to their assistance, and to assure them of the friendly dispositions of their neighbors in the United States."

Citizen Genet must have been breathless if he read all that rapidly. Actually he had informed Jefferson of his plan to send Michaux west a fortnight earlier. Jefferson could not have been surprised. Only Michaux was added to the French plans about which Colonel Smith had told him in February. At this June meeting Genet had asked for an Exequatur or written authorization of Michaux as "Consul of France at Kentucky." Jefferson shook his head at the young man as he must often have done. It was only in the ports he told the ardent young man that his country was entitled to consuls. If France should have a consul in Kentucky, England and Spain would soon demand the same and the interior of the country would be "filled with foreign agents."

Genet agreed and asked for the return of the commission he had given the botanist. But now on July 5, significantly just after Jefferson's friends had organized the Democratic Club in his support, the Minister had a modified request. He asked Jefferson to give Michaux a letter of introduction to Governor Isaac Shelby of Kentucky. A day or two later (the sixth or seventh of July), while the Cabinet was excited about Genet's privateering activities from Philadelphia itself, Jefferson sent him such a letter, mentioning Michaux only "as a person of botanical and natural pursuits." This did not satisfy Genet. So two days before he described Genet's appointment as "calamitous," Jefferson acceded to his request that he add in the letter that the botanist was a French citizen possessing the confidence of the French Minister. Obviously with the Secretary of State's letter vouching for his French connection, Genet's man was set up with the prestige if not the title of Consul. Jefferson could not have been so gullible as not to realize that.

The Secretary indicated no concern that Genet had carried off his explorer, forcing further postponement of his own Western plans. He warned Genet but did not try to deter him. He only told him that "enticing officers and soldiers from Kentucky to go against Spain, was really putting a halter about their necks; for that they would assuredly be hung if they commenced hostilities against a nation at peace with the United States." Leaving out "that article," he said, "I did not care what insurrections should be excited in Louisiana." War with Spain seemed all too likely for the United States then. Genet who could not get help in the East might give it in the West.

"I excite the Canadians to free themselves from the yoke of England," he had written home two weeks before; "I arm the Kentuckians, and I prepare by sea an expedition which will support their descent on New Orleans."

The project was not as fantastic as it seemed to some in the East— and to the new government hostile to Genet in France. Hatred of Spain was endemic in the West. Tough frontiersmen with their long guns were ready to push down on the Spanish who had too often denied them access to the sea. And the fanaticism of liberty, showing itself in Liberty Caps in Kentucky towns, might be contagious in Louisiana also.

Almost symbolically, on July 15, Michaux set out westward in the dark, leaving Philadelphia at 10 P.M., traveling by moonlight to avoid the heat of the day. Transformed from botanist to secret agent, he showed some of the delirious confidence of his superior. Unfortunately, however, his mission had become common knowledge. And his intoxication was said to be matched in actual inebriation by the man named by Genet as field commander in the scheme. George Rogers Clark had conquered and saved the West in the American Revolution. Now, however, he was reported to have turned to the bottle. He had reasons for it. Scarcely forty, his career seemed at an end. He was an early victim of the slanderous tongue of James Wilkinson. Wilkinson had come to Kentucky with a checkered career behind him. In the Revolution, as a heavy drinker with a passion for intrigue, he had been involved in the cabal to remove Washington as commander-in-chief. Then as Clothier General, he was forced to give up that position because of serious irregularities in his accounts. However, keeping his rank as General, he had married Ann Biddle of the prominent Philadelphia family. He moved to Kentucky in 1784 as trader and land speculator. There he pushed Clark aside as leader of the region and won the enmity of Humphrey Marshall, rich and arrogant Federalist relative of John Marshall, later Chief Justice of the United States. More significantly, in 1787, he made a voyage to New Orleans seeking a trading monopoly and there took an oath and received a pension as agent No. 13 in the service of Spain. Suspicions were aroused by mule loads of gold which came to him in Lexington. Still Spanish agent, he went back into the American army as Brigadier General in March 1792. As such a double-dealer in the West he passed on to his Spanish employers information about the plans of Genet and Clark.

Clark was a bitter if besotted man. Virginia owed him and did not pay twenty thousand dollars for his services and for supplies he had bought for his troops. He was not forgotten, however. In 1791 Jefferson had written about him to his friend Harry Innes, who was to be suspect with Wilkinson of treasonable dealings with Spain. In this letter the Secretary of State wondered if Innes could not help Clark.

"I know the greatness of his mind," Jefferson wrote, "and am the more mortified at the cause which obscures it. Had this not unhappily taken place, there was nothing he might not have hoped: could it be surmounted, his lost ground might yet be recovered. No man alive rated him higher than I did, and would again, were he to become again what I knew him."

Genet was ready to bring him forward and Clark was ready to show his greatness again. The Revolutionary hero was fired by the cause of France "against almost all of the despots of Europe." He wrote from Kentucky, "I can raise abundance of men in this Western country—men as well Americans as French. . . . Out of Kentucky, Cumberland, the settlement of Hilston, the Wabash and the Illinois I can (by my name alone) raise fifteen hundred brave men, or thereabouts—and the French at St. Louis and throughout the rest of Louisiana, together with the American Spanish subjects at Natchez, would, I am sure of it (for they all know me) flock to my standard. . . . With the first fifteen hundred alone I can take the whole of Louisiana for France." With the aid of frigates he could take Mexico. But he must have money: "if France will be hearty and secret in this business my success borders on certainty."

In Philadelphia, Genet wrote his government that he had the Secretary of State's support: "Mr. Jefferson seemed to me to be quickly sensible of the utility of the project, but he told me that the United States had begun negotiations with Spain [concerning a warehouse] below New Orleans, and as long as this negotiation was not broken off, the delicacy of the United States did not permit them to take part in our operations; nevertheless he made me to understand that he thought that a little spontaneous irruption of the inhabitants of Kentucky in New Orleans would advance matters. . . . And he put me in contact with several Congressmen of Kentucky . . . who . . . adopted our plans with as much enthusiasm as an American is capable of manifesting. He showed me the ways of acting with success, gave me the addresses of many reliable men, and promised me that he would apply all his influence to the success of our projects."

Genet may have been, as Jefferson wrote, "all imagination." But the agent he sent westward was the explorer Jefferson had chosen. Clark was a man in whom Jefferson still had great hopes. One of those enthusiastic in support of Genet's plan was John Breckinridge, later Jefferson's agent in a matter important to him in Kentucky. What the French Minister did not know—nor Jefferson—was that U. S. General Wilkinson was furnishing the Spanish with all information about the plans in Kentucky. Not until August 29, nearly two months after Genet had told him of his Western plans did Jefferson send a letter, not introducing Michaux but warning Governor Shelby to be on his guard and take such measures as necessary to suppress any enterprise against the Spanish territories. This was sent only a day or two before the Cabinet decision to ask the Minister's recall. Also in after years he wrote a private memorandum in his *Anas*, on March 27, 1800, that he had only given his letter to Michaux "as a botanist, which was his real profession." Even later he wrote, referring to Michaux as "a professed botanist," and that he was employed by the

French government for "botanical inquiries." Genet's plans of conquest died aborning. Michaux returned to the study of plants. Clark, whom Jefferson had hoped could be brought forward, became a still bankrupt exile in St. Louis when he refused to give up his commission as Genet's General.

Jefferson's fingers were at least scorched in this fiery enterprise. Some of his friends, including Harry Innes and George Nicholas, were loudly charged with conspiring with Spain by Humphrey Marshall. Indeed, Marshall so stirred up Kentucky with his cries of conspiracy that the Jeffersonians there were temporarily routed and Jefferson's own close associate, Breckinridge, was defeated for re-election to the Senate by Federalist Marshall. Genet's international plotting had American political repercussions all too real to please Mr. Jefferson.

Burr had written his letter about the rumors of Genet's recall on the day after Michaux set out for Kentucky in the dark. There was nothing imaginary then about the conflict of the politicians in the East. Jefferson was increasingly realizing that Hamilton and his friends were eager to use the behavior of Genet as a weapon for attack upon the republicans. They were insisting that radicalism and terror in France might be imported into the United States. Jefferson scoffed at suggestions of any overthrow of the American government. Hamilton had begun to write for the press along such lines, when, on July 7, Jefferson, who insisted he never engaged in press propaganda himself, urged Madison to answer in such a way as to "cut him to pieces." The debate was joined. The exchanges of Hamilton and Madison ran on the high road of discussion above furious party struggle in the United States. Under their debate and beside it, editors and politicians were engaged in verbal fisticuffs which often involved the sacred person of Washington himself. Jefferson wrote in his *Anas* that he believed some of the most violent attacks on the President were written by Federalists—probably Izard—pretending to be furious republicans. But Washington pointed his angry finger at Jefferson's Freneau and his friend Bache.

"The publications in Freneau's and Bache's papers," the President cried on July 21, "are outrages on common decency." He spoke of their "arrows of Malevolence." Angers in the Cabinet had risen to new heights at the beginning of August when the final decision about the fate of Genet was made. Knox, whom Jefferson regarded as a fat fool, wanted to hand the Frenchman his papers and send him off. Others disagreed but

Hamilton wanted to publish to the world all the evidence of Genet's impudence and folly. Then Knox, as Jefferson reported in his *Anas,* made a long incoherent speech to which he added the display of a cartoon depicting the funeral of a guillotined Washington. The old General exploded.

"The President was much inflamed:" the Secretary of State wrote, "got into one of those passions when he cannot command himself; ran on so much on the personal abuse which had been bestowed on him; defied any man on earth to produce one single act of his since he had been in the Government, which was not done on the purest motives; that he had never repented but once the having slipped the moment of resigning his office, and that was every moment since; that *by God* he had rather be in his grave than in his present situation; that he had rather be on his farm than to be made Emperor of the world; and yet that they were charging him with wanting to be a king. That that *rascal Freneau* sent him three of his papers every day, as if he thought he would become the distributor of his papers; that he could see in this, nothing but an impudent design to insult him; he ended in this high tone."

At the same meeting Hamilton spoke for three quarters of an hour, Jefferson said, on the subject of the Democratic Societies founded by Jefferson's philosophical friends. Some of these societies, indeed, had joined in intemperate opposition to neutrality, even against Washington's government which proclaimed it—and against Washington himself. If such societies were proscribed, Jefferson answered in the presence of Washington, the action would seem to make the President "assume the station of the head of a party, instead of the head of a nation."

Genet did not know he was a ruined man. The chiefs of the party in France which had sent him to America had been guillotined. Now in America, Jefferson, in whom he had placed his confidence as friend of France, had made his decision which he described later in a letter to Madison: "Finding at length that the man was absolutely incorrigible, I saw the necessity of quitting a wreck which could not but sink all who should cling to it."

Genet refused to consider himself or his cause a wreck. On the day the Cabinet was discussing the best procedure for getting rid of him, he announced, "I am going to New York, and the whole town will come out to meet me. Since I landed on this continent, there has not been a day that I have not received similar proofs of the love of this people here for our country, but my zeal will only be satisfied when I shall have profited from it. The whole of the New World must be free, and America must help us in this sublime design."

And the trip to New York was a triumphal tour. Crowds greeted him all along the line. In some towns the militia stood long under arms for the opportunity to salute him. He crossed the Hudson in a boat decorated with American and French flags. A huge crowd greeted him in the city. Undoubtedly in it were the representatives of Tammany. Soon, though Federalists scorned it, young Theodosia Burr would call that organization her father's Tenth Legion. He was not evident in the reports of the reception. He had already heard the reports that Genet would be recalled more than two weeks before. Later Hamilton undertook to show that Burr was a headlong Francophile.

"I dined with him lately," Hamilton wrote of Burr to a friend. At the Senator's table his hostility was masked. But quickly afterwards he reported on the private occasion. Burr had proposed several toasts to revolutionary France. And, added the friend of Britain, "His doctrine is, that it would be the interest of this country, to permit the indiscriminate sale of prizes by the belligerent powers, and the building and equipment of vessels; amounting to nothing more nor less (with the semblance of equality) than to turn all our naval resources into the channel of France, and compel Great Britain to war. Indeed, Mr. Burr must have war, as the instrument of his ambition and cupidity. The peculiarity of the occasion will excuse my mentioning, *in confidence*, the occurrences of a private table." Why Burr needed war then was not made clear.

At other private tables Mr. Hamilton worked against France and its minister. He was undoubtedly behind the formal charges against Genet emanating from the two great Federalists, Senator King and Chief Justice Jay. It was that the young French Minister had threatened to appeal over Washington to the people. Then Jay and King secured certificates to the truth of the charge from Hamilton and others. Undoubtedly Genet had made some indiscreet statements which came close to such a threat. But in this case the evidence lay in a line of hearsay back through Hamilton to Knox to Governor Mifflin to Secretary of the Commonwealth Dallas of Pennsylvania. And Dallas, the primary source, later denied that Genet had used the language attributed to him. Genet was at first inclined to dismiss this solemn charge as a joke. He called those who had attested to it "certificate men." Then, concluding that "this imposture might have deep roots," on August 13, 1793, he wrote a peremptory letter to the President himself.

"It has become necessary, Sir, to dissipate these dark calumnies by truth and publicity. I dare therefore to expect from your candor and probity an explicit declaration that I have never intimated to you an intention of appealing to the people." There was more and worse. He got a cold, brief reply back not from Washington, but from Jefferson. His recall by France was requested this same month.

For many reasons this was a season of unpleasantness for Jefferson. He understood his unpopularity in the top social circles of Philadelphia "where the laws of society oblige me always to move exactly in the circle which I know to bear me peculiar hatred." And now he found that many of his republican friends were not prepared for any such action as he proposed to put an end to the antics of Genet. To his dismay Freneau, who had written poetry for the young Minister's welcome, began to publish a series of satirical verses attacking Washington. Freneau, after Hamilton's charge that he was the hireling of the Secretary of State, had made an affidavit that Jefferson had neither written nor dictated anything for his papers. Some of the diatribes Freneau published against Hamilton had the sound of Jefferson's statement to Washington that the Secretary of the Treasury was a man whose history "is a tissue of machinations against the liberty of the country which has not only received and given him bread, but heaped its honors on his head." Many felt that the invisible hand behind the blows was Jefferson's. Even some of those who welcomed Jefferson into their houses were uncertain about him in this feverish summer. The brilliant Deborah Logan, Quaker wife of his friend Dr. Logan, entertained the Virginian at their great estate, Stenton, near Philadelphia, but she wrote that she saw "that he wanted sincerity Towards General Washington, whom I revered."

Jefferson spent many pleasant hours at Stenton. Once, at least, young Genet was there with him. Also in the ostracism he described he found refuge in the library of the American Philosophical Society. But he felt most secure in his own house on the Schuylkill where in this hot summer there were generally breezes under his plane trees. It was really a refuge this summer when young Genet justly complained of the heat and swarming flies in Philadelphia. And there, after the contentions in the Cabinet, Washington showed his faith in Jefferson despite his display of fury at the attacks from Freneau and Bache.

Washington drove out from Philadelphia to call at his restive Secretary's house in this hot August of 1793. Now again he hoped that Jefferson would remain in office. His trouble was doubled now because he had also recently received a letter from Hamilton informing him that he must retire because of "private as well as public reasons." Hamilton had told the President that he found it necessary to repair his private fortunes. In this conversation by the Schuylkill, Washington and Jefferson then repeated and compared their common repugnance to public life. Jefferson assured the President that there were no dangers to the government from "what is called the republican party."

"The manoeuvers of Mr. Genet," Jefferson said, "might produce some little embarrassment, but that he would be abandoned by the republicans the moment they knew the nature of his conduct. . . . No crisis existed which threatened anything."

The harassed Washington was not so sure about the situation.

"He said he believed the views of the republican party were perfectly pure, but when men put a machine into motion, it is impossible for them to stop it exactly where they would choose, or to say where it will stop."

Jefferson was having some such trouble then. Some of the anti-Federalist motion he had started or served was running headlong beyond the position he wished to take. Monroe had been slow in willingness to condemn Genet. Dr. Hutchinson agreed with Jefferson about the French Minister but within the group of republican philosophers Hutchinson was hated and opposed by Dr. Rush.

Then, assuming that Jefferson this time was fixed in his determination to retire, Washington talked with him about a successor. Jefferson must have been shocked, though he made no note of it in his *Anas*, that one of those Washington was considering was Congressman Smith of South Carolina, whom Jefferson regarded not only as a monarchist and speculator but also as a possible defector to Britain. Jefferson made some alternative suggestions. Washington, still worrying about the replacement of the two men, who had seemed to Jefferson as one of them like two cocks in a pit, got up to go back to his great house in the hot city.

"And," Jefferson noted, "he concluded by desiring that I would take two or three days to consider whether I could not stay in till the end of another quarter, for that like a man going to the gallows, he was willing to put it off as long as he could. . . ."

Mr. Jefferson only took five days after this conversation in which to

compose a letter to Madison which reads less like a prelude to retirement
than a plan for the political future.

"I believe it will be true wisdom in the Republican party to approve
unequivocally of a state of neutrality, to avoid little cavils about who shall
declare it, to abandon G[enet] entirely, with expressions of strong friendship & adherence to his nation & confidence that he has acted against their
sense. In this we shall keep the people on our side by keeping ourselves
in the right."

The fevers of partisanship had not cooled and to them came an im-
partial fever. Though people accustomed to pests paid less attention to
them than to the summer flies, mosquitoes swarmed out of the stagnant
ditches and ponds of the city's dirty waterfront. Yellow fever first appeared
at the end of August and by early September hundreds had already been
stricken. Bodies were piled in the death carts making ominous sounds on
the cobbles and those able to escape fled in such numbers as to depopulate
the city. Even some physicians hastily departed, but those two republican
stalwarts, Dr. Rush and Dr. Hutchinson, made their rounds in heroism
much praised. Rush's therapies of much purging and bleeding was not
questioned in this epidemic as it would be later. This time in rough confidence he was quick with a diagnosis of the fatal illness of Hutchinson
who seemed to many the chief martyr of the horrid visitation. His colleague, Rush said, did not die of yellow fever. He attributed his death to
his "dining too heavily with Jefferson down at Gray's Ferry in the open
air." Hutchinson had dined with Jefferson in a brief respite from his heroic rounds with the sick and was stricken that night. He died on September 6.

Jefferson had not suffered from the meal. He commented, "It is difficult to say whether the republican interest has suffered more by his death
or Genet's extravagance." Hutchinson was a giant not only as a republican
but as a man. Charles Biddle wrote that he could have played the role of
Falstaff without stuffing. Possibly his death came from the combination of
his obesity and his heroic exertions in the epidemic.

Other republicans were dying. Years later John Adams said that only
the fever saved the government from the adherents of Genet. This almost
delirious statement included Adams' claim that during this spring and
summer there were ten thousand people in the streets, day after day threatening to drag Washington from his house and effect a revolution in the
government. Certainly many of the so-called rabble rolled in the death

carts. But the plague was no respecter of persons. The epidemic had not reached its height when, in accordance with earlier announcement, Washington departed for Mount Vernon, on September 10. But when Knox departed, Jefferson described it as flight. The Secretary of State had announced that he would not leave town until the beginning of October. And, on September 8, he wrote Madison that he was staying because "I do not like to exhibit the appearance of panic." Still he moved his office to his house in the country. From there he wrote a letter neither philosophic nor benign.

"Hamilton is ill of the fever as is said," he wrote, "he had two physicians out at his house the night before last, his family think him in danger, & he puts himself so by his excessive alarm. He had been miserable several days before from a firm persuasion he should catch it. A man as timid as he is on the water, as timid on horseback, as timid in sickness, would be a phenomenon if the courage of which he had the reputation in military matters were genuine."

This was not only a bitter but a very strange letter from Jefferson. He was sensitive about the fact that his own wartime record included charges of ignominious flight. He sought the fairest weather for sea voyages. And certainly now he did not continue calm about the advance of the epidemic. Four days after he scoffed at Hamilton's illness, he was writing Madison again: "The fever spreads faster. Deaths are now up about 30 a day It is in every square of the city. All flying who can. Most of the offices are shut or shutting. The banks shut up this day. All my clerks have left me but one: so that I cannot go on with the business. I shall therefore set out in 3. or 4. days."

On September 17 (half a month short of the time he had announced he would leave), he left or fled too. Apparently he would have left sooner but he had to get a loan of one hundred dollars for traveling expenses from the Bank of the United States. Eight days later he reached salubrious Monticello.

Perhaps panic marked the yellow fever for Hamilton. Jefferson showed in the epidemic pernicious pique for his stricken adversary, who fortunately recovered. Burr's comment on yellow fever was afterwards presented by Hamilton's grandson as an evidence of his "casual feeling in regard to serious things." Burr wrote at the time of another visitation, "We die reasonably fast. Mrs. Jones died last night; but then Mrs. Smith had twins this morning; so the account is even."

Not all the casualties of the epidemic in Philadelphia in 1793 were human. Freneau's *National Gazette* died too. Though Jefferson had said that he would not let him go, the editor resigned from his position as translating clerk in the State Department on October 11. He was hard up. Printers had joined others in the flight from Philadelphia. Evidently he was as disturbed by Jefferson's attitude toward Genet as Jefferson was troubled by his. The shop of the *National Gazette* had become a headquarters of French sympathizers. Freneau collected money for the French government. He may have given up in disgust as well as despair.

Freneau was not the only republican who was not happy about Jefferson's repudiation of Genet, which momentarily made the Secretary of State almost popular in Philadelphia society. As late as February 1794 Congressman Smith, who scorned all republicans, wrote: "notwithstanding the conduct of Genet towards this country & the information received that his conduct has been disapproved by his employers & that his recall may be hourly expected, yet a party still adheres to him, among whom are men, called by some, virtuous, respectable, & the best friends of the people: Mifflin, Dallas, Giles, Taylor, Monroe, &c. associate with him or dine at his house & thus countenance him in his measures."

Perhaps, as has been said, Jefferson "noted with sorrow" the passing of the paper he had promoted. He did pay up his own arrears to the paper and collected sums due from Madison and others. To his daughter he wrote only that "Freneau's and Fenno's papers are both down forever." His report of the demise of Fenno's publication was premature. The recovered Hamilton and Rufus King raised two thousand dollars to bail him out lest they "lose his services." There was no such support forthcoming for Freneau. He left without any blast at supporters who to him must have seemed to have become timid. But later in his life, according to his biographer, Mary S. Austin, he acted like the burnt child who wanted no more of the uncertain fire. Jefferson in power later apparently wanted to give him belated reward. He sent for Freneau to come to Washington on "important business." Freneau sent word back: "Tell Thomas Jefferson that he knows where Philip Freneau lives. Let him come to Philip Freneau's house and transact it."

The pugnacious poet wanted no job from Jefferson. Indeed, in lasting disenchantment he recanted the statement he had sworn to that the Secretary of State had written nothing for the *National Gazette*. With marked files of the paper, he pointed to pieces which he said Jefferson had secretly written or dictated. But if he remained bitter, on his farm and on the sea which he loved he found peace. So in surprising fashion did Genet.

The young Frenchman had some good luck at the end of his days as Minister. At least Washington's government declined to turn him over to the new Terrorist government of France which had the guillotine waiting for him. Also, like a happy ending to a tumultuous tale, on November 6, 1794, he married gentle Cornelia Tappan Clinton, daughter of the crusty old Governor Clinton of New York. As an American citizen, the once flaming Frenchman lived with her in quiet retirement which was interrupted only by one great explosion in recollection three years later.

Then from "Cornelia's Farm," Long Island, on July 4, 1797, he wrote a long blast to Jefferson. He was aroused by a speech in Congress by Jefferson's aggressive friend Congressman Giles. Giles had been one of Genet's ardent supporters in 1793, though now he spoke of those who supported the French Minister as "turbulent citizens." He recalled Genet's conduct as "so rude towards the executive branch of our government that his recall was demanded."

Until he had read this speech by Giles, Genet wrote in a very long and very passionate letter to Jefferson he had been "tranquil and content in my peaceful retreat, occupying myself only with agricultural labors, with literary amusements. . . ." But now he told Jefferson he addressed himself to him as "my principal accuser" and "the real author of all my ills." He recalled the contrast at the outset of his ministry between the warmth of the welcome of the people and the coldness of his reception by Washington. He expressed his astonishment at the contrast to Jefferson, he said.

". . . then, although you spoke to me of the President always with a profound veneration, you confessed to me that unfortunately that excellent man was controlled by the English and the aristocrats, that you were the only one in the Cabinet who still took an interest in France, but that your voice was entirely powerless; that the people, however, was for us, that your friends would have a majority in the next Congress, but that the convening of that legislative body must not be hurried because all the idle speculators and brokers in the towns would come crowding while the cultivators occupied with their labors would be slow to respond and would leave time for the former to take contrary measures. . . .

". . . soon, however, . . . all the gazettes of the continent swarmed with articles each stronger than the others in favor of our cause, the people of its own accord constituted itself the general advocate of republican France before the Federal Government; and the Democratic Societies, composed of the patriots of '76, of the most respectable citizens, were formed as if by magic from one end of the continent to the other, and set down as a foundation for their association these powerful words, Liberty, Equality, Rights of Man, Country, France, Republic. . . .

"Then, Sir, that sentiment so common to philosophers . . . fear, took possession of your soul. Like those Indians whom images formed by their own hands intimidate and terrify, you trembled with all the shudders of the Union and of the Cabinet of St. James, and you sought only to deprive me of the weapons which you had given me, to unpopularize me and to smother the republican fires which were being kindled on all sides."

Though he still demanded reparation for mistreatment this was not a persuasive letter. It was written in anger and emotion as an indictment of Jefferson rather than a defense of himself. In it he paraded the jibes which he knew stung Jefferson. He spoke of "the useful however timid role that you had played in the American Revolution." He wrote of Jefferson's abandonment of his "dreams of Kentucky" for mammoth bones which he was sending as relics to placate enemies of that dream. His own fault, Genet told Jefferson, was "having preferred the great interests of liberty to your petty political views." He associated Jefferson with "the fable of my appeal to the people . . . an insidious artifice and a perfidious lie."

It is doubtful that Jefferson paid much attention to the letter. He was busy at this time writing letters more important to him. Just before Genet wrote Jefferson from his farm, Jefferson had written a very friendly letter to Aaron Burr. The Virginian needed his aid in "the preservation of our republican government." More than any other single action, Malone wrote, this letter "marked Jefferson's assumption of the leadership of the Republican party. . . ." Burr sent a prompt and gracious reply.

In making complaint at this time, Genet was not talking to the mob but to the wind.

2.

Between Mountain and Sea

Behind Jefferson's heels when he departed from Philadelphia, on January 5, 1794, to some the capital of the United States seemed beset between the mountains and the deep blue sea. Heading homeward, the retiring statesman was happily freed from angers aroused by frontiersmen in the West and by the British fleet off the shore. He had not favored the excise taxes on whiskey about which the Pennsylvania farmers were loudly complaining. Much as he had been irritated by Genet, he more resented the supercilious arrogance of the British in their seizures of American ships and seamen. He had left behind him proposals that America retaliate against British commercial restrictions. Madison presented resolutions embodying them. Smith of South Carolina, in a speech quickly recognized as having been written by Hamilton, gave a powerful answer.

Emotions exploded in a debate which Smith had blandly insisted should be a commercial discussion. One member of the House rose to declare that if a stranger had heard Smith's speech he might have thought he was listening to a British agent. And from such furious republicans, as even Jefferson deplored, to the South Carolina Congressman came an anonymous threat of assassination signed "15 Republicans and boys of Liberty to exterpate Torys."

The angers certainly were not all on one side. Less than a month later the same sort of high feeling attended the debate over a motion to unseat Albert Gallatin as Senator from Pennsylvania. There was some similarity in the grounds brought against him and those raised in opposition earlier to the seating of Congressman Smith. Gallatin's sin was that he was a republican. Worse than that, he came from the region where farmers were refusing to pay Hamilton's excise tax on whiskey levied to provide the revenues required by the assumption of state debts. Some suggested that Gallatin had participated in what would be called the "rebellion" of those who defied the tax collectors. Undoubtedly Gallatin understood the outrage of farmers about the tax on this only commodity they could ship from their farms down the mountains and more easily down the Monongahela, Ohio, and Mississippi rivers. But the cudgel with which Gallatin was hit was the charge that he was a foreigner.

Though he had arrived as a cultured Swiss immigrant in 1780, Federalists insisted that he had not been a citizen of the United States for the nine years constitutionally required for service in the Senate. As one who, though a city man, sympathized then and later with the problems of the West, Aaron Burr made a strong speech in favor of Gallatin's keeping his seat which he had taken on December 2, 1793.

Burr knew young Gallatin well and his wife better. Just a month before he took his seat in the Senate the Swiss-born Pennsylvanian had married Hannah Nicholson, daughter of a wealthy Revolutionary naval officer, Commodore James Nicholson. Though a strong republican, the Commodore had commanded the decorated barge in which Washington had been brought to New York as President. In his house on William Street, one of the most valuable in the city, he lived like a patrician but made it a headquarters for followers of Burr and Jefferson. He had come close to a duel with the much younger Hamilton. Naturally his son-in-law Gallatin had Burr's eloquent support. But the Federalist Senate, on February 28, voted fourteen to twelve to unseat the Pennsylvania republican. Federalists voted the more enthusiastically to oust him because he had in his brief stay wanted more scrutiny of Hamilton's activities as Treasury chief.

Burr was a busy man in this session. In January he had favored a bill to bar personnel of the Bank of the United States from membership in Congress and to sever connections between the government and the bank. Both bills were defeated by a majority of one. But a month later he joined in the victory for open sessions of the Senate which he had long been urging. Other significant personal and political matters marked this season for him.

He had been too busy, or the legislative recess too short, for him to get home for Christmas. He was much worried about his wife. As a lonely man on Christmas Day, he complained to young Theodosia about her not

writing. On the last day of the year he asked her again for news of her
mother. She was, he told her, "my only correspondent respecting the concerns of the family." Apparently the child reassured him. It gave him great
pleasure, he said, to learn that the elder Theodosia was better. Yet except
for his worries about her, his life in Philadelphia at this time seemed particularly pleasant. He had moved to more congenial quarters than the
house presided over by the deaf old lady. Now he was living in a very select
boardinghouse two blocks east of the State House in Chestnut Street. It
was kept by two widows, Mrs. John Payne and her daughter, pretty Mrs.
John Todd, christened Dorothea (after her relative, Patrick Henry's second wife), but known in variant spellings as Dolly or Dolley. Also, the
Senator was on very friendly grounds with his two fellow republicans from
Virginia, Madison and Monroe. Two incidents, one romantic and the
other political, point or confuse the position and character of Burr this
winter and spring.

Mrs. Payne's boardinghouse was no ordinary establishment. Though
the Senator visited in many Quaker homes at this time, this one was not
quite Quaker plain. Mrs. Payne's husband John had not come up to all
the expectations of the Friends in Philadelphia. He had been expelled
from meeting for failure to pay his debts. Mrs. Payne had been taking
boarders before he died in 1791. His death somewhat eased family burdens. So did the marriage of Dolley, at almost the old maid's age of twenty-
two, in January 1790, to lawyer John Todd, a Quaker presumably in good
standing. The couple had one son, John Payne Todd. Then in the yellow
fever epidemic which had carried off republicans and Federalists alike,
Todd died. Dolley, who had recently had a second child, was stricken. She
slowly recovered but the child died.

More than death had marked the household in 1793. From it Dolley's
much younger sister, fifteen-year-old Lucy Payne, eloped with George
Steptoe Washington, the President's nineteen-year-old nephew and ward,
then a college student in the city. Burr's residence there added high spirits
to the house. Evidently he also became the trusted counselor and friend of
Dolley Todd. This is documented, almost like a valentine, in a letter the
blue-eyed, dark-haired Dolley wrote a friend in this spring: "Thou must
come to me. Aaron Burr says that the great little Madison has asked to be
brought to see me this evening."

The great little Madison was forty-three at the time, nearly twenty
years older than Dolley and short beside her. Moreover, he was not only

small but prim. Heretofore he had not had much luck with the ladies. Long before, a Virginia girl had broken her engagement to him to marry a clergyman. There could hardly have been anything serious about his attentions to the brilliant but strongly Federalist Mrs. Colden in New York. Dolley was to be a young lady who preferred peacock appearances to gray Quaker garb. Burr, who introduced them, was thirty-eight and at the peak of his charm.

Many, including Madison's principal biographer Irving Brant, have found the situation involving gay Burr, pretty Dolley, and plain Madison incongruous. Brant wrote, "Because of Burr's later reputation as a lady killer and the trust Dolley placed in him, their friendship has led to many harmless sentimental conjectures. . . ."

Actually Burr was a man of the highest repute at the time. Nothing would seem to indicate that better than the support given him then by republicans in general and Madison and Monroe in particular for the delicate post of American Minister to France. An able man and a friend of France was needed in that post. The French government had been as eager to get rid of the scornful aristocratic Gouverneur Morris as Washington's government had been to see the last of Genet. Burr seemed an ideal choice. But the story of his consideration has been presented generally as evidence of the supposed distrust in which he was held by so sacred an authority as George Washington.

Burr's unfortunate choice of Matthew L. Davis as the keeper of his papers and his fame made the story told by Davis seem authoritative. In his *Memoirs of Aaron Burr,* published in 1838, Davis wrote the version of this incident picked up by Parton in the first objective biography published twenty years later. Most other historians have adhered to it. Davis wrote that Washington told Congressional republican critics of his foreign policy, as exemplified by the sending of Jay to England, that he would name a republican to the Paris post "if they would designate a suitable person." Thereupon a caucus of Democrats "resolved on recommending Colonel Burr."

Madison and Monroe took this recommendation of the party to the President. And Davis wrote: "General Washington paused for a few moments, and then remarked, that he had made it a rule of life never to recommend or nominate any person for a high and responsible situation in whose integrity he had not confidence; that, wanting confidence in Colonel Burr, he could not nominate him; but that it would give him great pleasure to meet their wishes if they would nominate an individual in whom he could confide."

The Democrats met again but came back to the President saying that they "adhered unanimously to their first nomination."

"Whereupon General Washington, with some warmth, remarked that his decision was irrevocable; but immediately added, 'I will nominate you, Mr. Madison, or you, Mr. Monroe.'" The Democrats declined to agree to any other man. Madison declined the offer. But on May 27, 1794, Monroe was appointed by Washington.

"This incident," wrote Davis, "demonstrates, on the one hand, the strong and unchangeable prejudices of General Washington against Colonel Burr; and on the other, the firm and unbounded confidence reposed in him by the democracy in those days." Washington's prejudice, if it existed, has been attributed to the whispers of Hamilton at his ear. The whole story about Washington's announced prejudice against Burr on this occasion is questionable. Davis attributed his version of the story to his conversations with Burr but added that "it was confirmed by the written statement of a gentleman of high standing to whom Monroe repeated all the details." He did not publish this statement or give the gentleman's name. Monroe himself told a very different tale.

Washington, Monroe wrote Jefferson, was placed in a difficult position by the demand of the French government that Morris be recalled. Another Federalist would be no more welcome in Paris than Morris was. Robert R. Livingston, Monroe heard, had been offered the post. He also heard that Burr was considered but as a remote possibility. Then on May 26 Monroe reported to the man at Monticello that both Livingston and Madison had declined appointment leaving Burr the strongest candidate. He had hardly dispatched this letter to Jefferson before Edmund Randolph, the new Secretary of State, called to ask whether Monroe would accept the assignment. Significantly Randolph said that Burr had been rejected by Washington, not on any grounds of lack of integrity but because Washington felt that, Livingston having declined the offer, it might seem that only New Yorkers were being considered. Monroe told Randolph that he had supported Burr and could not consider the post unless Burr were clearly out of the running. Randolph promised to "satisfy the friends of Colo. Burr on this head." Only after "this point of delicacy" was removed did Monroe agree to accept "upon the necessity of cultivating France; & the uncertainty of the person upon whom it might otherwise fall." A point of delicacy would have been involved if the man he first supported was the person upon whom he feared it might otherwise have fallen.

Monroe was named on May 27, 1794. Until a few days before that time Burr could not have contemplated such a mission. All through this spring he had been increasingly worried about the illness of his wife. He had proposed resigning from Congress to be with her in New York. Her illness was evidently terminal but her death was not expected when it came on May 18. It had required two days to get the news to Burr in Philadelphia. It must have required as long a time for him to get to New York for the funeral. The necessity of making some new arrangements for his beloved little Theodosia could not have been quickly accomplished. He must have been off the Philadelphia scene while the decision to make Monroe the Minister was reached. Monroe reported that he had only been offered the appointment on May 26. He was named the next day. Certainly Burr could hardly have been in town when Monroe resolved his "point of delicacy" and accepted the job.

Burr was not a man to display his loss or injury. Only later did the most vicious anonymous calumnists undertake to describe him as heartless and degraded at the time of Theodosia's death. If he had wanted the French post at this difficult period in his life and Monroe abandoned him to take it himself, it was strange that when Monroe returned from France Burr was the man he turned to in the serious matter of his honor and possibly his life. But trust in Burr at this time was gently demonstrated when Dolley Payne, on May 13, the day after her twenty-sixth birthday and five days before Theodosia's death, named Burr as the one to whom she wished her child to go if she should die.

From New York, Burr himself wrote, with no cry for sympathy at this tragic time in his life, to his cousin Timothy Edwards: "I came here on Tuesday last having been summoned by an express which brought me at Phila. the afflicting news that my once amiable and accomplished wife had died on the Sunday preceding. Though her situation had long been considered as helpless, yet no apprehension was entertained of any immediate danger until a few hours before her death; she then sank calmly and without pain into her last sleep. My little daughter though much afflicted and distressed, bears the stroke with more reason and firmness than could have been expected from her years."

Little is known about this sad period in New York. It is not

even known where the elder Theodosia was buried. One presumption is
that her grave is in Trinity Churchyard. By this time old Revolutionary
furies were subsiding. It would still be some years before her cousin's husband, the once rejected Reverend Benjamin Moore, would take his place
as rector of Trinity Church without opposition. He was evidently prominent in that parish, which would summon him to that position in 1800.
Certainly Theo's position in the community and the church is suggested
by the facts that this relative would become both Episcopal Bishop of New
York and president of King's College now reorganized as Columbia University. Unfortunately the burial records of Trinity Church from 1784 to
1800 have been lost.

There were other relatives and friends to help the Senator care for his
ten-year-old child. His fears for her loneliness would soon suggest his almost adoption of a little French girl refugee from revolution as her companion. He meant, however, for her early to become the mistress of
Richmond Hill. Burr was thirty-eight. There were many ladies ready to
take care of him and the child. None of them seemed necessary. The tie
between father and child was strengthened. In absence his letters to her
increased in frequency, so did his eagerness for hers. On the way back to
the Senate in Philadelphia he wrote her a long letter on the road. Communications being what they were then, he was not sure that she had received it two days before the end of the session on June 9. But he
did receive from her two very little letters in the French she was learning.
Apparently the lonely child had been sick. Her father wrote her that she
must fight all her ailments until he would be home in a few days. Then,
"I will engage to keep them at bay."

Even after he got home at the end of the session, however, he was
the driving man whom the elder Theo had so long before begged not to
ride so fast. Business apparently occupied him in the city in June and July,
but in August he was off again riding the circuit of the courts seeking the
means to maintain such an establishment as Richmond Hill. He wrote
young Theo long letters from his travels to Albany, Ballston, Troy, Kingston, Poughkeepsie. There were references in his letters to Madame De S.
(An aristocratic French refugee who opened a school in New York which
Theodosia attended.) Also, he began the amusing reports of his activities
to his daughter which were to mark their lasting intimate correspondence.
In one he indicated his fastidiousness about traveling companions. A rough
voyage up the Hudson was made "in a small cabin, with seven men, seven

women and two crying children—two of the women being the most splenetic, ill-humored animals you can imagine." (Of course, Theodosia, who
was only eleven in June, was expected to know the meaning and the spelling of "splenetic.")

Politically it was a relatively quiet summer for Burr as it was for the
retired gentleman at Monticello. Mr. Jefferson was rebuilding his château
on his hill, manufacturing nails for profit as well as his own purposes,
and once more trying to make financial sense out of his tangled affairs. He
contemplated his debts and planned his palatial cupolo. Soon after his retirement he had written Madison, "We are here in a state of great quiet,
having no public news to agitate us." By March, however, he was aroused
by Congressman Smith's by-Hamilton pro-British speech in the House. In
May, Monroe was corresponding with him about the French mission.
Also in May he wrote Washington that "My opinion of the British government is that nothing will force them to do justice but the loud voice of
their people, and that this can never be excited but by distressing their
commerce."

This was a busy season for Hamilton who saw the adversary of his
government not in the British but in tumultuous people at home. He had
long pressed for stern measures against the farmers, particularly in western Pennsylvania, who were resisting the tax on whiskey. Undoubtedly
these frontiersmen used rough measures in their opposition to the tax—
roaring, rioting, even burning down the house of a tax collector. Nobody
suggested that the tax on whiskey then seemed as much an infringement
of liberty to these men as the British tax on tea had seemed to the Sons of
Liberty before the Revolution. It was certainly distressing to the commerce
of people who could only transport their grain by distilling it, and to whom
whiskey was almost the medium of exchange. So excited, the furious farmers gathered around liberty poles. They set up placards bearing inscrip-
tions, "An Equal Tax and No Excise," and the device of a writhing snake
cut squarely in two. There was a don't-tread-on-me threat of secession in
their symbols.

Many of them, Hamilton declared, were members of the Jacobin
Party. Slowly he convinced a reluctant Washington that the violent resistance had been stirred up by the Democratic Societies which had first
been organized in Philadelphia by Jefferson's respectable friends the year
before. He at last made the President believe that these "self-created" societies had been "laboring incessantly to sow the seeds of distrust, jealousy,

and of course discontent, thereby hoping to effect some revolution in the government."

At Hamilton's urging, twelve thousand militia were called to duty to quell the "rebellion." And Hamilton, who, with the resignation of Knox, had taken on the duties of the Secretary of War along with his Treasury tasks, felt the old call to arms and glory. He went along with *his* troops, said to be composed in important degree by young men "possessing the first fortunes in the country, standing in the ranks as private men." Not all were plutocratic Pennsylvanians. Jefferson's young friend Meriwether Lewis saw his first military service with militia drawn from Virginia. He wrote his mother that he was "quite delighted with a soldier's life." Some of the troops turned out not to be either Pennsylvania or Virginia gentlemen but pillagers who in overrunning the country "did not leave a plate, a spoon, a glass or a knife."

They found no rebellion to suppress. Gallatin and other moderates had already persuaded the angry back-country people to make their protests in peaceful fashion. Still under Hamilton's direction the army made hundreds of arrests. The Secretary of both Treasury and War himself harshly questioned prisoners. Two were convicted of treason but pardoned by Washington. If not covered with glory, Hamilton came home confident that Federal authority had been asserted in a way that would not be forgotten. He disdained the attacks and the ridicule of the Democratic press. Still soon after this adventure he sent Washington his resignation to take place on December 31, a year to the day after Jefferson had left his post.

That Virginia gentleman, who preferred "indefinitely to contemplate the tranquil growth of my lucerne & potatoes," took note of the militant march. He spoke of "such an armament against people at their ploughs." Furthermore he resented the effort to make the protest of the farmers an evidence of agitation by the Democratic Societies. The President had permitted himself, he wrote, to be made the organ of an attack upon "the freedom of discussion, the freedom of writing, printing and publishing." He was amazed that the government should be patient under the "kicks and scoffs" of the British and yet rise "at a feather" against people at home. But he only criticized from a distance. He suggested a hope that Madison might become President. For himself, he said, "I would not give up my own retirement for the empire of the universe."

With Monroe off to France, the whole Virginia triumvirate seemed ready to leave the governmental scene in Philadelphia. Madison was blissfully married in a very private ceremony to his Dolley, on September 15, at the home of her sister Lucy at Harewood in what is now West Virginia. The great little man was already talking of retiring with his bride to his Orange County estate and devoting his life to scientific agriculture. On a visit to Monticello just before his marriage, Madison listened to Jefferson's expressions of dismay at his plan of retirement. Yet at the same time Jefferson himself, suffering acutely from rheumatism, was writing almost in pain of a proposal that he himself come back into service as Minister to Spain. Hardly hiding his irritability, he told his successor, Randolph: "No circumstances, my dear Sir, will ever more tempt me to engage in anything public. I thought myself perfectly fixed in this determination when I left Philadelphia, but every day and hour since has added to its inflexibility."

With their three great Virginia antagonists ready to leave the scene of battle, Federalists were already putting aliens and sedition together in their conservative views. Gallatin, for whom Burr had spoken in the Senate, was as a foreigner maligned as the arch-instigator of the Whiskey Rebellion, despite the fact that he had been, before and after his rejection by the Senate, the chief of those who saved western Pennsylvania from a civil war. Suspicions were directed also against the Irish and Germans who were changing the Quaker quality of Pennsylvania.

Different foreigners were feared for different reasons. While Genet was suspect as dangerous agitator as well as impertinent young man, many republican-Democrats had been more disturbed by reports that Washington had secretly seen Vicomte de Noailles, said to be the representative of the French Bourbons in exile. Washington might well have seen Noailles without sinister significance. As a soldier in the American Revolution, he had represented the French army in negotiating the surrender of Cornwallis at Yorktown. He was welcomed in Philadelphia by the Cincinnati whom Genet scorned. Still he was such an émigré as opponents of aristocracy and monarchy feared. Others like him came. Some, from the horrors of the Negro revolution in Santo Domingo, brought reports which strengthened the Federalism of Smith in his slaveholding state.

Also there were radicals coming in haste from repressions in Britain. There sympathy for the French Revolution became almost a crime even when not carried to the extreme of attack on the monarchy as in the case of Tom Paine. Moreover, almost unrealized at the time, another revolution was taking place. Labor disturbances in England had grown about the introduction of power-driven textile manufacture in growing factory towns. In them conditions increasingly justified Jefferson's antipathy to cities. Certainly, in 1794, few realized how much this revolution would be speeded from an American source. Just the year before Eli Whitney, the Yankee in Georgia, had invented the cotton gin which would speed the growth of the lint to English mills and perpetuate, as more than ever profitable, slavery particularly in the American Southwest in the new Natchez region. Planters there were eager to buy slaves who were less needed or useful on the worn lands of Virginia.

To meet his mounting debts Jefferson reluctantly and sometimes secretly sold slaves on occasion. He also set some free, particularly members of the handsome and talented family of Hemings. They had come to Jefferson, along with much debt, in his Wayles inheritance. Strong tradition and slave testimony reported them as people of very "bright" color and the children of Betty Hemings by Jefferson's father-in-law, John Wayles, and so the half brothers and sisters of Jefferson's wife. Late this year he permitted Bob Hemings to buy his own freedom at a valuation of £60. James Hemings, whom he had had taught "the art of French cookery" in Paris at great expense, was freed and given thirty dollars after he had fulfilled the condition of teaching another slave his art. Others remained, including Sally who like her brothers and sisters was noted for her looks and intelligence. According to the dictated recollections of Isaac, another Monticello slave, Sally, who had accompanied Polly Jefferson to Paris, was "very handsome, long straight hair down her back."

It seemed strange to some like the Federalist William Plumer, who was the author of the remark that he wished Jefferson's French politics were as good as his French wines, that the great republican leader presided like a feudal baron over his slaves. He noted the number of slaves in Virginia which had more than any other state and made an entry in his diary: ". . . strange & inconsistent as it may appear, in those very states where slaves are most numerous, the people are most vociferous for *liberty & equality.*"

Others seemed inconsistent too. Burr, who had been put forward as a friend of republican France when Washington sought a replacement for Morris, drew no line against French aristocrats. Indeed, François Alexandre Frédéric, Duc de La Rochefoucauld-Liancourt, agriculturist and social reformer, in his well-reported travels in America noted: "While I was at New York, I made an excursion to the beautiful country-seat of Colonel Burr. . . . He is one of the most amiable men I ever saw." Later at the end of his traversing of the republic the Duke spoke again of his friend Burr as "one of the most distinguished characters in the United States, for the extent precision, and clearness of his judgment, for his acquired knowledge, and for the delicacy and generosity of his sentiments."

Some of his pro-French supporters in the Tammany Society were regarded as the equivalent of sans-culottes by Federalists. Burr was a man with appeal to the Democratic Societies, sneered at as Jacobin Clubs. Yet he made a precious and lasting tie with French aristocracy. He wanted his young Theodosia to be no mere lady of fashion. But in the summer after his wife's death he was depending much on Madame de Sénat who, as French émigré, had opened her fashionable school for girls in New York. He wrote Theodosia from Albany in August 1794, "Imitate as much as you can the manners of Madame de S."

Through this lady and for an often lonely Theodosia, he made one of the loveliest relationships of his life in the practical adoption of young Nathalie de Delage who became in effect his second daughter. This child, "Nat" as she was called by Burr, was the daughter of Admiral Comte Joseph-Paul-Jean de Delage de Volude and Béatrix Stéphanie Renard de Fuchsamberg d'Amblimont. The length of their names proclaimed their patrician lineage. Nathalie's mother, the Marquise Stéphanie, had been from youth attached to the court of Louis XVI and Marie Antoinette. There ironically she must have been intimate with the sisters of republican Genet. In 1782 she became Dame d'Honneur to the Princess Marie Thérèse Louise de Savoy-Carignano de Lamballe, superintendent of the royal household. The salon of the Princess became, as the revolution began, the meeting place for the Queen and the members of the Assembly whom she wished to gain over. The people believed the Princess to be the center of all royal intrigues. On September 3, 1791, having refused to take the oath against the monarchy, she was delivered to the fury of the mobs. She died on no neat guillotine but her head was placed on a pike and paraded before the windows of the imprisoned Queen.

The Marquise Stéphanie had better luck. She escaped to Portugal by disguise, bribery, and the "assistance of the notorious Comtesse de Fontenay." (Though an imprisoned aristocrat, this Countess had become the mistress of a terrorist and cooled his revolutionary ardor as she enflamed his passion. For saving others as well as the Marquise Stéphanie she was hailed as "Our Lady of Thermidor" in relation to her part in the fall of Robespierre.) In Lisbon the Marquise Stéphanie entrusted her child to Madame de Sénat who was fleeing to the United States. It is not clear exactly when Nathalie entered the household at Richmond Hill. Neither is it certain that Burr legally adopted her, as Davis said he did. Certainly, however, she was educated by the Colonel as his child and as Theodosia's sister. Nothing better indicates the charm of the Burr household containing these two lovely girls than a playful letter he wrote Nathalie a few years later.

"You and Theodosia craze me with your jealousies," he wrote. "She always accuses me of writing you the longest letters—and you accuse me of writing her the oftener. As I do not keep very accurate accounts of the number of letters or the number of lines which they contain, you may for aught I know be both right, but I suspect not—There is but one way to satisfy both, & that is to write neither of you."

That was a threat he would never carry out. The two girls made the charm and warmth of Richmond Hill. And the great house was a set for him as a man who had no intention of retiring. More and more he loomed on the American scene. Soon, on the subject of Burr's ascendancy, Oliver Wolcott, who succeeded Hamilton as Secretary of the Treasury, would be quoting an unnamed Virginia Federalist who evidently knew the New York Senator.

"The two most efficient actors on the political theatre of our country," Wolcott said this gentleman told him, "are Mr. Hamilton and Mr. Burr. . . . I have watched the movements of Mr. Burr with attention, and have discovered traits of character which sooner or later will give us much trouble. He has an unequalled talent of attaching men to his views, and forming combinations of which he is always the center. He is determined to play a first part; he acts strenuously with us in public, but it is remarkable that in all private conversations he more frequently agrees with us in principle than in the mode of giving them effect. . . . I shall not be surprised if Mr. Burr is found in a few years, the leader of a popular party in the northern states; and if this event ever happens, this party will subvert the influence of the southern states."

Some Virginia republicans, including the greatest among them, had come to know Burr well, too. There was a danger to them in his talent and appeal. Yet he was essential to their plans. Hamilton's reaction to this report about Burr was simpler. He both hated and feared this rival in his own city and state with a revulsion he carefully concealed except in most confidential letters. Burr was aware of antagonism. Still, he had many blessings. Carefully he kept young Theodosia and Nathalie at their lessons. But it was a joy to watch them, not quite captured by instruction in languages, literature, and science, running at play in the elaborately landscaped gardens at Richmond Hill.

3.

The Inner Circle

Accompanied only by a single servant, Senator Burr, in the early fall of 1795, set out on a journey southward over rough roads and through dark woodlands. This trip was an excursion at least as mysterious as the "botanizing expedition" of Jefferson and Madison in fair summer weather in New England a few years before. Burr was at the height of his republican popularity then as the man who had made the fight against Senate approval of the violently opposed Jay Treaty with England. And evidently he was also looking confidently to amassing the fortune he required as the master of Richmond Hill, which to Abigail Adams had seemed so sublime. He meant to keep it so.

He moved south through the settled regions of New Jersey, by Elizabethtown and Princeton. In this state where he had been born and educated, he showed the easy manner and charm which kept him on friendly terms with many Federalists. He enjoyed himself at Sunday dinner with the staunch Federalist Senator Frederick Frelinghuysen. He saw friends in Philadelphia. Beyond Baltimore the road became a mystifying way through woods. The capital-to-be was little more than a surveyed expanse. In the city of projected avenues and planned buildings, he wrote Theodosia that he was "at home" in the "house of our friends, Law and Duncanson."

The names indicate Burr's interest in the land speculations in which so many Americans were involved. Thomas Law was a brother of Edward Law, first Baron of Ellenborough, who had defended Warren Hastings against charges of corruption and misconduct in India. Whatever was the guilt or innocence of the great Hastings in enriching himself in India,

Lord Ellenborough's brother, Thomas, was said to have amassed a great fortune there which he was investing in America. He was prominent on the small social scene. A year after Burr's visit he married Eliza Parke Custis, granddaughter of Mrs. George Washington.

The other of Burr's hosts was evidently William Mayne Duncanson. Before the Potomac site had been chosen for the permanent capital, Duncanson, a tobacco planter, had built one of the emerging city's first substantial residences. His place, The Maples, stood not far from the Capitol which was slowly rising when Burr came upon the scene. Law and Duncanson were buying lots in the platted city. So was Burr's political friend and business associate John Nicholson of Philadelphia. The biggest buyer was Nicholson's partner, Robert Morris, financier of the Revolution, friend of President Washington, and owner of millions of American acres. On a modest scale Burr was associated with them and others in a million-acre tract in the "Presque Isle angle," the northwest corner of Pennsylvania fronting on Lake Erie. Shortly before this visit to Law and Duncanson, the Senator had been hard up, but he wrote one of his creditors that he had no doubt that he would weather the storm and "be as rich as a reasonable man need wish."

In his letters home Burr mentioned no real estate transactions. He indicated no enthusiasm about his surroundings. He told Theodosia, "My remarks on this city are reserved till we meet." He wrote her instead about a sudden, startling illness. His face and eyes were inflamed. His ears buzzed. His throat was sore. At the sight of him his valet, Alexis, repeatedly cried, "Diable!" As usual, however, Burr described his troubles with more humor than complaint.

Two days later, on September 27, he wrote Theo, "I am so much better today, that, if the weather was good, I should prosecute my journey if I could find the means of getting on; but the rain, which is continual and very heavy, keeps well and sick within doors."

His destination, though he did not mention it, was Monticello. His visit there then has not been mentioned often since. None of Burr's major biographers refer to this trip. Malone, who briefly touched upon it in his multivolumed life of Jefferson, apparently attached little significance to it. Still it must have been important to Burr. The journey from the Potomac to Albemarle County was not one to be lightly undertaken then. Even in fair weather the travel from Monticello to Washington normally took Jefferson three days. The road was little more than a trail. On it, the Virginian reported half a dozen years later, there were eight rivers, "five have neither bridges nor boats." Those streams must have been swollen this fall by the continual rains. Underfoot was the mire of Piedmont red clay under the dank autumn trees.

No man recently devilishly ill would have undertaken this laborious enterprise to make a mere social call or, as Burr put it in connection with another significant journey, "pour passer le temps." Later he told Jefferson that he had always found his company and conversation fascinating. Fascination could hardly have pulled him across Virginia in this chill, drenched fall. It is not known whether Burr made this visit by invitation or set out on the basis of his own determination. He was still in Washington on September 28. He planned to be back in New York on October 24. Mail should be directed to him at Washington until October 10. The date of his visit to Albemarle County is only fixed by a letter Jefferson wrote his friend and neighbor, Wilson Cary Nicholas, on October 19. In it he said that Burr had left two or three days before after only one day's stay.

Burr might have been very welcome at Monticello in the fall of 1795. Though Jefferson was insistently more and more out of politics, he sometimes stirred restlessly on his hill. In this fall when the Virginia legislature was condemning the Jay treaty and by implication Washington, the former Secretary of State was watching with approval. Indeed, as of this time Albert J. Beveridge, biographer of John Marshall who was then defending the treaty and the President, spoke of Jefferson as "the Republican commander in Monticello." Certainly Jefferson had been aroused by the news of the treaty Jay had brought back from England. It seemed to him a complete surrender of the American position he had advocated before his retirement. So far as American rights were concerned it appeared to be an abdication to arrogant Britain. Its provisions also seemed an almost deliberate slap at France where Monroe was then laboring to heal the wounds created by Gouverneur Morris in Paris and by Genet in Philadelphia. It was to Jefferson a "monument of folly and venality." To Federalist insistence that at least the treaty prevented war, he growled of "the eternal truth that acquiescence under insult is not the way to escape war."

Burr, coming across the hills and rivers to visit him, shared such views. In the Federalist Senate he had marshaled the republican opposition to it. Gallatin wrote his wife of Burr's "most excellent speech" in opposition to ratification. The Senator had offered amendments. He had proposed postponement. Nevertheless, the treaty had been pushed through the Senate behind closed doors, on June 24, 1795, by a vote of twenty to ten. But a violently reverse sentiment sounded outside the chamber in the streets, at mass meetings, in the halls of the Virginia and other state legislatures. When Hamilton tried to defend the treaty in New York, the crowd answered with "stones and clubs and beat him and his party off the ground." Eleven days after the Senate had voted, Burr wrote Monroe in Paris that "the Country is considerably agitated. Many of the merchants who were most devoted to Mr. Jay and to the administration, express themselves decidedly and warmly against it." He could have been coming to Monticello, in October 1795, to make a similar report about the mounting opposition to the administration and its treaty.

This seemed unlikely to skeptical Virginians. Other republicans were using the mail for the dispatch of such information. Why not Burr? Some Virginia Federalists, who resented Burr's opposition to the treaty and suspected that Jefferson was still politician as well as rusticating philosopher, saw sinister implications in the Burr visit. One such was Levin Powell, staunch Federalist, Revolutionary soldier, and an opponent whom Jefferson could not disregard. Powell saw a plot against Washington's government in the Burr visit. He described the New York Senator as a man of "considerable talents" but a violent opponent of the administration. Burr came to Monticello, Powell charged, to meet in Jefferson's house with other extreme republicans to plan "rash and violent measures" against the government.

Monticello was to be the scene of many republican strategy conferences. Now, however, Jefferson was, as he endlessly reiterated, only a retired country gentleman. True, he was writing much in his private correspondence about what he regarded as the capture of the President by the Federalists around him. Yet, quickly he wrote Washington himself, denying a report that he was "still engaged in the battle of politics and in turbulence and intrigue against the government." Anybody who said that he was so engaged, he declared, was a "miserable tergivesator." Still the Powell charges seemed sufficiently disturbing to prompt two of Jefferson's friends and neighbors to swear to a deposition that there had been no such meeting of republican plotters as Powell reported. There is no evidence that Jefferson inspired this affidavit which he left in his papers. He did not repudiate it. Malone regarded as correct the sworn statement that there were no other political strangers at Monticello when the New Yorker came. That fact makes the visit even more mystifying. Why should the Senator have made this difficult journey for so brief a stay?

Only supposition is possible about the visit now. It could hardly have been connected with land speculations. Many Virginians, including neighbors, associates, and some opponents of Jefferson, were seeking riches in wilderness acres as well as in city lots. Washington and Patrick Henry were investors. At this very time the rich Morris was aiding the strong Federalist John Marshall and his brother, a Morris son-in-law, in acquiring a great Virginia tract. But Jefferson already owed more money on land than he could pay.

Possibly Burr, as one of the chief republican leaders, along with Madison and Gallatin in the House, made his journey to Monticello to put in an early bit of persuasion that Jefferson run for the Presidency in 1796. Three months after the New Yorker's visit to the rusticating philosopher on his Virginia hill, Madison wrote Monroe in Paris that he and others planned to "push" Jefferson as the only man they could elect as Washington's successor. Madison was afraid, however, that reluctant Jefferson might "mar the project" by "a peremptory and public protest." Certainly persuasion by Burr or anybody else at this point would have been premature. This was nearly a year before Washington finally said his farewell in eloquent words prepared for him by Hamilton. His wish for retirement was as real as Jefferson's often expressed preference for it. Yet no hopeful successor would want to seem to be pushing the stubborn and sensitive old man into it.

If Burr's career, as some believe, is to be explained by ambition only, ambition could explain this arduous journey. When he wanted something he never spared efforts or energy to get it. He had been considered by republican chiefs for their Vice-Presidential candidate in 1792. He believed he was entitled to it now. Jefferson and others, he indicated to Mrs. Gallatin later, had agreed to such an arrangement when he stood aside for Clinton four years earlier in the caucus which Beckley had reported. Burr had abided by his word in supporting Clinton then. Now he did not want to be forgotten by a recluse engaged in rebuilding a mansion on a hilltop. Burr was either satisfied in what he heard in his one day visit at Monticello or he only heard what the Virginian was telling everybody else that he had abandoned politics for farming and philosophy and so was not one to be consulted about the matter. Possibly all Burr got was good company and fascinating conversation.

Jefferson was farming in the summer of 1796 when Rochefoucauld-Liancourt came to receive a "wholly kind reception." The French aristocrat found him in the harvest fields. Still he regarded Jefferson as a book farmer "little accustomed to agricultural pursuits." The Frenchman spoke in admiration of the great house under construction on the hill. But from the vantage of Monticello he made his observations on slavery. He wrote: "The Virginia mongrel negroes are found in greater number than in Carolina and Georgia; and I have even seen, especially at Mr. Jefferson's, slaves, who, neither in point of color nor features, showed the least trace of their original descent. . . ." Rochefoucauld was more impressed with the farming of David Meade Randolph, at Presqu'ile, a much smaller plantation at the junction of the James and Appomattox rivers.

Only cultivating three hundred and fifty acres with eight slaves, Randolph, farming and fishing, was making thirty-five hundred dollars a year. Rochefoucauld regarded him as "fully entitled to the reputation he enjoys of being the best farmer in the whole country." The region was sickly, however, as Jefferson had suggested to his daughter. Indeed, when Rochefoucauld was there, he reported that David M. Randolph's "young and amiable wife has not enjoyed one month of good health since she first came to live on this plantation." Randolph was ready to sell but could not get the twenty thousand dollars he felt the place was worth. Lands were falling in value in Virginia.

While Jefferson rusticated in a political retirement at Monticello, others, in the months following Burr's visit there, seemed vague in recollection of the 1792 caucus at which Burr had voluntarily withdrawn. Now in 1796 Beckley, in his reports as political intelligence agent to the three great Virginians, soon to be described as a dynasty, seemed now to blow hot and cold on the Burr candidacy. He wrote of suggestions to put Chancellor Livingston in the field. He reported the views of others in the months between Burr's visit to Monticello and the choice of a republican candidate for the Vice-Presidency. He appeared to be fixed for Burr as the time of final selection approached. The New Yorker, he said, had the support of Gallatin, Rittenhouse, and Chancellor Livingston, which assured him Pennsylvania and New York. Finally he wrote that "if no great schism happens in Virginia, I think it morally certain that Mr. Jefferson and Col. Burr will be elected." Yet, on October 15, 1796, shortly before the election he made a cryptic suggestion to Madison.

"Burr has been out electioneering these six weeks in Connecticut,

Vermont, R. Island & Massach. But I doubt [not] his efforts are more directed to himself than anybody else. You well know him; would it not be prudent to vote one half of Virg for Clinton. *Consider this.*"

The provisions for the Presidential elections, as provided in the Constitution then, seemed to set up a system almost designed to promote confusion or connivance. Various election procedures were followed in various states. But in none was there separate voting for President and Vice-President. The candidate with the most votes took the Presidency, the one with the next greatest number became Vice-President. Thus a man supposedly running for Vice-President might be chosen President and vice versa. In effect, under a Constitution which did not contemplate political parties, the election was a popularity contest in which the selection was made by a strictly limited body of electors who could do pretty much as they pleased.

The vigilant Hamilton saw this. He preferred the supposed Vice-Presidential candidate of the Federalists, Thomas Pinckney of South Carolina, to the first Federalist candidate John Adams. Pinckney had much to commend him to the South and West. Only recently he had negotiated the treaty of San Lorenzo el Real under which Spain granted the free navigation of the Mississippi which, to the fury of men beyond the mountains, Jay years before had been willing to relinquish. What was more important to Hamilton, he believed he could more easily dominate the South Carolina aristocrat than the hardheaded Massachusetts Puritan. Hamilton was aware of his own unpopularity with the masses of the people. He had spoken of the populace as a "great beast" and the people were readier to return the compliment with stones than with votes. The former Secretary of the Treasury wanted the power of the Presidency, not the place.

So secretly, in a confidential correspondence which was as voluminous as Jefferson's, he urged his Northern and Eastern friends to give Adams and Pinckney equal votes, expecting that the Yankee Adams would get fewer votes than Pinckney in the South and West. Thus he hoped Pinckney might run ahead of Adams and be elected President. Something of the same sort was proposed in Beckley's *"Consider this"* counsel to Madison in regard to Burr.

Apparently Beckley did not entertain such ideas alone. Some Federalists, who were quiet about Hamilton's design, heard reports of republican finagling. Hamilton's Wolcott wrote that the "antis," as he called the republicans, did not expect Burr to win and secretly hoped Adams would run second to Jefferson. Smith of South Carolina discovered that without his knowledge some sly maneuvers were going on there. He wrote that Burr would only have the support of Jeffersonians "in some of the states."

Smith was a busy man in this election, apparently too busy to realize what was going on behind his back at home. His arrogance repelled republicans. Even his friend Hamilton said that "he is popular with no description of men, from a certain hardness of character." Still he brought to the Federalist cause a powerful pen. Indeed, while Jefferson and Adams stayed aloof in dignity, Smith and Beckley seemed to symbolize the furies stirred by loud politicians and the violent press. Beckley was so active around Philadelphia in this campaign that Malone called him the "chief organizer of the Republican campaign in Pennsylvania."

The two men collided in violent political pamphleteering. They were brought to pen-to-pen fighting by events in Virginia where efforts were made to create such a "schism" as Beckley had feared. One who mightily endeavored to create such a cleavage was the same Levin Powell who had tried to make something sinister out of Burr's brief visit to Monticello. Charges were renewed against Jefferson concerning his conduct as Governor at the time of the British invasion in 1781. He had abandoned his post of trust a second time, it was shouted, by quitting his place as Secretary of State when the nation faced a foreign crisis. Hostile writers outside the state took up these charges and added others to them.

Smith brought scorn and ridicule to the debate. Under the name of PHOCION he wrote a series of newspaper articles which were gathered in a pamphlet called *The Pretensions of Thomas Jefferson to the Presidency Examined*. The savage Smith had been irritated by some apparently mild piece in a Virginia paper arguing that Jefferson would make a fine President because he was a philosopher. Smith's production was a sharp satire. What kind of philosopher was the Virginia writer talking about? he demanded.

He answered his query: As "moral philosopher" Jefferson had never condemned the atrocities of the French revolution. Certainly there was nothing to recommend a "natural philosopher" for President. An important visitor might come to see him only to find him mounting butterflies or working in his whirligig chair "which has the miraculous quality of allowing the person seated in it to turn his head, without moving his tail." Even as a philosopher he was inconsistent, the violently pro-slavery Smith declared, first discovering in his *Notes on Virginia* that blacks were inferior to whites and then "*fraternizing* with negroes, writing them complimentary epistles, *stiling* them *his black brethren,* congratulating them on the evidences of their *genius,* and assuring them of his good wishes for their speedy emancipation."

Angry pro-Jefferson answers came fast. One reply was that Smith had become hysterical because he knew he would not be able to favor the British under Jefferson as he could under Adams. Most significant was the reply of Beckley, then beginning years of effective writing for the republican leader in Virginia. Beckley could exchange verbal blows. But he found the occasion and had the background to array the facts in answer to slurs at Jefferson's behavior as Governor long before. As a sensitive man the great Virginian cherished this defense by Beckley after the campaign as well as in it. He would depend much on Beckley's writing in the future. Sometimes the House Clerk wrote over the signature CALM OBSERVER. Often that seemed a really euphemistic label on his letters. He worked quietly but he could swing in writing from dignity to bombast. In partisanship he was the match for Smith. Their enmity was to be unforgiving.

The election returns came in slowly and uncertainly in 1796. When the votes were finally counted Adams had won with seventy-one electoral votes. Jefferson was close behind him with sixty-eight. Pinckney had fifty-nine. Burr received only thirty votes, including only one vote from Virginia where Jefferson and his friends were clearly in command. Indeed, Virginia instead of voting for Burr threw away fifteen of its votes to seventy-four-year-old Samuel Adams of Massachusetts who was no candidate at all. Jefferson's great admiration for this early Revolutionary agitator strongly suggests that it was he who chose this Adams as one to whom votes could be thrown like an unexpected bouquet. Obviously the votes were not so much to old Sam Adams as from Burr. One Virginia vote also went to the real candidate John Adams. It was cast by the single Federalist elector, again the same Powell who had smelled something almost like republican sedition when Burr visited Monticello.

There was not much room for cheering or hooting on either side. Still Hamilton, who had not managed to sidetrack Adams, found basis for elation. He wrote his friend King, recently appointed as Ambassador to Britain, that "it is now decided *that neither Jefferson nor Burr* can be President. . . . The event will not a little mortify Burr. Virginia has given him only one vote."

Congressman Smith put it more bluntly: "Burr's friends have betrayed him in Virginia—he had been so duped by them, that he has not yet showed his face here; tho his lodgings were engaged for him the first instant. They have made a complete cat's-paw of him."

Actually Hamilton had more reason for mortification than Burr. And Smith felt that he had been betrayed in his own house. Hamilton had not succeeded in making Pinckney President, but he had pointed a loop-hole in the plan devised by the Constitution makers for Presidential elections. That should have been warning that what Hamilton had proposed to do by design could happen by accident with almost venomous results. Indeed, in this election something of that sort was almost brought about in South Carolina. Pinckney's friends there also preferred him to Adams. So playing it smart to put their man ahead, they cast the state's eight votes, not for Adams and Pinckney but for Pinckney and Jefferson.

If the eight votes they gave to Jefferson had gone to Adams, the Massachusetts man would have had a more respectable majority. Furthermore Congressman Smith, on the basis of early returns, thought Pinckney had three New Hampshire votes which actually he did not receive. If Jefferson's total had been cut by eight and Pinckney's increased by three, Pinckney would have been elected Vice-President with sixty-two votes to Jefferson's sixty.

On the assumption that Pinckney had the three New Hampshire votes, on December 22, Smith scrawled his indignation at the South Carolina electors and particularly Edward Rutledge, who he felt had brought their own man down. He spluttered at the "folly and mismanagement" in his own state. Pinckney, he said, had been hit at home by the "ridiculous & wicked conduct of his own state & particular friends."

Burr made no public protest over the similar finagling in Virginia. He would not have been elected Vice-President if he had received all of Virginia's republican votes. Still, its vote gave him reasons, not for mortification but for present resentment and future suspicions. He made no precipitate cry that he had been betrayed. His political attitude then reflected some instructions about her writing which he sent to twelve-year-old Theo soon after the election: "Arrange a whole sentence in your mind before you write a word of it; and, whatever may be your 'hurry' (never be in a *hurry*), read over your letter slowly and carefully before you seal it." He was not now sealing himself off in hasty dudgeon.

Despite Smith's suggestion that Burr was ashamed to show his face in Philadelphia, he held his head in a way which always seemed to augment his height. Disappointments had not slowed his stride. He had reasons to believe he had been badly treated. Yet, if he had wished the post of Minister to France, he had shown no chagrin when his supporter Monroe took the post himself. Indeed, he (interestingly along with Beckley) remained one of those to whom the beset Monroe in France poured out his troubles. As friend of France, like Burr, Monroe was placed in an almost impossible position by the Jay negotiations and the treaty which emerged from them. The Minister's kindness to irascible Tom Paine, whose release from prison he had secured, only brought him embarrassment. That old agitator was now ready to accuse Washington of bad faith. Monroe's difficulties were increased when Jay's assistant, the artist Trumbull, wearing his military title of Colonel, came to Paris showing the American Minister no sympathy and adding to the suspicions of the French that the United States was becoming the perfidious friend of its old ally while turning in new subservient agreement to Britain. From Washington's government in Philadelphia, now totally top-staffed by Hamiltonian Federalists, Monroe received communications in the tone of "an overseer on the farm to one of his gang." As a humorless and partisan man, Monroe made some almost comic mistakes. There was, however, nothing funny about the fact that his harsh recall coincided with a stiff announcement by the French government that it would no longer recognize any American envoy. Burr, reading Monroe's letters, must have felt relieved not to be in his place. Still possibly his grace and tact, his suppleness of which many of his enemies were suspicious, might in Paris have prevented personal hurt and reduced international inflammation.

No sense of escape attended the Colonel's defeat when he came up for re-election to the Senate in the same year in which he ran for Vice-President. At this time of Federalist ascendancy, Hamilton and Schuyler were not to be surprised by any such combination against them as had put Burr in the Senate six years before. Burr certainly was not surprised when Schuyler grabbed back his Senate seat. Neither Schuyler nor Hamilton, however, could any longer regard Burr as a political upstart or as one who could be considered as finally swept aside. Even before he was defeated, Burr, pocketing his pride or, as one of his biographers has put it, stooping to conquer, was planning to return to power where he had begun twelve years before as a member of the New York Assembly. He was building strength with the rank and file of people who predominated in numbers in New York City. An organization of young and ardent republicans was increasing in numbers around him. Some who had sneered at Tammany were aware of its political potential. Old Schuyler's health, which would force his retirement from the Senate two years later, was already failing, but he gave perceptive warning to his son-in-law. Even as he was preparing to say his thanks to the Assembly for his election over Burr, he wrote Hamilton.

"Mr. Burr, we are informed," he warned, "will be a candidate for a seat in the Assembly; his views it is not difficult to appreciate. They alarm me, and if he prevails, *I apprehend a total change of politics in the next Assembly*—attended with other disagreeable consequences."

Others recognized that if Burr was down, he could not be counted out. Among them was Jefferson as he entered on his duties as Vice-President in March 1797. Much as he opposed the "commercial states" and feared the city masses, he had seen in the recent election that the agrarian South could never win alone. Only with the help of Pennsylvania had he won the Vice-Presidency. Also he knew that everywhere he had enemies. They would not allow him to be content even as philosopher. As he became Vice-President, he also became president of the American Philosophical Society succeeding his staunch political and scientific friend Rittenhouse who had died the year before.

Now even as head of that group of the elect, he was reviled and ridiculed as philosopher by a tough and able Maryland lawyer who was to be his long-time enemy. Hard-drinking and hard-hitting Federalist Luther Martin charged that the sage of Monticello had slandered his wife's family in his *Notes on Virginia*. Jefferson was sensitive about criticism of this book which provided the basis of his position as scientific observer. He was disturbed when Martin charged that in the book he had lied about the family of Martin's wife, calling one of them a "man infamous for many murders" of Indians. Also, the Maryland man whom Jefferson was to call later the "Federalist Bulldog," made fun of the Vice-President. He ridiculed Jefferson's efforts to prove that American native men and native beasts, even fossil bones, were bigger than their European counterparts. Martin roused ribald laughter at the philosopher and must have flushed the philosopher's cheeks. He quoted the sage as saying of the natives of the New World that *"les organes de generation ne sont plus faibles ou plus petits."*

Jefferson, who would meet Martin again in mounting antagonism, sought the facts to justify his book. In one of his letters seeking information he got into deeper trouble by a critical comment on Adams' handling of the French situation.

Adams exploded: "It is evidence of a mind, soured, yet seeking for popularity, and eaten to a honeycomb with ambition, yet weak, confused, uninformed and ignorant. I have been long convinced that this ambition is so inconsiderate as to be capable of going great lengths."

Jefferson was as unaware of this outburst as he was of the fact that Adams knew of his criticism. He did not know that Washington's faith in him as a friend had been whittled away. Their relationship had terminated, even in correspondence, by the time Jefferson became Vice-President. Also Jefferson was acutely conscious of criticism by newspapers. He complained, "I have been for some time used as the property of the newspapers, a fair mark for every man's dirt."

Now prompted by principles, antagonisms, or ambition, he was evidently ready to fight. If old friendships were to be broken, more recent acquaintances needed to be strengthened. So in June 1797, less than three months after he had been in office, he made a "conciliatory gesture" to Burr in a letter which Malone wrote "marked Jefferson's assumption of the leadership of the Republican Party." Certainly on this occasion he was sending an invitation to Burr to join him. In many ways it was a strange letter, written as if to one who was both a recent companion and a stranger who might have forgotten him. He thought, he told Burr, that "some general view of our situation and prospects, since you left us, may not be unacceptable. At any rate, it will give me an opportunity of recalling myself to your memory, and of evidencing my esteem for you."

In many ways this was similar to that letter his friend Dr. Rush had sent Burr introducing Beckley and calling for political aid several years before. Jefferson now told Burr that he was interested in the trends of affairs in his state. Because of Federalist gains there, he feared that "little is to be hoped." Yet the great need was to awaken the Eastern states, particularly New York. He wished Burr could give him "a comfortable solution" of "certain painful and doubtful questions." That would "relieve a mind devoted to the preservation of our republican government in the true form and spirit in which it was established."

Burr replied promptly and graciously. Perhaps, as has been said, Burr was "grateful" for the letter, though considering his recent treatment it is not easy to understand why. Certainly the ex-Senator was ready to be cooperative. His letter indicated no despair about the situation in New York. He told the Vice-President that "the moment requires free communication among those who adhere to the principles of our revolution. The conduct of some individuals of the [Jay] Treaty Majority has disappointed me a good deal. That of the executive something also, but less." He had, he said, been "led to hope that a more temperate system would have been adopted. All expectations are now abandoned. The gauntlet I see is thrown and the fruit of our War with Britain is again in jeopardy. . . . It would not be easy neither would it be discreet, to answer your inquiries or to communicate with you my ideas with satisfaction to either of us, in the compass of a letter. I will endeavor to do it in person."

Despite his increasing private schedule at the bar and in land speculations, Burr was again as good as his word. He was in Philadelphia within less than a fortnight. Evidently he came to join others in welcoming home, in June 1797, his much maligned friend Monroe. The recalled Minister was being treated almost like an undesirable alien by Federalists, including their petty customs authorities. Republicans meant to match what they regarded as Monroe's mistreatment by demonstration of their affection and regard. He was cheered in the streets. A great banquet was held for him to which all good democrats were invited. Friends of the Adams Administration and some others scorned it. John Rutledge, Jr., who was one of those who switched their votes from Adams to Jefferson in South Carolina to help Pinckney, described the banquet in distaste. This indicated his increasing antipathy to Jefferson which would be later apparent. On the Fourth of July he wrote home to Charleston:

"The invitation was very generally accepted & (it is with much sorrow I mention it) our friend the Vice-President was of the Party. . . . It was a complete medley. Perhaps there never was a company in any country (in the most democratic times) which was more completely mosaic. Here you saw an American disorganizer & there a blundering wild Irishman—in one corner a banished Genevan & in another a French Spye—on one side a greasy Butcher & on the other a dirty Cobler."

As the "banished Genevan," Gallatin got no such impression of the dinner. He wrote his aristocratic wife that fifty Congressmen, the Governor of Pennsylvania, and other dignitaries attended. Mr. Jefferson may have been present in the plainer clothes he was wearing—no ruffles, no great topaz ring. His enemies said he costumed his hypocritical democratic pretenses. Burr at this time, though closer to the masses, including cobblers and butchers, was as always the perfectly groomed gentleman of fashion.

More important than the banquet was the assemblage at the time of a smaller group. Even before he presented himself to the President and the Secretary of State, Monroe conferred with his greatest republican friends. For two hours at one session, he met with Jefferson, Gallatin, and Burr. Of the great republicans, as Malone wrote, only Madison was not present in person. At this meeting Burr undoubtedly shared with the others those ideas which he had told Mr. Jefferson he felt it would be indiscreet to discuss by mail There was time in the talk to cover more of his information and opinions than could be encompassed in a letter. But perhaps more important than anything at this conference was the fact, observed by Malone, that "the inner Republican circle" had been reformed.

Within it Burr had come by invitation to Jefferson's embrace. His trip back to New York in July weather was much more pleasant than the quick, strange journey he had made to Monticello nearly two years before. Yet now, though he could only have been aware of brewing personal-political trouble, he was headed toward the task of dealing with the results of sleazy political manipulations in the making of which he had had no part. As innocent certainly then, he moved to the role of peacemaker when an old scandal threatened fresh blood.

V.
THE
MOUNTING STORM

1.

Wall of Separation

On repeated occasions Jefferson expressed his determination not to cross the Atlantic Ocean again. A diverse company seemed to be crossing it to him. In 1797, when he welcomed Monroe home from France and called Burr into the inner circle of republican leadership, various such travelers brought him nostalgia, concern, and some still mysterious relationships. Earlier he had found congenial companions in such erudite refugees from British reaction as the philosophers and scientists, Joseph Priestley and Thomas Cooper. Philadelphia seemed filled with French émigrés and French revolutionists, European land speculators, journalists, tourists, secret agents, and plain Irish and German immigrants.

Some Americans, both rich and obscure, who had traveled much abroad, were returning. Late in May, Jefferson wrote home to his younger daughter Polly of seeing his former Monticello slave Thomas Hemings, who had traveled much since he had been given his freedom. With relief the Vice-President found that young Tom was "not given up to drink as I had before been informed." As former master he was urging the young Negro to stay in Philadelphia and save some money. Evidently, however, he was not confident of his persuasiveness.

"He tells me," he wrote, "his next trip will be to Spain. I am afraid his journeys will end in the moon."

In the same letter he mentioned more prominent acquaintances among Atlantic travelers: "I see by the newspapers that Mr. and Mrs. Church are arrived at New York. I have not heard from them, and therefore am unable to say about your friend Kitty. The situation in England is so unsafe that every prudent person who can quit it is right in doing so."

Obviously he was much interested in the arrival in America of Angelica Church, who had been a member of his choice coterie in Paris, and her daughter Kitty, who had been the schoolmate of Polly there. Mr. Church was the "prudent person" in this family group. He was moving his family and his money (some of which he had made in America earlier) from "unsafe" England. War with France was so spiraling the national debt that the Bank of England had been forbidden to pay its notes in gold. There was the prospect of an income tax. America seemed a safer place for such an elegantly tough man of fortune as Church.

He had already, through his brother-in-law Hamilton, loaned eighty thousand dollars to the great land speculator Robert Morris. Hamilton, who was useful to Church, had a special charm for Angelica. Some thought he was more to her than a gallant brother-in-law whom she gaily called her *petit Fripon*. Hamilton's solemn friend Troup resented both hearing his political idol called a little rascal and the lady who gaily called him that. Apparently her sister Eliza Hamilton, who was pregnant with her fifth son at this time, did not resent Angelica's flirtatious familiarity with her handsome husband. The brusque Church, who, with his money, had brought along a pair of dueling pistols which were to become famous later, found Hamilton only an admirable aide in his financial operations.

The rich Morris was making a Philadelphia monument for himself in the American society to which the Churches returned. He seemed the embodiment of the greater riches Church wished to gain. For one Philadelphia lot, in Chestnut Street near Seventh, he had swapped seventy-four thousand acres at the mouth of the Tennessee River. That was a small deal for a man who counted his acres in western New York alone by the million. Now with L'Enfant, who had laid out the lots he owned in Washington, as his architect he was building a marble palace in Philadelphia. Yet in his personal correspondence Morris was already speaking peevishly of republicans as anarchists and some capitalists as usurers.

Jefferson, as a republican who sometimes complained of money lenders too, expected less welcome to great houses in which Angelica would move with flippant grace. He kept no such establishment in Philadelphia now like that one he had maintained in Paris. He lived in no such elaborately remodeled house as the one which, as Secretary of State, he had rented from his esteemed friend, the ardent republican

Thomas Leiper. With rooms in Francis's Hotel, where critics said he was lodged with "a knot of Jacobins," he wore the careless garb of a Virginia planter. Yet back home in Virginia, not prompted by any special prosperity, he was continuing his incessant rebuilding of his Monticello château.

He hated to leave it. He had even thought that he might take the oath as Vice-President there. When, instead, he went to Philadelphia for the inaugural ceremonies, he had only stayed eleven days in the city before moving back to his building operations. Then reluctantly he prepared to go North again for the opening of the first session of the Fifth Congress, on May 15. Albemarle was beautiful then though the flowering spring was settling into the green-swarthed summer. There already he must have suspected romance on his hill.

His young, not-quite-nineteen-year-old Polly was prettier than her sister, Patsy, now Mrs. Randolph. She had more beaux. One had been her father's Congressional aide, the pugnacious Giles, though he was sixteen years her senior. Long afterwards the slave Isaac, in his dictated recollections of Monticello, left a vignette of Giles's last visit in courtship:

"Billy Giles courted Miss Polly, Old Master's daughter. Isaac one morning saw him talking to her in the garden, right back of the nail factory shop; she was lookin on de ground. All at once she wheeled round and come off. *That* was the time she turned him off. Isaac never so sorry for a man in all life—sorry because everybody thought she was going to marry him. Mr. Giles give several dollars to the servants, and when he went away dat time he never come back no more. His servant Arthur was a big man. Isaac wanted Mr. Giles to marry Miss Polly. Arthur always said he was a mighty fine man. He was very rich; used to come to Monticello in a monstrous fine gig—mighty few gigs in dem days with plated mountin's and harness."

Polly, to her father's "inexpressible pleasure," turned closer home. She had spent years in her childhood in the house of her mother's half sister, Mrs. Francis Eppes of Eppington, before she reluctantly joined her father in France. In that household then, as a boy only five years older than herself, was her cousin John Wayles Eppes. In her family's almost addiction to consanguinity she promised her hand to "Jack" Eppes. Old Isaac, who had rooted for Giles, said that Eppes was "a handsome man but had a harelip." There is no other report of this defect and portraits show no sign of it.

If Jefferson had any intimation of the pleasure this betrothal would give him before he left Monticello in May, he moved to pain and possible infliction of pain in Philadelphia. Those who worshiped Washington already, and possibly unjustly in a guilt by association process, regarded the Vice-President as his traducer. Jefferson's friendship for Tom Paine was recalled the year before when that bitter publicist had turned on Washington while he was the guest of Monroe in Paris. All who honored the first President were outraged when, in October 1796, Bache's *Aurora*, now Jefferson's chief organ, had published a violent open letter Paine had written to Washington. To his great former friend and benefactor Paine cried, "And, as to you, Sir, treacherous in private friendship (for so you have been to me, and that in the day of danger) and a hypocrite in public life, the world will be puzzled to decide whether you are an apostate or an imposter, whether you have abandoned good principles, or whether you ever had any."

On his own Bache was equally violent. While Jefferson was in Philadelphia taking his oath as Vice-President, Bache's republican organ had screamed at the retiring Washington. America had been debauched by him, the *Aurora* roared. Happily the old General and President no longer "possessed power to multiply evils upon the United States. . . . This day ought to be a JUBILEE in the United States."

Mr. Jefferson could be associated with such statements but not held guilty of them. On May 2, 1797, however, three days before he set out from Monticello, in New York the Federalist *Minerva* published a letter he had written a year before, on April 24, 1796, to Philip Mazzei, a man of many vocations and residences. A Florentine by birth, Mazzei had been by turn and in intermixture physician, author, merchant, horticulturist. He was to become the intelligence agent for princes. Jefferson had known him as the agent of Virginia in Europe during the Revolution. And, more intimately he had had Mazzei as neighbor in Albemarle County where the Italian was experimenting with the culture of grapes, olives, and other foreign fruits. To him, in Pisa, Jefferson wrote a declamatory report on the political situation in America.

With apparently the best intentions, Mazzei translated the letter into Italian and gave it to a paper in Florence. It was reprinted in France. Now translated from Italian into French it was turned back into English. Slightly distorted in the process it was published in the *Minerva* of New York and widely reprinted by other American papers.

Under indignant criticism Jefferson squirmed in his correspondence but did not squeal in the newspapers. He stuck to his often stated refusal to engage in newspaper controversy. Actually no explanation could have satisfactorily explained. Jefferson, evidently in anger at the time of the first republican furies over the Jay Treaty, had indulged in extravagant language, which without naming him appeared to damn Washington along with other Federalists. It was loudly charged that he included Washington in his reference to apostates "who were Sampsons in the field & Solomons in the council, but who have had their heads shorn by the harlot England." Years later Jefferson said that he was referring to the Society of the Cincinnati. In 1797, however, it must have been difficult to explain even to himself the writing of this letter, which certainly referred to Washington's government if not to Washington personally. Just two months before he wrote it, he was assuring the man of Mount Vernon that any person who tried to sow tares between them was a "miserable tergivesator."

Jefferson was secure, if not comfortable, in his seat as presiding officer of the Federalist-controlled Senate. In the mood of the moment, however, in the more evenly divided House, his opponents struck at him through his friend, informer, and aide Beckley. Led by Congressman Smith on the first day of the session, May 15, that effective politician was defeated for re-election as Clerk of the House. The vote against him was forty-one to forty with twenty-five Congressmen absent or not voting. Smith apparently had taken advantage of a situation which Jefferson had noted before. City Federalists, as he had told the impertinent and impatient Genet, were more apt to be present at the beginning of a session than the largely agrarian republicans.

In indignation he wrote to Madison: "Besides the loss of the ablest clerk in the US & the outrage committed on the absent members . . . it excited a fear that the republican interest has lost by the new changes."

Bache's *Aurora* described the defeat of Beckley as "a specimen of party rancour." Though Beckley had performed his duties as Clerk well in the eight years he had held the job, he certainly had not been free of "party rancour" himself. Men like Smith, who was soon to bow off the Congressional scene as Adams' Minister to Portugal, had good reason to regard him as a political henchman in the service of Jefferson rather than a non-partisan House functionary. Still the move left Beckley angry and, as a jobless man with a family, hard up. He found himself the partner in difficulty of another man whom Smith had helped remove from his livelihood in connection with the Congress, the radical journalist James Thomson Callender.

Callender was another of those who, in the 1790s, crowded the Atlantic passage to America. Unlike Church, he had come to America not to protect his money but his hide. In England, where not even such men as Priestley and Cooper were safe from the attentions of both repressive government and angry mobs, he had been indicted for sedition, in January 1793, for radical views he had expressed in a publication in Edinburgh called *The Bee.* As a man in his mid-thirties with a wife and four children, he fled to the United States.

He could hardly expect leniency in the British courts. In his radical writing, titled *The Prospect Before Us,* he had described Parliament as "a phalanx of mercenaries" and the English Constitution as "a conspiracy of the rich against the poor." He directed his barbs even at the King. In an advertisement of the second American edition of the *Prospect,* dated November 14, 1794, the author said that one reason for this republication was the encouragement of Jefferson and other gentlemen. He wrote of himself and other such pamphleteers in "the van of every revolution" as composing "a kind of forlorn hope on the skirts of battle; and though they may often want experience, or influence, to marshall the main body, they yet enjoy the honor and danger of the first rank, in storming the ramparts of oppression." Evidently he was sometimes reckless in this role. Later he was to remind Jefferson, who was sometimes fastidious after the fact, that "it is not by beaux, and dancing masters, by editors, who look extremely well in a muslin gown and petticoat, that the battles for freedom are to be fought and won."

His story in America was afterwards told with no sympathy and much scorn. Worthington Chauncey Ford in a study of Jefferson and Callender published in 1896 began with the sentence: "Of all the foreigners who were connected with journalism in the United States at the beginning of the century, James Thomson Callender was easily first in the worst qualities of mind and character." Other historians have almost in chorus used about him the phrase "a hack writer." Actually, though some of his longer productions were turgid and long-winded, his writing showed him to be a well-educated man with some gift for phrase. He had studied medicine. He was an expert shorthand reporter. He had been, he wrote, once "one of the happiest of human beings." Perhaps it was only additional evidence of Mr. Jefferson's credulity that he first regarded him as "a man of genius suffering under persecution."

Callender's sense of persecution was sharpened in Philadelphia.

There early he had found such friends as Leiper, Senator Stevens Thomson Mason of Virginia, and such a Beau Brummel of revolution as Alexander Dallas—and, at a date uncertain, Jefferson. In addition he found a market for his talents. He was employed, he wrote, by the *Philadelphia Gazette* to report the proceedings of Congress apparently at a salary of four thousand dollars a year—almost as much as that paid the Vice-President of the United States. In this position, of course, he knew Beckley who shared his radical views. He brought a merry malice to his work, reporting all too accurately the pompous phrases and idiotic comments which sometimes marked debate. He particularly offended Congressman Smith upon whom he stuck the nickname "British Agent." Sometimes he was indiscriminate in his darts, hitting and angering even such an extreme republican as Giles of Virginia whose aristocratic arrogance matched that of the Federalist Smith. Others winced under Callender's reports. Still, as he wrote later, "Dr. Smith" was "far more rancorous than the other gentlemen collectively." Efforts to end Callender's employment were begun, especially by Smith, as early as January 1794, Callender said. Congress, providing part of his pay, assumed a right of approval of his work. Efforts to fire him were renewed in March 1795. He was out of a job in May 1796 when he appealed to Madison for a position as a schoolmaster in Virginia.

It is difficult to date the beginning of Jefferson's acquaintanceship with Callender. The British newcomer stated that Jefferson among others had encouraged the American edition of the *Prospect* before its appearance in 1795. Jefferson wrote that it was "probably not till 1798" that he first saw Callender. He was not in Philadelphia between January 1794 and March 1797. Years later he described his first awareness of Callender's presence there both vividly and vaguely.

"When the Political progress of Britain first appeared in this country," he wrote Monroe in 1802, "it was in a periodical publication called the bee, where I saw it. I was speaking of it in terms of strong approbation to a friend in Philadelphia, when he asked me if I knew that the author was then in the city, a fugitive from persecution on account of that work, and in want of employ for his subsistence. This was the first of my learning that Callender was the author of the work. I considered him as a man of science fled from persecution, and assured my friend of my readiness to do whatever could serve him. It was long after this before I saw him, probably not until 1798. He had in the meantime written a second part of the political progress much inferior to the first and history of the US."

Unfortunately for this recollection, Jefferson's own notebooks show that, in June 1797, he gave Callender for fifteen copies of his "history of the US" $15.14—a small sum certainly but more than he contributed to the Philosophical Society's first plan for the exploration of the West. Also in that month, on June 19, the Vice-President called on the writer at the shop of Snowden & McCorkle, a new firm of printers which was publishing the provocative pamphlet to be entitled *The History of the United States for 1796*. Word about this project was already getting around. On June 24, just before Monroe's return, Hamilton's friend Senator Sedgwick of Massachusetts wrote to King in London. Beckley's ejection from the clerkship, he reported, was "resented not only by himself but the whole party [Republicans], and they were rendered furious by it. To revenge, Beckley has been writing a pamphlet mentioned in the enclosed advertisement. The 'authentic papers' there mentioned are those of which you perfectly know the history, formerly in the possession of Messrs. Monroe, Muhlenberg, and Venable. This conduct is mean, base and infamous."

It was also mysterious. The full *History* was dated July 19, 1797, but, first published in parts, its critical Nos. V and VI appeared weeks earlier. They had little to do with 1796 but presented the documents of Hamilton's "confessions" to the informal Congressional committee in 1792 about the Reynolds affair. In addition they repeated and amplified charges that Hamilton had made money on inside information as Secretary of the Treasury. Callender was the admitted author but behind him was Beckley. Beckley in many things was the agent of Jefferson. Callender, in a preface to the complete edition, undertook to refute the early rumor that Beckley was its author. Moreover, the preface seemed almost deliberately to point to Monroe who, like Beckley, had a grievance against the Federalists. Callender wrote: "Attacks on Mr. Monroe have been frequently repeated from the stock-holding presses. They are cowardly because he is absent. They are unjust, because he displayed, on an occasion that will be mentioned immediately, the greatest lenity to Mr. Alexander Hamilton, the prime mover of the Federal Party."

There was no intimation in the preface or the book that Jefferson had any connection with it. He was presented only in fulsome praise. His *Notes on Virginia*, Callender wrote, "unites the sweetness of Xenophon with the force of Polybius, information without parade, and eloquence without effort." The government had sagged when he left Washington's Cabinet. Some indication of Callender's bias appeared in his description of Hamilton as "a thread-bare lawyer, forgetting to earn daily subsistence for his family, that he may write two hundred newspaper columns for nothing." This suggestion of Hamilton's poverty was ridiculous. He was making the then amazing income of more than twelve thousand dollars as attorney, but there was something factual as well as prophetic about mention of the brilliant Federalist's readiness with the pen.

The former Treasury head directed his fury not at Callender or Beckley, certainly not at Jefferson, but at the innocent and surprised Monroe who knew nothing about the *History* until he landed in Philadelphia late in June. A few days later, on July 5, 1797, Hamilton wrote to all three of the members of the self-appointed Congressional Committee to whom he had told his tale of adultery and blackmail four and a half years before. Muhlenberg and Venable replied promptly regretting the publication and denying any part in it. When Monroe failed to answer, Hamilton was sure of his guilt. Accompanied by his newly arrived brother-in-law Church, on July 11, he came stiffly to call on Monroe then visiting in New York. Monroe had beside him David Gelston, republican politician and Surrogate of the County of New York, who was one of Burr's chief political aides. Gelston left a dramatic account of the meeting.

Hamilton was "much agitated." Monroe declared upon his honor that he knew nothing of the publication of the papers. He was sure his copy of them "remained sealed" where they had been "deposited in the hands of a respectable character in Virginia." A fiery dialogue followed.

Hamilton: "This as your representation is totally false!"

Monroe: "Do you say I represented falsely, you are a scoundrel."

Hamilton: "I will meet you like a gentleman."

Monroe: "I am ready. Get your pistols."

Church: "Gentlemen, gentlemen, be moderate."

The angry men seemed ready for fisticuffs then and there without any formalities of the code duello. Their friends quieted them. Monroe agreed to secure a statement from his earlier associates and himself denying all responsibility for the publication. But the statement which he sent six days later did not satisfy Hamilton. He was particularly infuriated by one item in the published papers signed by Monroe alone which quoted Clingman as saying that Mrs. Reynolds was innocent and that Hamilton's "Defense was an Imposition." This amounted, Hamilton wrote to Monroe, to giving a "sanction of credit" to Clingman's word over his own. And that, he said, merits the "severest epithets I could apply."

Monroe, engaged in writing a defense of his ministry in France, replied in irritation. It was proper for Hamilton to remember, he told him, "that we admitted your explanation upon the faith of your own statement and upon the documents you presented. . . . I do not recollect that they were proved or that proof was required of them." In Hamilton's eyes this amounted to a declaration that Monroe felt that he was not merely a confessed adulterer but a possible liar about the whole business.

The gentlemen named their seconds. Hamilton chose as his representative "Major Jackson." Evidently this was Hamilton's old friend Major William Jackson whom he had nominated as secretary of the Constitutional Convention in 1787. He was later one of President Washington's personal secretaries. In full uniform he had attended Washington when he delivered his first address to Congress. Declining the President's appointment as Adjutant General of the Army, he had become a business associate of the rich William Bingham, former Morris partner, and had married a daughter of Thomas Willing, first president of the Bank of the United States. Of course, he was a Federalist. For twenty-eight years he was secretary of the Society of the Cincinnati.

Ironically, in view of future events, Monroe called on Burr as his second. They had served together in the Revolution though Burr was to speak disparagingly later of the Virginian's military activities. They had served in the Senate together. They had recently met in high republican conclave. Monroe knew the kind of man he required in this difficulty. He turned to Burr because he had "entire confidence in your judgment, honor and friendship for me." Also, like others, he understood both Burr's diplomacy and his steady nerves. Monroe himself seemed almost hysterical. He believed, he told Burr, that Hamilton had been "pushed on by his party friends here, wo'd be very willing to hasard him. Of this I have many reasons to be well assured of."

There were differences among Federalists as among Democrats. Adams' friends and particularly his wife rather resented a High Federalist festival in a ball given on Washington's birthday. Many Adams people did not attend. And Hamilton had more direct lines of power to Cabinet members whom Adams had kept in office than the President then knew. Burr's view of the intra-party perfidy which Monroe reported is not known. He urged Monroe to burn any papers in the case he might possess. He undertook to settle the quarrel and prevent a meeting. Monroe he recognized wanted no duel but if Hamilton issued a challenge he was ready to meet him. In the surface amiability which Burr and Hamilton maintained toward each other, the two New Yorkers met. Hamilton was not eager to assume the rough role of challenger either. So Burr deftly drew up a statement which Monroe could in honor sign and Hamilton could in honor accept.

Pistols were lowered, but Hamilton, to the delight of Callender, Beckley, and Jefferson took up his pen. Swiftly he produced a pamphlet long-windedly titled: *Observations on Certain Documents contained in Nos. V and VI of "The History of the United States for the Year 1796," in which the Charge of Speculation against Alexander Hamilton, late Secretary of the Treasury, is fully refuted*—written by himself, Philadelphia, 1797.

In the introduction to this amazing work of confession in avoidance (fifty pages of text and fifty more of appended documents), Hamilton wrote:

"The charge against me is a connection with one James Reynolds for purposes of improper pecuniary speculation. My real crime is an amorous connection with his wife for a considerable time, with his privy and connivance, if not originally brought on by a combination between the husband and wife with the design to extort money from me.

"This confession is not made without a blush. I cannot be the apologist of any vice because the ardor of passion may have made it mine. I can never cease to condemn myself for the pang which it may inflict in a bosom eminently entitled to all my gratitude, fidelity and love. But that bosom will approve, that, even at so great an expense, I should effectually wipe away a more serious stain from a name which it cherished with no less elevation than tenderness."

Eliza evidently did approve. She bore his fifth child with pride. George Washington in Virginia sent his friend a wine cooler in testimony of his continuing faith in him. But some of Hamilton's friends shook their heads over this detailed report of his amorous affair. Many readers were titillated by the sexy story. Callender chortled with delight. He wrote Jefferson that the *Observations* were "worth all that fifty of the best pens in America could have said against him. My sale has been repaid beyond all hope. In less than five weeks, 700 have gone off, and some commissioners and subscribers are yet unanswered." He reported with delight that the Episcopal Bishop of Pennsylvania, William White, brother-in-law of Morris, declined at a public function to drink to the health of Hamilton, a confessed and almost ostentatious sinner.

Despite what Madison called "malignant insinuations" against Jefferson in the *Observations,* the Vice-President was evidently pleased by Hamilton's astounding literary performance. He wrote John Taylor of Caroline, his friend in politics and agriculture, about it expressing his opinion in classical metaphor.

"I understand that finding the strait between Scylla and Charybdis too narrow for his steerage, he had preferred running plump on one of them. In truth, it seems to work very hard with him; and his willingness to plead guilty to adultery seems rather to have strengthened than weakened the suspicions that he was in truth guilty of speculations."

This result was evidently what Jefferson wanted. And there is basis for belief that he brought it about. Beckley, who had brought the Reynolds affair to Monroe's attention in the first place, seems certain to have put the papers in the hands of Callender. Beckley was Jefferson's agent in a variety of activities. W. P. Cresson, in his biography of Monroe, wrote that "it is not too difficult to link the names of Beckley, Jefferson and Callender into a chain of evidence that gives us a simple solution of the case." Jefferson, he said, was "almost certainly" the "respectable character in Virginia" with whom Monroe believed the papers "remained sealed." Schachner, in his biography of Hamilton, reported the suspicion that this character was Jefferson. Malone, however, while regarding Cresson's account of the Reynolds affair as excellent, felt that he involved Jefferson in it "to a greater degree than seems warranted."

Certainly Jefferson did not regard what Callender had done to the character of his adversary as reprehensible. He not only bought fifteen copies of Callender's pamphlet obviously for distribution. He also began at this time a series of contributions to the writer which continued to 1801 when Callender thought he owed him more than he gave. Moreover, he encouraged others to make contributions to the journalist. His gifts were "charities," he said later, though, as he added, they were "considered as rewards for his calumnies." He wrote: "Nobody sooner disapproved of his writing than I did, or wished more that he be silent."

Mr. Jefferson himself was officially silent about another matter which came at about this time before the Senate over which he presided. On July 3, two days before Hamilton made his first demand on Monroe,

President Adams sent to the Senate an intercepted letter written by Senator William Blount of Tennessee which exposed his plan to incite the Creeks and Cherokees to aid the British in conquering the Spanish territories of West Florida and Louisiana. Blount was surprised at the "damnable fuss" this made. Jefferson took no part in it. As Vice-President he was above that fuss or battle. Also Blount was a republican. Many of his friends and supporters were republicans and Jeffersonians. Still the Senate voted to expel Blount by a vote of twenty-five to one. The indignation in the Senate was not matched in Tennessee. There Blount was given a vote of confidence in his immediate elevation to the Speakership of the State Senate. The West was restless in its feeling that the Eastern states were careless of the fortunes of men in the Mississippi country. Indeed, the feeling was so real that in this year when Blount was ready to back the old British enemy with a force of frontiersmen and Indians, even the hated Spanish hoped to take advantage of the discontent. Carondelet, Spanish Governor of Louisiana and West Florida, made the proposal to General James Wilkinson, then both the ranking officer in the American army and secret pensioner of Spain, that he make himself "the Washington of the West" by setting up an independent Western nation free from the distant government in Philadelphia. Wilkinson, who was wary as well as perfidious, declined. Burr, who had been vigorous for Tennessee statehood, was no longer in the Senate to vote in the Blount case. Jefferson washed his hands in the matter, leaving Philadelphia two days before Blount was expelled. Later, when impeachment was proposed, he showed himself sympathetic to Blount. Indeed, still later, Jefferson wrote, scoffing, that liars against him spread reports that he was "involved in Blount's conspiracy." As in the case of Genet, Michaux, and George Rogers Clark, he was, of course, insistently innocent.

Burr, this summer of 1797, not only well served Monroe and gave Hamilton a respite from danger. Also he was adept in other dealings. He made friends and showed no hustling enmity to anybody. He was at this time too busy to bluster. And the friends he accumulated covered a wide range in society and in geography. In New York he was attracting young men to him who would later make a political phalanx for him. His interests were not bound to that city. Busy in the courts, he was also concerned in far-flung real estate investments. The West to him now seemed not only sublime but full of profitable promise. This year while the boom in western lands was faltering, he corresponded with an agent he and other

speculators had sent abroad to interest European investors. He wrote that
he and Theophile Cazenove, a representative of Dutch speculators in
land, initiated the dispatch abroad of able James Wadsworth. Wadsworth
and his brother Charles were to be the most successful land developers in
the Genesee Valley. He had a tough assignment now. Looking to him
hopefully were not only Burr and Cazenove but Robert Morris, DeWitt
Clinton of New York, possibly others. Hamilton and Church were also
investors in great tracts in western New York—Church often as money-
lender rather than landowner.

Burr in this year and others traveled much in this western domain.
He surveyed Niagara Falls with an early vision of its possibilities in hy-
draulic power. Also, in 1797, he wrote to his friend Robert Morris' able
son, Thomas, then handling his father's domains in western New York.
He mentioned his plans to establish a bank in New York to young Morris
who was later to help him get it established. Perhaps his expansive operations and his charm in conducting them were best illustrated by his
lavish hospitality to the famous Mohawk chief Thayendanegea or, as he
came to be called, Joseph Brant. A remarkably well-educated Indian, Brant
had fought on the British side in the Revolution and with such violence
that his name had been regarded with terror in the Mohawk Valley where
Burr had first regarded the West with infatuation. All that was forgiven
now. Brant, who had been twice to England where in full regalia his portrait had been painted by Romney, was now concerned with the welfare
and religion of his people. He was also guarding the titles to their lands
where more and more speculators and settlers were pushing in. He gave
his friendship to young Morris and Burr for their fair dealings with his
tribesmen.

In 1797, at Burr's invitation, according to Brant's biographer, the
Chief came to Philadelphia and New York. In the Pennsylvania city Burr
gave a "brilliant dinner party" for him, including among his guests
not only American dignitaries but such foreign figures as the French
Minister, the French scientist Volney, and the great political chameleon
Talleyrand who between service to Bourbons and Bonapartes was specu-
lating in the United States. Then demonstrating both his affection for his
Indian friend and his faith in his fourteen-year-old Theo, Burr arranged
for her and Nathalie to give another dinner for him in New York. Theo
had been a little appalled at first as to what to serve the Indian. She wrote
her father that she "had a mind to lay the hospital under contribution for

a human head, to be served up like a boar's head in ancient hall bar-
baric." Instead she presided with grace at the dinner for the highly cultivated Chief, having among other guests Dr. Samuel Bard, Dr. David
Hosack, and Bishop Samuel Provosts—three of the most distinguished citizens of the city.

In this, as in other matters, Burr was mixing pleasure with business.
On business affairs he was corresponding with Wadsworth, who in England was finding fears that French influence in the United States might
make investments unsafe. He wrote about books which, as always, he required. Also, in gay gossip he told about himself and others: "I have it
from the very best authority that your friend Linklaen is soon to be married to a daughter of Major Ledyard, a pretty and agreeable girl. Not a
bad match I think on either side. I continue an inflexible bachelor, but
have been much smitten by Dge-gx of Naef-az, who is at present indis-
putably at the head of the list." Who the fascinating Dge-gx of Naef-az
was remains a mystery. In another letter he wrote, ". . . am not married,
nor have made any approaches to it, though shall not probably pass another six months single, though no particular object has yet engaged my
attention."

Gay as to possible matrimony, he was finding pleasure in business.
Evidently he was not as much troubled in 1797 as some of his fellow politicians and fellow speculators were. In one of his letters to Wadsworth he
wrote, "Upon the whole I am quite satisfied with the state of things."

Jefferson was less than content presiding over the Senate which contained so many hostile Federalists. He was anxious as always to get back
to Monticello. The formal news of Polly's engagement came on June 8
He was anxious to get home to congratulate the young couple in person.
Also, it took him away from Philadelphia at the time when the uproar
caused by the publication of Callender's *History* was at its height. He
was the busy builder again spending on construction at a rate he could
hardly afford. The roof was apparently on by October 13, 1797, when
Polly was married.

One who was undoubtedly a guest at the wedding and often was
sheltered by the roof at Monticello was Dabney Carr, son of Jefferson's
sister Martha. At this time he added mystery to marriage at Monticello in
a letter he wrote under the assumed name of John Langhorne to President
Washington. It pretended to be a letter of deep sympathy to Washington
for the "united calumny" he had received. If this was a prank it was a

peculiar one. And one of the enemies Jefferson had even at his door exposed it to the old man at Mount Vernon. This informer, who described himself as living "in cannon shot of the very headquarters of Jacobinism," convinced Washington that Carr was engaged in a "nefarious plan" to ensnare the former President into an unguarded statement which might be used to his embarrassment. Historians early and late have described this strange business as a "cobweb conspiracy." There is no evidence that Jefferson was the author or inspirer of the ridiculous letter. But it was to bring from Washington, as the Mazzei letter had not, an angry expression of his conviction of the insincerity of the pretensions of friendship Jefferson had shown him.

While Monticello was rising to its ultimate domed palatialness some other building operations sagged. In Philadelphia the half-built mansion of Burr's great associate in land speculations was now described by Morris himself as "that unfortunate building on Chestnut Street." The marble house L'Enfant designed lacked a roof. The rain poured in to run down the unfinished walls. The palace, which was to have been finished in 1795, in 1797 lacked roof, floors, and plastering. Workmen declined promises which were now all that the great financier had to give them.

One of Burr's biographers described his operations at this time as "financial legerdemain." Certainly Morris needed some sort of sleight-of-hand help at this time when the heavy hands of his creditors came with the deflation of the land boom. Two years before, on December 15, 1795, he had written Hamilton, "I want ready money sadly but it is not want of property. Property, however, cannot command ready money at this time without great sacrifice. I do not like to sacrifice if I can help it, because I have worked hard to get what I have, and will fight a good battle to keep it!"

Evidently it was after this time that he secured the eighty thousand dollars from Church. That was not all he needed for the interest and taxes on his great holdings. In April 1797 he declared, "I am plagued most cursedly for want of money, but since the Bank of England cannot pay, how the devil can anybody expect that individuals should do it unless in the same way by giving a new for an old note."

He and his partner Nicholson, who was watching the properties on the site of the permanent capital on the Potomac, were increasingly beset. So were others who had invested with them. Burr was energetically seeking endorsers for his notes, evidently successfully. But, in July 1797, Morris, pushed by Hamilton who was pushed by Church, offered a mortgage on fifty thousand acres of land near Pittsburgh. Hamilton showed little patience with his old friend. But Morris asked his help against Church.

"I would fain hope that he does not wish to take advantages of my necessities and obtain my property at less than its worth," Morris wrote.

Other creditors were pushing the great land speculator. Church could hardly have been expected to stand aside when others hounded Morris, kept him a furtive prisoner in his suburban residence, and waited in hope of catching him unawares. Business was business even if Morris had been the financial hero of the Revolution. Apparently Church was ready to join in the pressure. In a last lament Morris cried to Hamilton, "Your agency in it astonishes me. . . ."

The debtor's prison called Prune Street was waiting for Morris and for Nicholson too. Others were involved in this American land boom. Some lost in great and doubtful deals like the Yazoo Fraud in Georgia in which many prominent persons played a part. It was a game which went on after Morris' fall. Dangers connected with it at the last awaited Jefferson. At this point certainly Burr and Hamilton escaped. One of the great long-term financial gainers was Wadsworth. But in his speculations in western New York Burr gained friends whom he would depend upon to the last. These were times of stress in politics and finance. Old friends could seem Shylocks. Political antagonists appeared as rascals.

Some were saddened by conflict. Once again Mr. Jefferson expressed his dislike for the abrasions of politics. As the New Year began he wrote a nostalgic letter to Angelica Church now happily settled near her *petit Fripon*. He also wrote an affectionate note to Kitty Church telling her about her old friends Patsy and Polly.

"Party animosities here," he wrote Angelica from Philadelphia where he had joined his "knot of Jacobins" in Francis's Hotel, "have raised a wall of separation between those who differ in political sentiments."

This was a sort of farewell note to a lady tossed sadly over a wall.

2.

Tenure and Terror

The distinguished visitors entertained by Burr at Richmond Hill enjoyed not only its large library and its collection of works of art. After they shared Burr's fine food and wines, they often joined him in a special sport he provided. Apples were hung from the tall trees about the great house. From the porches host and guests tested their marksmanship with pistols. Hunters and duelists tried their hands. Burr seldom missed.

Though he was to own the beautiful estate for several years more, some thought the elaborate entertainments there constituted a brave show in the first years after his retirement from the Senate. He was still adding to his books and pictures. He was still supporting in his studies abroad the promising artist John Vanderlyn. The Colonel had been so impressed with a copy that Vanderlyn, as a twenty-year-old young man, had made of the Gilbert Stuart portrait of himself that he sent the young artist to Philadelphia to study under Stuart. Then, when Stuart told the younger artist that "I have taken you as far as I can," Burr brought him to Richmond Hill where he secured commissions for the young man to paint Gallatin; Pierre A. Adet, the French Minister; and others. He and Theo, of course, sat for him.

Interestingly the Colonel had made arrangements, in the summer of 1795, for his patronage of the young artist through Peter Van Gaasbeck, an anti-Federalist politician and Congressman from Vanderlyn's home town of Kingston, New York, to whom Burr then was in debt. Characteristically, however, patronizing the arts while unable to pay his debts, it was at this time the Colonel wrote Van Gaasbeck that "if I weather the storm, of which there can be no doubt, I shall be as rich as a reasonable man needs to wish."

Such patronage of the arts seemed expected of prominent persons, as both Jefferson and Church had shown in their aid to Trumbull. When the impecunious and dissolute painter Ralph Earle was in debtor's prison in New York during this period, Hamilton had his wife Eliza sit for him there. She was so pleased with the portrait that her recommendation of the artist made his prison a studio much frequented by ladies of fashion. Burr certainly appeared as a gentleman of fashion in a Vanderlyn portrait of him.

As ex-Senator he was described in more threadbare terms by both Adams and Jefferson. President Adams wrote of the Colonel at this time that being "somewhat embarrassed in his circumstances, and reluctant to return to the bar, [he] would have rejoiced at an appointment in the army." Jefferson wrote more testily later of the ex-Senator that "whenever a great military appointment or a diplomatic one was to be made, he came post to Philadelphia to show himself, and in fact that he was always at market if they wanted him."

At this time he was certainly not embarrassed alone. Difficulties with both England and France were troubling merchants. War and other troubles abroad had slowed the stream of immigrants and land buyers. Robert Morris was dodging the creditors who would put him in Prune Street early the next year. From Philadelphia, two days after Christmas 1797, Jefferson was writing home that he was relieved of the pressures of society "for partly from bankruptcies partly from party dissensions society is torn up by the roots." Even he, needing cash for clothes, taxes, and his interminable remodeling of Monticello, was embarking on an increase in tobacco culture which would lead him to losses which he called "a tragedy." Even the glittering Hamilton had his troubles. To an importuning friend he wrote that "if it were convenient to me nothing would make me happier than to accommodate you with the entire sum [of a note] by way of loan; but the truth is that my public engagements have not only left me bare of cash but have lain me under a necessity to use my credit at the Bank as far as consistency with delicacy in my station of director I ought to go."

There was nothing poor in the dress or spirit which Burr showed when he took his seat in the Assembly at Albany on January 2, 1798. Some wondered why one who had served in the Senate of the United States would stoop to a place in a state legislature. He was welcomed with regard and respect. He was at home in a society which neither in New York nor Albany was entirely torn up by the roots. He did not let his political views make a wall between him and good company. He had no antipathy to ruffles and lace. Neither did they awe him. Behind him in Manhattan he had the strong support of many old Sons of Liberty who kept intact their ardor about liberty even as they became substantial citizens.

Such men as Melancton Smith and Marinus Willett, who had brought him first into politics, and Colonel John Lamb, who had fought with him on the Heights of Quebec and was now Collector of Customs at the port of New York, gave solidity to his strength. The company of younger men behind him was growing, too. They did not disdain the men of Tammany. Neither did Burr in the Assembly treat as beneath his notice men in homespun dress from the back-country counties. One such, Judge Jared Peck from Ostego, he would put forward later in his unsuccessful effort to have Presidential electors chosen directly by the people. But by no means were all the back-country members bumpkins. Thomas Morris, to whom Burr had first confided his plan to establish a bank, was in the legislature. So was his fellow land speculator or developer, Charles Williamson, manager of the vast Pulteney properties.

A man of about Burr's own age, Williamson, of a noble Scottish family, had served as British officer in the Revolution and as secret agent in the Middle East before he returned to the United States as land developer in 1791. He was the sort of man of bold enterprise to whom Burr would be attracted and upon whom, in his own bold enterprises, he would depend. Others regarded him as more than dependable. Rochefoucauld, in his visit to the Pulteney properties, wrote: "Captain Williamson is here universally respected, honored and beloved. How glorious in my esteem is his career. How fortunate and enviable is his destination." At this time that destination was not quite so clear as the Frenchmen saw it.

Such men as Williamson and Morris could understand the interest Burr showed in more liberal bankruptcy laws, even if to them he seemed a little too idealistic in his renewed efforts for the abolition of slavery. Actually, other matters at this time concerned Burr and other members. One was a safety short of bankruptcy for great land speculators in the West. The other, which has been given much more attention in history, was the safety of the young United States in the face of almost paraded dangers of war with France. In this session Burr handled both matters with dexterity. Also, he kept in the back of his mind that bank he wished to establish.

Once more it was a feverish time. The national temperature rose almost to the boiling point, in March 1798, when the Congress and the country received the astounding tale of the treatment in Paris of American commissioners sent there to negotiate peace. The Jay Treaty had been considered in Europe as practically an alliance between the United States and Great Britain. In fear of such a combination Spain signed a treaty with the United States easing the strangle hold, which it held at New Orleans on American trade down the river, and adjusting its border with the American Southwest. Affairs with France had reached a crisis level when Adams dispatched his commissioners (Charles C. Pinckney, Elbridge Gerry, and John Marshall). No welcome awaited them in Paris. In the spring of 1798, from dispatches which they sent back to the President, the Congress and the country were told an amazing tale. Insulting proposals had been made to them, they reported, by three agents of Talleyrand or intermediaries with the French government whose chief officials refused to receive the American commissioners. These manipulators they designated only as X, Y, and Z.

Possibly this alphabetical designation helped arouse American indignation. Anger might have been complicated if it had had to be directed at such strangers as Hottenguer, Bellamy, and Hauteval. Not even Beveridge in his four-volume life of Marshall gave the first names of these agents of Talleyrand. Bellamy was, Beveridge wrote, "a Genevan now residing in Hamburg but in Paris on a visit." Hauteval was a man "whose fortune lay in the island of St. Domingo." Hottenguer was "a native of Switzerland who had been in America." Indeed, before Marshall met Hottenguer in Paris this Swiss manipulator had been involved in the desperate efforts of John and James Marshall, through Robert Morris, to secure loans which would save their investment in 160,000 acres in Virginia. When Morris' financial empire collapsed the Marshall brothers were still loaded with debt on the lands. Marshall's appointment was, as his critic Jefferson was to write later, "the greatest God-send that could ever have befallen a man."

These XYZ characters, who came almost as deviously into the American story as Rosencrantz and Guildenstern came into that of Shakespeare's Denmark, had approached the stranded commissioners as fixers in diplomacy. As a preliminary to possible peace they proposed that the commissioners of President Adams repudiate fiery words about France spoken by President Adams. More to the point they wanted America to buy peace with a bribe of a quarter of a million dollars for the members of the Directory.

Possibly, as X, Y, and Z told the innocent and indignant Americans, there was nothing strange about such under-the-table operations in European diplomacy. Undoubtedly some hands were greased. Even Washington took seriously supposed information from the British that Edmund Randolph as Secretary of State had his hand out in an XYZ manner. The British had intercepted a letter from the French Minister Fauchet which, in a rambling account, seemed to imply that Randolph made revelations to him and indicated that French money would be welcome in return. Fauchet denied he had meant any such reflections upon Randolph. Randolph himself later wrote an elaborate vindication. But when Washington coldly confronted him with the report, he resigned. He remained a leading and respected figure in Virginia where he later served as senior counsel for Burr in the great trial over which Marshall presided.

Few dared to defend the reportedly perfidious French in America in 1798, though Jefferson first thought or hoped that the XYZ affair was a hoax. Any defense of France in the instant indignation which rose about it in America would have been a whisper in a whirlwind. And when Marshall, as the greatest of the commissioners, returned home in June, significantly on a ship named *Alexander Hamilton,* the Federalists had inflamed the war spirit and all but routed "the French party," as they called the republicans.

Marshall was the hero of the hour. New Yorkers, including, of course, Hamilton, were disappointed that he stayed so briefly in that city that they could not do him honor. In Philadelphia a parade was followed by resounding toasts. The reported response to X, Y, and Z in Paris of "No, no, not a sixpence" was amplified to "Millions for Defense but not a Cent for Tribute." Marshall took his honors with grace and gratitude. He had reason for the last. He drew for his eleven months service in France $19,963.97, an immense sum in those days—not much less than the annual salaries of the President and his entire Cabinet, three times as much as Marshall's earnings in the practice of law. This made it possible for him to save the land holdings in Virginia which he and his brother had bought with the help of poor old Morris, now in Prune Street.

The war fever and other fevers mounted together. Both Jefferson and

Marshall, already fashioned as great antagonists, retreated to Virginia before the fevers of that summer came. Apparently in Philadelphia cholera appeared first. The wife of William Duane, who was soon to become the indomitable editor of the republican *Aurora*, died supposedly of this disease, on Friday, July 13, 1798. This was the same day on which the "war hawk" Federalists in the Congress passed the Sedition Bill which, as it was to be enforced, made criticism of the President and other officials a crime. This did not seem an unlucky day to Federalists then.

The yellow fever like the undeclared war with France became a political issue. In Philadelphia the fierce Federalist editor of *Porcupine's Gazette*, William Cobbett, charged that Jefferson's philosophic and political friend Dr. Rush was not curing but killing fever patients by his therapy of copious bleedings. Cobbett was right but in the courts Rush ended this editor's American career with a successful libel suit. The indiscriminate plague seemed intent on silencing the editorial clamorers of contention when it killed off within a week both Bache of the *Aurora* and his Federalist antithesis Fenno of the *Gazette of the United States*. In the same week the editor of Burr's chief organ in New York, Thomas Greenleaf of the *Argus, & Greenleaf's New Daily Advertiser*, was one of the 1524 New Yorkers who died in the epidemic.

Jefferson had reason to retreat to Monticello soon after the triumphal return of Marshall. In the excitement at the beginning of the summer he estimated that the majority sharing the Federalist fervors had become three to one in the Senate over which he uncomfortably presided. Some republicans had gone over to the "war Hawks." Even such an ardent republican as Giles had temporarily left the scene. And the Vice-President understood that even among the Senators before him were some to whom he was suspect as in "a criminal correspondence with the French Directory." Marshall's biographer Beveridge, who wrote with little sympathy for Jefferson, said that as the Federalist belligerency gained support he was "frantic with disappointment and anger. Not only did he see the Republican Party, which he had built up with such patience and skill, going to pieces before his very eyes; but the prospect of his election to the Presidency as the successor of Adams, which until then appeared to be inviting, now jeopardized if not made hopeless."

Certainly the deterioration of Jefferson's party, which recently in Monroe's ministry had shown its friendship for France, had gone on swiftly after the XYZ exposure. Between March and July, Congress passed twenty acts to improve American defenses against what Hamilton was calling the flagitious, vindictive, atheistic, and depraved government of France. And without mentioning Jefferson by name Hamilton denounced his Virginia adversary as "the high priest of this sect" who was "of so seditious, so prostitute a character" as to hope "to be the proconsul of a despotic Directory over the United States, degraded to the condition of a province." Other Federalists went beyond this in stories of invasion in the South where the French and their American sympathizers would incite slave insurrections. Violence and rapine and Jacobins were mixed in stories of threatened atrocities not only by invaders but by traitors within. And in response to these cries of havoc Congress passed a series of acts historically lumped together as the Alien and Sedition Laws. In addition to strictly curbing freedom of expression by native editors and others, they gave the President the power to deport any alien whom he regarded as dangerous.

Just a month before this Jefferson's friend Dr. George Logan of Stenton had quietly set out for France. This rich Quaker physician-farmer had not only conscientious convictions against all wars but also a particular determination to prevent this one. On June 13, Logan slipped out of Philadelphia carrying as a sort of passport letters attesting to his good citizenship from Jefferson and Chief Justice Thomas McKean of Pennsylvania. Eight days after he departed Jefferson heard that Federalists were saying that Logan's trip was a secret mission from American Jacobins "to solicit an army from France, instruct them as to their landing, etc." A more specific rumor was that Jefferson had given the Quaker letters to Talleyrand and to Philippe Antoine Merlin, chief of the French Directory.

Jefferson was uncomfortable under these charges. He denied that he had known the purpose of Logan's journey. Certainly Logan was not, he insisted, his envoy. He wrote to Burr about his strictly limited communications with persons in Europe which certainly did not include letters to Merlin and Talleyrand. Less sensitive to criticism than Jefferson, Logan's other sponsor, McKean, boldly showed his pro-French and anti-British sentiments. He was rougher in his politics than Jefferson professed to be. Soon after this episode when he became republican Governor after a bitter campaign, he was accused of establishing the spoils system in Pennsylvania. Not bothering to deny it, he admitted a strong preference in appointments "to a friend before an enemy . . . for it is not right to put a dagger in the hands of an assassin." He not only joined Jefferson in giving a letter to Logan; but also when Jefferson asked him to give a job to his henchman the then unemployed Beckley as a man of "talents, diligence and integrity," he gave him not one job but two. Beckley, as both knew, was a man who could be trusted with the dagger.

In this Logan episode Jefferson was painfully aware of the suspicions directed at Logan—and at him. The traveling Quaker's brilliant wife, Deborah, who had noted the big topaz ring which the great Virginian wore on his return from France nine years before, had some doubts about him later despite her husband's affection for him. She had felt earlier that he lacked sincerity in his relations with Washington, whom she admired. In her memoirs of her husband, she wrote of a visit by the harassed Vice-President to Stenton while Logan was still abroad.

Then he told her that he "could not have believed it possible that the utmost bitterness of party spirit could have invented, or given credit to, such calumnies" as were being circulated. Moreover, he reported that "he was himself dogged and watched in the most extraordinary manner; and he apologized for the lateness of his visit (for we were at tea when he arrived) by saying that, in order to elude the curiosity of his spies, he had not taken the direct road, but had come by a circuitous route by the Falls of Schuylkill, along one of the lanes to Germantown, and passing by the house and gate, had come in by the entrance on the York Road."

Deborah Logan added a parenthetical comment on Jefferson's round-about journey to her house. His devious approach, she thought, was "an excess of caution which seemed to me quite unavailing, for his Federal inspectors did not impute an iota less of evil designs to him, for all his care to avoid suspicion."

Others, with Federal spies or Federal prosecutors at their heels under the Alien and Sedition Laws, were making careful journeys too. Jefferson's then friend Callender, who once described himself as his "assistant writer," left Philadelphia in a hurry. Thomas Leiper, Jefferson's old friend and former landlord, agreed to take care of the writer's four children whose mother had died. Jefferson's lieutenant, Senator Stevens Thomson Mason, who was writing Jefferson in concern about "political persecutions," offered Callender sanctuary at his plantation, Raspberry Plain in Loudon County, Virginia. Ironically, Loudon County was the seat of many Federalists. One of them was Jefferson's enemy Levin Powell, who, in 1796, had charged that Jefferson and Burr were at Monticello plotting "rash

and violent measures" against the policies of the Washington administration.

Evidently hard up, Callender walked all the way to Virginia. He
found hiding place there. He enjoyed the use of Mason's good library.
His health improved. Both he and Mason were subjected to abuse in this
neighborhood. Callender wrote that the aristocracy there was "one of the
vilest in America." Mason was not only ready to shelter Callender, he also
gave aid and comfort to such other victims of the repressive laws as Thomas
Cooper and republican Congressman Matthew Lyon of Vermont.

From Raspberry Plain, in the early fall of 1798, Callender began a
long correspondence with Jefferson. He wrote as a much mistreated man
who has "engaged in American controversies not from choice, but necessity; for I dislike to make enemies, and in this country the stile of writing
is commonly so gross." He hoped to be able to go back to England. He
spoke of Philadelphia as "the sink of destruction" and "the porch of per-
dition." Even republicans there, including Giles who had joined Congressman "Phocion" Smith of South Carolina, had treated him shabbily in his
dismissal as reporter, he said. Jefferson asked Senator Mason to draw on
his Richmond agent, George Jefferson, for fifty dollars for Callender. But
he wished "to keep his name out of sight." By November 1798 Callender's
health was much improved. He was talking of writing and told his Monticello correspondent that he would write "such a Tornado as no Govt ever
got before."

Ready to write again, he moved to Richmond where he was connected with the republican *Examiner*. Even there, he told Jefferson, he
was in danger: "While I am in danger of being murthered without doors,
I do not find within them any very particular courage to proceed." Jefferson reassured him: "The violence which was meditated against you lately
has excited a very general indignation in this part of the country. Our
state from its first plantation has been remarkable for its order and sub-
mission to the laws."

Callender began to send Jefferson advance proofs of another book he
was preparing, called *The Prospect Before Us*, damning Adams in particular and Federalists in general. The writer hoped that from it and
successive volumes he could "save some money, and then come up the
James River . . . and try to find 50 acres of clear land, and a hearty Virginia female, that knows how to fatten pigs, and boil hominy, and hold

JOHN VANDERLYN
Presumed self-portrait.

THEODOSIA BURR
By C.B.J. Fevret de Saint-Mémin.

NATALIE DE DELAGE DE VOLADE
By C.B.J. Fevret de Saint-Mémin.

10

THOMAS PAINE
After a painting by Romney.

JAMES MONROE
After a painting by Gilbert Stuart.

her tongue; and then adieu to the rascally society of mankind for whom I feel an indifference which increases *per diem*."

Such idyllic retirement was not for Callender. He went on with his writing. Jefferson wrote him of the advance sheets he sent him: "Thank you for the proof sheets you inclosed me. Such papers cannot fail to produce the best effect. They inform the thinking part of the nation; and these again supported by the taxgatherers as their vouchers, set the people to rights." But Jefferson added: "You will know from whom this comes without a signature; the omission of which has been rendered almost habitual with me by the curiosity of the post offices. Indeed, a period is now approaching during which I shall discontinue writing letters as much as possible, knowing that every snare will be used to get hold of what may be perverted in the eyes of the public." However, Mr. Jefferson subscribed for copies of the forthcoming book.

Callender and Jefferson were both to be shocked later when rough Federalist Judge Samuel Chase, sweeping aside the arguments of republican lawyers, fined Callender two hundred dollars, sentenced him to jail for nine months, and ordered him to provide a bond of twelve hundred dollars for his good behavior for two years. Jefferson not only believed that Chase had been a judicial tyrant. He also was sure that, at the instigation of Chase, his cousin David Meade Randolph, as die-hard Federalist U. S. Marshal, had packed the jury.

Callender's letters to Jefferson continued from "Richmond Jail." From it, in a vivid contribution to history, he wrote of racial furies and fears. He composed a letter while listening to "the bellowing of the Bandetti downstairs." The cries came from the followers of black Gabriel Prosser who had led an abortive slave insurrection. Much mythology grew about this revolt. One queer item was that Prosser meant to make Mrs. David Meade Randolph his Queen because she was the best cook in Virginia. The fact was that executions continued until it was protested that there was danger of "the annihilation of the blacks in this part of the country." The event shook Virginia and shaped the ideas there of liberty or servitude.

Mr. Jefferson was much concerned about liberty at this time. With even more successful secrecy than he enjoined upon Callender he was preparing greater blows against Federalist repressions than any poor journalist in a strange land could prepare. He called on the collaboration of Madison to help him prepare some special "Tornados." Not until many

years later did he admit the drafting with his neighbor of Montpelier
resolutions condemning the Alien and Sedition Laws for introduction in
the Virginia and Kentucky legislatures. Certainly, even though Vice-
President, he might have seemed, if known in the matter at the time,
guilty under Federalistic interpretations of sedition. In the mood of the
times, impeachment would have been possible. Also, even in his indignation at this time he may have been embarrassed in the use of the same
method of state opposition to national action which Patrick Henry had
employed in the Virginia legislature in 1790. Then Virginia had impo-
tently undertaken to express a state veto on Federal legislation approving
Hamilton's assumption plan to which Jefferson, as a self-reported innocent, had agreed in exchange for the site of the national capital beside
Virginia.

Madison drew the milder resolutions passed in Virginia describing
the laws as unconstitutional. Jefferson in his draft of the Kentucky resolutions went further, in effect asserting the right of a state to nullify national action—a position which Hamilton was ready to regard as rebellion.
Kentucky was ready for the stronger verbiage. There was little sympathy
there for any war with France. Many Kentuckians remembered and regretted the collapse of Citizen Genet's plan to free the West of a sort of
imprisonment between the British and particularly the Spanish power
above and below them. Indeed, John Breckinridge, who looked with favor
on Genet's plan for war in the West, handled the Kentucky resolutions
for Jefferson. He had promised a financial contribution to Genet's Western plans which Jefferson seemed in turns to have both served and
scotched. Later it was to be charged that Breckinridge was treasonously
involved in the adventures of Aaron Burr in the West.

The chief aides of Jefferson and Madison in this enterprise in inter-
position were the brothers George and Wilson Cary Nicholas. Like Breckinridge and others, including some of Jefferson's close kin, they had
been speculators in Western lands. Indeed, already Wilson Cary Nicholas'
investments in lands constituted a slow fuse to disaster which would
at last involve his friend and neighbor at Monticello.

Jefferson hoped to have other states fall in line with other resolutions in protest against—or nullification of—the Alien and Sedition Laws.
One to whom he naturally turned was Burr. In New York copies of
both the Virginia and Kentucky Resolutions had been laid before the

Assembly. On February 3, 1799, Burr wrote Jefferson that he expected them to be rejected.

"Under circumstances so inauspicious," the New York assemblyman wrote, "I have not thought it discreet to urge a determination in either house."

Colonel Burr was familiar with inauspicious situations and the necessity for discretion in them. As a New York legislator, in the feverish year of 1798 and in the following year, he found that his political and financial life both required all his vigilance and brilliance and, as his enemies said, a deviousness approaching genius. Certainly sometimes, like Jefferson, he moved in mysterious ways his wonders to perform. It was clear now that he had not come unscathed through the collapse in land values which had landed the richer Morris and Nicholson in Prune Street and brought even Marshall close to ruin.

Even before he left the Senate he was calling on friends for help as endorsers or lenders. Sometimes he had to pay usurers, like those against whom Morris had bitterly complained, as much as fifteen per cent interest. He got endorsements from Willett and from his cousin Pierpont Edwards. He had similarly been helped by the now bankrupt Colonel Nicholson. Two others who endorsed his notes or lent him money seem particularly significant.

One was Louis Le Guen, a French shipping merchant. Strangely, considering Hamilton's privately expressed opinions of Burr, Hamilton had invited Burr to join him as counsel for Le Guen in a famous and complicated lawsuit. Burr was regarded as instrumental in securing a large verdict for Le Guen. However, afterwards, the Frenchman was asking Hamilton's help in collecting money which, in May 1800, he said Burr owed him. He had paid Burr, he wrote, $4636.66 but the Colonel owed him $13,200. Burr, it was said, did not appreciate Hamilton's intervention in this matter.

The other man upon whom Burr much depended was his friend and old comrade in arms, Colonel Lamb. He was the sort of bold soul whom Burr as soldier and politician highly regarded. Lamb's beginnings were less than humble. His father, Anthony Lamb, had been transported to America for crime but had served his time, then became a respectable citizen as a manufacturer of mathematical instruments. Young John not only joined his father in this business but also became prosperous as a wine merchant. But as an ardent Patriot he was one of those who, when the news came of the Battle of Lexington, seized the customs house in New York. Then he began his service as Revolutionary soldier in the campaign against Quebec which brought so many characters in the Burr story together. Apparently he carried his ardor as a Son of Liberty into service to the displeasure of his commander who described him to General Schuyler as "a restless genius." He was courageous, intelligent, and active, but "very turbulent and troublesome." Furthermore, "He has been used to haranguing his fellow citizens in New York, and can not restrain his talent here." However, he was swiftly advanced to Colonel and at the war's end was brevetted Brigadier General. A year later, in 1784, he was elected Collector of Customs for the port of New York by the legislature of which he was a member. Opposed to ratification of the Constitution, he had corresponded with Patrick Henry and others. A Federalist mob threatened his house. But when the Constitution was ratified Washington promptly continued him as Collector.

Burr's financial relations with him went back at least to 1796 while he was still in the Senate. In that year Lamb was sixty-one and evidently prosperous. Late in the year, on December 9, Burr asked in haste for "the other 2000 before three o'clock." The next day he wrote Lamb, "it is with reluctance that I ask your endorsement to the enclosed." On December 17, Burr had reduced certain notes by twenty-four hundred dollars and he sent the renewal notes for the remainder along for endorsement. Evidently, however, no other reductions could be made by Burr. Soon Burr offered to sell Richmond Hill to Lamb in a settlement of their mutual accounts. On March 29, 1797, Lamb declined the offer. "However desirable it might be to me to have your house on the terms you proposed," Lamb wrote, "yet if it will as you say enable you to settle with the holder of one of your Notes, I consent to release you from your offer. At the same time I must entreat you to provide in some other Way for the balance due me." On June 7 the Colonel was again encouraged about his financial situation as he wrote Lamb: "You perceive by the enclosed, that I am nearly through with your endorsements. . . . In truth I could not see you with pleasure while these matters were unsettled." Apparently he had given a mortgage on all the furnishings of Richmond Hill to Sir John Temple, the vain and irascible British Consul, for thirty-five hundred dollars. Certainly this could not have been a true sale, as on any market the furniture, library, and paintings described in the "bill of sale" would have been worth much more.

Obviously—and not merely as an endorser of Burr's notes—Lamb was in trouble. To say, as Schachner wrote, that he "bore the brunt of Burr's financial legerdemain" seems hardly justified. Burr was Lamb's friend and aide in his financial troubles. From Albany as Assemblyman, in January 1798, the Colonel wrote to the embarrassed port official: "I will return to N York and superintend the Sales of my own property untill you shall be exonerated. That your peace of mind should be disturbed or personal safety endangered by an act of friendship and generosity to me is the most humiliating event of my life—and I shall be most wretched untill I hear the Course the business has taken. Though a writ of error can at any time be procured in an hour, yet the possibility of any inattention by which you might be for a moment exposed to indignity from people who would delight in torturing me through you, leave me no rest or peace."

Much is mysterious about this letter. What had happened was that a large shortage had been discovered in Lamb's office as collector. "It is supposed," wrote Frank Edward Ross in the *Dictionary of American Biography*, "that Lamb's deputy, a former criminal, was guilty." Lamb, however, was held responsible and sold all his property to cover the lost funds. He was arrested on May 6, 1799. Burr was active in his behalf. He offered himself and his political associate David Gelston as bail. As a result of his efforts Lamb was released. He was left a ruined man, though certainly not entirely due to Burr. Indeed, Burr's activities must have been responsible in some degree for the delay of sixteen months between the time he wrote Lamb that he was hurrying to help him in January 1798 and the day of Lamb's arrest in May 1799.

At this time Burr needed to demonstrate both political and financial dexterity. Certainly he operated effectively in a maze of interlocking and conflicting financial and political interests in connection with a law sought by Theophile Cazenove for the benefit of the Holland Land Company. In a letter to Cazenove, Judge Egbert Benson, member of the Council of Revision to which all laws passed by the legislature had to be sent for approval, described the situation. In connection with it he said, "there has been such a combination of views, objects & interests not only wholly dissimilar but even directly opposed to each other in promoting or at least acquiescing in this law as infinitely surpasses anything I have hitherto seen in the notable business of Legislation, as conducted with us."

Cazenove, as a bankrupt speculator in Franco-American obligations, had come to a second chance in America nearly ten years before as representative of Dutch financiers looking for profits in American state and Federal securities. He had been introduced to prominent Americans by Jacques Pierre Brissot, who had visited the United States previously in connection with his opposition to slavery. One letter from this French radical was addressed to Hamilton's assistant, Duer. Now in 1798, Brissot in the shifts of the French revolutionary struggle had been guillotined. Duer, despite Hamilton's aid, was still in a debtors prison where he would die in 1799. Cazenove was headed for trouble too. While living like a lord in Philadelphia, he had invested much of the funds of his Dutch backers in wild lands. The more than five million acres which he purchased in western New York and in northern and western Pennsylvania were put together in the Holland Land Company in 1796. Unfortunately for him and for others too, New York laws strictly limited the time of land tenure by aliens. So Cazenove turned for aid to Hamilton, then to Burr.

Hamilton managed to secure the passage of a law permitting aliens to hold land for a period of seven years. But Cazenove wanted an end to all such limitations. Hamilton agreed to push through a bill raising the term of alien holdings to twenty years, provided the Holland Company would lend the Western Inland Lock Navigation Company, which General Schuyler had formed, $250,000. Cazenove balked, resenting such a pay-off. Hamilton cautiously warned him that the Holland Land Company would be in trouble if he refused to make the deal involving his father-in-law's company.

The Dutchman turned to Burr. The Colonel and his legislative associates, Morris and Williamson, were obviously also much interested in removing this barrier to foreign land sales. On April 2, 1798—three months after he entered the Assembly—Burr got Hamilton's legislative deal set aside and put through a superseding law granting unrestricted tenure. In the process Cazenove put up sums to grease the legislative process, small he told his principles in comparison with the $250,000 Hamilton's proposal required. In the Holland Company records listed as counsel fees were $3000 to State Attorney General Josiah Ogden Hoffman, $1000 to Senator Morris, $1000 to an unidentified Mr. L———, and $5500 to Aaron Burr. These were odd bribes to men already bribed by their own interests. Hoffman was not only the aristocratic Federalist leader in the Assembly. Also he was the owner of extensive tracts of land in St. Lawrence County on the sale of which he could have wanted no restrictions. In Burr's case, records seem to indicate that this was regarded as a loan. Loan or sweetener, it was a fraction of the quarter million the Hamilton-Schuyler combination demanded. Coupled with other matters, however, it was soon to be a part of charges involving Burr in one of the very few whispers against him which he ever deigned to explain and deny.

The bill regarding alien land tenure in New York passed as the furies about the XYZ papers were preparing the way for the Alien and Sedition Laws and for the creation of an army headed ostensibly by the aging Washington but actually by Hamilton as his second in command. Burr's position on these national matters puzzled more people than his former friend Troup who made himself a sort of chronicler of his activities. As one who always looked back to glory as a soldier and hopefully ahead also, Burr worked for expanding military measures which Jefferson deplored and against the Alien and Sedition Laws which Jefferson was making the issue.

3.

War and Water

In politics and finance Burr carried himself like the soldier he had once been. All his life, indeed, he took pride in his military services. Even as ardent democrat, he joined in the festivities of recollection of the Society of the Cincinnati which Jefferson disapproved as the possible cradle of a hereditary aristocracy. His military ardor accounted for some of his behavior in the legislature after his re-election despite a Federalist sweep in the state in 1798. His sense of realism was also undoubtedly involved in some of his activities as a man who meant to survive in politics at this time of much fury against both France and democrats in America.

His conduct puzzled some friends and enemies. Troup, who by turns was both, was perplexed. Noticing his activities for defense Troup wrote King: ". . . his conduct very different from that you would imagine. Some conjecture that he is changing his ground. He concurs with us decidedly in measures for the defense of our port." Others saw Burr as the most ardent advocate of state defenses. In this matter he was ready to co-operate with Hamilton. He wanted in the defense of New York "an *impregnable castle* to contain from 75 to 200 Cannon, Howitzers & Mortars." And when one influential Federalist demurred at the cost he suggested to the army officer in command in the area that "A letter from Genl Hamilton to him might be useful." In the Federalist-controlled Assembly he was made chairman to deal with the message of Governor Jay relating to the defenses of the city. Those defenses were entirely inadequate, Burr reported, and he brought in a bill calling for $1,200,000 to improve them. Vigorously pressing the measure he did secure an appropriation for $300,000 from the reluctant legislature. Indeed, he went further than this in associating himself with the belligerent ideas of the Federalists. He joined in the unanimous passage of an address to the President on the conduct of France.

Troup, who considered Burr as "much superior in talents to any of the opposing party" (his own Federalists), was bewildered. "No doubt," he wrote, "is entertained that after the publication of the dispatches from our envoys to France his conduct showed strong symptoms of a wish to change his ground. He was active & apparently zealous in our measures for defending our harbour. He was particularly courteous to Hamilton, and some of the most intelligent of his party have gone so far as to say he certainly expected an appointment in the army."

Yet, wrote the puzzled Troup, "before the appointment of general officers took place, and in the midst of conciliating appearances, he became bail for the appearance of one Bourk who was apprehended upon a warrant . . . for a most infamous libel upon the President." Evidently Troup was referring to John Daly Burk, a romantic young Irish playwright and editor of the New York *Time Piece*, who besides being termed seditious because of writings about President Adams was an alien who had escaped from political prosecution in Ireland in a woman's clothes. He had adopted his middle name after that of the woman who aided in his escape and apparently lent him the clothes. Perhaps the most puzzling thing about this may be that Burr had bail for Burk when he was worried about bail for Lamb.

He had time if not cash to spend in another case under the Alien and Sedition Laws. This involved his plain, back-country friend Judge Peck. Peck, possibly at Burr's instigation, added opposition to the laws to his pious preaching as itinerant land surveyor. He circulated a sarcastic petition against the laws which some believed was prepared by Burr. Ostego County Federalists brought about his arrest at Cooperstown. Sympathy for him and indignation at the authorities blazed as he was conveyed as prisoner to New York City by a Federal marshal.

"A hundred missionaries in the cause of democracy," wrote a historian of New York politics at this time, ". . . could not have done so much for the Republican cause."

In the face of popular disapproval this case was dropped. Burr's part in it did not endear him even to those Federalists who approved of his activities for defense. Certainly it did not reduce the still secret animus to him of Hamilton, now as major general embarked upon what he hoped would be a path to glory. He was certainly not prepared to share it with Burr. And when Adams, surrounded by a Cabinet more loyal to Hamilton than himself, suggested that Burr be given a position as Brigadier General, Hamilton's friends moved into action.

Adams later quoted Washington as saying, "By all that I have known and heard, Colonel Burr is a brave and able officer; but the question is whether he has not equal talents at intrigue." This may have been Washington's uninfluenced position. It was similar to that he reportedly had made when it was suggested that Burr be sent as Minister to France. And, indeed, at this time Washington had come to regard all republicans, including his neighbor at Monticello, as evil. He wrote the Secretary of War his opinion "that you could as soon scrub the blackamoor white, as to change the principles of a profest Democrat; and that he will leave nothing unattempted to overturn the government of this country."

In the face of Washington's implicit threat to resign as chief commander if Burr were named, the President capitulated. Only long afterwards did Adams express his feelings at this time that Hamilton, through Washington, had compelled him to elevate him over other officers and deny Burr any military position. Then the old Yankee ex-President described Hamilton as "the most restless, impatient, artful, indefatigable and unprincipled intriguer in the United States," and yet Washington "dreaded an intriguer in a poor brigadier."

When Adams wrote this outburst in recollection he added to his feeling at the time what he learned afterwards and put them together in one of the greatest "ifs" of history. It was Hamilton's intention, Adams wrote, to make an offensive and defensive alliance with England. *If* that had been permitted, he said, it was his opinion then "and has been ever since, that the two parties in the United States would have broken out into civil war; a majority of all the states to the southward of the Hudson, united with half New England, would have raised an army under Aaron Burr; a majority of New England might have raised another under Hamilton. Burr would have beaten Hamilton to pieces, and what would have followed next let the prophets foretell."

Adams' ominous "what-might-have-been" was perhaps written to underscore the credit he deserved for preventing any such possibilities. But there was basis in 1798 for his fears. Jefferson shared the President's view as to Hamilton's readiness to be the Man on Horseback. Indeed, the Virginian expressed the view that the only hope for American escape from a continuing military establishment dominating the nation was that Hamilton would find many ready to wear the braid of officers but few anxious to enlist as privates. Certainly at this time Hamilton was seeing the dream, vision, or hallucination of power and glory in the American West. Genet, Clark, Breckinridge, Blount, and others had been under its spell. Just the year before General James Wilkinson had prudently turned down the suggestion of Baron de Carondelet, whose Spanish gold he was taking, that he make himself "the Washington of the West" by freeing it from the Union.

Certainly, as instant Major General, Hamilton was listening to Francisco Miranda. This colorful soldier of fortune, who was the forerunner of South American independence, found sympathy in the militant American. General Hamilton wanted war with France, providing reason for a large standing army, then an attack on Spanish possessions from Louisiana and the Floridas to the rich and restless lands beyond. Confident of Hamilton's comradeship, Miranda for his part wrote him from England, "Everything is smooth and we wait only for the fiat of your illustrious president to depart like lightning." Hamilton was increasingly less certain of the greatness of the President.

He was soon complaining that the administration had "no general plan." He had one. He wrote to Secretary of War James McHenry, who acted almost as spy for him at the table of Adams. At least, he said, "we ought certainly to look to the possession of the Floridas and Louisiana and we ought to squint at Mexico." Adams was squinting in no such directions. He began to see clearly, however, that he was surrounded by a Cabinet who regarded Hamilton—not him—as the chief of the Federalist party and party cause. When Dr. Logan returned from his French mission the President listened to him though the "war hawks" welcomed the Quaker home with indignation and derision. In France, aided by Lafayette, Logan had been able to get beyond any X, Y, and Z characters and had talked with Talleyrand, who treated him with respect. He was able to mitigate some of the reasons for complaints Americans had against France and was given assurances that an American Minister would be favorably received. Other intelligence of the same kind was coming to the President. Soon, without confiding to his Cabinet, Adams, to the fury of Hamilton, named commissioners to reopen negotiations with France. The war spirit was deflated. In home affairs Adams even pardoned some Pennsylvania farmers who had been condemned to death for rising in almost comic rebellion against the taxes to support Hamilton's war plans. He fired Hamilton's friends in his Cabinet. That temporary General never forgave the independent President.

"Burr," wrote Adams when in 1815 he described his proscription as Brigadier General by Washington and Hamilton, "to this day knows nothing of this." Considering Burr's many sources of information, even within the Federalist party, this seems doubtful. Jefferson's early biographer, Randall, who wrote almost as Burr's prosecutor, said in connection with another incident that the Colonel "had in his interest a motley band of scouts and spies (male and female)." Certainly he seemed to have a gift for knowing what Hamilton was doing at crucial moments. From this grew the report that one basis for their enmity was a contest in gallantry for the favors of "a beautiful blonde with a superb figure and graceful carriage" known variously at this time as Eliza Brown and Betsy Bowen— later to be known as Madame Jumel and Mrs. Burr. She could have leaked information from one admirer to another.

Whatever Burr may have known about his rejection as Brigadier General, he showed no flaring resentment to his rival in New York. He moved serenely amid many slowly mounting resentments. In considerable measure the Alien and Sedition Laws had been drafted to curb the political impertinence of the poor. And bitterness came up to meet scorn. While the recurring yellow fever, in the summer of 1798, struck indiscriminately, the poor were less able to flee from the plague. They could bring in little wholesome water but had recourse only to water from shallow wells in the dirty city. Many began to believe it might be the cause of the pestilence. And many of the less fortunate, particularly the more articulate among them organized in Tammany Hall, added fever anger to their fever fears in this plague summer. Other grudges were remembered. Class feeling was sharpened in the tumult aroused by the Alien and Sedition Laws under which such a plain man as Jared Peck was led across the state as a prisoner into the town. People without property became more aware of their impotence as citizens without the right to vote to elect men to change such laws. And in class cleavage small workers and artisans were reminded that the only banks in the city were controlled by rich Federalists who could exercise power by controlling credit.

In a stroke of genius, which at first seemed a serious error, Burr put these factors together. It was said by his critics then and by some historians later that in the legislative session of 1799 he "quietly" introduced "An Act for Supplying the City of New York with Pure and Wholesome Water." It provided for the incorporation of the Manhattan Company, capitalized at two million dollars, with right to condemn lands, erect dams, turn streams and rivers, dig canals and trenches, build dikes and reservoirs, and lay pipes and conduits. But the act contained another provision: "And it be further enacted, That it shall and may be lawful for the said company to employ all such surplus capital as may belong or accrue to the said company in the purchase of public or other stock, or in any other monied transactions or operations not inconsistent with the constitution and laws of this state or of the United States, for the sole benefit of said company."

This was then and afterwards described as a Burr trick. The two existing banks—the Bank of New York and a branch of the Bank of the United States—were dominated by Hamilton and his friends. Through them, it was said, Federalist borrowers were favored with loans; republicans found themselves turned away unless they mended their political ways. This power, wrote Schachner, "*was* used with the necessary ruthlessness." Guile may have been necessary in the Federalist-controlled legislature to meet such ruthlessness.

It could not have been a secret, however, that Burr had been contemplating the creation of a bank since he wrote to Morris about the idea in 1797. The bill did go through swiftly. Introduced on March 28, it became law on April 2. It had been passed by the Assembly "quietly" without even a record vote. In the Senate it was considered by a select committee. It is true that on this committee was Burr's friend Morris. The other two Senators placed on the committee, Samuel Jones and Ambrose Spencer, were two of the most prominent citizens in this period in New York. Both Jones and Spencer were distinguished lawyers not to be deluded by a legislative trick. According to Burr's friend and biographer, Davis, they asked him about this proviso. He answered, possibly with a gift of overstatement which seemed a dismissal of the query as ridiculous, that, yes, the company "might have a bank or an East India Company." Jones reported the bill and it was passed. Some question was raised as to its unusual powers in the Council of Revision by the Chief Justice. The council as a whole, however, approved the law.

The long-lasting legend that this was a devious business deserves some scrutiny. Burr certainly set up no mere political bank for republicans. Its president was Daniel Ludlow who had built up the largest mercantile and importing trade in the city. He maintained not only an impressive marble house at 54-56 Broadway and an estate at Barretto's Point on the East River. Also he moved about New York in a four-in-hand equipage. John Stevens, brother-in-law of Chancellor Livingston, became not only a director. He was also consulting engineer of the company. As a famous inventor in the field of steam navigation by both water and rail, he convinced the company that steam pumping engines should be used. Samuel Osgood, director, had been Washington's Postmaster General. Brockholst Livingston was, indeed, a friend of Burr's but an eminent member of the distinguished family. And there on the same board of directors with Burr was the aggressive and acquisitive Church who had come over with his dueling pistols and would soon put them to use.

Trick or treat depending upon the point of view, the company did provide the city of New York with the supply of wholesome water it required. The bank, which was quickly organized under the supposedly tricky proviso, was a sound institution which long outlasted its founders. Indeed, as the Chase Manhattan Bank it is, as this is written, one of the great financial institutions of America one hundred and seventy years after its creation. The immediate result of Burr's legislative activities, however, was politically costly to Burr and came close to costing him his life.

Scarcely a month after the bill became law, it was made an issue in an election which drove Burr from the Assembly in a sweeping Federalist victory, setting back republican hopes not only in the state but in the nation, too. Troup, who made himself a sort of Federalist watchman over the activities of his once friend and now political opponent, reported again to King about Burr.

"Burr," he wrote on May 6, 1799, "has for two years past been a member of the assembly & by his arts & intrigues he has done a great deal towards revolutionizing the state. It became an object of primary & essential importance to put him & his party to flight. The Manhattan company bill . . . gave not a little strength to our opposition against him. The election was the most animated I have ever experienced. All men of property & respectability stood forth, and appeared to act as if they were persuaded that everything valuable in society depended on the success of their efforts. The

merchants in particular were zealous & active. The consequence was that
we have obtained a glorious triumph."

A month later he made a fuller report to the interested Federalist in
London. The news about the new bank, he said, had "seriously alarmed
the two existg banks—and induced them to curtail their discounts very
considerably." That meant political pressure on their borrowers. As a result, Troup added, "the opposition given to this company by the great body
of our monied & mercantile interests is astonishg. . . . The odium it has
caused against Burr had a powerful tendency durg the election to oust him
& his partisans. . . . We have at last prevailed upon the merchants to exert
themselves. In the last election they were essentially useful." Pressure on
the merchants and monied men went down the line to pressure on others.
"They told the cartmen that such of them as supported the democratic
ticket would be dismissed from their employ. The consequence was we
had a strong support from the cartmen. . . . Mr. John Murray spent one
whole day at the poll of the Sevth Ward sometimes called the cartmen's
ward or the Livingston stronghold—and his presence operated like a
charm."

John Murray then was the president of the New York Chamber of
Commerce and a director of the Bank of New York. As Quakers, he and
his brother Robert had stayed out of the Revolution but were enriched
and protected by the British. During the British occupation of New York
their country mansions on the "Heights of Inklenberg," soon to be called
Murray Hill, were not seized. English officers enjoyed lavish hospitality in
them. Both brothers were noted for their philanthropy as well as their acquisitiveness. And both epitomized the "monied & mercantile interests" of
the time.

In the election and afterwards the "odium against Burr" stirred gossip
about his conduct in connection with legislation with regard to alien tenure which he had secured for Cazenove. Evidently that land agent whom
he had helped was returning slander for assistance. Gossip had grown in
the complicated business. In 1796 Burr had contracted to purchase from
the Holland Land Company one hundred thousand acres in the Presque
Isle area of northwestern Pennsylvania, at twelve shillings an acre, pay-
able in installments. The transaction provided for a penalty of twenty
thousand dollars in case of default in performance on Burr's part. As security for this penalty Burr mortgaged to Cazenove, or the Holland
Company, twenty thousand other acres of land in the Presque Isle area.

As further collateral security he gave a bond, endorsed by a friend, for twenty thousand dollars. When the bottom dropped out of the land boom at the end of 1796, Burr was unable to pay and was threatened with demand for the penalty under the agreement. The convivial but gouty Cazenove at this point was confusing his Dutch employers' money with his own, and was soon to lose his job. He claimed to his employers that he did Burr a great favor in the settlement by which Burr conveyed the Presque Isle lands to the Holland Company. Also he claimed that the settlement involved "large compensation for his efforts in behalf of the alien bill."

Burr denied that Cazenove had done him any favor. But Cazenove talked, apparently to Hamilton. With the pot calling the kettle black Hamilton passed the report on to Church, who had not been averse to profiting from some of Burr's activities—notably the creation of the Manhattan Company. About the land tenure legislation gossip, however, Church talked to others too much. Burr was outraged. He wrote a letter in explanation of the whole affair to a friend.

"This, sir, is the first time in my life that I have condescended (pardon the expression) to refute a calumny. I leave my actions to speak for themselves, and to my character to confound the fictions of slander. And on this very subject I have not up to this hour given one word of explanation to any human being. All the explanation that can be given amounts to no more than this—*That the thing is an absolute and abominable lie.*"

Cazenove had departed for Europe never to return but to end his days eking out a precarious existence in Paris with the aid of Talleyrand whom he had entertained in Philadelphia. Burr sent his challenge to Church. The Bank of the Manhattan Company was established at 40 Wall Street on September 1, 1799. And on the same day two of its directors, Burr and Church, went to Hoboken where their fellow director, the inventor Stevens, had large estates. There Burr, with an inept second who failed to properly load his pistols, faced Church's beautiful dueling weapons for the first time. They were thick-barreled, of small bore, with hair triggers and a bulldog look.

Next day the incessantly reporting Troup wrote King: "Mr. Church fought a duel yesterday with Colonel Burr. A day or two ago Mr. Church in some company intimated that Burr had been bribed for his influence, whilst in the Legislature, to procure the passing of an act, permitting the

Holland Land Company to hold their lands. One of the company mentioned it to Burr. A challenge ensued. A duel was fought. Burr had a ball through his coat. Church escaped. After the first fire, and while the seconds were preparg to load a second time, Church declared he had been indiscreet and was sorry for it, thus the affair ended. Church wanted proof of the charge—but it has long been believed."

Troup, however, had no good word for Burr's antagonist in this duel. He disliked Angelica with whom he feared his idol, Hamilton, might become involved in a scandal less forgivable than his dalliance with Mrs. Reynolds. But Church, who had added the insurance business to his other financial operations, was particularly offensive to him. He wrote King on the same day he reported the duel: "Poor Church is fast declining in respectability. He talks too much—is too fond of premiums—and too unwilling to pay losses." Furthermore: "Church is said to be much pushed for money—and indeed family affairs are in a train which in my opinion will by & by cause an explosion which will spread general ruin around it—I mean the ruin of almost the whole connection. I consider it unfortunate that he ever removed with his family to this country."

In his duel with Church, Colonel Burr was lucky to have only a bullet through his coat. Or in terms of power to have a coat. He had been defeated as U. S. Senator, rejected as General. And he was now defeated in his own city. Hamilton's hand had been in some fashion behind all three —even behind Church's gun. And Hamilton was prepared to wear a Major General's cloak on the paths of glory both he and Burr pursued.

Hamilton declined to let what he regarded as the pusillanimity of Adams destroy his dream. He declined to see, as Troup saw, that the army was "progressing like a wounded snake" or see the lapse in ardor and zeal for war. He went on with his correspondence with Miranda. Also, in the summer of 1799, he was conferring with General James Wilkinson who had been summoned from the West for that purpose. Hamilton wrote to Washington about Wilkinson on June 15, 1799: "It strikes me as both right and expedient to advance this gentleman to the grade of Major-General. . . . I am aware that some doubts have been entertained of him, and that his character gives room for doubts. Yet he . . . is a man of more than ordinary talent, courage and enterprise . . . ambitious . . . apt to become disgusted if neglected . . . rendered what he is now suspected to be . . . It seems to me good policy . . . to make it the interest of this individual to practice his duty."

Washington replied: "I think with you . . . it will feed his ambition, sooth his vanity, and by arresting discontent, produce the good effect you contemplate."

So Washington and Hamilton, who had barred Burr as an "intriguer," were ready to give higher rank and greater power in the West to Wilkinson despite widespread doubts about his character and loyalty. Indeed, even at this time the subservient McHenry warned Hamilton while he agreed to the promotion of Wilkinson. "Of this, however, be assured," he wrote, "that until the commercial pursuits of this gentleman with and expectations from Spain are annihilated, he will not deserve the confidence of the government. Further, I recommend to you, most earnestly, to avoid saying anything to him which would induce him to imagine government had in view any hostile project, however remote, or dependent on events, against any of the possessions of Spain. I require this caution on good grounds."

Hamilton disregarded the warning. He had a very congenial conference with Wilkinson in which each played effectually to the vanity of the other. Wilkinson later told a story of the termination of their talk.

"Well, sir," said the strutting soldier from the West to the New York gentleman now second in military command under the physically failing Washington, "having fatigued you with my prattle, I now propose to visit an old friend whom I have not seen for several years; but I hope there is no disagreement between you which might render the renewal of my acquaintance with him indecorous to my superior officer."

Hamilton asked if he meant Colonel Lamb who had been arrested a month before.

"No," said Wilkinson, "Colonel Burr."

Hamilton smiled in depreciation. "Little Burr! O no; we have always been opposed in politics, but always on good terms. We set out in the practice of law at the same time, and took opposite political directions. Burr beckoned me to follow him, and I advised him to come with me. We could not agree, but I fancy he now begins to think he was wrong and I was right."

VI.
SECOND
AMERICAN
REVOLUTION

1.

The Election

In his correspondence, as dark 1799 turned into 1800, "Little Burr" did not seem cast down. His chief complaints in his letters to Theodosia related to her failure to write or to tell enough when she wrote. Sometimes he told her they reminded him of one from a French lady to her husband: *"Mon cher mari, je vous écrit parceque je n'ai rien à faire; je finis parceque je n'ai rien à dire."* He protested particularly in one letter because she had not mentioned "the beauty's ball."

"For which," he threatened in a note from Trenton on January 2, 1800, "I owe you much ill will, and therefore my next shall be to *Natalie,* to whom all good wishes."

He put his love in gay messages to both Theo and Nathalie de Delage, now contrasting blond and brunette belles of sixteen in the society of New York. Certainly they would have been included in any dance of the beauties. They added much to the charm of Richmond Hill which the Colonel so much missed on his many journeys as attorney, sometimes even now practicing in association with Hamilton in important cases. He was always impatient to return to their company from whatever places law and politics carried him. Romantic stories grew about the two girls almost as lushly but more gently than the malignant legends which grew about him.

In France, Nathalie's mother, the Marquise Stéphanie, worried about her lovely daughter in American society. She was urging her to return to her native land where, under the stern rule of Napoleon, terror no longer threatened aristocrats, even if the Bourbons remained in exile. The Marquise Stéphanie was troubled about Nathalie in America where she might even marry a republican.

The name of dark beautiful Theodosia was romantically linked with a variety of acceptable beaux. One mythmaker even wrote of the beginning at this time of a long, unrequited love affair between Theo and young Meriwether Lewis, of Virginia, though he was not on the scene. More likely have been reports which joined her name to that of Washington Irving. Though biographers have often since spoken of the Irving family then as "middle class," the many Irving children grew up in a house with a garden on William Street, not far from the mansion of Burr's great friend Commodore Nicholson. Washington, at this time unenthusiastically studying law, was only a year older than Theo. Also, his oldest brother, Peter, was one of the young men stirred in politics by Colonel Burr and a few years later would be the editor of *The Morning Chronicle*, a Burrite newspaper. As Washington began to write, Theo's father commended his contributions to her as "very good for so young a man."

That would have been a match. It seems unfortunate to have to relegate this story of young love of such luminaries to romantic limbo. Clearly, however, in 1800 the young gentleman certainly seeking the pretty prodigy's hand was the rich South Carolinian Joseph Alston. Diverse descriptions have come down about this Palmetto plutocrat. Prepared for college by private tutors, he had entered the junior class at Princeton in 1795, but left without graduation. Then he studied law under Edward Rutledge, signer of the Declaration of Independence and Governor of South Carolina. Alston himself summed up his education in a letter to Theo: "From my father's plan of education for me, I may properly be called a hot-bed plant. Introduced from my infancy into the society of men, while yet a boy I was accustomed to think and act like a man. On every occasion, however important, I was left to decide for myself; I do not recollect a single instance where I was controlled even by advice; for it was my father's invariable maxim, that the best way of strengthening the judgment was to suffer it to be constantly exercised. Before seventeen I finished my college education; before twenty I was admitted to the bar. Since that time I have been constantly traveling through different parts of the United States; to what purpose I leave you to determine."

Some determinations about him were not complimentary. Evidently in his travels he enjoyed society in the North and made variant impressions in it. From the great house of her father the Commodore, Maria Nicholson wrote her sister Mrs. Gallatin what she had heard about him.

"Report does not speak well of him," she said, "it says that he is rich, but he is a great dasher, dissipated, ill-tempered, vain and silly."

Evidently Burr had no such impression of the young man, only twenty-one in 1800. Even in this year Alston's Federalist associations in South Carolina did not trouble the republican candidate for Vice-President. Indeed, he may have been politically courting Joseph while he and Theo talked of Aristotle and Cicero, the comparative charms of New York and South Carolina, and certainly of more intimate matters. Sometimes Joseph thought she formed her impressions of South Carolina from persons who believed "every other place except the Park and the Battery a desert or a marsh," and Charleston a place where the fevers and the heat were "joined to the yells of whipped negroes." Theo thought he ought to learn French. And at seventeen she was reluctant about early marriage.

Burr may have been more impressed by Alston's wealth than Theo was. Joseph's father, William Alston, already had accumulated great wealth in lands and slaves. George Washington, on his Southern tour in 1791, wrote of the Alston rice plantations on the Waccamaw River as "entitled to be styled a fairy land." Wealth aside, Burr had come to regard young Alston as dependable. He sent him, in 1800, on his way homeward, to Virginia with letters of introduction on a mission to Jefferson at Monticello and Madison at Montpelier. He took them information from Burr about political affairs in the North in general and New York in particular. The Virginians were eager for such news. Early in the year Jefferson was doubtful about republican hopes in New York where the year before the Federalists had swept the city and the state. For republicans to win now would require the overturning of a Federalist majority of nearly a thousand out of a vote of only about six thousand. On that depended the election of a legislature which would choose the Presidential electors Jefferson needed.

The Virginians to whom Alston took Burr's letters and his news were well aware, as Jefferson put it, that "the vote of the city of New York . . . would decide the vote of the State, and that again the state of the Union." Only "Little Burr" had thought it could be done. And to do it he brought energy, patience in the patching up of party factions, boldness, skill in organization. No one, of course, then knew that in the campaign he would receive required and unexpected aid from "little Hamilton."

Later, as seemed a set historical pattern, every skillful and democratic step he took was given an ugly explanation. He did turn, as the fastidious have steadily emphasized, to Tammany Hall. This, of course, was not his first connection with that organization which in a real sense was the successor society to the Sons of Liberty, as it also constituted the opposition to the Society of the Cincinnati. Burr, as a Revolutionary officer, was by war record, position, and manner a proper member of the Cincinnati who joined in its lofty patriotic celebrations.

Historians of the Tammany Society doubt that he was ever a member of that organization. He never attended its sometimes rowdy gatherings. He directed its operations, however, through a group of devoted young men who took their places around him. The Swartwout brothers, Samuel, Robert, and John, of old Dutch descent, were scarcely of voting age. William Peter Van Ness, who had studied law in the office of Edward Livingston, was only twenty-two. Van Ness was described as an almost clientless lawyer then. Soon he was to take into his office young Martin Van Buren who showed his ardent republicanism this year before he was of voting age. Davis, Burr's biographer-to-be, was only twenty-seven. Other such young men were ready to take leadership from and give devotion to Burr. Jacob Barker, who was to make and lose fortunes as merchant, financier, and lawyer, was only twenty-one. Daniel G. Tompkins, later Governor of New York, was twenty-six. Older men joined these devoted youths behind Burr. One of his principal assistants in communication with Jefferson in this campaign was David Gelston, who had been a member of the last Continental Congress and at this time was Surrogate of the County of New York. He was fifty-six. Commodore Nicholson was sixty-four.

Such men constituted no rabble. Federalists in classical scorn called them Burr's "myrmidons" or subordinates who carried out the superior's orders without mercy or consideration for others. With equal ease in classical terminology, Theodosia called such men her father's Tenth Legion. But under them Burr was concerned with the masses disenfranchised by property qualifications for voting. Many of them as Irish, French, and German immigrants had been disturbed by the deportation provisions of the Alien and Sedition Laws. With the aid of the new Bank of the Manhattan Company which Burr had supposedly gotten by trick, he brought them to the ballot box by another much denounced device. To evade the election laws disqualifying the poor, the Bank of the Manhattan Company made loans with which poor men, "mainly penniless students and mechanics," clubbed together to buy property which qualified them for voting. This seemed outrageous to Troup who had applauded the coercion of the cartmen in 1799.

Even with such an expanded electorate, Burr needed a break to secure him the victory. Hamilton gave it to him in double measure. Never forgiving Adams, who had demolished his dream of military glory, Hamilton apparently had learned nothing from the failure of his attempted trick in the 1796 Presidential election to put Thomas Pinckney ahead of Adams. He had only feared that he could not dominate Adams then. Now that had been demonstrated to his dismay. So with greater ardor he undertook to try the trick again with Charles Cotesworth Pinckney, brother of Thomas, who was the supposed second man on the Federalist ticket. This would require some quiet manipulation. Therefore he put up as legislative candidates men—or myrmidons—who would be docilely subject to his directions in the choice of Presidential electors. His operations could not be entirely secret. Even Adams heard that at a Cincinnati assembly he inspired Federalist cries: "We must sacrifice Adams, We must sacrifice Adams!" Adams thought that Hamilton was pushing himself for President. One of those echoing this cry, he said, was the Reverend Timothy Dwight, president of Yale, who shared none of the republican ideas of his first cousin Burr.

Adams later wrote that he had heard of Hamilton's plan to give him "the go-by" before the New York Federalist leader selected his legislative slate. When it was named it constituted an assembly of his stooges. He had, Adams wrote later, "fixed upon a list of his own friends, people of little weight or consideration in the city or the country." Even in recalling his own injury Adams seemed pleased with the reaction of Burr when he saw this ticket. He reported that Burr looked at the list, stuffed it in his pocket, and made only one terse comment.

"Now," said he, "I have him hollow."

Both swiftly and patiently the Colonel undertook to shape a republican ticket which would not only pull the warring factions of the republican or Democratic Party together but also confront Hamilton's nonentities with the most distinguished body of candidates ever presented to the state. It was easier for Burr to select the candidates he wanted than to get them to run. He topped the ticket with an eminent trio: Governor Clinton, Brockholst Livingston, and General Horatio Gates.

Under Burr's pressure his friend Livingston agreed to run if Gates and Clinton would. Gates was a close friend of Burr's and a strange figure in American history. During the Revolution the so-called Conway Cabal against Washington centered around a proposal to substitute Gates as commander-in-chief. Whether Gates actually shared in this conspiracy is not historically clear. As a result of its disclosure he fought a duel with his disloyal aide Wilkinson, then only beginning a career of betrayal. Burr, who had been on the fringes of this cabal, kept Gates's friendship if he also won Washington's antipathy. Gates, who had loomed as possible first soldier after his victory at Saratoga, slipped in esteem after his costly defeat at Camden. Yet he was honored as president of the Virginia Society of the Cincinnati. Then he moved to New York in 1790, where his sympathies were decidedly with liberals like Burr. In 1800 his name as war hero was politically negotiable. As a warm admirer of Burr, he reluctantly agreed to run—if Governor Clinton would.

This old crotchety democrat was the tough one. Not only was he quoted as saying to Burr he did not care to run on a ticket designed to help Jefferson. Also, Burr's man Davis, in a much disputed passage in his memoir of Burr, quoted Clinton comments at a conference at Burr's house at length. They were remarkable in the light of future Jefferson-Clinton alignments. The tough old politician had, so Davis quoted him as saying, "long entertained an unfavorable opinion of Mr. Jefferson's talents as a statesman and his firmness as a republican. That he conceived him an accommodating trimmer, who would change with times, and bend to circumstances for the purposes of personal promotion. Impressed with these sentiments, he could not with propriety, he said, acquiesce in the elevation of a man destitute of the qualifications essential to the good administration of the government." To this, wrote Davis, "he added other expressions too vulgar to be repeated here."

When Davis wrote this years later he was aware that subsequent events in the relations of Burr, Jefferson, and Clinton made it almost incredible. So he listed others whom he said were present and listening then as witnesses. They heard, too, he said, an even more remarkable statement which he credited to Clinton.

" 'But,' said he, with energy, 'if you, Mr. Burr, was the candidate for the presidential chair, I would act with pleasure and with vigour.' "

These expressions attributed to Clinton were later sharply questioned by partisans of Jefferson. Some did seem suspect. As early as 1792 Burr had written that Clinton regarded him "with jealousy and malevolence." Randall, in his life of Jefferson, described this whole report by Davis as "a characteristic specimen of effrontery." Yet Parton regarded as correct the report of Clinton's low opinion of Jefferson at this time. He gave reasons for it. In 1792 Clinton had received fifty electoral votes out of one hundred and thirty-two while Jefferson had but four. Then it seemed that it was Clinton, not Jefferson, who was headed for the Presidency. But Clinton had dropped to only four votes in 1796 when Jefferson was chosen Vice-President. And that year young Burr received thirty votes. Clinton did not like to ride behind Jefferson, certainly not Burr. Still, Commodore Nicholson, in a letter to Gallatin soon after this occasion, confirmed Clinton's good opinion of Burr at this moment. There is also other basis for the possibility of his unfavorable opinion of the Virginian.

In his own household Governor Clinton had heard expressions of bitterness and distrust toward Jefferson. The Governor had undoubtedly heard the expressions of resentment from his son-in-law and the father of his grandson, now American Citizen Genet. One reason for this former French Minister's outburst to Jefferson three years before, he had said then, was that he owed a defense of his honor "to the respectable family which has received me in its midst." The Governor may not have seen his son-in-law's angry letter. He could not have failed to know of the animosity toward Jefferson which his daughter Cornelia shared. Politicians may not hearken to their women; they can hardly fail to hear them.

The certain fact is that Clinton, at Burr's insistence, agreed not to protect the use of his name on the ticket. Also, so Davis said, he promised reluctantly not to use such language about Jefferson during the campaign. In the campaign, however, said Davis, his son talked of Jefferson with "vulgar severity" and his rising nephew DeWitt Clinton showed the "most shameful indifference and inactivity in the democratic cause."

Burr had the names to top his ticket even if reluctantly given and precariously secured. He added strength below them. One was Osgood, former Postmaster General and now president of his Bank of the Manhattan Company. Quite as eminent was Henry Rutgers, brewer, land magnate, and philanthropist, who later was to raise a large sum for the construction of Tammany Hall's Great Wigwam. Other men of more than ordinary prominence represented every branch of the republican party in the city. And, of course, on it there was Burr's aide John Swartwout. Burr himself was not on the ticket. Various reasons have been given for this. If, as has been said, he did not want the ticket to share the "oblyquy" resulting from his supposedly tricky creation of the bank, it would seem odd that he had put the bank's president on it. Perhaps, as has also been said, in ardently supporting the New York City republicans, he did not wish to seem to be too much supporting himself. He was put forward as candidate from Orange County.

The ticket was unveiled to republicans in general at the house of "J. Adams, Jr., on William Street." This Adams was, of course, no close connection of the Adams who would move briefly to the unfinished President's House in Washington in the fall. Federalists, not all of whom wanted any Adams to win, were dumbfounded. With such personages on Burr's ticket it was difficult to make the contest seem one between the rabble and the respectables. Still, then and later, Burr was described in Hamilton's favorite term as a Cataline, a dissolute aristocrat who stirred and rode the discontent of the masses. As one of the well-born he was far ahead of many of his contemporaries in his views on democracy. He was willing to lead the city poor by whom Jefferson was repelled. Still, an early biographer, who lived and wrote in Burr's lifetime, left a vivid description of his methods with the electorate.

"Colonel Burr," said Samuel L. Knapp, "never courted the mob by mingling with them, and sharing their movements; for it was seldom they met him. He made no converts by *pewter mug* stories, and they liked him the better for all this abstraction from the great body of democracy; but whenever he came in contact with the humblest of his admirers, it was well known that he treated them so blandly that his manners were remembered when the whole conversation was forgotten. His manners were the most courtly of any of his age."

That other certainly courtly gentleman, Hamilton, declined to be appalled by Burr's imposing list of candidates. He arrayed the merchants. He put on pressure through his banking relationships. On the three-day election in April, he dashed from poll to poll, an intense, pale rider on a white horse. No description of the equally hard-ridden mount of Burr survives. It is recorded that sometimes they met on their rounds and maintained perfect courtesy toward each other in their arguments. Such politeness was not strange. The two men appeared on the same side in a famous murder trial in New York in this same month. They saved their client, then rode to battle. Hamilton was the man dismounted. The Federalist majority of the year before was wiped away and a republican majority elected assuring the choice of republican Presidential electors.

Immediately after the election Nicholson wrote his son-in-law in Congress that the campaign had been "conducted and brought to issue in so miraculous a manner that I cannot account for it but from the intervention of a Supreme Power and our friend Burr the agent. . . . His generalship, perseverance, industry, and execution exceeds all description, so that I think I can say he deserves anything and everything of his country. . . . I shall conclude by recommending him as a general far superior to your Hambletons [sic]; as much so as a man is to a boy; and I have but little doubt this state, through his means and planning, will be as Republican in the appointment of electors as the State of Virginia."

If "a Supreme Power" had aided Burr, Hamilton prepared more mundane intervention. Within the week after the election he composed one of those documents which in his life as a writing man appear like ink blots on his brilliance. He proposed to Governor Jay that, though the new legislature had been chosen, he call back into special session the old lame-duck Federalist legislature to nullify the election by changing the method of choice of the Presidential electors. Mr. Hamilton understood that what he proposed to do was to cheat the victors out of their victory. But, he said, in the face of "the very high probability" the New York election would mean the election of Jefferson as President, he thought it was no time for "a strict adherence to ordinary rules."

"In observing this I shall not be supposed to mean that any thing ought to be done which integrity will forbid; but merely that the scruples of delicacy and propriety, as relative to a common course of things, ought to yield to the extraordinary nature of the crisis. They ought not to hinder the taking of a legal and constitutional step to prevent an atheist in religion and a fanatic in politics from getting possession of the helm of state."

And in this long letter he piously added: "In weighing this suggestion, you will doubtless bear in mind that popular governments must certainly be overturned; and, while they endure, prove engines of mischief, if one party will call to its aid all the resources which vice can give, and if the other (however pressing the emergency) confines itself within all the ordinary forms of delicacy and decorum."

This letter, according to Davis, was discussed only at a "select and confidential federal caucus" on May 3, the day after the full election returns were known. But on May 4 the news of the planned proposal was sent to Editor Duane of the Philadelphia *Aurora* from Burr's headquarters in New York. The letter itself was published in the *Aurora* on May 6—a day before the date upon it. Quickly a Federalist paper in New York denounced it as a Jacobin fabrication. It demanded: "Where is the American who *will not detest the author of this infamous lie.*" Yet, the letter was not only printed later in Jay's papers but also with a notation the Governor had made upon it in his own handwriting: "Proposing a measure for party purposes which I think it would not become me to adopt."

Certainly, if not "a Supreme Power" as Commodore Nicholson suggested was working with Burr, mysterious powers were available to him in espionage with regard to Hamilton's activities. Repeating the current gossip, Parton wrote that "the whisper at the time was that Hamilton and Burr were both enamoured of the same frail woman, who really loved Burr but endured Hamilton only that she might beguile him of secrets with which to ingratiate herself with his rival." Parton dismissed "this wretched gossip." He wrote: "Neither Hamilton nor Burr was blameless toward women; but neither of them, I am sure, ever addicted himself to the kind of debauchery which is implied in the story. . . ."

Jefferson also seemed to have mysterious sources of information. He required no intelligence organization, however, to learn that the Federalists did not conceal their despair as the result of the election. But possibly he heard from Beckley of some "hocus-pocus maneuvers" in a Federalist caucus, perhaps the same one in which Burr had a spy. In it Hamiltonians were pushing Charles Cotesworth Pinckney with the hope that they could put him ahead of Adams in the voting.

Such shenanigans were possible under the Constitution in both parties. And at this time Burr did not conceal his feeling that the Virginians had made him a victim of similar ones in 1796. On the same day that Jefferson wrote of Federalist "hocus-pocus maneuvers," Commodore Nicholson and Mrs. Gallatin were reporting Burr's fears of "hocus-pocus maneuvers" by republicans.

Jefferson's friends had by this time decided that his running mate should be a New Yorker. So the choice lay only between the chiefs of the three great factions there—Chancellor Livingston, Governor Clinton, and Burr. Livingston, as a man almost stone deaf, seemed hardly a man to preside over the Senate. For Jefferson, Gallatin asked his father-in-law to sound out both Burr and Clinton. Commodore Nicholson reported on May 7: "I have conversed with the two gentlemen mentioned in your letter. . . . George Clinton with whom I spoke first declined. His age, his infirmities, his habits and attachment to retired life, in his opinion, exempt him from active life. He (Governor Clinton) thinks Colonel

Burr is the most suitable person and perhaps the only man. Such is also the opinion of all the Republicans in this quarter that I have conversed with; their confidence in A.B. is universal and unbounded. Mr. Burr, however, appears averse to be a candidate. He seems to think that no arrangement could be made which would be observed to the southward; alluding, as I understood, to the last election, in which he was certainly ill used by Virginia and North Carolina.

"I believe he may be induced to stand if assurances can be given that the Southern States will act fairly.

"Colonel Burr may certainly be governor of this state at the next election if he pleases, and a number of his friends are very unwilling that he should be taken off for Vice-President, thinking the other the most important office. Upon the whole, however, we think he ought to be the man for V.P., if there is a moral certainty of success. But his name must not be played the fool with. I confidently hope that you will be able to smooth over the business of the last election, and if Colonel Burr is properly applied to, I think he will be induced to stand. At any rate we, the Republicans, will make him."

Mrs. Gallatin added her report on the following day: "Papa has answered your questions about the candidate for Vice-President. Burr says he has no confidence in the Virginians; they once deceived him, and they are not to be trusted."

Five days later from Philadelphia Gallatin wrote his wife: "We had last night a very large meeting of Republicans, in which it was unanimously agreed to support Burr for Vice-President." Certainly in the five days between the report of Burr's reluctance to Gallatin and Gallatin's report of his nomination by the caucus no such "arrangement" of reassurance as Nicholson reported Burr wanted with the Virginians could have been made. Whatever his reluctance may have been, however, as one who had recently dragooned Clinton, Gates, and Livingston to head his ticket in New York, he was in no position to turn down republican determination on his nomination.

Jefferson later wrote cynically of any reluctance on Burr's part. Then after a cold conversation in the White House the Virginian wrote that Burr had told him that he had not expected the nomination, and had "acceded to it" only to help Jefferson's election. Jefferson snorted in his *Anas:* "Colonel Burr must have thought I could swallow strong things in my own favor, when he founded his acquiescence in the nomination as

Vice-President, to his desire of promoting my honor, the being with me, whose company and conversation had always been fascinating to him."

Certainly, however, in 1800 Burr had become, as Malone wrote, "an invaluable accessory" to republican plans and Jefferson's hopes. And, reluctant or headlong, "Little Burr" had come a long way forward from the time when Hamilton so described him. That incessant chronicler of his activities from the Federalist point of view, Troup, reported him moving this summer with almost Napoleonic confidence.

"Burr," he reported to King, "whom Mr. Church calls our first consul, is in very high glee. He entertains much company with elegance. I understand he is in a day or two going to the Eastward & I presume on business of the coming election."

A month later Troup reported again: "Burr has just returned from the Eastward where he has been for the purpose of effecting a division of the New England vote. . . . I recollect no period of Burr's life in which he has been more complacent than since our last election in the city."

Hamilton had written almost prophetically on the same subject, on August 6. He was certainly not in high glee or a state of complacency then. The three men he hated most—Jefferson, Burr, and Adams—were candidates for the highest offices in the land. And there seemed to be too much probability that Jefferson and Burr would be President and Vice-President. He had spoken earlier of the necessity to save the country from the "fangs of Jefferson." Now he reported that Burr was intriguing in New Jersey, Rhode Island, and Vermont. There was a "possibility of some success in his intrigues." Burr was counting on all the republican votes and it was possible "that by some adventitious aid from other quarters, he would overtop his friend Jefferson."

Hamilton scribbled his fury: "Admitting the first point, the conclusion may be realized, and, if it is so, Burr will certainly attempt to reform the government à la Bonaparte. He is as unprincipled and dangerous a man as any country can boast—as true a Cataline as ever met in midnight conclave."

Hamilton's suspicions are the more easily understood because he was himself at this time engaged in his own operation—or intrigue—to put the second man first in the Federalist party by maneuvers to elect Pinckney instead of Adams to the Presidency. What he proposed to some of his close Federalist friends was that the New England states, where Adams was strong, give equal votes to Adams and Pinckney but that some of the

Southern states cast ballots for Pinckney and Jefferson. As a result, he hoped, Pinckney would run ahead of both Adams and Jefferson.

This was an ambitious maneuver, requiring skill and secrecy. Adams' friends whom Hamilton called Federalists of "the 2nd class" might, if they learned of it, throw votes away from Pinckney. The response to his confidential letters was not all that he wished. So as the election approached he turned from his pen to the printshop. He prepared a pamphlet called *A Letter from Alexander Hamilton, concerning The Public Conduct and Character of John Adams, esq., President of the United States.* In the midst of an election, it struck at the candidate of his party whose "disgusting egotism, distempered jealousy, and ungovernable indiscretion" had sowed the seeds of discord at home and reduced the reputation of the nation abroad.

This, of course, was to be a very confidential publication. Its timing suggested that it was meant to be circulated and have its effect in the South without being known in the North before the election.

Once more Colonel Burr in his mysterious way caught Hamilton "hollow." He got a copy of the printed pamphlet even before Hamilton did. Nobody will ever know how. One tale is that he got it by chance from a young delivery boy who had no idea of how confidential was his load. There may have been one of his myrmidons among the printers. There were whispers again about the woman he and Hamilton were supposed to share on unequal terms.

The certain fact is that he quickly called Robert and John Swartwout and Davis to his house. They read the pamphlet, picking out the choicest items of the invectives Hamilton had written against Adams. Then Davis was given the job of getting them quickly to Duane of the *Aurora* in Philadelphia and Charles Holt, editor of *The Bee* in New London, Connecticut. The results were immediate. The united republicans confronted a fragmented Federalist Party. Adams wrote that "Cicero was not sacrificed to the vengeance of Anthony . . . more egregiously than John Adams was to the unbridled ambition of Alexander Hamilton. . . ."

Some historians have suggested that Burr was engaged in the same sort of shenanigans on the republican side when he sent his daughter's fiancé Alston to see Jefferson and Madison in Virginia. In the letters he sent by Alston, some said, he was undertaking to make sure that he would get all Southern votes while willing that some Northern votes would be dropped from Jefferson, thus putting him ahead in the republican voting.

The letter Alston carried to Jefferson on this occasion was one reassuring the Virginian about republican prospects in New England. Burr evidently wanted similar assurances as to himself in the South—that this time he would get the whole republican vote in Virginia and other Southern states. In addition to letters from Burr, Alston brought a letter from Burr's lieutenant, Gelston, again stating doubts of Southern integrity in supporting Burr. This letter may have veiled a suggestion that the pot could play as black as the kettle, that something like that which happened in Virginia in 1796 could happen in New York in 1800. The result of this letter, wrote Malone, "was to strengthen Madison's determination that Burr be fully supported in the South." Jefferson shared this determination that there would be no repetition of Virginia's tricky treatment of Burr in 1796.

Possibly young Alston brought some copies of Hamilton's blast at Adams on this trip in October, though it is presumed that Jefferson saw only extracts in a Richmond paper early in November. It is even more probable that Alston carried some copies on to South Carolina where Hamilton hoped they would do the most good and where they actually did Adams and Pinckney most harm. Certainly in his native state where there had been trickery involving one innocent Pinckney in 1796, more trickery was in process to the injury of another Pinckney now. At his age Alston could not have been a power in the politics of the Palmetto State. He had been absent in August when efforts apparently were made there to ditch Adams. Offers were made to organize a Jefferson-Pinckney ticket but General Pinckney haughtily rejected them.

Then came Hamilton's violent pamphlet against the head of his own party. It did not result in putting Pinckney ahead, even in his own state, but in the choice there of electors for Jefferson and Burr. If both Federalists had won in South Carolina, Adams and Pinckney would have been chosen President and Vice-President, not Jefferson and Burr. Though this election has often been described as a revolution, it was no landslide. The final vote was 73 for Jefferson, 73 for Burr, 65 for Adams, 64 for Pinckney, and 1 for Jay. A Federalist victory in South Carolina would have made the result 65 for Jefferson and Burr, 73 for Adams, and 72 for Pinckney. There were no defections from Jefferson in New England which Burr was charged with seeking. And this time Virginia did stand by its promises not to cut Burr in the South. Burr got all of the 21 votes in Virginia as Jefferson did all of the 12 votes from New York.

The total results did not come in swiftly. When they did come, republicans, caught in a tie, were almost as much in a state of consternation as the Federalists were cast down in defeat. Jefferson had heard from South Carolina early in December that one South Carolina elector had cast his vote for Clinton instead of Burr to prevent the possibility of a Jefferson-Burr tie. Similar arrangements were supposed to have been made in other states. But Jefferson must have learned, as Hamilton was informed this month, that, in anticipation of a tie, Federalists were suggesting that an election might be prevented by throwing the government into the hands of the President of the Senate.

Jefferson moved in flattering fashion to make sure that his running mate not take any advantage of the situation. On December 14, assuming his election, he strengthened his ties with the New York Livingstons by offering Chancellor Livingston the post of Secretary of the Navy. And on the next day he wrote to Burr. He had already then, he told the New Yorker, heard that "several high-flying Federalists have expressed their hope that the two Republican tickets may be equal, and their determination in that case to prevent a choice in the House of Representatives (which they are strong enough to do) and let the government devolve on a President of the Senate." Carefully, however, Jefferson swept such a possibility aside.

"While I must congratulate you, my dear sir," he wrote his running mate, "on the issue of this contest, because it is more honorable, and, doubtless more grateful to you than any station within the competence of the chief magistrate; yet, for myself, and for the substantial service of the republic, I feel most sensibly the loss we sustain of your aid in our new administration. It leaves a chasm in my arrangements which cannot be adequately filled up. I had endeavored to compose an administration whose talents, integrity, names, and dispositions should at once inspire unbounded confidence in the public mind, and insure a perfect harmony in the conduct of the public business. I lose you from the list, and am not sure of all the others. Should the gentlemen who possess the public confidence decline taking a part in their affairs, and force us to take persons unknown to the people, the evil genius of this country may realize his avowal that 'he will beat down the administration.' The return of Mr. Van Benthuysen, one of your electors, furnished me a confidential opportunity of writing this much to you, which I should not have ventured through the post-office at this prying season. We shall, of course, see you before the 4th of March."

This letter may have been written, as Davis said in his memoirs of Burr, with "the *tact* of the ostrich and the *sincerity* of a refined Jesuit." Burr in his cordial and prompt response did not seem to regard it so. He had believed he had made arrangements for one vote to be dropped from him in Rhode Island. There were no Burr votes there.

"I do not, however, apprehend," he wrote, "any embarrassment even in the case the Votes should come out alike for us. My personal friends are perfectly informed of my wishes on the subject and can never think of diverting a single Vote from you. On the contrary they will be found among your most zealous adherents. I see no reason to doubt of you having at least nine States if the business shall come before the H. of Rep."

As to Mr. Jefferson's regret with regard to his loss of Burr from a "list" he had already made of those officials he required about him, Burr was even more emphatic. He told Jefferson that "as far forth as my knowledge extends, it is the unanimous determination of the Republicans of every grade to support your administration with unremitted zeal: indeed I should distrust the loyalty of any one professing to be a Republican who should refuse his services. There is in fact no dearth of Talents or of patriotism as ought to inspire a doubt of your being able to fill every office in a manner that will command public confidence and public approbation. As to myself, I will chearfully [sic] abandon the office of V.P. if it shall be thought that I can be more useful in any active station. In fact, my whole time and attention shall be unceasingly employed to render your administration grateful and honorable to our Country and to yourself. To this I am impelled by the highest sense of duty as by the most devoted personal attachment."

Burr had not waited for Jefferson's letter to make his position clear. On December 16 he wrote from New York to tall, handsome Senator Samuel Smith of Maryland. Smith, a friend of Jefferson, who was to have more than one part in this Presidential imbroglio, quickly published Burr's letter.

"It is highly improbable that I shall have an equal number of votes with Mr. Jefferson," it read, "but, if such should be the result, every man who knows me ought to know that I would utterly disclaim all competition. Be assured that the federal party can entertain no wish for such an exchange. As to my friends, they would dishonor my views and insult my feelings by a suspicion that I would submit to be instrumental in coun-teracting the wishes and the expectations of the United States. And I now constitute you my proxy to declare these sentiments if the occasion should require."

In Washington then Jefferson seemed more than ever the embodi-ment of the plain democrat. At Conrad's boardinghouse on Capitol Hill, though Vice-President and the oldest in the company, he insisted on a place at the foot of the table and farthest from the fire. Also, according to Mrs. Margaret Bayard Smith, whose husband he was establishing as editor of his organ, the *National Intelligencer,* this much denounced "atheist" regularly attended Sabbath Day services in a humble Episcopal Church which had been remodeled from a tobacco house. Mrs. Smith was an important friend and witness in Jefferson company in Washing-ton. Not only do her letters attest the closeness of her tie with the Jef-fersons. In addition, Jefferson's daughters in their letters to him were constantly referring to her as a close family friend. This was a little strange since Mrs. Smith's people, the Bayards, were staunch Federalists and her cousin, Representative James A. Bayard, was soon to show himself as one of Jefferson's special opponents. She had been pleased when Jefferson set up her husband as his editor. But her admiration for Jefferson became like that of a convert to a religion. Her own people had described him as a violent democrat, a vulgar demagogue, a bold atheist, and a profligate man. She found him instead a man "meek and mild, yet dignified in his manners, with a voice so soft and low, with a countenance so benignant and intelligent" that she could scarcely believe her ears and eyes.

Some other ladies seemed more contained in their enthusiasm, or coolly devoid of it. Early in January, Jefferson went to Mount Vernon, where he had not been welcome during Washington's last years, to pay a call on the widow Martha. As he reported it, the talk was largely about the ailments of Washington's sister, Mrs. Fielding Lewis. The redoubt-able Martha he only quoted as inquiring "very kindly" after his daughter Polly.

He wrote Polly in doubt as to whether he was "destined to remain here." On January 4, 1801, he told her of his confidence in Burr: "The Federalists were confident at first they could debauch Colo. B. from his good faith by offering him their vote to be President, and have seriously proposed it to him. His conduct has been honorable and decisive, and greatly embarrasses them."

On January 16 Jefferson was less sanguine. He longed to be home in the midst of his grandchildren where he would "have more pleasure in their little follies than in the wisdom of the wise.

"Here too there is such a mixture of the bad passions of the heart that one feels themselves in an enemy's country. It is an unpleasant circumstance, if I am destined to stay here, that the great proportion of those of the place who figure are federalists, and most of them of the violent kind. Some have been so personally bitter that they can never forgive me, tho' I do them with sincerity. Perhaps in time they will get tamed."

Colonel Burr was days away from the Washington scene. He and Theo were preparing to go farther away—up the river to Albany to which his duties as Assemblyman called him. She wrote young Alston, "My father laughs at my impatience to hear from you, and says that I am in love; but I do not believe that to be a fair deduction, for the post is really very irregular and slow—enough to provoke anybody." And she ended, "Adieu, I wish you many returns of the century."

Alston made no detour by Piedmont Virginia this time. Theodosia had written him a letter proposing an "interview."

"I shall therefore sail certainly in a few days," he wrote her on December 28. "Winds be propitious!"

The century was not a month old when he reached dark and finally determined Theo and victorious Burr. To them the new century seemed full of promise for men and democracy, for officials and lovers. Yet, it would scarcely be begun before Burr would be charged with a willingness to debauch his country and a heartless willingness, too, to force this child he loved and who adored him into the service of his ambition. In Albany, to which they had come by sleigh, the weather was bitter cold as they awaited the slowly arriving news from Washington and the arrival of Alston up the frozen shores of the Hudson. Theo had been suffering from an injured ankle. Also, she had been visiting at Ballston Spa near the then inferior Saratoga Springs. There doctors sent "invalids of elegance and opulence." But well and vital people also came to drink the waters and dance with the assembly. Malady and merriment were often side by side. That could be in the new century which had been welcomed by the ascent of balloons and the booming of guns.

2.

The Tie

"The Prospect before Us" was Callender's phrase but he wrote about it in no wilder language than the thunderous warnings of distinguished, highly educated Federalists in 1801. Among his own neighbors Jefferson had enemies. Families were divided in the furies. Burr's first cousin, the eminent Calvinist Theodore Dwight, saw the republican victory the Colonel had helped make as almost the arrival of the Beast of the Apocalypse.

"The object of Jacobism," he proclaimed, "both in its political and moral revolution, is to destroy every trace of civilization in the world, and to force mankind back into a savage state. We have now reached the consummation of democratic blessedness. We have a country governed by blockheads and knaves; the ties of marriage with all its felicities are severed and destroyed; our wives and daughters are thrown into the stews; our children are cast into the world from the breast and forgotten; filial piety is extinguished, and our surnames, the only mark of distinction among families, are abolished. Can the imagination paint anything more dreadful on this side of hell?"

And some republicans, like the imp of the devil Dwight conjured up, met the anathema hurled at them with suspicions of evil of their own. On November 8, when the republican victory was becoming evident, fire in the War Department ran through the files. The victors voiced suspicions that this was an incendiary cover-up by the Federalists. Callender, languishing though not quietly in the Richmond jail, predicted that this would not be the last of the burning of the records. Then, on January 20, 1801, a blaze broke out in the Treasury Department.

Callender chortled to Jefferson: "The singular accuracy of my prediction, as to the *second* fire produced such a roar of laughter, and such a pang of indignation in Richmond, as I would not have lost the satisfaction of for an hundred dollars. I would not for the price of an estate, be divested of the self-congratulation that I feel, in being able to go straight through this great national crisis, without having to look back upon one moment of trimming, or flinching."

Callender was ready to settle for less than an estate. What he expected from Jefferson was pardon from his jail sentence and the remittance or payment of the two-hundred-dollar fine Judge Chase had given him under the Sedition Law. After that he was ready to receive other rewards for his services.

Others were turning to Mr. Jefferson with congratulations and with expectations which met and increased Federalist fears. Also, many were coming to him with reports of manipulations to keep him from the Presidency. Some gossip like that he often got from Beckley he put down in his *Anas*. Even President Adams told him, he wrote later, that he thought the Federalists in Congress would be justified in using the crisis caused by the tie Presidential vote to secure some promises from him which they felt the safety of the republic required.

They wanted, as Adams put it, promises from Jefferson that he "would not turn out the Federal officers, nor put down the navy, nor spunge the national debt." Otherwise the Federalists proposed the substitution in the Presidency of Burr, whom many of them preferred as a "vigorous, practical man . . . to courage he joins generosity." Jefferson, they thought, was "infected with all the cold-blooded vices." Gouverneur Morris of New York, however, who preferred Jefferson's assurances to a deadlock over the Presidency, realized the difficulties of the situation. He wrote: ". . . whatever may be Mr. Burr's conciliatory disposition, it will be impossible for him to assuage the resentment of the Virginians, who will consider his acceptance as treachery, for Virginia cannot bear to see any other man than a Virginian in the President's chair."

Resentment was already roaring even at the possibility of turning the choices of the people upside down. There were threats of state militia pouring in from Virginia and Pennsylvania. Jefferson himself spoke of the bitterness on the scene crowded with spectators, some of whom were ready to be the assassins of a usurper. He seemed serene in his bottom-of-table seat at Conrad's boardinghouse. But he left a record which seems credulous and confused.

He wrote home to Polly, on January 16, of his evident satisfaction that his old enemy Hamilton, who now hated Burr more, "was using his utmost influence to procure my election rather than Colo. Burr's."

Hamilton was, indeed, exerting his influence but discovering that his place as First Federalist had been shaken by his secret attack on Adams which Burr had forced into the open. With his able but sometimes unfortunate pen he rushed into the fight on the highest patriotic grounds.

"If there be a man in the world I ought to hate," he wrote Morris, "it is Jefferson. With Burr I have always been personally well. But the public good must be paramount to every private consideration."

There is no indication that Hamilton changed a single vote in the House. But at this time in private letters he did bring to completion his portrait in demonology of the Colonel who had beaten him in his own bailiwick. At the same time he was ready to use the situation to strike at both Burr and Jefferson. Burr must be rejected, "Yet it may be well enough to throw out a lure for him, in order to tempt him to start for the plate, and thus lay the foundation of disunion between the two chiefs."

In a fashion which he always concealed from Burr ("I dined with him lately," he wrote at this time), he let loose his venom in confidential letters. Burr was "bankrupt beyond redemption except by the plunder of his country. . . . To accomplish his ends he must lean upon unprincipled men, and will continue to adhere to the myrmidons who have hitherto surrounded him." Every move in Burr's career, he wrote, proved that he "has formed himself upon the model of Cataline, and that he is too cold-blooded and too determined a conspirator ever to change his plan. . . . Adieu to the Federal Troy if they once introduce this Grecian horse into their citadel . . . a profligate . . . a voluptuary . . . in his profession extortionate to a proverb. . . ." To meet his requirements he would be ready to have recourse to "unworthy expedients." And: "These may be a bargain and sale with some foreign power, or combinations with public agents in projects of gains by means of the public moneys; perhaps and probably to enlarge the sphere—of war."

Jefferson at this time quickly moved in insistence to Burr that he had made no critical references to him. Two weeks after he noted that Hamilton was coming to his assistance, he wrote the Colonel not to let the enemy "sow tares between us, that they might divide us and our friends." Specifically he denounced as forgery a letter which he was supposed to have written containing "sentiments highly injurious to you."

And he added, "A mutual knowledge of each other furnishes us with the best test of the contrivances which will be practiced by the enemies of both."

Yet soon he was recording in his *Anas* Washington gossip which was certainly not friendly to his running mate. He quoted an informant as telling him that Gouverneur Morris had "expressed himself thus. 'How comes it,' said he, 'that Burr who is four hundred miles off, (at Albany), has agents here at work with great activity, while Mr. Jefferson, who is on the spot, does nothing?'" Also he entered a strange note about Burr's close friend Edward Livingston, member of the great New York family and an ardent democrat who dressed so like a dandy that he was called "Beau Ned." In the *Anas* he wrote that Livingston told him that Congressman Bayard of Delaware, who was leading the Federalist fight, had tried to entice Jefferson's friend General Samuel Smith of Maryland to vote for Burr on the promise that he would be named Secretary of the Navy. (His brother Robert was afterward named to this position by Jefferson.) This Smith was the same gentleman to whom Burr had sent his early rejection of any plan to put him forward. Smith and Bayard were to be the chief figures in the much disputed matter as to whether through Smith Jefferson made a deal with Bayard.

Son of a rich merchant in Baltimore, Samuel Smith had become even more wealthy as merchant and land speculator before he entered Congress. His wife's sister had married William Patterson, another Baltimore merchant prince. Bayard, the Federalist, came from more solid and ancient background. He had come as Delaware's lone Representative to Congress at the age of thirty in 1787. He quickly showed his ability as manager of the case against Senator Blount of Tennessee for conspiracy with the British in the West.

On the same day Jefferson made his *Anas* note about supposed finagling by and for Burr, the Colonel replied to his letter about the forgery. "It was so obvious," he told Jefferson, "that the most malignant spirit of slander and intrigue would be busy that, without any inquiry, I set down as calumny every tale calculated to disturb our harmony. My friends are often more irritable and credulous; fortunately I am the depository of all their cares and anxieties; and I invariably pronounce to be a lie, everything which ought not to be true."

Mr. Jefferson might have taken some such similar position. Livingston, to whom he credited reports of bargains being offered for Burr's benefit, was actually Burr's friend and agent charged with preventing what Burr himself described as "usurpation." This is documented by the correspondence of Burr, Livingston, and Gallatin who came to lead the fight for Jefferson in the House. To Gallatin, who had been a little late in arriving on the Washington scene, Burr wrote, on January 16, from New York:

"I am heartily glad of your arrival at your post. You were never more wanted for it was absolutely vacant.

"Livingston will tell you my sentiments of the proposed usurpation, and indeed of all the other occurrences and projects of the day."

Also from Albany, on February 12, the day after the voting began in the House, Burr wrote Gallatin again: "My letters for ten days past had assured me that all was settled and that no doubt remained but that J. would have 10 or 11 votes on the first trial; I am, therefore, utterly surprised by the contents of yours of the 3d. In case of usurpation, by law, by President of Senate pro tem, or in any other way, my opinion is definitely made up, and it is known to S.S. and E.L. On that opinion I shall act in defiance of all timid, temporizing projects."

E.L. and S.S. were, of course, Edward Livingston and General Smith whom Burr had made his agents in opposing usurpation. They were also two whom Jefferson listed in his *Anas* as reporting an attempted deal of the Federalists to buy votes for Burr by the promise of office. Undoubtedly some of Burr's young friends were, as he put it to Jefferson, "irritable and credulous" about reports of Jefferson's disloyalty to Burr. Some were eager for Burr's ascendancy. But a letter, from Livingston to Burr's first lieutenant Davis a week before the voting, began, as it turned out, with undue optimism.

"I can now speak with some degree of confidence," he told Davis, "and have great pleasure in assuring you that all the little intrigues of falling ambition, all the execrable plans of violence and usurpation will in a few hours after you read this be defeated by the election of Mr. Jefferson." He went on to say that "if any unforeseen event should disappoint our hopes and wishes, you may rest assured that our city shall never be disgraced by any temporizing plan or acquiescence in usurpation on the part of its representatives and I think I may without danger give this pledge for all those with whom he acts."

Gallatin, as he took charge of the fight for Jefferson, wrote his wife that "A more considerable number [of Federalists] will try actually to make Burr President. He has *sincerely* opposed the design, and will go *any lengths* to prevent its execution."

He had gone to some length. He had publicly announced through Smith that he rejected and resented the plan. He had so informed Livingston and Gallatin. Yet as unwilling candidate, if the vote had been by members of the House, not as the Constitution required by the states, he would have won by fifty-four to fifty-one on the first vote. And with every Federalist except Huger of South Carolina voting for him, he was given the vote of six states to Jefferson's eight—nine states necessary to election. The shift of a single vote to Jefferson would have given him a majority. Bayard, as the only representative from Delaware, could have elected Jefferson on any vote. A shift of three votes would have given it to Burr. Without any shifts, the Federalists, as long as they stood firm, could prevent the election of either.

The voting, which began on February 11, has been often and dramatically described. Incessant balloting went on with brief recesses for six days. A blizzard raged. Weary men slept in their chairs. One member came ill on a stretcher to keep Maryland from going to Burr. Then, suddenly and inexplicably on the thirty-sixth ballot, Jefferson was elected.

From Philadelphia, Burr wrote Gallatin: "The four last letters of your very amusing history of balloting met me at New York on Saturday evening. I thank you much for the obliging attention, and I join my hearty congratulations on the auspicious events of the 17th. As to the infamous slanders which have been so industriously circulated, they are now of little consequence, and those who have believed them will doubtless blush at their own weakness."

But to this he added a paragraph about a possibility not soon to be forgotten by Jefferson or himself: "The Feds boast aloud that they have compromised with Jefferson, particularly as to the retaining certain persons in office. Without the assurance contained in your letter, this would gain no manner of credit with me. Yet in spite of my endeavors it has excited some anxiety among our friends in New York."

Obviously there were suspicions on both sides which have not yet been dissolved. Those who believed that Burr was ready to grab the Presidency by connivance with his party's enemies insisted that his apparently frank letters were actually those of a conniving and consummate villain. Knave or not, Burr was no fool. In the violent temper of the time he had more to lose than gain by letting himself be made a Federalist pawn. And it is certainly doubtful that Jefferson made any clear, firm deal with the Federalists who afterwards said he did. But subsequent events as well as subsequent testimony appear to make it evident that, if a deal was not made, an understanding was reached. Jefferson himself gave no direct promises. But Federalists believed then and later that they had dependable assurances through Jefferson intimates. And Jefferson, as later long explanations in his *Anas* indicated, was embarrassed about the matter, as he was earlier about his part in the bargain by candlelight to put the capital on the Potomac.

Bayard was later to swear, to Jefferson's indignation, that he had secured a deal through General Smith. He then said: "I told him I should not be satisfied or agree to yield till I had the assurance of Mr. Jefferson himself [on the promises Federalists wanted] . . . The general proposed his giving me his [Jefferson's] answer the next morning. The next day, upon our meeting, General Smith informed me that he had seen Mr. Jefferson, and stated to him the points mentioned, and was authorized by him to say that they corresponded with his views and intentions, and that we might confide in him accordingly."

Bayard at the time was anxious to avoid the appearance of a deal. In the few remaining days of his term Adams offered him the post of Minister to France. Bayard declined, saying that "as he would have to hold it during Jefferson's term to make it worth while, and if he did so he would be accused of having made an agreement with him." Adams tried, however, to show his approval of Bayard and his connections by making Bayard's father-in-law one of the "midnight judges" whose appointment infuriated Jefferson. Only Margaret Bayard Smith could spread nobility around at the end of the contest. She rejoiced in Jefferson's election and Bayard's withholding of his vote to let that occur. Bayard, she wrote, "gave up his party for his country." It did not seem that simple then or later.

Apparently nothing was too bad to be attributed to Burr. During the tie fight Gallatin had heard a suggestion sharper than a serpent's tongue or any politician's venomous whisper about him. Mrs. Gallatin during this period had received from her sister the letter about young Alston, who, she said, she knew was "ugly and of unprepossessing manners." She had a still uglier report about Burr.

"As I know you are interested for Theodosia Burr," she began, "I must tell you that Mr. Alston has returned from Carolina, it is said, to be married to her this month." Actually, when Maria Nicholson wrote, Theodosia and Joseph had been married three days before. The ceremony had taken place in Albany presumably because of Burr's duties there. Tradition, however, acidly adds that the marriage took place there because Burr was, as so often reported, broke and could not afford the sort of wedding and reception which would be necessary if he and Theo had been in residence at Richmond Hill.

Maria Nicholson put her gossip into a question: "Can it be that the father has sacrificed a daughter so lovely to affluence and influential connections? They say that it was Mr. A. who gained him eight votes in Carolina at the present election, and that he is not yet relieved from pecuniary embarrassments. Is this the man, think ye? Has Mr. G. a favorable opinion of this man of talents, or not? He loves his child. Is he so devoted to the customs of the world as to encourage such a matter?"

It is not quite clear whether in the last sentences Miss Nicholson was speaking of Burr or Gallatin. Evidently she was an ardent republican like her father and resented the Federalist machinations in which many suspected Burr was covertly involved. Burr was given the Congressional vote of South Carolina though none of its electors had been for him. But all but one of the members of its Congressional delegation were Federalists. Indeed, in the tie fight the only Federalist who voted for Jefferson was one from South Carolina. Maria had listened to tall tales about young Alston's part in his state's vote in Congress.

Still as late as 1878, Charles Burr Todd, historian and genealogist of the Burr family, repeated the story. In recollection of old tales and in rejection of them he wrote: "It was the gossip of the day, and still believed by some, that she was forced into this marriage by her father, for political and prudential reasons chiefly, while she was really in love with a young writer of the town, one Washington Irving, whose articles in the newspapers of the day were then attracting much attention. But the story lacks confirmation. Irving and lovely Theodosia were acquaintances, it is true, but there is no proof of any intimacy between them."

Burr's ambition for his daughter was certainly served by what his early biographer Parton described as "a marriage in every respect fortunate and suitable." The testy testimony about young Alston by Maria Nicholson at a time when she was suspicious of Burr is certainly not borne out by the character which emerges from one of Alston's last long love letters as suitor. There was humor, grace, evidences of erudition in it as in Burr's own letters. The young South Carolinian evidently had a love of beauty

and devotion to the Carolina country to which he wished to take Theodosia. But he was amusing even in his praise of it. And certainly this letter
did not show him pushing in—or willing to be pushed—upon a lady who
did not love him. She had, she wrote him, "intended not to marry this
twelvemonth." This was a month before she married him. And before this
he had been timid in love. He had not written he told her in one letter because "not knowing till you wrote me from Ballston how my letters would
be received, I was really afraid to venture writing."

On January 14, 1801, while plots and angers filled Washington, Theo
wrote Joseph from New York to come to her quickly: "I have already written to you by the post to tell you that I shall be happy to see you *whenever
you choose;* that I suppose is equivalent to *very soon;* and that you may no
longer feel doubts or suspicions on my account, I repeat the invitation by a
packet as less dilatory than the mail; but for these doubts and suspicions I
will take ample revenge when we meet."

Where Alston was when she wrote this letter is not known. Certainly
he must have already been hastening on his way from South Carolina
which Parton wrote was then twenty days away. At the same time from
New York, Burr wrote his son-in-law-to-be a formal letter beginning "My
dear Sir:

"Your two letters have been received, and gave me great pleasure. We
are about to begin our journey to Albany. I propose to remain there until
the 10th of February; possibly till the 20th. If you should come northward, you will find a letter for you in the post office of this city."

Then he added a paragraph which only the most prejudiced can think
he wrote as a part of a cover for secret plotting from the distance:

"The equality of Jefferson and Burr excites great speculation and
much anxiety. I believe that all will be well, and that Jefferson will be our
President."

On the day the Federalists finally agreed to the election of Jefferson
as President, Burr sent the couple on their way southward with letters of
introduction. He was now not only certain to be Vice-President but if tradition was maintained, as Adams and Jefferson had done, he might expect
to succeed to the Presidency. His children could count on cordial reception as they traveled. In Philadelphia they must see Charles Biddle, his
lifelong friend. In Wilmington, Delaware, he wanted them to see "Cesar
Rodney . . . a very respectable young man." His feeling about young Rodney at the time was reciprocated by Rodney who had recently written that

"I think Col. Burr deserves immortal honor for the noble part he has acted on this occasion." Burr certainly then could not look forward to the fact that Caesar Rodney's father, Thomas, as a Jeffersonian judge in Mississippi, would give him rough treatment in his court. He wanted the young Alstons to meet in Delaware also "the venerable Dickenson" apparently John Dickinson, known as "the penman of the Revolution." And in Baltimore he wanted them to call immediately on Mrs. Smith. Though the name is a common one, apparently he meant Mrs. Samuel Smith whose husband had published for him his early firm rejection of Federalist moves supposedly in his behalf. He promised to meet the honeymooners in Baltimore.

In Washington, on March 4, Theo and Joseph watched the ceremonies in the Senate when the significant trio of President Jefferson, Chief Justice Marshall (only recently appointed by the departing Adams), and Vice-President Burr stood together. The oaths of the new officials were given and taken in decorum. Yet they were a trio of distrust. Jefferson hated and feared Marshall as Federalist opponent in Virginia. Now he resented him as symbol of a clear Federalist purpose to perpetuate itself in the judiciary, regardless of changes the electorate might make in the legislative and executive branches of the government. Not a single republican had ever been appointed as a Federal judge. And now more Federalist judges, the "midnight judges" as republicans were calling them, had been added on the night before. On his side, Marshall had expressed the opinion, never to be changed, that the man who had written the Mazzei letter was not capable of truth.

As to Burr, Jefferson's expressed opinions extended from the fulsome to the fearful. He was, as the Virginian had written after their election in the winter before, one of those men of talent, integrity, name, and disposition whom he wanted about him to "inspire unbounded confidence in the public mind." Yet the suspicions were not erased which he had more recently noted in his *Anas*. In addition, and of longer standing, was his knowledge that Burr had distrusted him and his Virginia lieutenants as a result of their actions in 1792 and 1796. None are so suspicious as the suspected and Jefferson was no exception to that rule. Finally, at almost fifty-eight, Jefferson evidently saw Burr, just turned forty-five, as a man whose ascent might abort the plans for a Virginia succession in the Presidency.

As an imaginative historian Schachner wrote that Burr on this occasion watched the scene "with somber eyes and inscrutable thoughts." He had made no secret of his suspicions of possible perfidy about Virginians in earlier elections. He must have known now that some Jeffersonians doubted his loyalty in the tie fiasco. He may have been at this moment a disappointed plotter. It requires no imagination, however, to be sure that at the inauguration he impeccably played his role. First to arrive in the chamber of the Capitol, which was disparagingly called the "Oven," he had gracefully moved to give Jefferson the first place of honor when he arrived. Perhaps he was inscrutable. So in deportment were all three of these men who would be later the chief figures in the greatest American trial.

Jefferson's admiring friend and the wife of his new journalistic protégé, Mrs. Samuel Harrison Smith, described the occasion. He delivered his address, she wrote, in "so low a tone that few heard it." It was an address which, if few heard it, has been much remembered. Those who could hear listened to words which were pertinent not merely to history but to themselves. Some who had feared Jefferson as an atheist must have been astounded as well as reassured by his profuse profession of faith "acknowledging and adoring an overruling Providence, which, by all its dispensations, proves that it delights in the happiness of man here, and his greater happiness hereafter."

Another phrase caught most attention. The bitterness of the election and then the fight in the House had not abated. Republicans were already muttering about the action the night before when Adams, now ostentatiously absent, signed by lamplight the appointments of many Federalists to office, chiefly new judges for whom the expiring Federalist Congress had provided life tenure.

Still in his almost whispering voice the new President pronounced, "We are all republicans; we are all federalists."

Some of both political persuasions were astounded. Those Federalists who, like Hamilton, had regarded the new President as a "fanatic in politics" could not have been quite reassured. Some of the republican faithful, crowding to Washington in hope of reward, must have wondered if this total embrace verified the rumors they had been hearing of such a deal as Congressman Bayard later swore had been made: that except for the highest posts Federalist officeholders would not be removed for political reasons.

There was no evidence that Burr was disturbed though he later wryly repeated the sentence to his son-in-law. It was a joyful occasion for the victors. Pretty legends were made about the day such as the one about the unpretentious President riding alone to the Capitol and hitching his horse to a post as he went in to become chief executive of the nation. Actually, of course, he had only walked the little way from Conrad's boardinghouse, owned by Burr's friend Law. Probably visiting Law at this time, Burr must also have walked to the half-finished Capitol. Certainly there was about him no suggestion of an unruly and relentless Man on Horseback. He fitted snugly into the pattern of the new party in power. Within the week the Vice-President indicated his confidence in his place and in the friendship of other republicans, particularly the Livingstons. With Chancellor Livingston, the head of that powerful family who was going to France as Minister, he made arrangements for Nathalie and Madame Sénat to sail on his ship. In addition to such news he wrote Theo: "Would Mr. Alston be willing to go as secretary to Chancellor Livingston?"

Certainly the new President and Vice-President were contrasting figures. Citizens, before foreign envoys did, were already commenting on Jefferson's plain, even frayed and soiled dress. Without ostentation Burr was a figure of fashion. The contrast between them was also pointed in the quarters the New Yorker maintained during the sessions of the Senate. The Washington correspondent of the *Gazette of the United States* of Philadelphia, strongly pro-Federalist, wrote: "Instead of lodging and boarding (as Mr. Jefferson did when Vice-President) at an Inn, he [Burr] has taken a handsome suite of rooms and lives in the style of a perfect gentleman."

Burr himself described his Washington situation during the first session of the Senate over which he presided. "I live at Mr. Law's, not nominally but in fact. Mrs. Madison is distant one mile. Anne Payne is a great belle. Miss Nicholson ditto, but more retired; frequently, however, at Mrs. Law's." This set the Vice-President in a lively society. Anne Payne was Mrs. Madison's pretty sister. And Miss Nicholson was the young woman who had suggested or charged that the Vice-President had forced his daughter to marry Alston. Perhaps she seemed only "more retired" with Burr because of that.

Certainly the household of his old friend Law was a lively one. Since Burr visited him before on his way to Monticello in 1795, Law, described as eccentric perhaps because he was poet as well as land speculator, had built a new house at the corner of New Jersey Avenue and C Street. Eliza Law, Martha Washington's granddaughter, was presiding over it then though rumors about her euphemistically stated that "she loved the world and its admiration too much." She and Law were to separate in 1804 in the midst of scandalous reports of the lady's behavior with handsome military men. Law then denied any improprieties on the part of the lady and was reported to have provided for her at the rate of fifteen thousand dollars a year—three times the salary of the Vice-President. Certainly it was a delightful company even if Burr's Theodosia did later indicate a fastidiousness about its most romanticized member.

"Mrs. Madison and myself have made an exchange of visits today," Theo wrote on a visit to Washington. "She is still pretty; but oh, that unfortunate propensity to snuff-taking."

Dolley seemed a glamorous figure in Washington then—possibly too glamorous beside austere little Secretary of State Madison. The elegant Dolley and her husband, whom Washington Irving was soon to describe as "a withered little apple john," had not been able quickly to find quarters in the favored and congested area around the Capitol. So when Jefferson moved into the cavernous President's House, in which Abigail Adams had found it difficult to keep warm, he invited them to stay with him.

However plain his clothes may have been, he had no plans for parsimony in the White House. His $25,000 salary quintupled his Vice-Presidential income. Still he was deeper in debt than ever. He had hardly been inaugurated, however, before he sought a chef who would add perfection to his cuisine. He reached high. His statesmanship and his epicureanism were both testified to by Don Carlos Martínez d'Yrujo, Spanish Minister to the United States. Yrujo had married the daughter of Democratic Governor McKean of Pennsylvania who was then sweeping Federalists out of jobs to make places for republicans like Jefferson's man Beckley.

Only a little over a week after his inauguration Jefferson received a letter from d'Yrujo, who preferred Philadelphia to the callow capital on the Potomac. He told the President that "in my way I have conversed with tyrians and troyans, high and low; and all to a man consider your exaltation as the triumph of merit and virtu; your speech, which could not be easily heard in the room of the Senate, is making great noise and many conversations without doors."

Then he got down to the specific business which Jefferson had entrusted to him as a friend: the matter of a chef for the President's House. He had tried to lure away the cook of William Bingham, the richest man in America and husband of the greatest hostess, Anne Willing Bingham, who was soon to die as a result of social exertions too soon after bearing a child. The cook would be glad to go to Jefferson, Yrujo reported, but Bingham owed him eight hundred dollars in wages and he feared he would "lose every farthing if he was to leave him."

In the absence of such a chef Dolley did not have to do the cooking. There were plenty of black hands to do that. Eleven servants had been brought from Monticello. The presence of the plump wife of the Secretary of State added warmth to Jefferson's establishment. Also, in this age of easy slander, rumors spread that Jefferson's interest in boarding the Madisons was based on an undue familiarity with Dolley. Evidently the gossip was so widespread that Jefferson's friends heard it in Virginia and he felt it necessary to denounce it to such an intimate as St. George Tucker, stepfather of his legislative leader young John Randolph of Roanoke.

"I thought my age and ordinary demeanor," the President wrote, "would have prevented any suggestions in that form, from the improbability of their obtaining belief . . . I believe all persons concerned are too conscious of innocence to feel the burden."

His burden seemed greater when the Madisons found a house. Jefferson's daughters were not able to leave their families in Virginia. On May 28 he wrote his daughter Martha: "Mrs. Madison left us two days ago to commence housekeeping, so that Capt Lewis and myself are left like two mice in a church."

The big house must have been lonely, though sometimes it seemed besieged by republicans panting for office. Meriwether Lewis' appointment had not been a political one. Jefferson had known him and his people long as Albemarle County neighbors. The young man had made strong appeal to Jefferson when Western exploration had been planned in 1792 and then withered as a French adventure which Jefferson abandoned. Since then Lewis had served in the army where his record for honesty and industry had been noted though once he had had to face a court-martial on a charge that he had insulted and threatened to kill a fellow officer in a duel. He had been acquitted with honor, despite evidence of his easy anger. He had shown skill in intelligence work on the frontier. When Jefferson, before he was inaugurated, offered him the position as his secretary, Lewis, aged twenty-six, was serving under General Wilkinson, whose disloyalty to the country he served had already been suspected.

In selecting a secretary Jefferson wrote the young man, "I thought it important to respect not only his capacity to aid in the private concerns of the household, but also to contribute to the mass of information which it is interesting to the administration to acquire. Your knowledge of the Western country, of the Army and of all its interests and relations had rendered it desirable for public as well as private purposes that you should be engaged in that office."

The position paid only five hundred dollars a year, but Lewis could live in the executive mansion and keep his military rank. Others wanted the job, Jefferson told him, but, he would hold it open until he heard from him. Jefferson wrote on February 23. The long, sinewy Lewis, then en route to Detroit, received it at Pittsburgh. Quickly he obtained leave of absence from Wilkinson who at the moment was eager to do a service for the new President. Lewis moved swiftly and was in Washington about the time of the inauguration. When the President moved into the executive mansion, in March 1801, he went along.

Only legend—or fiction—suggests that Lewis met Theodosia in Washington then or later. Obviously he met Burr, who was a man careful to meet subordinates with grace. Moreover, in the White House, Jefferson noticed, as he said later, the moodiness which sometimes marked his aide. He expected that, the President wrote, from knowledge of the Lewis family. Definitely Meriwether was a mercurial young man, sometimes morose. But he understood the tasks of governmental housekeeping. He was qualified to take on a smooth job or a rough one. Neither he nor Jefferson were mice, however empty the great house about them seemed to be.

3.

Precarious Pinnacle

Reluctantly, on March 18, 1801, Vice-President Burr finally gave up plans to follow the Alstons south and headed for New York and the political hustings there. He had contentedly completed such business as he could with the new President, who looked like a carelessly dressed Virginia farmer in the huge, half-empty house in which he had only the company of Meriwether Lewis. Jefferson sometimes appeared vague in the firm possession of his new power. Burr had undertaken to be specific with him. With two representatives of the Livingston family in Congress, and with Gallatin, he had drawn up a list of New Yorkers whom they felt were entitled to rewards. Now he set off for New York to help old Governor Clinton who was vigorously opposed for re-election by the candidate of Hamilton.

The melting snows and the early spring rains made it a tempestuous journey. With his servants and horses Burr arrived at the Susquehanna River to find the stream so swollen that the ferryman pronounced it impossible to pass with horses and unsafe to attempt it. Burr was impatient.

"By the logic of money and Brandy," he wrote Theodosia, "I persuaded him to attempt it. We embarked; the wind was, indeed, too mighty for us, and we drove on the rocks; but the boat did not bilge or fill, as in all reason it ought to have done. I left Alexis and Harry to work out their way; got my precious carcass transported in a skiff, and went on in a stage."

The help of all Democrats was needed in this election in which Clinton was seeking his seventh term. Opposed to him Hamilton presented thirty-seven-year-old Stephen Van Rensselaer. He was one of the foremost men in the state in wealth and social prominence. Furthermore, he had married a Schuyler daughter. Here were embroiled again the three powerful families; Schuyler, Clinton, and Livingston—and the lone man Burr.

"Hamilton," the Vice-President wrote, "works day and night with the most intemperate and outrageous zeal, but I think wholly without effect." It turned out that Burr was right. Still he might not have joined in the Democratic celebration if he had known that a month before the election, which began on April 28, the Clintons had begun a determined campaign to destroy him. On March 24 Samuel Osgood, too briefly described by one Burr biographer as a "Clinton henchman," had written Madison asking for a job himself, and opposing the appointment of any friends of Burr. Their republicanism, said this associate of Burr on the board of the Bank of the Manhattan Company, "has been and still is questioned by many." Only Clintonites, he said, should be given Federal jobs, as they would soon be getting all the state ones.

Osgood was an old acquaintance of Jefferson's. Indeed, as far back as 1785 when the President was Minister in Paris, he had written this gentleman, then a member of the board of the Treasury, about his tangled finances as a diplomat. They had served together in Washington's Cabinet when Osgood was Postmaster General. He was no mere Clinton henchman but by a marital connection a member of the family. As a result of this letter he secured the first of two positions which Jefferson gave him. It may have been as a result of this word to Madison also that Jefferson sent to Governor Clinton the list of those men Burr had proposed as deserving political reward. Few of them survived the Clinton scrutiny. Almost like a bone thrown to a dog, John Swartwout, one of three brothers who were ardent Burr men, was made U. S. Marshal. But the name of Matthew L. Davis, whose appointment as supervisor of the New York port Burr most wanted, was disregarded. As he watched Livingstons and Clinton supporters almost gorged with reward, Burr grew restive. With some sharpness in June he wrote to Gallatin. "Strange reports are here in circulation respecting secret machinations against Davis. . . . He has already waived a very lucrative employment in expectation of this appointment. . . . The opposition to him, if any, must proceed from improper motives, as no man dare openly avow an opinion hostile to him."

Gallatin agreed as to the merits of Davis, but he could give no assurances as to his appointment. Jefferson was playing his patronage cards close to his chest. He was not indulging in any such sweep-out of job holders under former administrations as Federalists had feared. Indeed, more Democrats (as republicans were more and more being called) than

Davis and associates were muttering about Presidential ingratitude in leaving Federalists in jobs Democrats wanted. The President, in his first days in office, did engage in some bold favor, offensive to Federalists, as when he offered to bring "atheistic" Tom Paine, who had damned Washington, home from France on a battleship. Some wondered, however, why he had no reward for the faithful Beckley whose name was less a flag to fanatics. Surely the President could not forget that this able agent had brought him to the endorsement of Paine's *Rights of Man* which had first put him forward in the popular mind as the leader of the anti-Federalists. Furthermore, many recalled that Beckley, in his pamphlets in 1796 and 1800, had been, in effect, the President's first biographer in arraying the facts of his life against Federalist falsehoods. Admittedly the old Clerk had been pretty rough on the Federalists, particularly some of those who preached politics from pulpits. One explanation which went around was that if the President promptly gave Beckley an important post, it would seem to confirm the suspicion that he had been responsible for the Beckley-Callender revelation about Hamilton in the Reynolds affair.

The President was not forgetting Beckley. At this time evidently both he and Beckley were remembering Congressman Smith of South Carolina. Smith, an *Anas* note in 1797 said, had been appointed Minister to Portugal by Adams for his Federalist services. One item in that service had been the Congressman's action that same year in getting Beckley ejected from his position of Clerk of the House. Smith had enjoyed himself in this foreign post, entertaining lavishly and working smoothly with British diplomats. Some thought he moved too smoothly among elegant Britishers. Indeed, Commodore Barry of the Navy, visiting Lisbon, had described Smith as "the damndest Englishman he had met." He had sometimes seemed that way in Congress to republicans. Worse than that, Smith in his Congressional days had charged that Jefferson had been the author of a system of detraction which his press had sparked. In his inaugural mood of conciliation Mr. Jefferson was not firing Federalists because they were Federalists. But quickly "for reasons of economy," he decided to abolish the Portuguese post. Smith was not fired as, in effect, Beckley had been, but he was out—and forever out so far as national position was concerned.

Another situation involving Jefferson and Beckley could not be so deftly handled. As a man in trouble Callender required early attention. His prison term was expiring, but he could not go free until his two-hundred-dollar fine was paid. Jefferson, as a part of his determined repudiation of the Alien and Sedition Laws, remitted the unexpired part of the sentence. Callender, however, was under the impression that the President had promised to remit the fine, too. There was confusion about this. Callender himself finally scraped up the money with which to pay it. Furthermore, he piled up indignation in the process. He was in debt for the care of his children in Philadelphia; and Leiper, with whom they were staying, he said, was growing cool waiting for his money. In his destitute situation, he wrote, he had fled from ridicule in Richmond to Petersburg. From there, on April 27, 1801, he exploded to Madison.

It had been seven weeks since he had "a written message from Mr. Jefferson with a solemn assurance that he 'would not lose one moment' in remitting my fine." On the basis of this Callender had written Leiper that he would send him "this money on the part of the boys." Now, however, he wrote Madison, he had had to tell the Philadelphian: "Mr. Jefferson has not returned one shilling of my fine. I now begin to know what Ingratitude is."

He had, he said, written a letter to the President's cousin and agent George Jefferson in Richmond which should "have reached the heart of a millstone. I might as well have addressed a letter to Lot's wife." Others had intervened. Nothing happened. "I had no more idea of such mean usage than that mountains were to dance a minuet." He summed up his suspicions as follows: ". . . I have gone such lengths to serve the party, that I believe your friend designs to discountenance and sacrifice me, as a kind of scapegoat to political *decorum* as a kind of compromise to federal feelings."

Callender, however, was ready to be appeased. His hopes for changes in office which might involve him were lifted by the dismissal of the Federalist Marshal David Meade Randolph. Actually the final decision to remove Randolph was made four days after Jefferson came to power and more than a week before Callender was pardoned. Randolph was replaced by Joseph Scott, Jr., a fifty-eight-year-old Revolutionary veteran who had not enjoyed "the advantages of a liberal education" and with a constitution impaired by war service. He had very little property and a disabled arm.

Scott needed the job and Callender needed one too. The postmastership at Richmond (worth about fifteen hundred dollars a year) was held by a Federalist editor. Callender sought the job through Madison who found it difficult to deal with a man "whose imaginations and passions

have been so fermented." The Secretary of State wrote to Monroe, then
Governor of Virginia: "Do you know too, that besides his other passions,
he is under the tyranny of love. The object of his flame is in Richmond.
I did not ask her name; but presume her to be young and beautiful, in
his eyes at least, and in a sphere above him. He has flattered himself into
a persuasion that the emoluments and reputation of a post-office would
obtain her in marriage. Of these recommendations, however, he is sent
back in despair."

By May 26 Jefferson was writing Monroe about the matter. He
wanted to avoid "giving room for specious criticism." He thought Congress might well indemnify all sufferers under the sedition act. He believed that David Randolph, out of spite or because he had pocketed the
fine and was unable to refund it, was causing delays in repayment of the
fine. Evidently there was some question about Randolph's accounts.
Nearly four years after he was fired, he was, "with due humility," appealing to Jefferson to rescue him from "unjust approbrium." When he
was removed, he wrote, he "felt no emotion other than an ardent desire of
evincing to the world and to my friends, that I had in no instance betrayed the confidence of your predecessors, or abused the trusts which
belonged to that highly responsible office." He mentioned the President's
former "affability" toward him. He spoke to Jefferson's "own high sense of
honor, and sacred regard for character."

Whatever may have been the finagling about the fine, Jefferson, in
May 1801, wanted this irritant to the political writer promptly removed.
He told Monroe: "To take from Callender particularly all room for com-
plaint I think with you we had better refund his fine by private contri-
butions. I enclose you an order on Gibson and Jefferson for 50 D. which
I believe is one fourth of the whole sum."

This letter had scarcely been dispatched before the angry Callender
arrived in Washington. He avoided the White House; but the President,
"understanding he was in distress," sent his young aide Meriwether Lewis
with fifty dollars to see the writer. Lewis was directed to inform him that
"we were making inqueries as to his fine which would take a little time,
and less he should suffer in the meantime I sent him &c."

Only Jefferson told about the meeting of Lewis with the prison-pallid
journalist furious in frustration. The Captain had met some rough custom-
ers on the frontier. Still he had probably never encountered such a man
as this one. Callender, though destitute and fifty years old, acted like no

whimpering beggar. In perhaps wrongheaded righteousness he evidently regarded himself as a fighter in the vanguard for the rights of man—ready to fight for his own rights as well. Before the muscular Lewis, Callender though flabby, possibly sodden, was not intimidated.

Jefferson wrote Monroe: "His language to Captain Lewis was very high toned. He intimated that he was in possession of things which he could and would make use of in a certain case: that he received the 50 D. not as a charity but as a due, in fact as hush money; that I knew what he expected, viz. a certain office, and more to this effect. Such a misconstruction of my charities puts an end to them forever. . . . He knows nothing of me which I am not willing to declare to the world myself. . . . I gave to him from time to time such aids as I could afford, merely as a man of genius suffering under persecution, and not as a writer in our politics. It is long since I wished he would cease writing on them, as doing more harm than good."

Monroe evidently did not like the look of the business. As he saw it, Lewis had paid what would be interpreted as blackmail. On June 1 the Governor wrote: "It is to be regretted that Capt. Lewis paid the money after the intimation of the payer of his views &c. It will be well to get all letters however unimportant from him. . . . Your resolution to terminate all communication with him is wise, yet it will be well to prevent even a serpent doing one an injury."

The angry editor disappeared. The midsummer heat descended. Breezes from the Potomac brought mosquitoes from the fens beside it. The same miasmas Burr dreaded for Theodosia in the South Carolina low country slipped up from the boggy river rim. Jefferson was lonely in the "great stone house, big enough for two emperors, one pope and the grand lama into the bargain" as he described it. Down in Virginia his daughter Mary worried about "the unsafe and solitary manner in which you sleep upstairs" in the vast house. The sprawling city of few mansions and many slave pens was already then as the patronizing Thomas Moore later described it:

> The medley mass of pride and misery
> Of whips and charters, manacles and rights
> Of slaving blacks and democratic whites.

And in the heat, it was in the summer of 1801 "this desert city," forlorn as the tide of casual population rolled away, which Washington Irving found. Jefferson got away in July to the fresh air and high breezes of Monticello. To his irritation, not even there was his philosophic solitude undisturbed.

In the persisting heat of late summer, the disregarded Davis came down the rough road to the great house in Albemarle. He set out against Burr's advice. In Washington, Gallatin, now Secretary of the Treasury, also tried to persuade him not to go. However, Gallatin gave the job seeker a letter to Jefferson in which he lamented the "general spirit of persecution" among the Democrats in New York. At the same time Gallatin sent by post a long, private, and significant letter to the President which is revealing as to Jefferson's plans and purposes then.

There were two points, Gallatin said in this letter of September 14, 1801, "on which I wish Republicans throughout the Union would make up their minds." By "Republicans throughout the Union" the Pennsylvanian clearly meant their chief at Monticello.

"Do they eventually mean not to support Burr as your successor, when you shall think fit to retire? Do they mean not to support him at next election for Vice-President?"

Gallatin was writing before change was made in the provision of the Constitution which had made a Presidential tie possible. That would soon be changed. Still at this time he pointed risks to the President. He presumed that in the next election Jefferson would run again. He thought Madison would be preferable as Vice-President, but two Virginians could not be Constitutionally chosen. So "it seems to me that there are but two ways, either to support Burr once more, or to give only one vote for President, scattering our votes for the other person to be voted for. If we do the first, we run, on the one hand the risk of the Federal Party making Burr President, and we seem, on the other, to give him an additional pledge of being supported hereafter by the Republicans for that office."

Then Gallatin came back to the seemingly small immediate problem of Davis.

"I said before that I was led to that train of ideas by Davis's personal application," he went on, "although in writing to you by him I said, as I sincerely believe, he would nor could be influenced by B. or any other person to do an improper act or anything which could hurt the general Republican principle, yet it is not to be doubted that, after all that has been said on the subject, his refusal will by Burr be considered as a declaration of war. The Federals have been busy. . . . There is hardly a man who meddles with politics in New York who does not believe that Davis's rejection is owing to Burr's recommendation."

Mr. Jefferson had considered all such contingencies. He had long had ideas about the Presidential succession. He did not amplify them to Gallatin now. Blandly he answered his close associate's letter: "Mr. Davis is now with me. He has not opened himself. When he does, I shall inform him that nothing is decided nor can be till we get together in Washington."

Burr wrote Jefferson about the Davis matter on September 4 and 23, and November 10. Though Jefferson noted the receipt of these letters, they disappeared from his papers. Indeed, between February 24, 1800, and January 25, 1802, Jefferson noted in his register of correspondence the receipt of fourteen letters from Burr which have been lost or destroyed. However, to Burr's letters in September and November 1801, he made one reply on November 18. "These letters," he told his Vice-President, "all relating to office, fall within the general rule which even the very first week of my being engaged in the administration obliged me to establish, to wit, that of not answering letters on office specifically, but leaving the answer to be found in what is done or not done on them. You will readily conceive into what scrapes one would get by saying *no*, either with or without reasons; by using a softer language, which might excite false hopes, or by saying *yes* prematurely; and, to take away all offense from this silent answer, it is necessary to adhere to it in every case rigidly, as well with bosom friends as strangers. . . .

"Accept assurances of my high respect and consideration."

Davis was never appointed though Gallatin described him at this time as "a man of talent, particularly quickness and correctness, suited for the office, of strict integrity, untainted reputation and pure republican principles." The holdover Federalist in the office Davis sought, one Rogers, was said to have been a Tory in the Revolution. Gallatin's father-in-law, the Commodore, was hot for Davis and called Rogers "a British Tory to say the least." Gallatin was not able to help Davis. And soon, with the backing of DeWitt Clinton, the Commodore applied to Jefferson for the post of supervisor of loans, though Gallatin was said to have opposed it. He got the job. Thenceforth his voice for Burr was silenced. Indeed, later he wrote a revised version of his part in the selection of Burr as Vice-Presidential candidate which presented the Colonel as not reluctant but demanding. Other mouths were being closed. Significantly the

job Burr had sought for Davis was later given to Osgood who had opposed the appointment of any of Burr's friends.

In his letters to Theo in this period, the Vice-President did not seem
like a greatly troubled man. Soon after he reached New York from Washington, he was reporting loneliness as his only trouble. His house was
"Dreary, solitary, comfortless. It was no longer home." It did not suffice
to have Nathalie and Madame Sénat there, though he seemed to be
clinging to Nathalie. He had been opposing earlier plans for their sailing
which had been made by his stepson J. B. Prevost, now a substantial lawyer in his own right. The ladies did not really want to go to France, Burr
thought. Evidently he did not want Nat to go. And he concurred in the
decision of the Alstons not to consider a post there. He was happy that
after a month in South Carolina they were planning a Northern tour,
though he questioned the wisdom of Alston's leaving his business for such
a trip. He was staying "in Broadway" and would not open Richmond Hill
until they came.

Their coming was a joy which he dramatized by opening wide the
doors and windows of the great house near the city. Also he made part of
their visit a pilgrimage to the western New York country in which he had
many dependable friends. They moved through the Genesee country on
the way to Niagara Falls. Burr was particularly pleased that they saw the
falls which he was soon to send his protégé Vanderlyn to paint. He was
glad they saw and much pleased Chief Brant whom Theodosia as a girl
had entertained. Burr enjoyed the friendship of the Indian with whom
he had recently been corresponding about the improvement of his people.
Brant sent Indian products to the Alstons after they visited him.

Almost certainly on this trip, too, the Alstons saw Burr's friends in
western development, Williamson and Morris. Williamson, in his efforts
to further immigration to the vast Pulteney properties, for which he was
agent, had built a substantial hotel at Geneva at the foot of Seneca Lake,
staffed it with trained European chefs and other personnel. He had laid
out roads, built bridges. He promoted horse races, provided a theater,
and published a local newspaper. All in all he spent sums varyingly
estimated at one half to one million dollars on promotion, including a nationally advertised fair which brought three thousand people across difficult roads to his town of Bath. Some of them, including Virginia gentry, it
was reported lost so much on a horse race that they had to stay. Others

came back again to buy lands. As a result of his exuberant promotion the wilderness could already provide comforts for such a couple as the Alstons.

Williamson's imaginative extravagance was in the next year to lose him his place with his English principals. His friendship for Burr was to last through greater, more disastrous adventures. Son of the greatest of the speculators, Morris, now serving in Congress, was a special Burr friend. The year before, the Colonel had described his close relations with him. On one of his journeys he wrote Theo, lamenting that he would be delayed in coming home.

"But our friend Thomas Morris," he told her, "has entreated in such terms that I would devote this day and night to certain subjects of the utmost moment to him, that I could not, without the appearance of un-kindness, refuse. He would, I know, at any time, devote a week or month, on like occasion to serve me."

The period of this Alston visit in the North and their journey to the falls, which Burr was to say Vanderlyn painted so well that the beholder of his picture could almost hear the roaring of the cataract, was on its surface an idyllic interlude for the Vice-President. Sadly he saw Theo go South again. He was much concerned about Nathalie when she set out in late September with Livingston's party on the long, perilous Atlantic crossing.

In politics in New York, however, he was reassured or lulled. With-out his initiative he was elected a member of the New York Constitu-tional Convention of this year from the County of Orange. And apparently to his surprise, he wrote Alston, he was chosen president of that assemblage. He was the picture of prestige as he presided over the con-vention. Later he was to make light of the occasion saying to Alston that he had not "expected that fifteen days would have been consumed in accomplishing the business of six hours."

Actually in those fifteen days, some historians have thought, he held the limelight while his opponents took the power. Some felt that he pre-sided over his final political emasculation in the state. The principal prod-uct of the convention was a definition of the powers of the Council of Appointments, which, with the Governor, controlled the patronage of the state in such fashion as to put it in control of the Clintons—notably young DeWitt who would bring a greater ruthlessness to politics than his uncle had ever shown. Burr, who had recently helped make George

Clinton Governor again, now presided over the doubling of Clinton power.

Danger could not always be foreseen. Despite his defeat in the gubernatorial election, Burr's rival Hamilton walked in elegance with his head and his hopes still high. He showed no depression, though the placating course which Jefferson had adopted toward the Federalists seemed to be working altogether too well. He got little response to attacks he made in the newspapers on the President's policies. Perhaps overextending himself financially, he was building a fine country seat to be called The Grange after the estate of the aristocratic Scottish family to which he clung despite the irregularity of his birth. It was to be a place where he could entertain the great and beautiful as Burr did at his precariously held Richmond Hill. Hamilton's personal trouble came like lightning striking.

On November 23, 1801, Burr wrote Theo of the death of young Philip Hamilton: "Shot in a duel with Eacker, the lawyer. Some dispute at a theatre, arising, as is said, out of politics. The story is variously related." Burr sent her newspaper stories giving "a concise summary of the facts, in fifteen sheets of paper, with comments, and moral and sentimental reflections." One such reflection at the time came from William Coleman who in the same month had become editor of Hamilton's organ, *The New York Evening Post*. He spoke of the "horrid custom" of dueling which "fashion has placed upon a footing" that nothing short of law could control. A detail of the encounter was that the same pistols were used as had been fired in Burr's duel with Church and which would be used again. To Hamilton's grief for his son was added the fact that the shock of Philip's death brought on the lifelong insanity of his sister Angelica, named after her lovely and charming aunt, Jefferson's old friend. Burr seemed casual about this tragedy. He proposed no change in the fashion. Hamilton was coming to the dark mood which he would describe a few months later, in February 1802, to Gouverneur Morris.

"Mine is an odd destiny," he said of his increasing political isolation. "Perhaps no man in the United States has sacrificed or done more for the present Constitution than myself; and contrary to all my anticipations of its fate, as you know from the very beginning, I am still laboring to prop the frail and worthless fabric. Yet I have the murmurs of its friends no less than the curses of its foes for my reward. What can I do better than withdraw from the scene? Every day proves to me more and more, that this American world was not made for me."

Burr had no such fated sense when the first session of the Democratic Congress under Jefferson convened on December 7, 1801. Indeed, the President's message, carried to the Capitol by Captain Lewis, suggested that this should be a happy time for everybody. In it Jefferson wrote of peace, prosperity, order, and liberty. There were few clouds in the sky: "The assurances, indeed, of friendly disposition, received from all the powers with whom we have principal relations, . . . inspired a confidence that our peace with them would not have been disturbed."

There were no wrongs that could not be righted. Indeed, on the day before the President's message was read, certainly with his approval, if not his insistence, the House righted one. It overwhelmingly elected Beckley to his old post. Burr undoubtedly was pleased by this. Beckley had been one of those who had never questioned his loyalty. During the tie fight in the House Beckley had presented a unique version of the roles of Hamilton and Burr in this crisis. Beckley had written to Gallatin on February 15, 1801, of "the movements of A. Hamilton in New York—his overtures to Col°. Burr disdainfully rejected by the latter." Possibly as Jefferson had written years before Beckley was "too credulous as to what he hears from others." Others may have been.

The Vice-President at this time of republican elation in Washington was certainly not aware of a correspondence between the President and James Cheetham. This recent English immigrant in the summer before had been set up by the Clintons as the editor of their new organ the *American Citizen* designed from the start for the defamation of Burr. Cheetham's background was much like that of Callender. An Englishman, he had like Callender been arrested, in 1793, in connection with radical activities. He was released for lack of evidence but when repression mounted to rioting in Manchester, in 1798, he was forced to move to America. He must have been more than the hatter he was said to have been. However, when he came to America he had written no such work against tyranny as that which recommended Callender to Jefferson and others as a persecuted genius and as one whose talents they might turn to the cause of the rights of man in the United States. Still, in New York, Cheetham found sympathizers. One of the first of these was said to have been Burr, who had aided other such refugees—some as tutors for Theodosia. The tradition is that Burr first suggested that he edit a paper but as the Clintons turned on Burr, Cheetham chose to go with them.

In the opening week of the Congress, Jefferson was receiving—and not repulsing—communications from Cheetham outlining plans for increasing attack on Burr. Much of the outlined journalistic strategy in detraction involved allegations that Burr had deliberately and stealthily tried to steal the Presidency in the tie fight. Jefferson had already noted gossip about this in the *Anas*, much of it incorrect. Cheetham wrote him on December 10, again on December 19, 1801. There may have been other communications. Perhaps as Schachner said, Jefferson receiving these "confused and wholly garbled accounts" of Burr's supposed efforts to supplant him in the Presidency and merely "silently filed them for future reference and reprisal." Still, as the campaign against Burr about which Cheetham had informed Jefferson in advance mounted, the President carefully wrote the editor in April 1802. "I shall be glad hereafter to receive your daily paper by post, as usual. . . . I shall not frank this to avoid post office curiosity, but pray you to add the postage to your bill."

Burr gave no impression of a man beset as 1801 drew toward its end. His chief desire seemed to be the happiness of Theodosia in South Carolina. He followed her with gifts: "You shall have apples, and nuts, and a cook, and lucerne seed." He had put in motion, he said, the whole French republic in the matter of a *femme de chambre*. The cook he described sounded at least as good as the one Yrujo had tried to steal for Mr. Jefferson from Mr. Bingham. *Monsieur le Cuisinier*, he wrote her, "is the best I ever had in the house." Superior to any he knew, he said, "for cakes, pastry, and jimcracks." He was of a mind to keep him himself. With him "you will be forever giving good dinners." And he added, irrelevantly as it seemed at the moment, "he has something of the manner and phisiognomy of Wood, your teacher." Neither then dreamed what this teacher Wood might be cooking up.

To Alston about the same time, the debonair Vice-President wrote a tongue-in-cheek letter mixing politics with his hope for a grandchild. He sent him a bill of lading for the things he had dispatched on the ship *Protectoress*. With it he enclosed a copy of the President's recent message to Congress in which along with peace he had spoken enthusiastically of population. Some merriment had been made over the President's report on the recent census showing great growth in the nation. In his report, the President had seemed to enjoin his fellow citizens to "the multiplication of men." Burr echoed the frivolity which greeted this Presidential utterance.

"One idea contained in this message," the Vice-President told his son-in-law, "is much applauded by our ladies. They unite in the opinion that the 'energies of the men ought to be principally employed in the multiplication of the human race,' and in this they promise an ardent and active co-operation. Thus, then, is established the point of universal coincidence in political opinion, and thus is verified the prophetic dictum, 'we are all republicans, we are all federalists.' I hope the fair of your state will equally testify their applause of this sentiment; and I enjoin it on you to manifest your patriotism and your attachment to the administration by 'exerting your energies' in the manner indicated."

Actually, though Burr did not know it, Alston and Theo had already carried out this injunction of the President and the Vice-President. Theo was four months pregnant at the time. Indeed, she had apparently conceived in the August before when she and her husband were visiting and traveling in the North, perhaps in the western country which her father loved so much.

Her condition may have been responsible for her absence from Charleston just before Christmas in 1801. Then the ship carrying the many things her father was sending her from New York arrived at the port. Apparently all were received safely, however, though Burr wondered how the cook and the maid he had sent with the cargo got along in the absence of the Alstons in a city strange to them. Theo in writing her father her thanks evidently spoke a little doubtfully about her ability to provide the hospitality expected of her among the South Carolina gentry.

"Mighty meek and humble we are grown," her father answered. "You really expect to do the honours of your house *equal* to &c. I know better. It will be one of the most cheerful and amiable houses in the United States."

And he added: "I am gratified that you do not start with splendour; to descend with dignity is rare."

VII.
CROSSFIRE
OF CALUMNY

1.

"Incurable Schism"

Western lands were an old passion with Vice-President Burr, ever exciting and appealing. So it was no wonder that in January 1802 he arranged his "affairs of *all kinds* for six months absence." He planned to preside over the Senate, go thence to South Carolina. And he added his heart was set on "running over the mountains with Mr. Alston in the spring." In his letters to Theo about his plans he added a sentence, however, which remains mysterious: "Yet you know that *a single letter may take me in a contrary direction,* and mar all my plans of pleasure."

Two weeks after he told his plans to Theo he was expressing concern about what was happening in the Southwest to which so many Americans were trekking. To Alston he wrote then: "It has for months past been asserted that Spain has ceded Louisiana and the Floridas to France; and it may, I believe be assumed as a fact. How do you account for the apathy of the public on this subject? To me the arrangement appears to be pregnant with evil for the United States. I wish you to think of it, and endeavor to excite attention to it through the newspapers."

Evidently at this time he did not feel free to excite interest in the matter through the President. Indeed at this time the West itself seemed "pregnant with evil" to Jefferson in terms of his own personal life. That region which had been a bright philosophical prospect suddenly seemed a dark threat to his happiness. He was no longer concerned about it in terms of great fossil bones found there or herds of wild horses roaming its ranges. He was appalled by the sudden probability that his brilliant but erratic son-in-law Randolph, "allured by the immensely profitable culture of cotton," might take Martha and her children to Mississippi.

Other people were going. Some guests at Monticello early this year were on their way. As early as 1792 one of his Dabney nieces had gone to Kentucky with her husband. Jefferson had been disturbed then only because their move required money from him which he could not well spare. His sister Lucy, Mrs. Charles Lilburn Lewis, would in 1808 make a "dreadful journey" to settlement there.

Jefferson undertook to exercise no veto of Randolph's plans. Indeed, he bought him a "beautiful blue Casimer, waterproof . . . as a traveling coat for his journey" of investigation about moving. Still the President drew an adverse description of the new country: "The distance 1500. miles of which 600. are through an uninhabited country, the weakness of that settlement, not more than 800 men, with a population of blacks equal to their own, and surrounded by 8000. Choctaw warriors."

Randolph did not go. Instead, turning from pioneering to politics, to the President's embarrassment, he narrowly succeeded in getting himself elected to Congress over one of Jefferson's most loyal supporters. There were dangers along the Potomac as well as the Mississippi. There could be ambuscades in Washington as in the wilderness. Vice-President Burr, in his letters to his daughter, seemed not aware of them or was unwilling to disturb her about them. Indeed, his letters to Theo were more sprightly than serious all his days. He wrote in early February, "We make a pleasant society here, so that one may get through the winter without ennui." Yet, already then, though he might not be bored, he could not have failed to see that efforts were being made to make his situation unpleasant if not untenable.

The year had hardly begun before his friend William P. Van Ness in New York wrote him that "the affair with Wood has assumed a very singular aspect." James Wood, a young Scot who looked prematurely aged, before Theo's marriage had been her tutor in mathematics and languages. After her wedding he had done some political writing for Burr. Now he had written a book, *The History of the Administration of John Adams*. Before Burr left New York he had read it in copy or proofs. He described it to Theo as "being principally low scurrility and illy told private anecdotes; with about 30 pages of high eulogium of A. B." He decided that the book, coming from his apparent protégé and viciously attacking Adams, would do more harm than good to himself and his party. He undertook to suppress it by buying up the edition. Now the "singular aspect" of the matter was that Cheetham of the *American Citizen* had somehow

EDMOND CHARLES GENET
By Ezra Ames.

GOVERNOR GEORGE CLINTON
By C.B.J. Fevret de Saint-Mémin.

DE WITT CLINTON
By C.B.J. Fevret de Saint-Mémin.

JAMES A. BAYARD, SR.
After a painting by Wertmuller.

MERIWETHER LEWIS
By C.B.J. Fevret de Saint-Mémin.

16

got a copy and was loudly charging that Burr had suppressed the book to curry favor with the Federalists.

Soon the same charge was directed at him in connection with votes he cast as Vice-President to break ties in the closely divided Senate over the repeal of the judiciary bill under which Adams had packed the courts with Federalist "midnight judges." Actually, Burr saved the administration plan when he broke a tie for it on a vote on its passage. His sin to his enemies was that subsequently he voted after another tie vote to recommit the bill for further study. The anti-Burr press lifted its hue and cry in the charge echoed later by Jefferson's eulogist Randall that "in this matter as presiding officer of the Senate Vice-President Burr coquetted with the Federalists, but had not the power if he had then the will to effectually aid them." Gouverneur Morris better understood the action from the Federalist point of view. Not long afterwards he wrote that there was "a moment when the Vice-President might have arrested the measure by his vote, and that vote would, I believe, have made him President at the next election; but there is a tide in the affairs of men which he suffered to go by."

Certainly efforts were being made within his own party to stir a tide against him. Friends and enemies were aware of it. A variety of politicians and personages were speaking of antagonistic reports about him apparently emanating from the President's House. Perhaps most revealing as to the situation and the feeling of Burr's friends about it at the time came from an unnamed lady, Mrs. ****, of New York. Her letter Burr saved among his papers. Fortunately it escaped the censorous editing by Davis of letters to Burr from ladies. This lady certainly did not feel discarded in ruin as his enemies were to charge was his fashion in affairs with the fair sex. She was angered by newspaper assaults upon him when she wrote him in Washington to recall to him "the impression I once flattered myself to have made on your memory." Her wrath at such articles, she said, subsided "when I consider that my anger can no more check their calumnies than the splendour of your reputation be clouded by their impotent attempts."

In erudite affection she wrote what may have been a prophecy or warning—or a portrait: "Tell me how you do, and how you pass your time. Taking lessons in Wisdom from your Minerva? or flying after the Atalanta's of Virginia, more swift than their celebrated racers? or, more probably, pouring over musty records; offering your time, your pleasures, your health, at the shrine of Fame; sacrificing your own good for that of the public; pursuing a chimera which ever has and ever will mock the grasp; for however the end may be crowned with success, the motives will be questioned, and that justice which has been refused to a Regulus, a Brutus, a Publius, who can hope for?"

Two weeks later Burr seemed almost deliberately to show his defiance for what he regarded as rag, tag, and bobtail republican editors snarling at his heels and the greater figures behind them. Federalists then annually celebrated the birthday of Washington whom they regarded as their patron and possession, never more precious than at this time in the capital captured by Democrats. Tricked or intriguing, the Vice-President appeared at the banquet honoring Washington whom he had no reason to remember with appreciation. At its conclusion he lifted his glass high in a toast.

"To the Union of all honest men!"

Democrats were startled at what Hamilton called this "strange apparition" at a Federalist feast. Both Burr's presence and his imputation puzzled some and angered others—including, it was said, "a certain great personage." Hamilton saw the situation with both delight and apprehension. There was, he wrote not long afterward, "certainly a most serious schism" between Jefferson and Burr—"the chief and his heir-apparent." He hailed it as "a schism absolutely incurable, because found in the hearts of both, in the rivalship of an insatiable and unprincipled ambition." A more bitter animosity, he thought, was already ripening between the partisans of the two men "than ever existed between the Federalists and the anti-Federalists."

As a man who hoped for the Democratic row he predicted, Hamilton went on cautiously about Burr: "Several men, of no inconsiderable importance among us, like the enterprising and adventurous character of this man, and hope to soar with him into power. Many more, through hatred of the chief, and through an impatience to recover the reins, are linking themselves to the new chief almost without perceiving it, and professing to have no other object than to make use of him; while he knows that he is making use of them. What this may end in, it is difficult to perceive."

Burr gave no indication that he had used the Federalist occasion to demonstrate that he could strike back, if necessary, or that he intended in any way to upset the Democratic apple cart. He wrote instead to Theo of a runaway of General Samuel Smith's carriage horses and the narrow escape of three Smith ladies and Mrs. Law. Indeed, on the day of the dinner his chief concern seemed to be the news that Nathalie had arrived at Orleans after a passage of twenty-six days. Her letters, he said, "are full of good sense, of acute observation, of levity, of gravity, and affection. No news of her mother." That news would be coming slowly.

The Vice-President passed on to his daughter the story of Nathalie's progress which she reported in letters which he described as "far superior to any of our diplomatic communications." Yet in the slow mails it came as a tantalizing tale.

"She is to travel," he wrote, "from Nantz to Paris (about four hundred and fifty miles) *with her maid and postillion only*: an enterprise which no woman in France under forty hath executed without shipwreck during the last hundred years. Yet Natalie will do it without injury and without suspicion. I have taught her to rely on *herself*, and I rely on her pride."

Then: "Natalie arrived in Paris . . . ; her mother not there; but numerous friends, who fatigue her with civilities. Her heart is in the United States."

He did not realize how true that was. Actually on the long voyage Nathalie had fallen in love with Thomas Sumter, Jr., going to France as Livingston's secretary—the post Burr had mentioned as a possibility for Alston. When mother and daughter actually met it was a dramatic occasion attended by tears of joy, then for the mother, tears of shock. The lady had built high plans or dreams about her returning child. She had anticipated correctly that she would be fascinatingly beautiful with perfect manners, with exotic charm which comes from a long sojourn in a foreign country. (". . . d'une beauté séduisante et de manières parfaites, avec ce charme exotique que donne un long séjour dans un pays étranger, un coeur non moins distingué que l'esprit et le visage. . . .") The girl was all she expected. But her hopes were broken. She had dreamed that she could arrange for Nathalie a marriage with a Frenchman of fine name and, if possible, great fortune, who would be able to aspire to everything when the King should remount his throne and arrange his court.

The Marquise's chagrin might have been greater had she known that Sumter's father, though honored as a signer of the Declaration of Independence and a Revolutionary War hero, was not aristocratic even by American standards. Young Sumter's grandfather had come to America as an indentured servant who became a miller and married a midwife. Nathalie's suitor, the Secretary of Legation, was son of General Thomas Sumter. Nathalie's mother would have been really shaken had she known more about the General. The guerrilla forces he had led in the Revolution were described as "a motley group of men clad in hunting shirts, deerskin breeches, Indian moccasins, and animal skin caps, whose weapons were anything from pitchforks to hunting knives." They must have looked like the forest equivalent of the mobs of the Terror. However, the General, who had left Virginia as a debtor, had in South Carolina found a rich widow. As an enthusiastic trader he extended his lands. Now, however, his fortunes were fluctuating. Payments of even small debts had to be extracted from him by lawsuits.

Still at Stateburg, which he had founded and pushed as a possible future capital of the state, a pleasant society flourished. It was located in the "High Hills of Santee" to which low-country aristocrats resorted for their health from the miasmic shores. Theo would be one of them when Nathalie came.

In Stateburg young Sumter had grown into a "handsome polished youth." He was not quite a youth when Nathalie fell in love with him. He was fourteen years older than she was. Also, years before he had sired two illegitimate children. They had been accepted into the family and bore its name. Nathalie, at nineteen, knew nothing of all this. Theo's marriage may have given her some romantic feeling about South Carolina. She fell in love under the stars of a wide sea. In France she made her declaration of independence from her mother's *ancien régime* ideas. Burr gave the marriage his transatlantic blessing. Now with both Theo and Nat married to South Carolinians he was going to spend much time there.

"Which is my favorite daughter," he wrote the bride in France, "I have not been able to decide."

He added a postscript to this letter which might have seemed another example of heresy to those who were questioning his democratic principles. He sent a message to Nat for her mother: "I am not at all surprised at her repugnance to your marriage with a democrat, the son of a rebel. She must hate above all things, democrats and rebels. But tell her, as doubtless you have told her a thousand times, that she is wrong; and that we are not all like your French democrats."

Some American democrats seemed increasingly dissimilar to each other. Yet if there was schism, there was dissemblance. Less than a month after Burr's startling toast he wrote to Alston: "I dine with the President about once a fortnight, and now and then meet the ministers in the street. They are all very busy: quite men of business. The Senate and the vice-president are content with each other, and move on with courtesy." That certainly was a broad and bland statement for the Vice-President to make about a Senate which now contained DeWitt Clinton.

Clinton had assumed the seat graciously abandoned for him by General Armstrong of the Livingston tribe. Senator William Plumer of New Hampshire, who kept a vivid diary in these times, drew contrasting portraits of the two New York antagonists. "Mr. Burr, the Vice-President," he wrote, "presides in the Senate with great ease, dignity & propriety. He preserves good order, silence—& decorum in debate—he confines the speaker to the point. He has excluded all spectators from the area of the Senate chamber except the members from the other House. A measure which contributes much to good order."

When a year later, in 1803, like changing partners in a dance, Clinton left the Senate and Armstrong came back, Plumer summed up his opinion of Clinton. "His absence will not be the object of regret to a single member of the Senate," he wrote. "He is a man of violent passions, of a bitter vindictive spirit,—unfeeling—insolent—haughty—and rough in his manners."

This was hardly an adequate portrait of Clinton. At this time he was only thirty-three but already ambitious to outmatch his uncle and ready to be ruthless in the process. He was a physical giant beside Burr, six feet tall and of such proportions as to justify the complimentary nickname of "Magnus Apollo." Coming into politics without the necessity of apprenticeship, he was overbearing in manner, preferring assault to intrigue in his operations. Yet he was to be a creative figure in the American story, man of expansive mind, patron of arts and letters. It was said of him, as some said of Burr, and others of Jefferson, that while his principles associated him with democrats, his tastes were those of aristocrats. Strangely, like Burr, he was to dislike and distrust Virginians. But at this point he provided alliance for Virginians in their joint feeling of the necessity to get Burr out of the way on the path to power in New York and America.

If Burr presided with ease and dignity, he did so with impatience, too. He was still anxious to get over the mountains with Alston, more eager to be with Theodosia at the time of her delivery. Politics could be put aside for that. Before Congress adjourned he was on his way to South Carolina with horses which drew the admiration of Jefferson's friend, John Taylor of Caroline, with whom he stopped on the way. Every prospect seemed promising there. Aaron Burr Alston was born on May 29, 1802. Theodosia, however, was much depleted. Less than a month after the child's birth, Burr brought them by boat to New York.

She had never seen the city so beautiful, she wrote Alston after a drive from Burr's town house to Richmond Hill. At the same time her letter indicated a passionate devotion to her husband which belied any suggestion that her marriage had not been one of love. "God knows," she told him, "how delighted I shall be when once again in your arms." Still, if Manhattan Island with its "variety of vivid greens," its "finely cultivated fields and gaudy gardens" looked beautiful to her, an ugly situation there confronted her father.

On May 26, when Burr in South Carolina had been anxiously awaiting the birth of his grandchild, Cheetham in New York had begun the stepped-up assault on Burr about which he had informed Jefferson in the winter before. He repeated the charges about the suppressed Wood book and the Washington's birthday toast as proving that Burr was trying to ingratiate himself with the Federalists. Then on July 16 he brought on his heavy artillery with an advertisement of a pamphlet entitled *A View of the Political Conduct of Aaron Burr*. In a venomous summation of Burr's career Cheetham charged that he had been a poor soldier, an undependable politician. His part in the republican victory of 1800 had been only "listless." But the violent assault, now supposedly documented for the first time, was that Burr had conspired to defeat Jefferson in the election and seize the Presidency for himself. The book was a mass of inaccuracies, innuendoes, and lies, but dressed in blatant dogmatism, it confused or convinced many readers. Evidently such political charges were not to be enough. Burr was going to have to be proved to be not merely an apostate but a monster as well. Something of the same sort was in store for Jefferson.

On July 16, when Cheetham announced his anti-Burr pamphlet, Jefferson in the White House in Washington was searching for Callender letters as he writhed under Callender attack. In New York, Burr, solicitous of Theodosia, had sent her and the boy upstate to the springs. Jefferson was much concerned about the frantic fears of his daughter Mary, herself in poor health, about the danger to her teething child from an epidemic of measles in Virginia. The President had been concerned about this daughter earlier in the year. She seemed to be withdrawing from the world which he told her he knew from experience led to "an antisocial and misanthropic state of mine." He himself, the President told her, had been in danger of being rendered "unfit for society, and uneasy when necessarily engaged in it" during the years between his retirement as Secretary of State and his election to the Vice-Presidency.

Now, however, respecting the fears of Mary whom he wanted to visit him at Monticello, on July 2, 1802, he ordered the removal from the mount of all children who might carry the contagion, including the children of Betty and Sally Hemings. On the same days on which he made these arrangements, he was writing Monroe about malignant charges Callender was making against him. He was, he wrote, "really mortified at the base ingratitude of Callender. It presents human nature in a hideous form." As a start, as Jefferson put it, the disappointed journalist had imputed to him responsibility for all the scurrilities in his writings about "genl. Washington, Mr. Adams and others." There was nothing particularly new about this. The President had been suspected of Freneau's and Bache's attacks on Washington, Duane's on Adams. But now as *particeps criminis* Callender was undertaking to prove that Jefferson had subsidized him in slander of Presidents under whom he had served. Jefferson's explanations to his friends that all his payments to Callender were only charity to the unfortunate were neither candid nor convincing. Monroe thought this excuse would not suffice. It was clear to Abigail Adams, as she wrote Jefferson later, that he had now been bitten by a serpent he had "cherished and warmed"—and used.

This serpent in Jefferson's Eden was only beginning to pour its poison. Increasingly he was carrying out the threats which he had made to outraged young Captain Lewis when he took the fifty dollars from him not as charity but as inadequate hush-money. There was no place for Callender now on the *Richmond Examiner*, distinguished for its friendship for Jefferson. As an ardent apostate, he was soon at work on the *Richmond Recorder,* a four-page Federalist weekly. There was a market for mounting attacks on the President who had recently swept away Presidential defenses against literary assault in the Alien and Sedition Laws. Soon the paper prospered. Randall reported that the *Recorder* "which was an obscure paper, scarcely known out of the city, rapidly attained a circulation throughout the United States!"

Old charges against Jefferson were repeated: of his cowardice in war, of his cheating a friend by paying off a sound money debt in depreciated currency. Jefferson might have shrugged these off. Readers may have found them stale. Haters of Jefferson asked for more and out of his own reservoir of hatred Callender provided it. Specifically and naming names, he told two scandalous stories neither new but never published before. The first was that as a young man between 1768, when he was a bachelor, and 1779, after he was married, Jefferson had made a series of improper advances on Elizabeth Moore Walker, wife of John Walker, close and trusting Virginia friend. The second, more unsavory Callender story was that the President had long maintained an amorous liaison with at least one of his slaves, the Sally Hemings who as a girl had accompanied Jefferson's youngest daughter to Paris.

The first story about Elizabeth Walker seemed improbable since the friendship of Jefferson and Walker continued long after the former's allegedly multiple improper advances on the latter's wife. Years passed before Walker made a statement that even after his marriage Jefferson "renewed his caresses [and] placed in Mrs. W! (sic) gown a paper tending to convince her of the innocence of promiscuous love." He stole into the "room where my wife was undressing or in bed." He "attempted to seize her on her way from her chamber—indecent in manner." He only learned of these things, Walker said, after Jefferson had gone to France. Then Walker's wife, in objecting to his naming Jefferson as an executor in his will, told him of the incidents. Whatever may have been the lady's reactions at the times of Jefferson's advances, she said she had remained silent then from fear that Walker might have become involved in a fatal encounter. Apparently her husband's indignation toward Jefferson was sharpened when Monroe, as Jefferson's closer friend, replaced Walker in the United States Senate in 1792. Whatever may have been the details of this affair, Jefferson, in referring to the charges of immorality first loosed by Callender, admitted guilt.

"You will perceive," he wrote Robert Smith, his Secretary of the Navy, "that I plead guilty to one of their charges, that when young and single I offered love to a handsome lady. I acknowledge its incorrectness [i.e., the incorrectness of his own behavior]. It is the only one founded in truth among all their allegations against me." Malone believed it virtually certain that he gave the offended Walker a statement wholly exculpating the lady's behavior. Still some attributed her long silence to something different from fear of danger to her husband.

Callender's other, uglier charge cannot possibly be proved false or true. Miscegenation did go on at Monticello, involving at least some of the young men, friends and relatives, who frequented the place. The observant Duc de La Rochefoucauld-Liancourt, who visited Jefferson's plantation in 1796, reported the presence of blue-eyed, blond slaves with no African features. In his recollections, Captain Edmund Bacon, long Jefferson's overseer and a continuing admirer, spoke about the matter. He gave special praise to young William Cabell Rives, later political leader and diplomat. He was always a very modest boy, Bacon said: "The other boys were too intimate with the Negro women to suit him." Also of Jefferson's emancipation of some slaves, he said, "He freed one girl some years before he died, and there was a great deal of talk about it. She was nearly as white as anybody and very beautiful. People said he freed her because she was his own daughter. She was not his daughter; she was ———'s daughter. I know that. I have seen him coming out of her room many a morning when I went up to Monticello very early. When she was nearly grown, by Mr. Jefferson's direction I paid her stage fare to Philadelphia and gave her fifty dollars. I have never seen her since and don't know what became of her. From the time she was large enough, she always worked in the cotton factory. She never did any hard work."

The slave Isaac in his dictated recollections indicated the prominence of the Hemingses in the Jefferson ménage. He not only spoke of Sally's beauty. Also he said, "Folks said that these Hemingses was old Mr. Wayles's children . . . Sally had a son named Madison, who learned to be a great fiddler." Evidently this was the Madison Hemings who in March 1873, giving his address as Pec Pec, Pike County, Ohio, published in the *Pike County Republican* of Waverly, Ohio, his recollections as a child of the President's by Sally.

Speaking confidently of himself as Jefferson's son born in 1805, Hemings said that his grandmother, Elizabeth or Betty Hemings, was the daughter of a full-blooded African slave woman belonging to John Wayles and a British Sea Captain Hemings. When Betty was born around 1735, the Sea Captain, acknowledging the child as his own, tried to purchase her from Wayles. Wayles refused, his putative grandson said, not from any compunction about separating mother and child "but he was restrained by the fact that just about that time amalgamation began, and the child was so great a curiosity that its owner desired to raise it himself that he might see its outcome." As the girl grew Captain Wayles became more than curious. When Mrs. Wayles died in 1748, shortly after the birth of her Martha who was to become Mrs. Jefferson, Hemings said, "she (Elizabeth) was taken by the widower Wayles as his concubine, by whom she had six children," including the Sally of Callender's tale. Betty Hemings was only thirteen at this time, evidently not too young for concubinage. (Virginia genealogists credit Betty with having twelve children "presumably" by four different fathers.)

Along with her mother, brothers, and sisters, Sally, in 1773, the year of her birth, became the property of Mrs. Jefferson by inheritance from her father, who was Sally's father, too. Then at fourteen Sally accompanied Mary Jefferson to Paris. Madison Hemings' story proceeds matter-of-factly: "Their stay (my mother and Maria's) was about eighteen months. But during that time my mother became Mr. Jefferson's concubine, and when he was called home she was *enciente* by him. He desired to bring my mother back to Virginia with him but she demurred. She was just beginning to understand the French language well, and in France she was free, while if she returned to Virginia she would be re-enslaved. So she refused to return with him. To induce her to do so he promised her extraordinary privileges, and made a solemn pledge that her children should be freed at the age of twenty-one years. In consequences of his promises, on which she implicitly relied, she returned with him to Virginia. Soon after their arrival, she gave birth to a child, of whom Thomas Jefferson was the father. It lived but a short time. She gave birth to four others, and Jefferson was the father of all of them. Their names were Beverley, Harriet, Madison (myself), and Eston—three sons and one daughter. We all became free agreeable to the treaty entered into by our parents before we were born."

Certainly it seems incredible that a sixteen-year-old slave girl could have exacted such a "treaty" from such a personage as the American Minister. Yet all the children were freed by Jefferson during his life or in his will except Beverley who, in 1822, apparently freed himself by running away. Sally was given her freedom in 1827. Her daughter Harriet, who ran away, possibly with Beverley in 1822, was later set free. And in his will Jefferson not only provided for the freedom of Madison and Eston when they reached twenty-one but "I humbly and earnestly request of the Legislature of Virginia a confirmation of the bequest of freedom to these servants, with permission to remain in this State, where their families and connections are. . . ."

Most scholars since have been as disdainful of this tale of Sally—

even of a black seraglio—as Jefferson's friends were outraged by Callender's blurt of it in 1802. Madison Hemings evidently believed what he said though it is doubtful that he himself wrote the published statement. As a result of casual, even secret, education at Monticello he only claimed at the time the statement was prepared that "now I can read and write." His attainment in life was that of a small-town carpenter. It is doubful that such a man would have used such a word as *enciente*. Still similar statements, accepted by scholars, as the recollections of Isaac and Bacon, were prepared by dictation. Furthermore, while not so elaborate as to dates and other facts, the Madison Hemings' statement corresponds remarkably with the scholarly genealogy of this slave family published in *Jefferson at Monticello*, edited by James A. Bear, Jr., curator of the Thomas Jefferson Memorial Foundation at Charlottesville, Virginia. If Madison's statement was faked, there must have been a remarkable Jefferson scholar operating in Pike County, Ohio, in 1873. As early as 1874 Parton, in his life of Jefferson, accepted the authenticity of the Ohio carpenter's belief in his story. He only dismissed it by saying that the "respectable Madison Henings (sic) . . . has been misinformed."

Parton went on: "The record of Mr. Jefferson's every day and hour, contained in his pocket memorandum books compared with the record of his slaves' birth, proves the impossibility of his having been the father of Madison Henings. So I am informed by Mr. Randall, who examined the record in the possession of the family. The father of those children was a near relative of the Jeffersons, who need not be named."

This mathematics of gestation upon which Randall and Parton depended (apparently first advanced as proof of Jefferson's innocence by his daughter Martha to her sons) has not gone unchallenged. In a carefully documented article in the *Journal of Negro History*, in April 1961, Pearl Graham came to the flat conclusion that Sally Hemings was Jefferson's concubine "for at least ten years, and probably more than twice this time." In the case of Madison particularly, she was sure that Jefferson was at Monticello just nine months before his birth in January 1805. The records bear her out. He was there from April 4 to May 11, 1804. This, however, was two years after Callender's recital and would suggest that no publicity shook Mr. Jefferson from stubbornness in miscegenation.

The supposition has grown that the man whom Parton described as "a near relative of the Jeffersons, who need not be named" was Peter Carr, a well-loved nephew of the President. He was said to be enamored of the woman who, though described as "Black Sal" and "Dusky Sally" by the impertinent, was fair-skinned. At first blush this seems quite plausible. In 1802, when Callender loosed his venom in print, Peter was thirty-two and Sally twenty-nine. Jefferson was fifty-nine. Yet at this time Peter was apparently happily married to a sister of Senator Samuel Smith and the father of legitimate offspring of his own.

Jefferson's granddaughter, Ellen Randolph Coolidge, however, wrote that the "general impression" was that all four of Sally's children were sired by another Jefferson nephew, Samuel Carr. She described this Carr brother as "the most notorious good-natured Turk that ever was master of a black seraglio kept at other men's expense."

Madison Hemings, said to have startled guests by his resemblance to Jefferson as he waited on Jefferson's table, made his statement when there was eagerness to believe it. In 1873 the furies about slavery were strong in the Reconstruction years. Long after the tale was injected into Federalist-republican politics it was picked up by abolitionists as an evidence of the evils of slavery even on such a plantation as Monticello. One such Alexander Ross, who claimed to be a personal friend of Abraham Lincoln, wrote that two of Jefferson's daughters "by an octoroon slave were taken to New Orleans, after Jefferson's death, and sold in the slave market at $1500 each to be used for unmentionable purposes. Both these unfortunate children of the author of the 'Declaration of Independence' were quite white, their eyes blue, and their hair long, soft and auburn in color. Both were highly educated and accomplished. The youngest daughter escaped from her master and committed suicide by drowning herself to escape the horrors of her position." The remarkable fact about this tale was that it was still accepted as true by a French philosopher, R. L. Bruckberger, in his book, *The Image of America*, published by the Viking Press in 1959.

Madison Hemings told no such tale. Beverley, he said, went to Washington as a white man and married into a white family of good circumstances. Harriet, "whose name I could give, but will not for predential (sic) reasons," also moved away and married a white man. Eston married a colored woman in Virginia and moved on to Ohio, thence to Wisconsin. Madison himself, he said, married a product of miscegenation like himself whose mother had been set free by her master-father, Stephen Hughes, of Albemarle County. They had thirteen children, one of whom as a Union soldier "died in the Andersonville prison pen."

Possibly this story has significance today only as it indicates the extremes to which political "debate" could descend in the early American republic—and not only in regard to Jefferson. Much as the behavior of Callender may have been entitled to the dismay, disapproval, and considerable disregard which it has received in history, the indisputable truth is that many were much pleased with his supposed revelations in 1802. Beside Jefferson's indignant friends, there were plenty who hoped to see punctured the philosophic pretensions of the President. The saint, they hoped, was stripped by snickers. Soon Callender's bitterness was turned into badinage. Those who regarded themselves as far above vulgarity found in the "vile tale" materials for amusement. Federalists certainly did not cancel their subscriptions when the *Portfolio*, leading literary magazine of the time, in October 1802, burst into bawdy lyrics to be sung to the tune of *Yankee Doodle*. Its lines, which have left generations of historians aghast, ran:

> *Of all the damsels on the green,*
> *On mountain, or in valley,*
> *A lass so luscious ne'er was seen*
> *As Monticellian Sally.*

> *Yankee doodle, who's the noodle?*
> *What wife were half so handy?*
> *To breed a flock, of slaves for stock,*
> *A blackamoor's the dandy.*

> *When press'd by load of state affairs,*
> *I seek to sport and dally,*
> *The sweetest solace of my cares*
> *Is in the lap of Sally.*

> *Yankee doodle, (etc.) . . . .*

> *What though she by the glands secretes;*
> *Must I stand shil-I-shall-I?*
> *Tuck'd up between a pair of sheets*
> *There's no perfume like Sally.*

> *Yankee doodle, (etc.) . . . .*

Possibly Jefferson's moral solemnity made even those who did not believe the stories ready to be amused at his expense. No comic touch was given to the equally dirty stories told about Burr. He pretended to no purity which could be ridiculed and so was attacked instead with a Puritan savagery. Disreputable as he may have been, Callender at least took responsibility for his tales, while Cheetham *et al.*, when going to the extremes of defamation in the case of Burr, generally put the worst charges on unsigned handbills. Burr's levity about sex even in his letters to Theodosia perhaps helped a belief that he might be guilty of abominations. His reputation in history has suffered not only at the hands of contemporary calumnists. His own friend Davis, when he wrote Burr's memoirs, gave sanctimonious support to the charge that Burr, who was moderate in all other things, was a master philanderer. Davis wrote piously that he had destroyed all letters to Burr which might injure any of the ladies who wrote them. Randall, who in eulogizing Jefferson felt it necessary to demonize Burr, snorted his doubts that there were any letters from "ladies." He wrote: "Burr's amours were generally low." At the same time he dismissed Callender's stories about Jefferson as "old gossip, exploded calumnies and base suspicions" put together by "a common blackguard." But even Randall grudgingly admitted that Callender was "well educated and possessed much coarse, vigorous ability." Cheetham had only bold coarseness to recommend him. His style was pretentious and verbose. In his vindictiveness he did not pretend to have any personal reason for the blows below the belt which he aimed at Burr. In a real sense he was a hired political assassin, certainly not a discarded friend.

Burr made no pretensions to the Puritanism of which he was the exotic product. As gay widower he never made any show of monasticism. Among his many witticisms, always dangerous in a politician, he was once supposed to have said, "when a lady does me the honor to name me as the father of her child, I trust I shall always be too gallant to show myself ungrateful for the favor." There was never anything in his life, however, to suggest the bestiality and brutality in sex which his enemies imputed to him. Concupiscent, he may have been, cruel he never was. Indeed, a fairer critic said of him that he was always a man of charity—"of the heart spontaneous, promiscuous, and usually misdirected."

Still, the Clinton-Cheetham company flung charges like offal: "His ABANDONED PROFLIGACY, and the NUMEROUS UNHAPPY WRETCHES who have fallen VICTIMS to this accomplished and but too successful DEBAUCHEE, have indeed been long known to those whom similar habits of vice, or the amiable offices of humanity have led to the wretched haunts of female prostitution." But the names of none of the supposed victims of his "SATIATED BRUTALITY" were given. Only the ugliest charge permits some scrutiny. That was that he was "the disgraceful debauchee who permitted an infamous prostitute to insult and embitter the dying moments of his injured wife."

Nothing is more clear in the record than Burr's tenderness and concern for his wife. Furthermore, though she had long been ill, her death when it came was unexpected and the then Senator was not present during her "dying moments." The Cheetham who attacked him in the service of the Clinton-Jefferson-Livingston alliance against him in the republican party can hardly be regarded as more respectable than the Callender whom Jefferson used before he himself was the subject of his venom.

Neither Jefferson nor Burr made any public answer to the attacks of Cheetham and Callender. Burr brought a libel suit against Cheetham whom he did not regard as a gentleman worthy of his challenge. Jefferson later stopped a legal action in Massachusetts which would have hung Callender's dirty linen up to public gaze again. In 1802 Jefferson remained much cloistered and Burr was apparently too confident. It was not, he wrote Alston, "worth while to write anything by way of comment or explanation" in response to the scurrilities of which he said DeWitt Clinton was the instigator.

Burr was subjected at this time not only to charges of sexual immorality. He was put also under financial pressures. Church, his onetime antagonist on the dueling field, and Hamilton were increasingly prominent in the affairs of the Bank of the Manhattan Company which Burr had created. The Vice-President, though a director, was engaged in complicated transactions with the bank. One, involving at least $120,000, was related to property in the Seventh Ward, including a mansion house—apparently Richmond Hill. He dealt with the bank and Secretary Gallatin in a transaction about Dutch guilders. On September 7, 1802, records of the bank show, Daniel Phoenix, onetime city treasurer, was elected a director "in place of Aaron Burr."

Yet almost at this time the Vice-President was writing to welcome Theo to Richmond Hill which he was readying for the reception of her "and encumbrances."

"We are all in the bustle of moving. Heighho! for Richmond Hill. What a pity you were not here, you do so love a bustle; and then you, and the brat, and the maid, and thirty trunks would add so charmingly to the confusion."

Soon, however, even Burr's exuberance was shaken by the illness of the returned Theodosia. She had been restless at the springs to which he sent her for her health. But she had hardly left the health resort before she was taken seriously ill. He had been over-optimistic about her recovery. Now he wrote that her complaint had continued from the period of her confinement. Three doctors were called into consultation about her debility and lack of appetite. Their proposal that she wean her baby only brought refusal and floods of tears. At last she did agree. But her worries grew about her husband. She feared he would be doomed to live with an invalid all his days. She clung to her boy, "If Heaven grant him but to live, I shall never repent what he has cost me." Fortunately colder weather had a happy effect upon her. Her father was able to send her back to Charleston in the same brig, the *Enterprise,* upon which they had come North in June. When news came of her safe arrival her father and the artist Vanderlyn, who was finishing his Niagara paintings, celebrated over a bottle of champagne. Good things remained in the world. Vanderlyn was also completing his portrait of Theodosia which he was sure would be "the best work I have ever done in America."

Then far-off an event occurred which stirred many Americans including the Vice-President, whose dreams of military glory had never faded. Suddenly, in October 1802, startling news came from Louisiana about which Burr earlier in the year had sensed a situation "pregnant with evil." The Spanish Intendant, Don Juan Ventura Morales, had closed the port of New Orleans to the passage of goods from the whole upriver West. Foreign occupation of the river mouth was the basis of ancient angers on the frontier. Spanish arms there had seemed like iron fingers at the throat of the West which might relax by Spanish whim or favor, or contract in arrogant strangulation. Report of its secret transfer to Napoleon's France had increased fears before the great gateway was shut.

The Intendant's action now surprised not only Jefferson's government but also his friend the Spanish Minister Yrujo, who insisted that the river had been closed without authority. Actually the French had pressed this move on Spain, preferring to take over with the Americans already shut up in the river. The long resentful West clamored more loudly for war. Jefferson minimized the belligerence of the transmountain country where so many of his friends lived. He gave chief responsibility for the war cries to the Federalists in the East. There was, however, no doubting the temper of men like Andrew Jackson. Kentuckians threatened to move against New Orleans and West Florida if the Federal government did not force the port open. Jackson was ready to move his frontier militiamen and cut "through the damned greasers to Mexico City."

Some on the seaboard shared such feelings. Burr kept a letter which he received not long after this from his friend Biddle, of Philadelphia. At this time Burr was doing all he could to advance Biddle's son James, who became a famous Commodore. Also Biddle had sent Burr the thanks of his cousin Mrs. James Wilkinson for his aid and friendship to the General who was now in the troubled West dealing with Indian tribes and, as was even then suspected, operating on the side with Spanish officials whose pensioner he was. Burr, Mrs. Wilkinson believed, had helped Wilkinson keep his high military post, perhaps with the help of Secretary of War Henry Dearborn who had also been a comrade in the famous Quebec campaign.

Biddle wrote in belligerency: "The business of New Orleans is much talked of here. In my opinion, and it is the opinion of many others, we should immediately take possession, and then treat about it. We have no business to make excuses for the conduct of the Spanish government, by saying that they gave no orders to treat us in this manner. For my own part I do not fear a war with France and Spain. We could do more injury to them than they could do to us. If we were at war with them, and Great Britain did not join us, we should have our ports filled with their seamen, and the coasts of France and Spain would soon swarm with our cruisers."

This was by no means a solitary view. Yet the Presidential message which Captain Lewis carried up to Congress when it convened on December 15, 1802, reflected no national indignation. All was well· "Another year has come around and finds us still blessed with peace and friendship abroad; law, order, and religion at home; good affection and harmony with our Indian neighbors; our burdens lightened, yet our income sufficient for the public wants, and the produce of the year great beyond example."

Jefferson hardly mentioned the shift of Louisiana from Spain to France or the closing of the port. He only cautiously admitted that these things might make "a change in the aspect of our foreign relations." So mild were his words that the eccentric John Randolph of Roanoke, until then his House leader, in disgust demanded the documents relating to the whole business. Fortunately for Jefferson he at this time received a very welcome document—a letter quoting Spanish authorities as saying piously that the Intendant at New Orleans had indeed acted without authority in closing the port. Jefferson sent it promptly to Congress on December 30. Tempers were cooled by the opening of the river. The danger that it might be closed again remained.

The French Minister sensed that many Americans were not satisfied. A veteran in international affairs, he was possibly an innocent in American politics. He thought that the pacific President was dangerously put into contrast with Burr who even in his largely impotent place in the Senate stood like a man of arms or, as Hamilton had briefly put it earlier in the year, an "enterprising and adventurous character."

"However timid Mr. Jefferson may be," M. Pinchon reported to Talleyrand on December 22, "and what price he may put on his specific policy, one cannot foresee precisely what his answer will be. . . . I find in general a bad temper as regards us, and I cannot help seeing that there is a tendency toward adopting an irrevocably hostile system. This circumstance will be decisive for Mr. Jefferson. If he acts feebly, he is lost among his partisans; it will be then time for Mr. Burr to show himself to advantage."

It would be interesting to know what was the reaction of Talleyrand who later indicated a hostility to Burr. Mr. Jefferson did not publicly act as if he were in a precarious position. Indeed, he appeared at this time more bookish than belligerent. He was working on plans for a library for Congress and would soon make his friend Beckley first Librarian of Congress. His feeling about the war spirit at home would soon be expressed in a letter to Monroe. Asking that old friend to go to France, he said such a mission was necessary because "the fever into which the western mind is thrown by the affair at N. Orleans stimulated by the mercantile, and generally federal interest threatens to overbear our peace."

This December was a crucial month for Burr as well as his country. On the day before Congress convened in Washington, a much smaller company met in New York. A committee, of which Church was a member, made a report to the board of directors of the Bank of the Manhattan Company showing the total indebtedness of the Vice-President to the bank as $98,036. It recommended:

"Considering the very liberal advances which have been made to Col. Burr, and the time which has been consumed in disposing of his various proposals, it is proper to avoid importunity, that he should be given to understand, that no further loan will be made to him on any security whatever, until his present debt be extinguished."

The resolution was adopted by the directors, including members of the Livingston and Schuyler clans, who at this time were planning to add a new member to their board. In effect he slipped his big frame into the chair which Burr had occupied. He was, of course, DeWitt Clinton.

In Washington as the new year began, Burr maintained the same establishment as in the past, only adding a chariot to his possessions, hoping that the Alstons might come and ride in it with him. He wanted to know Theo's plans. He himself was looking again beyond the mountains. "If you are not to go northward," he wrote, "it is not probable that I shall see you in some time, for I have thoughts of going on a tour through the western country, which, if executed, will consume the whole summer."

He still owned and meant to keep Richmond Hill. In his letters he seemed content. Possibly he smiled over one he received from John Taylor of Caroline who had so admired his horses.

"My time goes along tolerably enough one way or another," Taylor wrote him. "Fancy furnishes me with passions and amusements, and about one hundred dollars a year more than meets every want I have which money can buy."

That would never be the fortune of Burr—or Jefferson. Both confronted power from mortgaged mansions against which filth was thrown.

2.

"Tant Mieux"

On July 15, 1803, President Jefferson wrote Meriwether Lewis, who had left Washington ten days before on his great exploration of the West. Lewis had arrived that same day in Pittsburgh after a dusty journey through the back country. The President's news was important to Lewis. It meant that in the country to which he was going he could nowhere be considered a spy. Last night, the President told him, "we received the treaty from Paris ceding Louisiana according to the bounds to which France had a right." And two days later an event occurred about which apparently the President did not write his former secretary, much as that young man might have been expected to be interested in it. On July 17, in Richmond, the body of Callender was found in the muddy fringes of the James River.

The corpse lay in shallow water or, as one of the many who scorned the dead man said, "in congenial mud." A coroner's jury, quickly empaneled, found that while drunk he had drowned in three feet of water. The body was buried the same day in the Richmond Church Yard, though no record of the burial remains. Conjecture continued about the cause of his death. Ten days after he was drowned and buried, the *Richmond Examiner,* on which Callender had first worked in Virginia, took the view that the unfortunate man had killed himself. The *Examiner* had no reason to like Callender. He had turned upon it as well as Jefferson. Still this paper stated that he had sunk to depths of misery after being cheated by his last partner in journalism.

Slander was not silenced. Calumny could be immortal. It followed Lewis. To his successor in the President's House the President wrote:

"I have delayed writing you because my great regard for Captain Lewis made me unwilling to show a haste to fill his place before he was gone, and to counteract also a malignant and unfounded report that I was parting with him from dissatisfaction, a thing impossible from his conduct or my disposition toward him." Lewis certainly had then no feeling of rejection. He was feeling "much benefitted by the exercise the journey has given me, and can with pleasure announce, so far and *all is well*." He was not inconvenienced because he had left his dirk behind at the White House: "the knives that were made at Harper's ferry will answer my purposes equally as well and perhaps better." Also figuratively a President might use a dirk in Washington. Already Burr's friends were fearing it was driven in his back to the hilt.

Democratic celebrations over the Louisiana Purchase were to continue for months. Of one especially lively one at Stelle's Hotel in Washington the observant Federalist Senator Plumer noted: "After the President and Vice-President retired, this toast was given 'The President of the United States'—& accompanied with three cheers. The next toast 'The Vice-President', few cheered him, & many declined drinking it," particularly, he noted, some from Virginia. However, "A number of guests drank so many toasts that in the night they returned to their houses without their hats."

Not everybody was intoxicated by the Purchase. Plumer wrote: "We have already without Louisiana, more uncultivated lands than we can sell. . . . And I am confident that the ratification of this treaty & the possession of the immense territory will hasten the dissolution of our present government. We must form different empires and the form of our governments will then result more from the circumstances of the times in which the change is effected, than the will of the people or the fitness and propriety of the measure."

Other Easterners, already seeing the determined dominance of Virginia, feared the loss of trade and population and power. Men, like Senator Timothy Pickering of Massachusetts and Congressman Roger Griswold of Connecticut, were talking about peaceful secession. Some thought that if Burr could be persuaded and put forward by Federalists he could bring New York into an independent Northern confederacy.

The idea did not seem fantastic then. The danger of disunion had been brought forward in the assumption fight soon after Jefferson returned to the United States to be Secretary of State. And when he agreed to assumption his own Virginia, at Patrick Henry's behest, had declared that a state was not bound by a Federal law which it regarded as unconstitutional. Jefferson had taken much the same position in regard to the Alien and Sedition Laws. Even in geographical terms, after the acquisition of Louisiana, he wrote his fellow philosopher Dr. Joseph Priestley: "Whether we remain in one confederacy, or form into Atlantic and Mississippi confederacies, I believe not very important to the happiness of either part. Those of the Western confederacy will be as much our children and descendants as those of the Eastern, and I feel myself as much identified with that country in future as with this." His complacent attitude about separation would not last long. Indeed, as the months passed after the Purchase, suspicions grew, many of them centered in the White House, that Burr, pushed from place in the republican party, might be ready to lead Federalists in a dismemberment of the Union across the middle and not, as was later charged, on the Western frontier.

Hamilton, who, like Jefferson, was ready to believe any evil thing about Burr, was one Federalist who hailed the acquisition. This West had been part of his dream of power and glory when he conferred with Wilkinson about the war of which Adams deprived him. Almost uniquely in the Federalist press, his organ, the New York *Evening Post,* edited by Coleman, hailed the Purchase. Coleman only undertook to minimize the credit due Jefferson and to ridicule some of his solemn reports about the vast area. The President, in recounting the wonders of the Purchase, spoke of a tribe of giant Indians, of river bluffs carved into antique towers, of prairie lands too rich to produce trees, and of a huge saline mountain, said to be 180 miles long and 45 miles in width, composed of solid salt rock.

Coleman added his pinch of salt to this tale. The President, he said, should have added that "some leagues to the westward . . . there was an immense lake of molasses, and that between this lake and the mountain of salt, there was an extensive vale of hasty pudding, stretching as far as the eye could reach, and kept in a state of comfortable eatability by the sun's rays, into which the natives, being all Patagonians, waded knee deep, whenever they were hungry, and helped themselves with salt with one hand to season their pudding, and molasses with the other to give it relish."

Burr was always expansive in his enthusiasm about the West. The wilderness was not filled with fears for him. He looked back with most pride to his adventures, as the soldier he always felt himself to be, in the Revolutionary march across northern forests and mountains to Quebec. He continued to regard the wild lands with some of the ecstasy he had expressed to his wife when he first regarded the mountains beyond the Mohawk. He had no regrets about the faith he had put in his speculations with Williamson, the Morrises, Cazenove, the Wadsworths in the settlement of the West as the path to fortune. He was recognized as a man with much knowledge about the West and its settlement. In the year of the Purchase one who came to consult him about such things was the young, idealistic, and optimistic Earl of Selkirk who was planning great settlements for displaced Scottish peasants on Prince Edward Island and at Baldoon in Upper Canada.

In the summer of the Purchase, however, he had put off his plans for a "tour through the western country," which would take all summer. Theo decided to come North again. Burr's affairs in 1803 were not as easy to arrange for absences as they had been the year before. Furthermore, as he reported in long letters to Theo, he was tentatively in love with the young lady of Philadelphia named Celeste. He had every right to be, as a vigorous widower of forty-seven. Theo urged his remarriage. Certainly in the letters about this affair, which he described as the "Loves of Reubon and Celeste," he appeared far from any confident lady killer. He described himself as a trembling swain. Indeed, casting himself as Reubon, he made the story seem a kind of comic parlor pastoral. Sometimes his letters on the subject seem more like a literary exercise to amuse his daughter, than a recital of events.

Celeste, he wrote, was "pensive and interesting." His pointed attentions met a cheerful return. Her sprightliness moved him, after meditation, to "take the fatal step." Formally he asked and received her father's permission to address her. The young lady, however, demurred.

"I recollect to have heard you express surprise," she told him, "that any woman would marry, &c, and you gave such reasons, and with so much eloquence, as made an indelible impression on my mind."

The whole business, he wrote, "is finished—concluded—forever abandoned—*liber sum*." But not quite. A few days later he received a note from Celeste saying that she would be happy to see him, though she expressed "an unalterable determination never to listen again to his suit, and requesting that the subject might never be renewed." At their meeting

Celeste said that perhaps she had not been sufficiently polite and respect-ful ". . . here she stuck."

"Reubon," the letter continued, "ought in mercy and politeness to have taken up the conversation; but he, expecting no such thing, was taken by surprise, and remained dumb, with a kind of half grin. The duette, at this moment, would have made a charming subject for the pencil of Vanderlyn. Celeste was profoundly occupied in tearing up some roses which she held in her hand, and Reubon was equally industrious in twirling his hat, and pinching some new corners and angles in the brim."

The lady invited him back again but his proposal to renew his suit was "*faintly opposed*." During this interview, Reubon Burr reported, Ce-leste, "having no roses to occupy her hands, twisted off two corners of a pocket handkerchief." The little drama was over. But a year later when he saw her casually he exclaimed that "truly her hand and arm are hand-some."

Theo, evidently taking the affair as realistically reported, gave her verdict:

"As to Celeste, *voilà mon* opinion. She meant, from the beginning to say that awful word—*yes*; but not choosing to say it immediately, she told you that *you* had furnished her with arguments against matrimony, which in French means, Please, Sir, to persuade me out of them again. But you took it as a plump refusal, and walked off. She called you back. What more could she do? I would have seen you in Japan before I should have done so much."

Evidently Colonel Burr, keeping his freedom, was not much dis-turbed. He was pleased when Theo, bringing the boy both loved, came North. In July 1803 she was reporting from Ballston: "Behold us, cher père, at this fountain of health; and now my wish is to leave it as soon as possible." Some other guests were bored, including Burr's Maryland friends, General Smith and his family. However, Theo went from the private house she maintained at the spa to a ball, which "surpassed my expectations in brilliancy. I danced twice, but I am unable to tell you whether I looked well or danced well." Her father was sure how she looked and delighted at the new signs of health and spirit.

"Lord, how I should have liked to see you dance. It is so long; how long is it? It is certain that you danced better than anybody and looked better."

Except for a foray into Rhode Island early in August, Burr himself stayed in the city despite the recurrence of yellow fever there. He presumed the intolerable heat had prepared an atmosphere for the disease which, he said, killed three fourths of those who contracted it. He was evidently active in both business and politics. His financial steps are difficult to follow. He was "negotiating for the possession of Richmond Hill, by exchanging with Colonel F. for my house in town." He added, "in the sale of this estate I reserve the house and a due portion of the ground about it; yet a good price will tempt me to part with it." Later in the year he wrote about his failure to write, "I have been too busy selling."

"All is sold, and well sold; not all, however," he told her on November 7, 1803. "The house, outhouses, and some three or four acres remain. Enough to keep up the appearance, and all the pleasant recollections of your infantine days, and some of your matronly days also, are reserved with interest. This weighty business, however, is completed, and a huge weight it has taken from the head and shoulders, and every other part, animal and intellectual of A. B."

Yet soon he was reporting that he was thinking of acquiring the "Roger Morris's place." This was the great house built in Harlem by Morris, an English army officer who had married New York's richest heiress, Mary Philipse. Though he remained neutral in the Revolution, he had been unable to prevent the confiscation of their huge estate in New York and up the river. Apparently Burr did not make this trade. This house was bought a year later by Jumel, the wine merchant, for his wife, the beautiful woman who had been known variously as Eliza Brown or Betsy Bowen. Ultimately the Morris property went to John Jacob Astor as did Richmond Hill. The Vice-President this year was on very friendly terms with this forty-year-old German immigrant who was building his vast fortune in western fur operations and New York real estate.

Possibly more significant, though he treated it lightly, was his hospitality to "Mr. and Mrs. Harper of Baltimore." The gentleman was Robert Goodloe Harper who had come to Congress as a republican from South Carolina. In the rich society of Philadelphia he became almost a fuming Federalist. He was described as the "most insolent man in the House," vigorously supporting the Jay treaty and the Alien and Sedition Laws. A dandy in dress, he became a social lion. Then he married Catherine Carroll, daughter of Charles Carroll of Carrollton who violently opposed the match. Harper had ardently supported Burr over Jefferson in the contest in the House. Later he was to be attorney for some of Burr's comrades in the "conspiracy." Now he was one of those Federalists who looked to Burr as a possibly useful "instrument" against Jefferson.

Burr, who invited the Harpers to breakfast, wrote to Theo of no Federalist flirtation. The only indication he gave of any coquetry was his note that with the Harpers was "a pretty looking, black-eyed lass, whose name I did not hear. I hope she is coming to breakfast for I like her." She did come. She proved to be a Miss Chase of Baltimore. It seems not only possible but probable that she was the daughter of Judge Samuel Chase who had tried—or mistried—Callender and for whom Jefferson was now proposing impeachment.

Some of Burr's law business this summer was "extremely troublesome and disagreeable." There were other troublesome matters. Late in September he was persuaded to break his contemptuous silence under attack. He wrote then to his friend Governor Bloomfield of New Jersey a letter for publication describing as "false and groundless" any and all suggestions that he had "advised or countenanced" the opposition to Jefferson's choice as President in the House of Representatives. Such simple denial no longer sufficed against the tumult of his enemies. Counterattack seemed essential. So it seems probable that at this time Burr was engaged in helping his friend Van Ness prepare an assault on his enemies.

Nothing of his concern at the time appears in his letters. Theo had written him as she moved southward of an accident to her carriage near Washington when at the top of a hill broken harness sent the horses crowding down upon one another. Except for luck, she said, "the *poor world* would have been deprived of the heir-apparent to all its admiration and glory." She found no social sign in Washington, however, that her father was not still an heir-apparent. The Gallatins had her to tea. She and Mrs. Madison exchanged pleasant visits. Apparently this was the only occasion upon which Theo visited Washington after her father became Vice-President. Unfortunately for the fragile fable about her and Captain Lewis, that tall Jefferson agent was already in St. Louis forming the band of his companions in exploration.

After she had passed on her way South, Burr came to Washington, too. Apparently, as was often the case, he arrived late to assume his position as presiding officer. Indeed, though the session had been called by the President to convene on October 17, 1803, the Vice-President first wrote from Washington on his arrival there on December 4. He seemed welcome in the city. Mrs. Law, not yet separated from her husband, warmly greeted him. To breakfast in his quarters, he had young Jerome Bonaparte, brother of Napoleon, who on Christmas Eve was to marry Elizabeth Patterson, kin of many of Burr's Maryland friends. He had been invited to spend Christmas in Maryland by his visitor of the summer before, the Federalist Harper. He was pleased with Madame Bonaparte, "a charming little woman; just the size and nearly the figure of Theodosia Burr Alston; by some thought a little like her; perhaps not so well in the shoulders; dresses with taste and simplicity (by some thought too free); has sense, and spirit, and sprightliness."

As to Madame Bonaparte's being "too free" in her dress, Jefferson's friend Margaret Bayard Smith wrote, apparently in shock, that "mobs of boys have crowded around her splendid equipage to see what I hope will not often be seen in this country, an almost naked woman." The Vice-President declined to become involved in the social debate as to the legality and propriety of the match. However, he inclined to agree with the approving, rather than scandalized, Mrs. Caton, apparently another daughter of Charles Carroll of Carrollton.

In one social conflict, however, the Vice-President disagreed with the President. Burr arrived in the capital almost immediately after a famous dinner party for diplomats and others at the President's House. Possibly with an election year ahead, Jefferson was eager to demonstrate his democracy in contrast to the lofty airs of representatives of monarchical governments. Diplomacy he considered "as the pest to the peace of the world." Though he had been one, he felt that way about diplomats. He had already much chagrined the British Minister Anthony Merry at his official reception. Then that gentleman in his glittering official costume was, he wrote home, "introduced to a man as the President of the United States, not merely in an undress, but actually standing in slippers down at the heels and both pantaloons, coat and underclothes indicative of utter slovenness and indifference to appearance, and in a state of negligence actually studied." This was not accidental but deliberate, Merry reported to the British foreign office.

At the dinner this December, the President appeared ready to offend the whole diplomatic corps. He disregarded all precedence and rank at his table in such a fashion that both the British Minister and Mrs. Merry had to fend for themselves for seats. On this occasion the Spanish Minister Yrujo was amused to see the discomfort of Britain's emissary. He saw nothing funny, however, when four days later he and his American wife got similar treatment at the table of the Secretary of State. The French *chargé d'affaires*, Louis André Pichon, joined them in an alliance of indignation.

"M. Yrujo," the Frenchman reported to his government, "who is vanity itself, blew the flames more vigorously." He and Merry planned social reprisals. Mrs. Merry, however, was apparently the most vocal. She was, wrote Margaret Bayard Smith, "so entirely the talker and actor in all companies, that her good husband passes quite unnoticed." Her audible protests were such that Madison gravely consulted Rufus King in London about the matter. What the administration wished to do, he wrote, was to "unfetter social intercourse as well as public business from ceremonious clogs; this may be rendered difficult by the pretensions & expectations opposed to it." Jefferson was adamant: "The principle of society with us, as well as our political constitution, is the equal rights of all; and if there be an occasion where this equality ought to prevail pre-eminently, it is in social circles collected for conviviality. Nobody shall be above you, nor you above anybody, pêle-mêle is our law." And as for Mrs. Merry, Jefferson said she was "a virago."

On the Washington scene of this table tempest, Burr wrote a very different opinion. Mrs. Merry was "tall, fair, fat—*pas trop,* however. No more than a desirable embonpoint. Much of grace and dignity, ease and sprightliness; full of intelligence. An Englishwoman who has lived much in Paris, and has all that could be wished of the manners of both countries. An amiable and interesting companion. . . ." The Colonel saw much of the Merrys at this time and later.

The pêle-mêle policy was to have more than comic consequences. On their recent arrival in America the Merrys had been accompanied by the young Irish poet Tom Moore, described by Randall as a "perfumed little Adonis," and by Adams as a "trifler and butterfly." He wrote home in high dudgeon about the treatment of the Merrys "with the most pointed incivility by the present democratic President, Mr. Jefferson." On his trip Moore visited Richmond where Callender had screamed and died. In all America he found no more congenial spirit than Joseph Dennie, editor of *The Port Folio* of Philadelphia. *The Port Folio* was continuing its impertinent lampooning of the President. In a paraphrase of Horace that publication jibed:

"Dear Thomas, deem it no disgrace with slaves to mend thy breed,
Nor let the wench's smutty face deter thee from the deed."

Moore went on from there:

> The patriot, fresh from Freedom's councils come,
> Now pleas'd, retires to lash his slaves at home;
> Or woo, some black Aspasia's charms
> And dream of freedom in his bondmaid's arms.

Callender's immortality in smear was to be further aided by a just
budding poet, William Cullen Bryant, later to be editor of the New York
Evening Post. Before he wrote *Thanatopsis,* Bryant provided lines which
many Federalists praised:

> Go wretch, resign the presidential chair,
> Disclose thy secret measures, foul or fair.
> Go, search with curious eyes for horned frogs,
> Mid the wild wastes of Louisianian bogs;
> Or, where the Ohio rolls his turbid stream,
> Dig for huge bones, thy glory and thy theme.
> Go, scan, Philophist, thy Sally's charms,
> And sink supinely in her sable arms;
> But quit to abler hands the helm of state.

Perhaps, as Randall said, Moore later became one of Jefferson's favorite poets. The President was not, however, enjoying the sometimes obscene
treatment he was receiving from the Federalist press. Despite some stories
of his laughter about it, he was humorlessly sensitive to criticism. He did
not, however, seem to be disturbed by the smut and smear being poured
upon his associate the Vice-President. This got belated answer in the December of the Merry-go-round dinner party. Then a pamphlet appeared
in New York entitled *An Examination of the Various Charges Exhibited
Against Aaron Burr . . . And a Development of Characters and Views of
his Political Opponents.* It was signed simply Aristides. This was no
such bland defense of Burr as Peter Irving had presented against the
whirlwind of vilification. In both savagery and artistry it exceeded anything that Cheetham had written. It struck at the "doddering" Governor
Clinton, the "perfidious" DeWitt. Osgood, who had been studying the-
ology before he asked for a Federal job for himself and opposed any jobs
for Burr's friends, was sarcastically called "that learned and pious ex-

pounder of the prophecies." Cheetham was dismissed with a contemptuous slap as a blasphemer. Spreading his target wide—perhaps too wide—Aristides presented the President as a weak and fickle visionary who had gone to improper lengths to assure himself of the Presidency. He could not escape his ties with Callender.

It is hardly conceivable that this pamphlet appeared without Burr's knowledge. Certainly it contributed to his final undoing. Designed not to convince so much as to condemn, Aristides' product increased the zeal for Burr's destruction by enemies it helped make more cohesive. Burr's elimination as Vice-President had undoubtedly been prepared long before the pamphlet appeared. Now it was made a personal satisfaction as well as a political move. Aristides, in denouncing the charge that Burr had been willing to make a deal with the Federalists to seize the Presidency, implicitly charged that Jefferson had agreed to a deal in order to assure his election. This hit Jefferson in his most tender spot. The pamphlet drew both blood and readership. Senator Samuel L. Mitchell of New York wrote his wife in shocked admiration that Burr's enemies were "flagellated without mercy, and scourged with a whip of scorpions."

Evidently, as a letter to Burr indicated, the pamphlet was circulated by Burr's own editor Dr. Irving. Also Jefferson later learned it was promoted by one of the few Burr men who had secured Federal appointment, U. S. Marshal John Swartwout. Swartwout, the President noted later, was "affirming every fact in it as holy writ." Only later was it discovered that the author was Van Ness. He was no Cheetham or Callender. Henry Adams described him as "socially well connected and well brought up." He was later to be named a Federal Judge by President Madison. Even his enemies gave grudging admiration to his pamphlet. Randall, who found no good in any Burr connection, wrote of Van Ness as a "brilliant pamphleteer." He added, however: "Van Ness was the confidant, newspaper champion, and instrument of Burr, and a keener and more terrible instrument—adding to the still tread, the deadly ferocity and power of the tiger—never served a congenial companion." In New York, DeWitt Clinton threatened the printers. Governor Clinton cried in anguish to Jefferson.

Despite the tumult made by Mrs. Merry this was a month of the greatest satisfaction to the President. His power in his party was more absolute than ever. And in the nation his prestige was crowned by the ceremonial transfer of the great Louisiana country to his representatives,

William C. C. Claiborne, Governor of Mississippi Territory; and General Wilkinson, chief American military man. The day after Christmas, Jefferson wrote his daughter Mary, about whose pregnancy he was concerned, of expecting the great news from the Southwest. Dispatches from Natchez had been delayed. On New Year's Day, however, "we shall hear of the delivery of New Orleans to us." There would be a great gala then.

On the eve of this gala Jefferson answered Clinton's letter. He assured the Governor that he was not disturbed by the pamphlet's allegation that he had spoken derogatively of him. Then in the manner of both a scornful politician and a bored literary critic, he went on: "I began to read it but the dullness of the first page made me give up the reading for a dip into here and there a passage, till I came to what respected myself. The falsehood of that gave me a test for the rest of the work, and considering it always useless to read lies, I threw it aside."

However, the charges in the pamphlet were not dismissed from his mind. On the same day, December 31, 1803, on which he wrote Clinton, he made a note in his *Anas* about it. He quoted a Congressman as saying in the discussion of the pamphlet that he had been offered a bribe to vote for Burr in 1801. Two days later he made another entry quoting a Massachusetts Colonel as saying that Burr, in effect, had told him that the Congress should elect him President and Jefferson Vice-President. These were the last entries he made before he wrote a long passage, on January 26, 1804, about a conversation he had had with the Vice-President at his request.

Burr left no record of the visit. That is a great pity. This episode in political courtship and rejection was, of course, nothing like the affairs of Reubon and Celeste. Yet in solemnity the President, even as self-described, played a role similar to the hard reluctance of Reubon to the belated eagerness of Celeste. It is doubtful that even Burr could have put the comic touch on any report of this occasion. The roles were reversed, Jefferson was Reubon, Burr Celeste, though Burr had come early and eagerly to Jefferson's aid in answer to invitations from Rush and Beckley and from Jefferson himself. Still there is a tragicomic aspect to this matter which Jefferson reported in self-righteous sophistry. The exchange was as cold as the weather Burr reported at the time. For him it must have been as unpleasant as the headache he had mentioned the day before, painful but "no mortal or alarming Symptoms."

Although Jefferson did not mention it, the situation surrounding the meeting was clear. The President had accomplished what Gallatin had suggested might be his plan as early as September 1801. Burr was to be dropped from the republican ticket. Burr, of course, now knew that. So did almost everybody else. Not certain that Jefferson had already arranged for his successor, however, some politicians were engaged in what even Beckley called "the dirty intrigues for the vice-presidency." Burr came to the White House, pocketing his pride. That required a big pocket. But he managed it, asking in return only that at least he not be dismissed in humiliation.

Evidently Jefferson watched Burr talking as Reubon had watched Celeste tearing up the roses and with no more sympathy. Burr went further than Celeste's pride could let her, speaking of the fascination of Jefferson's company and conversation, his eagerness to continue the attachment he had long felt for the President. Behind his mask Jefferson must have sneered at this then as he did in his *Anas*. Burr, he wrote, must have felt that he could "swallow strong things in my own favor." Burr did state his case in fulsome terms. But what he asked was simple and clear. He was ready to get out of the way. But:

"He observed, he believed it would be better for the interest of the republican cause for him to retire; that a disadvantageous schism would otherwise take place; but that were he to retire, it would be said he shrunk from the public sentence, which he never would do; that his enemies were using my name to destroy him, and something was necessary from me to prevent and deprive them of that weapon, some mark of favor from me which would declare to the world that he retired with my confidence."

Certainly Burr must have been expected to do some swallowing when Jefferson, as he himself reported, said, "that I never interfered directly or indirectly with my friends or any others, to influence the election either for himself or myself; that I considered it as my duty to be merely passive, except that in Virginia, I had taken some measures to procure for him the unanimous vote of that State, because I thought any failure there might be imputed to me. That in the election now coming on, I was observing the same conduct, held no councils with anybody respecting it, nor suffered anyone to speak to me on the subject, believing it my duty to leave myself to the free discussion of the public; that I do not at this moment know, nor have ever heard, who were to be proposed as candidates for the public choice, except so far as could be gathered from the newspapers. That as to the attacks excited against him in the newspapers, I had noticed it but as the passing wind. . . ." He suggested that this was particularly the case with Cheetham.

Jefferson ended the *Anas* note, however, with that earlier-mentioned declaration of his animus which involved an amazing lapse of memory or a deliberate disregard of the facts. He wrote: "I had never seen Colonel Burr till he came as a member of the Senate. His conduct very soon inspired me with distrust. I habitually cautioned Mr. Madison against trusting him too much. I saw afterwards, that under General Washington's and Mr. Adams' administrations, whenever a great military appointment or a diplomatic one was to be made, he came post to Philadelphia to show himself, and in fact that he was always at market, if they had wanted him."

Obviously there was to be no such post for Burr now. Of the end of this confrontation, the President wrote, "He left the matter with me for consideration, and the conversation was turned to indifferent subjects." It is difficult to think of the "indifferent subjects" which could have filled their conversation at this point. Possibly they spoke of fears Burr had expressed a few days before to Alston that regardless of the Purchase "the Spanish government will endeavor to limit our west bounds to the Mississippi, with the addition of the island of Orleans only." The day after this conference Burr wrote Nathalie about Louisiana in a letter largely concerned with the beginnings in New York of efforts to provide a museum or gallery to "create a taste for painting and sculpture." The same week he sent Theo some pieces by Washington Irving which he thought merited so high an honor as being perused by her eyes and touched by her hands.

The President had not been quite as remote from politics as he indicated to Burr. Indeed, two months before his meeting with the Vice-President, DeWitt Clinton had written him that Burr was planning to run for Governor. He thought the only candidate certain to beat him would be his uncle the present Governor but that, in his mid-sixties, he was unwilling to run again. DeWitt asked the President to prod him. Jefferson replied with characteristic caution that he thought it would be "a serious misfortune should a change in the administration of your government be hazarded before its present principles be well established through all its parts. Yet, on reflection, you will be sensible that the delicacy of my situation, considering who may be competitors, forbids my

intermeddling, even so far as to write the letter you suggest. I can therefore only brood in silence over my secret wishes."

Jefferson was silent but not quiet. Soon after this meeting with Burr,
according to his Postmaster General Gideon Granger, Jefferson sent
Erastus Granger to tell the younger Clinton that Burr was indeed planning to run for Governor. Perhaps that had been mentioned in the "indifferent subjects" Jefferson said they talked about. Clinton moved swiftly,
securing the republican nomination for Chancellor John Lansing, a much
respected figure. At a secret meeting of Federalists in Albany, Hamilton
urged his election. Shock followed when, on February 18, 1804, Lansing
withdrew declaring that he had agreed to run only in order to establish
a union of republican factions about which he now felt he had been
"too sanguine."

On this same day the Burr forces gathered in enthusiasm at the Ton-
tine Coffee House in Albany and formally nominated him. In such a way
he provided his own escape from public rejection. He had chosen to run
for Governor. Actually that was the only choice he had. He knew his
elimination as Vice-President had been arranged. He knew the President
had no favor for him. When the Congressional caucus met to choose the
Democratic candidates for President and Vice-President, Jefferson was
unanimously nominated for the first place. Votes were scattered for the
Vice-Presidential nomination: Governor Clinton, 67; Senator John
Breckinridge of Kentucky, 20; former Congressman Levi Lincoln of Massachusetts, 9; Senator John Langdon of New Hampshire, 4; Gideon
Granger, 4; former Senator William Maclay of Pennsylvania, 1. Not one
for Aaron Burr. The Jefferson-Clinton ticket suited Virginia to perfection
since Clinton, already feeling too old to run for Governor of New York,
seemed unlikely to provide any threat to the dynasty when the time came
to choose a successor to Jefferson. In New York it meant Jeffersonian
endorsement of the Clintons without the necessity of his writing any letter
to that effect.

Two days after Burr's nomination, DeWitt Clinton dictated the
nomination of another candidate who would not run out on him. He
strengthened the alliance with the Livingstons by the choice of Chief
Justice Morgan Lewis, who had married Chancellor Livingston's daughter, Gertrude. Long before Lewis and Burr had been friends at Princeton.
Later Lewis was to break with Clinton. Now, however, the lines were
drawn for a bitter campaign, and one which Jefferson afterwards said

threatened the Union itself. He wrote that during it he received "daily and confidential reports" from Gideon Granger as a sort of spy within the Burr camp. They related, he said, "to the intrigues which were in agitation, and at the bottom of which we believed Colonel Burr to be; to form a coalition of the five eastern states, with New York and New Jersey, under the new appellation of the seven eastern states; either to overawe the Union by the combination of their power and their will, or by separating themselves from it." A week before the election in New York, Jefferson was referring to the alignment behind Burr as one which might create "a bastard system of federo-republicanism."

There is no doubt that some desperate Federalists sanctioned such a scheme as the only means of escape from republican and Virginia domination. In January, Timothy Pickering was writing furiously: "I am disgusted with the men who now rule and with their measures. . . . The cowardly wretch at their head, while, like a Parisian revolutionary monster, prating about humanity, would feel an infernal pleasure in the utter destruction of his opponents." One particular Northern resentment was the Constitutional provision allowing Virginia and other Southern states to add three fifths of their Negroes to their white populations in determining their representation in Congress and their vote in Presidential elections. Pickering stormed: "Without a separation, can those states ever rid themselves of negro Presidents and negro Congresses, and regain their just weight in the political balance." Plumer wrote in his diary: "Strange and inconsistent as it may appear, in those very states where slaves are most numerous, the people are most vociferous for *liberty & equality*." Other influential Federalists shared such views. A Burr victory in New York, they believed, might provide the required leader for a separate American confederacy.

The evidence does not indicate that Burr was ready to be such a leader. Proscribed by the Clintons with Jefferson behind them, he was not turning down any votes. With no Federalist candidates in the field he would be glad to have Federalist votes. Early in the year in Washington he had dined with Pickering, Plumer, and other plotters. He listened to such sentiments as that the United States "would soon form two distinct & separate governments." He was gracious and courteous. He appeared interested in the ideas. But when Plumer got home he realized that in Burr's talking there was "nothing that he said that necessarily implied his approbation" of the plan. He wrote, "perhaps no man's language was ever more apparently explicit, & at the same time so covert & indefinite." Other Federalists got no more satisfaction.

Hamilton, who had lost much of his leadership in his party by his aid in the defeat of John Adams, was furious at Federalist finagling with his ancient rival. He threw all his weight to the Clinton-Livingston candidate—or against Burr. He repeated old charges that Burr was a dangerous man though as in the past in supposedly confidential utterances. He fought to keep away from Burr those Federalist votes he would need to win. In so doing he prepared for results none could foresee.

An ominous design was made. Henry Adams, in his classic history of the Jefferson administration, described the array of people and papers in the attack on Burr: "Never in the history of the United States did so powerful a combination of rival politicians unite to break down a single man as that which arrayed itself against Burr; for as the hostile circle gathered about him, he could plainly see not only Jefferson, Madison, and the whole Virginia legion, with Duane and his 'Aurora' at their heels; not only DeWitt Clinton and his whole family interest, with Cheetham and his 'Watchtower' by their side; but—strangest of companions —Alexander Hamilton himself joining hands with his own bitterest enemies to complete the ring."

In the settled East, Burr's situation was almost like one which Meriwether Lewis was moving to encounter in the wilderness West. One day wandering alone from his party Lewis found himself surrounded by a great bear, bull buffalo, and a creature "of the tiger kind." In the almost mystic poetry of which he was capable he wrote in his journal. "It now seemed to me that all the beasts of the neighborhood had made a league to destroy me, or that some fortune was disposed to amuse herself at my expense. . . . the succession of curious adventures wore the impression on my mind of enchantment; at sometimes for a moment I thought it might be a dream, but the prickley pears which pierced my feet very severely once in a while, particularly after it grew dark, convinced me that I was really awake, and that it was necessary to make the best of my way to camp."

Burr moved in no dream—or nightmare. He fought. Somehow he found the minutes in which to write Theodosia. He told her of "some new and amusing libels" against the Vice-President. He was not amused. Neither was he captured. Even in tumult he had time to speak of Montesquieu and Lady Mary Montague. However, on April 25, he told Theo that he wrote in the midst of a storm, "an election storm, of the like you have once been a witness. The thing began yesterday, and will terminate tomorrow." In the same letter he offered her Richmond Hill again. Then he closed with what seemed almost an afterthought: "I forgot to speak of the election. Both parties claim majorities, and there never was, in my opinion, an election, of the result of which so little judgment could be formed. A.B. will have a small majority *if to-morrow should be a fair day*, and not else."

That tomorrow was a fair day for Jefferson though one reported harshly by Plumer. Celebration marked the signing this day by the President of a law setting up the plan of government for the newly acquired Western empire. Not all celebrated the event. Creoles and others in Louisiana felt the legislation was harsh and undemocratic. The New Hampshire Senator wrote of the celebration in Federalist peevishness and possible distortion: "At twelve o'clock the Chamber was crowded with people of all classes & colors from the President of the United States to the meanest vilest Virginia slave. Mr. Jefferson took his jack knife from his pocket & cut & eat of the beef & bread & drank of the liquors. He compared this drunken frolic to the sacrament of the Lords supper. This motley collection made so much noise as to disturb the Senate." Only after difficulty did the president pro tem of the Senate, sitting in the absence of Burr, quiet the crowd.

Evidently it was not fair weather for Burr. He lost by 22,139 votes to 30,829 for his opponent. The Vice-President put his report of his defeat in one line in a long letter: "The election is lost by a great majority: *tant mieux.*" His situation could hardly have been worse. Perhaps he indicated that a week later when he reported, "Madame Bonaparte and husband are here. I have just seen them and no more. For reasons unknown to me (doubtless some state policy), we are suddenly become strangers." More backs were turned on him.

He was not so philosophic about the election as he suggested to Theo. Even before the votes were counted he told Charles Biddle "that he was determined to call out the first man of any respectability concerned in the infamous publications concerning him." That ruled out Cheetham. Indeed, this might have been only a flash of anger. Certainly there was room for cooling before he called his friend Van Ness to him on deadly serious business on June 18, 1804. Yet three days later with a party of friends he celebrated Theo's birthday—incredibly only her twenty-first. He reported we "laughed an hour, and danced an hour, and drank her health at Richmond Hill. We had your picture in the dining room; but, as it is a profile, and would not look at us, we hung it up, and placed Natalie's at table, which laughs and talks with us."

3.

Angel and Devil

Veterans were growing paunchy twenty years after war, on July 4, 1804. More gray hairs marked the company of the New York Society of the Cincinnati gathered at dinner to celebrate the great day. The one-eyed artist John Trumbull saw the scene as flat as his canvases of Revolutionary heroes and statesmen. He had grown more cantankerous but no less observant since he had attended another dinner at which, to his anger, Jefferson smiled at the vociferous expression of atheism by Congressman Giles. Trumbull had become more fixed in his Federalist sentiments in the service of John Jay abroad. But his turn to diplomacy and speculation in Europe had not served his art. He came back to disappointment in the patronage his painting would receive. But in his recollections rather than on canvas he drew a picture of this celebration of the patriotic and, to democrats, pretentious society. In its foreground was the most dramatic portrait of Burr and Hamilton together, now middle-aged veterans, too, but both sinewy and slim, with gray hardly marking their brunette and blond heads.

"The singularity of their manner was observed by all," Trumbull said, "but few had any suspicion as to the cause. Burr, contrary to wont, was silent, gloomy, sour; while Hamilton entered with glee into all the gaiety of a convivial party, and even sung an old military song."

None at the dinner knew that on the day before final arrangements had been made for the two gentlemen to meet at "Weehawk, on the Jersey shore, at seven o'clock A.M.," on Wednesday, July 11. The ceremonious exchange between the two gentlemen's seconds, Van Ness and Judge Nathaniel Pendleton, had begun on June 18. The bald facts in the case are much simpler than the true situation. During the election campaign certain letters had been published in the Albany *Register,* a republican organ which Schachner believed had been summoned into the campaign against Burr by Jefferson. The letters were written by Dr. Charles D. Cooper after Hamilton had spoken at a private dinner in the state capital.

Cooper wrote, on April 12, 1804, that Hamilton "has come out decidedly against Burr; indeed when he was here he spoke of him as a dangerous man and ought not to be trusted." Another letter, of April 23, contained the line "General Hamilton and Judge Kent have declared, in substance, that they looked upon Mr. Burr as a dangerous man, and one who ought not to be trusted with the reins of government." Then came the sharper line: "I could detail to you a still more despicable opinion which General Hamilton has expressed of Mr. Burr." Both letters were published in the *Register,* on April 24, on the eve of the election.

Certainly Burr could not have been surprised when the letters belatedly came into his hands. It is inconceivable that in the years before there had not come to him reports of the steady flow of invective which Hamilton poured upon him. The General had accused his rival of everything from private misconduct to a lack of probity, from a readiness for treason to talking "perfect Godwinism." Burr may well have been guilty of this last. He was a great admirer of the works of William Godwin, whose *Political Justice* was the most influential English expression of revolutionary ideas with the possible exception of Paine's *Rights of Man.* This charge would not have disturbed him. Here and now, however, was serious defamation in print, and "more despicable" meant dishonorable, even contemptible.

So, on June 18, 1804, Burr wrote to Hamilton: "You must perceive, sir, the necessity of a prompt and unqualified acknowledgement or denial of the use of any expressions which would warrant the assertions of Mr. Cooper."

Hamilton hedged. He complained in punctilious language that Burr's demand was too indefinite. Perhaps, as Trumbull thought, he should have replied, "Sir, a duel proves nothing, but that the parties do not shrink from the smell of gunpowder, or the whistling of a ball: on this subject you and I have given too many proofs, to leave any necessity for another, and therefore, as well as for higher reasons, I decline your proposal."

Hamilton's situation permitted no such sonorous solution. Certainly he had every reason to hate dueling which had recently brought about the death of his son and the insanity of his daughter. However, the files of his friends were packed with letters full of "despicable opinions" of his rival. In their eyes any denial now that he had indulged in similar opinions in Albany or anywhere else would make him seem both a liar and a groveler. His already shaken Federalist leadership would be shattered. He would be subject not only to contempt but laughter. And, though much isolated even in his own party, he still wished to be useful in public affairs which would be improbable without "a conformity with prejudice in this particular." A similar wish had made Burr's challenge seem essential to him.

Yet, the reasons for Burr's challenge were more complex. He had greater complaint against Cheetham, but could not condescend to notice him. Many years later when someone asked Burr if Hamilton was a gentleman he replied in hauteur, "Sir, I met him." Certainly, however, DeWitt Clinton was not beneath notice and Clinton had recently stirred more abuse of him than Hamilton. Isaac Cox wrote in the *Dictionary of American Biography* that "in addition to settling past grievances, Burr may have wished to forestall further unwelcome rivalry, either in a possible northern confederacy or on the southwestern border. The latter was the more probable field, for both Burr and Hamilton cherished the ambition to lead an army thither in an effort to free the Spanish colonies." In such a realm of conjecture it might be suggested that as some people may be made for devotion, Burr and Hamilton seemed almost designed to make even their antagonism perfect of its kind. They seemed almost men born to meet in decorous hostility.

Certainly these two are not to be clearly seen in the punctiliously correct formalities of their final correspondence. The men emerge truly in the personal, not frigidly polite, letters which each left for perusal by those who loved them after their possible deaths. Though thinking himself justified, Hamilton was much troubled that he may have gone too far in some "animadversions of mine which bore very hard upon him." He insisted that he was "conscious of no *ill will* to Colonel Burr distinct from political opposition." Burr, in his letters, made no reference to Hamilton except to say that he had called him out. Each man was conscious of his precarious financial situation. Writing Theodosia of his new will Burr said, "Tell my dear Natalie that I have not left her anything, for the very good reason that I had nothing to leave to any one." Hamilton, much overextended in the building of The Grange, was in similar financial condition. Despite a vast tract of land which he had acquired in western New York in speculations like Burr's, the solvency of his estate would be doubtful. Yet both men wrote from their great houses of Richmond Hill and The Grange. Burr in this period was not always the imperturbable assassin he was to be pictured. On July 1, while the city sweltered, though in perfect health, he so shivered that he had a fire built in his library.

The only dispute about the facts of their meeting on the sunlit heights of Jersey on that Wednesday morning was whether Hamilton did not fire, as in one of his letters he said was his plan. Possibly his pistol— one of the famous pair owned by Church—was discharged only accidentally when he received Burr's bullet. All else was indisputable and correct. There was even the charitably remembered moment when Burr advanced toward his fallen adversary with a manner and gesture which seemed to Hamilton's second to express regret. Lest witnesses see him, his own second urged his swift withdrawal from the scene. Almost immediately, malignant legends began to be nourished. Cheetham reported that Burr had gone to the encounter dressed in clothes which constituted a sort of suit of armor. Burr and his friends were depicted as drinking, joking, exulting while Hamilton lay dying. Very natural was Angelica Church's cry that Hamilton had been "wounded by that wretch Burr." She did not mention the often-used Church pistols.

In Washington, apparently Jefferson's only comment was in a postscript to a letter to his daughter Martha: "I presume Mr. Randolph's newspapers will inform him of the death of Colo. Hamilton, which took place on the 12th." But Beckley, calling Hamilton a "double adulterer," wrote that Burr was being "pursued with vindictive and unrelenting fury." After a great funeral, a strident hue and cry was set up. In proceedings so irregular that even Burr's recent opponent, Governor Morgan Lewis, described them as disgraceful, Burr was indicted for murder in New York where no shot had been fired. In the clamor New Jersey, with more right, followed suit. Burr wrote Alston that "the malignant federalists or tories" and the "most unprincipled Jacobins" had combined to drive him into "a sort of exile, and may terminate in an actual and permanent ostracism." He was leaving the city "but whither is not resolved. Perhaps to Statesburg." In the meantime Alston could "write under cover to Charles Biddle, Philadelphia."

To Biddle, who offered him sanctuary, Burr wrote his own story of the duel and its cause: "It is too well known that Gen'l H. had long indulged himself in illiberal freedoms with my character. He had a peculiar talent of saying things improper & offensive in such a manner as could not well be taken hold of. On two different occasions however, having reason to comprehend that he had gone so far as to afford me a fair occasion for calling on him, he anticipated me by coming forward voluntarily and making apologies and concessions. From delicacy to him and from a sincere desire for peace, I never mentioned these circumstances always hoping that the generosity of my conduct would have some influence on his. In this I have been constantly deceived, and it became impossible that I could consistently with self-respect again forebear."

Burr evidently was incensed by reports that Hamilton did not fire. Indeed, he wrote that his opponent had on the field given elaborate indications that he meant to fire—and fire accurately, adjusting his glasses and leveling "his pistol in different directions to try the light." And at the signal, Burr said, Hamilton fired first. In this letter, however, Burr used the language of the Federalists about those Democrats behind the Clintons and Jefferson.

"You will remark," he told Biddle, "that all our intemperate and unprincipled Jacobins who have been for years reviling H. as a disgrace to the country and a pest to society are now the most vehement in his praise, and you will readily perceive that their motive is, not respect to him, but malice to me."

Under cover of darkness ten days after the duel Burr boarded a barge anchored near Richmond Hill. Accompanied by John Swartwout, the Vice-President reached the home of his friend, Commodore Thomas Truxtun, the next morning. The Commodore thought he showed more sorrow than was generally the case with successful duelists. Monday morning Truxtun took him in his carriage to a town twenty miles away. From there the Vice-President was conveyed in a light wagon to the ferry at Bristol and on "by back roads, made his way, incog., to Philadelphia." There he found hospitality and shelter with Biddle and the staunch Democrat and noted dandy Alexander Dallas. Interestingly, Dallas was Jefferson's appointee as U. S. District Attorney in eastern Pennsylvania at this time.

Regrets Burr may have felt; he was certainly not repining. He wrote Theodosia not to believe the lies in the papers including one that he was threatened with assassination. He wrote: "Those who wish me dead prefer to keep at a very respectful distance." He was walking and riding as he pleased around Philadelphia. His letters suggest that at this time he was sentimentally engaged with two ladies, one "La G" and the old flickering flame Celeste. This summer he was especially confiding to Theo about the ladies—of one Clara, a Madame Sansay, who "has claims on my recollection," perhaps less sentimentally of Mrs. Law, who was this year separating from her husband.

"If any male friend of yours should be dying of ennui," he told his daughter, "recommend to him to engage in a duel and a courtship at the same time—prob. est."

Regardless of his letters to Theo, the Colonel was certainly not merely engaging in dalliance after a duel. He wrote that many visitors came to see him from New York and New Jersey. One of them was Burr's old friend in land speculations and the New York legislature, Colonel Williamson. Since those days he had returned to England and reassumed his British citizenship. In England his knowledge of the United States made him useful as a volunteer adviser to successive British Cabinet officers including his cousin Henry Dundas, Lord Melville, First Lord of the Admiralty.

In 1803 he was commissioned to raise a regiment for service in the West Indies or South America. In this one of many British schemes against the Spanish he was only partially successful. He established, however, a covert intimacy with William Armstrong, a later associate of Francisco Miranda, the perennial South American revolutionist. Now in Philadelphia he renewed his friendship with Burr. In this August of Burr's sanctuary there, ostensibly as Burr's agent Williamson had mysterious conversations with Merry who was spending the summer in this city. Williamson apparently was still a British agent and from Burr or others he knew of the Minister's hospitality to ideas of New England secession. After his conferences with both Merry and Burr he returned to England on a then mysterious mission for Burr—or in furtherance of his own anti-Spanish British operations in which Burr seemed the man required.

During this time Burr also saw Yrujo. This vain and explosive diplomat was becoming increasingly furious at American pretensions that the Spanish Floridas had been included in the Louisiana Purchase. Also he shared the bitterness of the Merrys about Jefferson's pêle-mêle social policies. As of this time, Henry Adams wrote that "the first effect of Jefferson's tactics was to ally the British minister with Yrujo; the second bound him to Senator Pickering and Representative Griswold; the third united his fortunes with those of Aaron Burr." Though Merry had heard the reports of Burr's "profligacy" recently paramounted in New York politics, he was sympathetic to Burr-Williamson schemes. Neither he nor Yrujo apparently were disturbed by the clamor set off by the duel. Merry came pêle-mêle to the support of Burr-Williamson proposals. Yrujo gave Burr a passport to the Spanish Floridas.

Burr could not linger to attend to any plotting. Swartwout came with the news that Burr had been indicted in New York for willful murder. A call was to be made to the Governor of Pennsylvania, Yrujo's father-in-law, Thomas McKean, to deliver the Colonel for trial. So Burr prepared for a journey South. His purpose was not merely flight. He was anxious to see Theo. He declined to be discouraged by reports that there was no going through the low country at this season without hazard of life. He hoped to find Theo in the "High Hills of Santee." Also he already had some special interest in the Spanish South. So he fixed his destination as Florida.

Earlier in the year he had inquired of a correspondent, one A. R. Ellery, about Daniel Clark, substantial merchant of New Orleans. Clark was a friend of Burr's close associate Jonathan Dayton, Federalist who was soon to be replaced by a Democrat in the United States Senate. Dayton, the year before, had visited New Orleans where Clark was a powerful and controversial character whose business often carried him to Mexico. Burr must also have heard of Clark through his old Revolutionary comrade General Wilkinson, who at this time was describing Burr as "the first gentleman in America." Wilkinson himself was being described to Talleyrand as "ambitious and easily dazzled, fond of show and appearances" who was complaining "rather indiscreetly, and especially after dinner, of the form of his government, which leaves officers few chances of fortune, advancement and glory. . . ."

A cast of characters was evidently being assembled even if not for a conspiracy. In March 1804 Burr had written Biddle expressing regret that he could not help Wilkinson. His "direct interference" would probably not be useful to him. Wilkinson, however, on May 23, 1804, thought Burr and himself might be useful to each other. On that day on a visit East he wrote Burr, a month after his defeat for Governor.

"To save time of which I need much and have but little, I propose to take a Bed with you this night, if it may be done without observation or intrusion."

Certainly as a man rejected as Vice-President and defeated for Governor, Burr would be interested in any plans the General might have. Whatever they were, they had been discussed before the Vice-President left New York, certainly before he left Philadelphia.

With Samuel Swartwout and a slave named Peter ("the most intelligent and best disposed black I have ever known"), Burr secretly embarked for Georgia. There on St. Simon's Island at the Hampton Plantation of his friend, rich former Senator Pierce Butler, he found refuge. Furthermore, this was a point from which Burr could make any forays into Florida he wished to make. He traveled under the name of Roswell King. His plan, he wrote Alston, was to visit "the Floridas for five or six weeks," then to meet his son-in-law at "any healthy point."

He got no such unhappy impression of the island as Fanny Kemble did a few decades later when she came as wife of Butler's grandson to denounce the slavery she found. Burr relaxed under the attentions of a chambermaid, a seamstress, two footmen, two fishermen, and four bargemen always at his command. All the products of field and orchard and sea came to his table. There was plenty of Madeira, brandy, and porter. Still both Florida and the best route to Stateburg were much on his mind. Then the disastrous hurricane of September 1804 intervened.

"The flood was about seven feet above the height of an ordinary high tide. This has been sufficient to inundate great part of the coast; to destroy all the rice; to carry off most of the buildings which were on low lands, and to destroy the lives of many blacks. The roads are rendered impassable, and scarcely a boat has been preserved. . . . the effects of the storm have defeated all my plans."

He still made it to Florida briefly, but only as far as the mouth of the St. Johns River about thirty miles from St. Augustine. Then he moved northward from St. Simon's to Savannah where to his surprise he was not stoned but serenaded. The South saw no murder in the honorable, if fatal, meetings of gentlemen. He had invitations it would take weeks to satisfy. His letters do not make it quite clear how he traveled beyond Savannah, but he arrived at Stateburg where Theodosia and Nathalie, Alston and the baby Aaron were waiting. Undoubtedly, as he said, he was yellowed by the sun but there was characteristic hyperbole in his statement that he had traveled four hundred miles in a canoe.

Before he made this Southern journey Burr had read—and recommended to Theodosia—the *Travels* of the botanist William Bartram through this region. Probably in Philadelphia he had known André Mi-

chaux who had botanized through South Carolina before Genet sent
him West as secret agent to join George Rogers Clark in a Western adventure for France. Before Burr, Michaux had come to the High Hills of
Santee, where the Sumters had their seat, to note alum root, wild vetches,
and phlox in bloom. Conveniently Stateburg was about halfway between
The Oaks plantation of the Alstons near Georgetown and their western
retreat at Clifton.

The Vice-President had long been acquainted with General Sumter,
as he told Nathalie at the time of her marriage. Possibly he had met her
husband when he sailed with Nathalie from New York for France. Certainly now as "Gamp" he was anxious to see little Aaron, a babbling two-
year-old. With them and Theodosia his whole world was in Stateburg.

Significant change was taking place around that little town. Planters
were turning from indigo to cotton in the vast demand for that fiber which
followed the invention of the cotton gin and the application of steam
power to textile manufacture. And, as in Virginia, men were talking of the
Western lands where the plant could be grown on wide acreages of un-
worn soil. Sumter's great neighbor Wade Hampton had already grown a
six-hundred-bale crop on his South Carolina lands and was looking to
the West with, as a biographer wrote, "the will to possess without any
overscrupulous regard for the means of acquiring possession."

Others besides Burr in South Carolina this year were seeking means
to make new starts. William Loughton Smith, who had lingered in
Europe after Jefferson abolished his post in Lisbon, had come back to improve his finances, if not his political prospects, by marrying a lady with a
large estate in land, money, and slaves. Burr then apparently never looked
at the ladies with an eye to their estates. He was looking for no comfortable
place on the piazza of a plantation mansion. Already he had those dreams
of the West which he had never lost since he first looked beyond the
Mohawk.

As precious as was the company in Stateburg to him, he pressed on.
According to the calendar and his estimates of travel time, he could not
have been with Theodosia in Nathalie's house more than a week. He
pushed on to Fayetteville, North Carolina, where the only person he knew
was former Congressman William Barry Grove, a Federalist who did not
call on him. At Petersburg, Virginia, however, the hospitalities of the republicans of the place detained him three days. A public dinner was given
for him, though he wrote Theo that it was the last town and Virginia the

last state "in which I should have expected any open marks of hospitality and respect." His journey ended at Washington on November 4. As one waiting for clamor to quiet, he had taken no part in the Presidential election which demonstrated the popularity and the power of Jefferson. The Virginian and Clinton received all the electoral votes except two in Maryland and those of Connecticut and Delaware. The President sneered at Bayard's Delaware as no more than an English county. The Federalist Party was as dead as Alexander Hamilton.

Apparently with his own last election behind him, Jefferson blossomed forth in dress equal to a British Minister's conception of proper costume for his reception. Senator Plumer wrote: "He has improved much in the article of dress; he has laid aside the old slippers, red waistcoat, and soiled corduroy small-clothes, and was dressed all in black, with clean linen and powdered hair." Possibly the pêle-mêle policy could be modified too. But Merry and Yrujo would not be modified soon.

Despite his triumph, this had been a far from happy year for the President. In the spring when Burr was going down to defeat, Jefferson made a note in his family Bible of the death after childbirth of Mary at the age of twenty-six. He wrote a friend that he had "lost even the half of all I had." The event brought a brief break in the hostility of Abigail Adams who had loved Mary as an unhappy child on the way to Paris. She wrote her sympathy. Jefferson eagerly answered but soon, in defending himself, made the New England woman more fierce in her bitter belief that he had nurtured Callender as a serpent to sting her husband.

Jefferson's journey back to Washington after the burial of his child seemed, as he described it to Martha, "a dreadful journey" in the rain over roads so deep in mud that his carriage horses could not make it. He finished the trip on horseback, sore and fatigued. He faced the election campaign sick at heart, running, he said, only because "the unlimited calumnies of the federalists have obliged me to put myself on trial of my country."

Burr seemed to some brazenly declining to be cast down, and unfatigued by a more difficult journey. Senator Plumer regarded him with distaste when, as was unusual with him, he arrived on the first day of the session on November 5. The Senator wrote in his diary: "I avoided him—his presence to me is odious—I have merely bowed and spoken to him—federalists appear to despise neglect and abhor him. The democrats at least many of them, appear attentive to him—and he is very familiar with them—What a line of conduct they will generally observe to him is yet uncertain."

Suddenly the administration and its forces in Congress seemed more concerned about Burr than Burr about them. As presiding officer he was a lame duck. Yet his term of office extended to March 3 of the following year. And within that period he would have important part in a matter close to the heart of the President. A crucial case was coming up in Jefferson's determination to purge the Judiciary of violent Federalists who filled the benches. As Vice-President, Burr would preside at the impeachment trial of Judge Chase. The House had arraigned that Judge for his allegedly extremely partisan conduct on the bench in several cases including the trial of Callender. Plumer suspiciously watched the scene about him. He reported to his diary on November 26:

"I am now satisfied with the course Administration and democratic members of Congress, intend to pursue in relation to Mr. Burr. I never had any doubts of their joy for the death of Hamilton; my only doubts were whether they would manifest that joy by carressing his murderer. Those doubts are now dispelled."

Since Burr had arrived, he noted, the President had shown the Vice-President more attention and invited him to his house more often than ever before. Gallatin had come calling on Burr at his lodgings and on one occasion was closeted with him for more than two hours. Madison, "formerly the intimate of General Hamilton," had taken the Vice-President into his carriage, on one occasion accompanying him to see the French Minister. And Giles of Virginia, now promoted from his leadership for Jefferson in the House to the Senate, was circulating a petition to Governor Bloomfield of New Jersey urging that a nol pros be taken in the case against Burr in that state. It was signed, Plumer said, by most of the Democratic Senators, "I presume by General Dayton." Dayton undoubtedly signed it. Though elected as a Federalist, he was the friend and close associate—some thought too close—of the Vice-President.

Burr was busy providing an impressive stage setting for the trial. Benches for the Senators sitting as judges were covered with crimson cloth. A temporary semicircular gallery was erected on pillars and draped with green cloth. Places were provided for ladies expected to be present in large numbers.

He himself was moving to simpler quarters or preparing to move from Washington altogether. Still he was apparently enjoying himself.

"You would laugh to know my occupation on New Year's eve," he wrote. "It cannot be written, but it shall at some time be told." His friends were coming back: "Mrs. Merry arrived a few days ago, and looks extremely well." He could not share Mr. Jefferson's view that "she has already disturbed our harmony extremely. . . ."

Burr's situation at the time was certainly complex and is still confusing. His house and furniture, he told Alston, had been sold for about twenty-five thousand dollars. Seven or eight thousand dollars in debts remained unpaid. His agents had not collected any of the debts due him, nor sold any of the "detached lots," presumably adjoining Richmond Hill.

"The library and wine remain," he told his son-in-law. "They will, I think, become your property."

In this economic and political situation, some saw cracks in his customary aplomb. Plumer was pious about this: "He appears to have lost those easy graceful manners that beguiled the hours away the last session—He is now uneasy, discontented, & hurried. So true it is, 'Great guilt never knew great joy at heart.' What course he will take after the 3d of March is very uncertain—He can never I think rise again. But surely he is a very extraordinary man, & is an exception to all the rules."

Burr meant to be. During this session of Congress, in the winter of 1805, Burr's movements attracted much attention. The new French Minister, Louis Marie Turreau, wrote about them to Talleyrand. Burr, the minister wrote, had conferred with a delegation of Louisianians disturbed about the rigidities of the new American rule. He added: "Louisiana thus is going to be the seat of Mr. Burr's new intrigues; he is going there under the aegis of General Wilkinson. It is even asserted that he might find the means there already prepared by a certain Livingston whom the disruption of his business has driven from New York City and who is closely associated with Burr."

As the country awaited the trial of Chase and the drapes were being hung in the Senate Chamber, Burr was absent for a few days. Present or absent, he was aware of a petition presented by General Benjamin Hovey of New York, on January 17, 1805. It asked for a Federal grant of twenty-five thousand acres of land on which Hovey and associates would build a canal around the falls of the Ohio. The petition was referred to a committee composed of three friends of the Vice-President: Jonathan Dayton, of New Jersey; John Smith, of Ohio; and John Brown, of Kentucky. No action was taken by Congress then. Still evidently at this time alternate

plans were being made under which later in the year the state of Indiana
would grant a charter to the Indiana Canal Company. It was set up to
carry out this project with a capital of a million dollars. Among its original
directors were Dayton, Brown, and Burr. As a sort of Burr hallmark, the
corporation, like the Manhattan Company, was empowered to establish
a bank as well as build a canal. Prestige was given to the project by the
selection as its chief engineer of Benjamin Latrobe who was to be both
Jefferson's architect in the capital and the designer of the house of Church
and his Angelica in the Genesee Valley. In this enterprise Latrobe was
to recruit five hundred men for the work.

In Burr's mind in his last days in office was the financial pyramiding
which was to have more reality than the canal. The bank would be
created, with the right to issue paper money. The same group would buy a
large block of stock in the Kentucky Insurance Company, which would
also issue notes. From it Burr would borrow twenty-five thousand dollars.
The plan went on to the acquisition by Burr and associates of a huge tract
called the Bastrop lands on the Ouachita River in the northern part of
what became the state of Louisiana. For this land of doubtful title, acquired through his old friend Edward Livingston, Burr would pay five
thousand dollars and assume a thirty-thousand-dollar debt. Only by settlement could he hope to validate his ownership. Undoubtedly he believed
he could do that. He had dealt with such title questions before. Some
were already suggesting that his plans beyond that—or in that—were not
merely financial but even imperial. Not even Burr was certain of all the
eventualities before him. To find a new opportunity he had to be an op-
portunist. Realistic persons, if they had known only the first steps of his
plans, might have wondered if he were not creating a one man Mississippi
Bubble.

In such complicated planning of a grand scheme, it is no wonder
that Burr was sometimes testy in his Vice-Presidential chair. The wonder
is how imperturbable he usually seemed there. The evident drama of the
Congressional session came when the impeachment trial of Chase began,
on February 4, in a Chamber packed with spectators, including many
fashionable ladies. It was understood that this was no mere trial of a man,
even such an arrogant partisan as Samuel Chase. Though Jefferson did
not appear openly in the matter, it was believed and feared that this was
only a first Presidential move to clear the Federal bench of Judges who
under John Marshall had presumed to a right to declare acts of Congress

unconstitutional and issue orders even to the Executive branch. If Chase could so be gotten rid of, other judges including Marshall could expect the same treatment.

Marshall's biographer, Beveridge, described Burr as presiding official of the court as "a short, slender, elegantly formed man, with pallid face and steady black eyes." He was "carefully dressed, and his manners and deportment were meticulously correct." As a man in so strategic a position at such a crucial trial, Beveridge wrote, "Jefferson determined that Aaron Burr must be captured—at least conciliated." At the outset of the trial Federalists feared his partiality. Indeed, Plumer described him as "very fretful and peevish." He was, the diarist wrote, "remarkably testy—he acts more of the tyrant—is impatient & passionate—scolds—he is in a rage because we do not sit longer." His treatment of Chase seemed harsh.

Burr left no descriptions of the trial over which he presided. But in the lawyers and witnesses a company was assembled which he would meet again when he was not on the bench but in the dock. Marshall appeared as an evidently fearful witness. Luther Martin, the brilliant drunkard of the Maryland bar, spoke for Chase in his implacable dislike of Jefferson. As witness came George Hay who had been the most aggressive of Callender's defenders before Chase and who would become Burr's chief prosecutor. Hay's associate in the later prosecution of Burr, William Wirt, was often mentioned in the testimony as having been outrageously treated in the Callender trial by Chase. Here, too, was John Randolph of Roanoke, already breaking with Jefferson, but chief of the House managers against Chase. Burr faultlessly presiding now would meet them all again.

Little attention was paid then and has been paid in history to another figure in the Jefferson-Burr story. It is not clear whether David Randolph's friendship with Burr had already been formed before Jefferson's antagonism was clear. Now in the Chase trial Randolph did not regain Jefferson's affection by appearing as a witness for the Judge on trial—and for himself as well. A Democratic witness testified that Chase in his presence had asked Randolph "if he had any of those creatures or people called democrats on the panel of the jury to try Callender." When Randolph replied that he had "made no discrimination," the Judge told him "to look over the panel and if there were any of that description, strike them off."

Now Randolph testified that he had never seen this witness in the Judge's chambers and that Chase "never at any time or place" gave him any such instructions by either word or letter. In effect, he called Jeffer-

son's witness a perjurer. The President, however, had held to his conviction that the Callender jury was packed and had fired Randolph for that
reason. Burr expressed no opinion about Randolph's testimony. Long
afterwards he was to describe him as a man of "truth and goodness."

As the Chase trial proceeded Federalist fears of Burr's partisanship
disappeared. Even Plumer wrote at the trial's termination that "Mr. Burr
has certainly on the whole, done himself, the Senate & the nation honor
by the dignified manner in which he has presided over this high & numerous court." On not a single one of the eight charges against Chase
were the republicans able to muster the two-thirds vote necessary to conviction. Burr was unanimously acquitted of partisanship. He was proud to
send to Theodosia a comment by *The Washington Federalist*, which had
been critical of him at the outset: "He conducted [the trial] with the
dignity and impartiality of an angel, but with the rigour of a devil."

Strangely not even Jefferson seemed to disapprove of his behavior.
Beveridge thought the President's feelings "were balanced between grief
and glee." He was, he thought, rather pleased that John Randolph, who
was becoming more and more critical of the administration, had not gained
a personal triumph. Furthermore, the result would quiet republican restiveness in the Northern states and strong arguments would be taken from
those still mouthing about secession in New England. Later the President
was to confide to Plumer, whom he would convert to republicanism, that
"impeachment is a farce which will not be tried again."

Certainly the President at this period showed Burr favor sharply in
contrast to the mood he reported of their meeting a year before. Burr
wrote Theodosia of a message from the President that "Dr. Browne may
have the office of secretary of the government of Louisiana (which means
the upper district, whereof St. Louis is the capital). General Wilkinson is
appointed governor of that territory." Dr. Joseph Browne had married
the elder Theodosia's half sister. Moreover, Burr's stepson, J. B. Prevost,
was appointed Judge of the Superior Court at New Orleans.

"Wilkinson and Browne," said Burr, "will suit most admirably as eaters
and laughers, and, I believe, in all other particulars."

In this letter of March 10, 1805, however, he added a line suggesting
both haste and apprehension: "Charles Williamson has not returned from
Europe, but is hourly expected." This may have been reflected in some of
the testiness Plumer had noticed. At the end of the Chase trial Burr was
not well. According to a newspaper he had a sore throat. Plumer wrote

that he was "afflicted with pain in the head." Still, on March 2, 1805, the
retiring Vice-President rose to say farewell to the Senate. He spoke quietly
in the Chamber which had so recently resounded with legalistic oratory.
His extemporaneous remarks were variously reported but by all in admiration.

He spoke in warmth of his relations with the Senators. He was sure
that at times he had wounded the feelings of some by his rulings. He had
not knowingly done or attempted any injuries to any of the Senate, "nor
had he any to complain of, if any had been done or attempted, he was ignorant of the authors, and if he had ever heard he had forgotten, for, he
thanked God, he had no memory for injuries."

Then, as the *Federalist* reported, he challenged the attention of the
Senators "to considerations more momentous than any which regarded
merely their personal honor and character—the preservation of law, of
liberty, and the Constitution."

He paused in the deadly still quiet of the Chamber.

"This House, said he, is a sanctuary; a citadel of law, of order, and of
liberty; and it is here—it is here, in this exalted refuge; here, if anywhere,
will resistance be made to the storms of political phrensy and the silent
arts of corruption; and if the Constitution be destined ever to perish by
the sacrilegious hands of the demagogue or the usurper, which God avert,
its expiring agonies will be witnessed on this floor."

In the stillness "he averted to those affecting sentiments which attended a final separation—a dissolution, perhaps for ever" of happy associations. So saying, John Quincy Adams wrote his father, he left the
room quietly. Plumer wrote, "He bowed & retired—several shed tears very
plentifully." And at the President's House two days later in a group discussing the speech a Senator was asked how long Burr spoke. The Senator
paused, then said "he could form no idea; it might have been an hour, and
it might have been but a moment; when he came to his senses, he seemed
to have awakened as from a kind of trance."

Burr with "no memory for injuries" was gone. Within the month, he
wrote to his son-in-law from Philadelphia, "In New York I am to be disfranchised, and in New Jersey hanged. Having substantial objections to
both, I shall not, for the present, hazard either, but shall seek another
country."

He wrote in no saintly resignation, however.

"You will not, from this, conclude that I have become passive, or disposed to submit tamely to the machinations of a banditti. If you should you would greatly err. ———— and his clan affect to deplore, but secretly rejoice at and stimulate the villainies of all sorts which are practiced against me. Their alarm and anxiety, however, are palpable to a degree perfectly ridiculous. Their awkward attempts to propitiate reminds one of the Indian worship of the evil spirit. God bless you ever."

Evidently he knew that Alston could fill in the name which he left blank.

VIII.
WEB OF ENMITY

1.

The Double-Dealers

Charles Williamson had still not returned from England in April 1805 when Burr, with "gayety and cheerfulness," set out for the West. Neither had Merry received any answer to his endorsement of Burr's plans. Possibly the apparent contradiction of each other by the two Englishmen in reporting Burr's intentions created confusion in England which served delay.

According to Merry, Burr had offered to "lend his assistance to his Majesty's government in any manner in which they may think fit to employ him, particularly in endeavoring to effect a separation of the western part of the United States from that which lies between the Atlantic and the mountains, in its whole extent." To effect it he wanted half a million dollars and some ships at the Mississippi's mouth.

Williamson reported no such plan. What he described and supported was a proposed operation by the retiring Vice-President to invade Spanish territory in the West—a project always popular with the American pioneers along the Mississippi. He urged Britain to act promptly. In February 1805, while Burr was presiding like an angel and devil over the Chase trial, Williamson gave his understanding of the Colonel's enterprise and his faith in its success. With a small naval force in the Gulf of Mexico and an expenditure of less than two hundred thousand pounds, England, he said, "could expect before next August to see 50,000 North Americans with Colonel Burr at their head, far on their march to the City of Mexico."

As one old land developer to another Burr may have also mentioned to Williamson his canal, bank, and other projects, including a settlement

like the Britisher had built in the Genesee Valley. These may now have
seemed irrelevant to the repatriated Briton. He had greater schemes
related to the war going on in the world.

No one will ever be able to say with any certainty the exact plotting
or planning for a future which went on in Burr's brilliant mind. He had
secured strategic positions for his friends. Wilkinson, who may have first
proposed Western adventure, was in place by the Sabine River boundary
between the United States and Spanish territory. There he might create
a border incident which would bring on war.

The West then would rally behind an adventurous leader ready to
lead. In that situation, if Jefferson were docile before the Dons, the West
might be ready to separate from the Union. If the President were pushed
into firmly facing the Spanish, he could hardly hold back Burr to whom
thousands might rally and follow even to Mexico City. In the absence of
either eventuality, Burr would have properties near the frontier which
might serve for a base or a settlement, an enterprise or an excuse, a mask
or an alibi. Certainly the possibilities were more exciting than the dull
business some suggested of his securing a Congressional seat from this
region where he was more honored than vilified. He had stooped to
conquer once, now he meant to soar.

Disturbed but not discouraged by lack of news from England, he
cantered across Pennsylvania in high spirits. He was delighted by an
"ark" which he secured in Pittsburgh for only $133: "a floating house, sixty
feet by fourteen, containing dining room, kitchen with fireplace, and two
bedrooms; roofed from stem to stern; steps to go up, and a walk on the top
the whole length; glass windows &c." He floated in style on his downriver
journey, a trip, as he told Theodosia, not undertaken "from mere curiosity,
or pour passer le temps."

It was, however, merely from curiosity that he first stopped at an island in the middle of the Ohio River which had been turned into a se-
cluded gardened retreat by Harman Blennerhassett and his pretty young
wife Margaret. It included a great house of "original ugliness." Blennerhassett, an eccentric, nearsighted Irishman, was not present at the time, but
Mrs. Blennerhassett insisted upon the former Vice-President's staying for
dinner. Burr not only enjoyed the fine food and wines and exotic atmosphere of the island in the rough and ready river country. Also he surveyed
with his eyes the strategic position of the island as a place where he might
converge any settlers, adventurers, traitors, or filibusterers he recruited for

any of his downriver purposes. On her part, Margaret Blennerhassett was fascinated with her visitor as apparently were almost all ladies and gentlemen in this middle American country.

Downriver even a Judge, presumably of a judicial temperament, described Burr as the West saw him: "a man of erect and dignified deportment—his presence is commanding—his aspect mild, firm, luminous and impressive. The eyebrows are thin, nearly horizontal, and too far from the eye; his nose is . . . rather inclined to the right side; gently elevated which betrays a degree of haughtiness . . . His eyes . . . are of a dark hazel, and, from the shade of protruding eye bones and brows, appear black; they glow . . . and scintillate with the most tremulous and tearful sensibility—they roll with the celerity and phrensy of poetic fervour, and beam with the most vivid and piercing rays of genius. His mouth is large; his voice is clear, manly and melodious; his lips are thin, extremely flexible, and when silent, gently closed . . . His chin is rather retreating and voluptuous." Burr would have edited that ornate passage as sharply as he had some of Theo's adolescent letters. But the effusion explains some of the fascination of Margaret Blennerhassett and others—gentlemen, ladies, level-eyed frontiersmen, adventurous boys and girls. Burr's chroniclers almost blaze his passages by babies he supposedly left behind him including, according to Wandell and Minnigerode, a "Fearing Burr" born on the island in 1806.

The Colonel was all business, showing no "phrensy of poetic fervour" when he met his partners in canal promotion, Senators Dayton and Smith, in Cincinnati. Smith, as a speculator in West Florida, had earlier followed what the Hispanic-American historian Isaac J. Cox called "the usual practice of taking an oath of allegiance to the Spanish King." From this conference the Colonel moved overland by Lexington, where, though many cheered him, a few regarded him in silent suspicion, then to Nashville. There he renewed his friendship with Andrew Jackson. This tall, gaunt Tennessean remembered Burr's efforts in Tennessee's fight for statehood. As a man ready with his fists or pistols to defend his honor, he was outraged by the denunciation of Burr for his duel at Weehawken. This "Old Hickory" of future fame and others paid the New Yorker honor and piled hospitalities upon him. Then in an open boat, provided by Jackson, he drifted down the Cumberland River to board his own ark again and to find General Wilkinson waiting at Fort Massac on the Ohio.

The slim Colonel and the bulbous General conferred for four days.

Burr, counting on his old and intimate friend, certainly could not have known of a transaction in which the General had been involved just a year and a half before. On December 20, 1803, in a post secured for him by Burr, Wilkinson had participated in the transfer of Louisiana from France to the United States. Shortly after the ceremonies the General got in touch with high Spanish officials still lingering in New Orleans. He complained that his Spanish pension was twenty thousand dollars in arrears. He made this move, he wrote the Marquis of Casa Calvo, because of the "anxious solitude which I feel for the prosperity of the two Powers, which I love equally."

After some bargaining Wilkinson agreed to accept a cash payment of twelve thousand pesos in lieu of the pension arrears and promised to send—in the greatest secrecy, of course—such information to the Spanish government as he believed would be useful to it. Soon he advised the Spanish to fortify the Texas and Florida frontiers against possible American attack, to placate the Indians, and to arrest the expedition led by Lewis and Clark.

Playing both strings of his bow, Wilkinson sent Burr South with reassuring letters to his Spanish bribers and other letters fulsomely introducing him to persons who wanted just such a movement against Spanish territories as the Dons feared. Wilkinson also provided Burr with an elegant barge. Under its colored sails, a military crew propelled the Colonel down the Mississippi by mansioned Natchez. Along the lower river he stopped for breakfast and dinner at a succession of hospitable plantations. There were new friends and old ones, some Revolutionary companions in arms. All greeted him with both respect and expectancy.

New Orleans opened its arms to him. Honors were paid him by Creoles, many of them discontented under the new American rule, and by settlers from the Eastern states as intent as he was upon restored fortunes. He had met in Washington the winter before the three Creole gentlemen who had come protesting to the Jefferson administration against laws which indicated a lack of faith in the ability of the people in the new territory to govern themselves. The system provided for the government of Louisiana seemed to some, even in the East, a lapse in Jeffersonian ideas of democracy. Without using the expression, the Creole deputies had protested in effect against "taxation without representation."

Minister Merry had written his government, on the occasion of the visit of these gentlemen to Washington, that he knew that they became very intimate with Burr. Certainly Creoles welcomed him in New Orleans like an old friend. Welcoming him too was Daniel Clark, in whom he had expressed so much interest. He was happy to see again his old friend "Beau Ned" Livingston who had come West after he was ruined by the defalcations of a subordinate in his post as Federal official in New York. While neither of these gentlemen admitted membership in it, they were sympathetic with an organization called The Mexican Association which desired invasion of that Spanish colony. Burr found possibly unexpected welcome from the Roman Catholic Church. Much of its revenues in Mexico had been cut by a decree from Madrid. A bishop took him on his arm to a convent of Ursuline nuns where, as he reported it, gay and witty nuns, with their veils thrown back, served him wine and cake. There were banquets and toasts. And everywhere to his acclaim were added glasses lifted *À la santé Madame Alston* whose place was first in all his plans. Somehow all seemed to expect that Burr's purposes in conquest, separation, or settlement were their own. Through Clark and Livingston he began to negotiate for the purchase of the Bastrop lands on the Ouachita River in what became the northern part of the state of Louisiana, close to the Spanish border.

Such were the attentions paid him that the Colonel found it hard to pull himself away on July 10 for the laborious overland journey northward. Possibly his reception in the Southwest after rejection in the East turned his head a little. He was, he wrote, in Natchez long enough to "leave some tears of regret when I left."

There was hard going ahead. In the deadly summer season on the Natchez Trace, he found traveling conditions worse than he had met in the aftermath of hurricane in Georgia and South Carolina. Then beyond hardships came greater hospitality in Nashville—banquets and parades in his honor. Jackson, to whom he poured out his vision of Mexican adventure (and certainly not one word of any secession plans), was, he found again, "one of those prompt, frank, ardent souls whom I love to meet."

While "lounging" for a week at Jackson's house, he wrote Theo a letter which amounted to part of a journal about his travels. He was cured of "all the evils of my wilderness jaunt." Playfully he addressed her as "hussey," one of the teasing terms like "baggage" which he used in writing her. He would not have been so playful had he known her state of mind at this time. She needed more than toasts "à la santé." The daughter whom he thought of as a princess was, in this August 1805, showing or hiding

definite signs of morbidity of mind. Secretly she disclosed them in a letter
to Alston for delivery to him "immediately" after her death.

Burr, who often worried about her health, did not know that she had
been ill while he was laboring up the Natchez Trace. But Theo was
then moving, she believed, on an even darker path than the Trace. At
only twenty-two, she wrote her much loved husband that "something whispers me that my end approaches." Standing on "the brink of eternity,"
she wrote, she had a few requests to make "ere I plunge in the fearful
abyss."

She directed the disposal of her possessions, including some things
which had belonged to her mother. "Return Natalie the little desk she
gave me, accompanied by assurance of my affectionate recollection, and
a ring of my hair. . . . To you, my beloved, I leave our child. . . . You
love him now; henceforth love him for me also. . . . I fear you will
scarcely be able to read this scrawl, but I feel hurried and agitated. Death
is not welcome to me . . . you have made me too fond of life. . . . Let
my father see my son sometimes. Do not be unkind towards him whom I
have loved so much, I beseech you. . . . I hope for happiness in the next
world, for I have not been bad in this."

And finally, almost madly she wrote: "I had nearly forgotten to say
that I charge you not to allow me to be stripped and washed, as is usual.
I am pure enough thus to return to dust. Why, then, expose my person.
Pray see to this. If it does not appear contradictory or silly, I beg to be
kept as long as possible before I am consigned to the earth."

All unaware of this delusion of his daughter which might make dust
of his dreams, the Colonel moved northward again by Lexington and
Frankfort where he had enemies as well as friends. Travel was slow,
stops frequent. He had written Theo that he expected to be in late October at Berkeley Springs, now West Virginia, one of those fashionable spas
at which she spent so much time. Just as he was unaware of Theo's dark
fears, he was ignorant of reports about himself behind him and before
him. Tongues were already wagging then with rumors apparently aroused
in the North by Yrujo and in the South by his agents. The Spanish Minister might be a fop, jealous of his position at a President's table. He was
no fool.

On Burr's way he conferred again with Wilkinson in St. Louis. What
passed between them then was only reported later by the General. Then,
in covering his own tracks, this military personage stated that on this

occasion Burr spoke of the imbecility of Jefferson's government: "It would moulder to pieces die a natural death." Wilkinson quoted himself as responding, "No person was ever more mistaken! The Western people . . . are bigoted to Jefferson and democracy."

This was a dramatic after-speech. The General was then, Burr believed, his enthusiastic ally. Soon afterwards, however, behind his blustering front, Wilkinson was secretly shaken. Two months after Burr left New Orleans to the music of cheers, his new friend Clark wrote his old friend Wilkinson a long letter. Written in bantering tone, it must have chilled the General to the bottom of his well-shined boots. Clark's letter was dated September 7, 1805. Possibly, as has been suggested, Burr was with Wilkinson when he received it. That seems improbable considering the pace of the mails at the time. Certainly the General did not then share its contents with the Colonel.

"Many absurd and wild reports are circulated here," the acquisitive and exuberant Clark wrote from New Orleans, "and have reached the ears of the officers of the late Spanish government, respecting our ex-Vice-President. You are spoken of as his right-hand man, and even I am now supposed to be of consequence enough to combine with Generals and Vice-Presidents. At another time but the present, I should amuse myself vastly at the folly and fears of those who are affected with these idle tales; But being on the point of setting off for Vera Cruz, on a large mercantile speculation, I feel cursedly hurt at the rumors, and might, in consequence of Spanish jealousy, get into a hobble I could not easily get out of." Clark's letter seemed almost deliberately designed to dangle the portly General in suspense.

"Entre nous," he went on, "I believe that Minor, of Natchez, has a great part in this business, to make himself of importance. He is in the pay of Spain, and wishes to convince them he is much their friend. This is, however, a matter of suspicion on my part, but the channel through which the information reaches me, makes me suppose it."

The region was rampant with suspicions. Clark mentioned a mutual acquaintance, one Power, "whose head is always stuffed with plots, projects, conspiracies, etc., etc., etc., and who sees objects through a millstone." He was going up to Natchez "to unravel the whole of this extraordinary business, and then God have mercy on the culprits, for Spanish fire and indignation will be leveled at them. What in the name of heaven could have given rise to these extravagancies?"

Finally he came to the reports which did seem of a Munchausen character: "The tale is a horrid one, if well told. Kentucky, Tennessee, the State of Ohio, and part of Georgia and Carolina, are to be bribed with the plunder of the Spanish countries west of us, to separate from the Union. This is but part of the business. Heavens! what wonderful things there will be in those days. But how the devil I have been lugged into the conspiracy, or what assistance, I can be to it, is to me incomprehensible. Vous, qui savez tout, can best explain this riddle. Amuse Mr. Burr with an account of it, but let not these great and important objects, these almost imperial doings, prevent you from attending to my land business."

He added a final fillip: "I hope you will not have Kentucky men for your masters of ceremonies."

Wilkinson was not amused. Later he described Clark's report as "the tale of a tub of Burr." As the chief among them, he knew that the West was replete with double-dealers. He knew that Minor to whom Clark referred was Stephen or Estevan Minor, who from service as a Spanish officer had moved to wealth as an American citizen and planter at Natchez. Obviously, with various sources of sinister information, Spain wished to immobilize Burr as an assailant by spreading the report that he planned treason against his own country. The florid and arrogant Wilkinson has not generally been regarded as a man with a conscience. Certainly he had the cowardice associated with a bad one. He was in danger of being exposed as a traitor to both Spain, which paid him well, and the United States, which had given him the highest rank in its army. He was in a position where he might lose both or set himself up as the savior of each.

Not only were rumors following Burr. Also questions were raised before him in the East. While he was still in the West a series of "Queries" appeared anonymously in the *Gazette of the United States* of Philadelphia. It has been suggested that they were inspired by Spanish Minister Yrujo who, on occasion, did use the press for his propaganda. Charging nothing but insinuating much, these "Queries" wondered about Burr as "the head of a revolutionary party on the Western waters" in a plan for the states there to "form a separate government."

The Colonel could not have failed to be disturbed by such speculations about his movements. Apparently he heard them when he reached Berkeley later than he expected. He was disappointed not to find the Alstons there. They had left bad news behind them at the springs. Burr was troubled by the information he received about Theo's health and not, as he wrote Alston, reassured by "the sort of recovery of which she advises me." His solicitudes about both her and her son, he said, "poison all my enjoyments, and often unfit me for business." He hurried on to Washington. From there he reported to Alston, without personal comment: "There will be no war with Spain unless we declare it which is not expected. England continues a course of malevolence, which will still continue and be borne. France, more courteous in words, under the pressure of her own affairs."

Burr evidently reflected the view Jefferson was taking of foreign affairs. Officialdom in Washington was paying little attention to the questions about the Colonel's activities in the arch-Federalist *Gazette*. The supposed inspiration of them by Yrujo added nothing to their credibility. Jefferson wrote, referring to the dinner party tempest, that Yrujo had been "soured on a question of etiquette against the administration." Yrujo's irritations could be disregarded since, as the President wrote to his daughter Martha shortly before Burr's arrival in the capital, "The almost certainty of a continental war in Europe gives us time to bring Spain to reason peaceably. . . ."

Already the United States seemed almost in the pinchers of an intercontinental and particularly a maritime war. The day before Jefferson wrote, Nelson's defeat of a Franco-Spanish fleet at Trafalgar had reduced Spain's ability to protect its possessions in the Americas. That would have seemed to make it simpler for Britain to provide the few ships both Merry and Williamson asked for Burr in the West. There Spanish provocations on the land equaled the British harassment of American shipping and the impressment of American sailors on the seas.

Publicly Jefferson talked more belligerently than he did to his daughter. In his message to Congress, on December 3, 1805, the pacifistic President spoke militantly against Spain. They were raiding into Orleans (as Louisiana was then called) and Mississippi, seizing citizens and plundering property, giving cause for the war for which Burr hoped. Such outrages, Jefferson said, must be met by force. But three days later, in a secret message to Congress, he indicated he had no idea of going to war. What the President asked in this second message was obscure. Inquiring about it, Randolph of Roanoke found out, at least to his own satisfaction, that Jefferson wanted two million dollars with which to pay again for the Floridas that Americans thought they had already bought—or, as Randolph regarded it, as a bribe to Napoleon to disassociate powerful France from feeble Spain. Ready for a break with Jefferson, Randolph denounced this as "backstairs government." There were some who thought that in wanting money to pay what the nation did not owe, Jefferson was reversing the old cry about millions for defense but not one cent for tribute.

Whatever the facts, Burr seemed about to be deprived of war as a way to glory. This appeared to be particularly true when the President arrayed his forces in Congress to silence opposition. A proposal was made that, instead of an appropriation for his use as the President asked, troops be raised to defend the Southern frontier "from Spanish inroad and insult, and to chastise the same." This was defeated seventy-two to fifty-eight. Still weakness in support of the President even among his own forces was indicated when twelve of Virginia's twenty-two representatives voted for the fiery resolution.

Shortly before the President sent these two messages to Congress, the nation had indicated its sentiments. New York had hailed the arrival of Miranda announcing his intention to liberate South America. This Venezuelan soldier of fortune was a flamboyant figure whose presence in itself was a sensation. As a young man he had gone to Europe to join the Spanish army, but he was charged with insubordination and misuse of funds. Crying his innocence he fled to America, arriving just as the Colonies were winning their independence. Here he had the friendship of such great ones as Washington, Paine, and Hamilton. As an adventurer with a cause, he was hounded by Spanish agents. He led them on a lively trail which included his service for the Revolution in France, a place as one of the lovers of Catherine the Great, and as ubiquitous agitator for South American independence. It was said of him that he had all the talents except ability to put them together. One item which does not seem to have detracted from his charm was that he was always picking his teeth.

As early as 1792 he had proposed to William Pitt a plan for the creation of an independent empire stretching from the Mississippi to Cape Horn. Pitt was not interested. Ten years later, finally with the aid of Burr's friend Williamson, he tried again. Pitt was still not interested. So, in 1805, he decided to set out singlehandedly with private aid.

His reception in Washington added to the confusion about Jefferson's attitude toward Spain. Secretary of State Madison, who had been quarreling with Yrujo about the boundaries of the Floridas, gave the exuberant South American a dinner. Jefferson invited him to dine at the Executive Mansion. Without reserve Miranda discussed with American officials his plan of forcibly expelling Spanish rulers from Venezuela. He went back to New York and with little effort at concealment acquired a ship, arms, crew, and military supplies. Also in Philadelphia he met Burr.

From Miranda, Burr must have received his first full report of the failure of Williamson to secure British aid for such an adventure as his. Williamson had had a long and dangerous voyage to England. There his position as the brother of a Scottish baron gave him access to the highest society. Even more important, his friend and patron Lord Melville put him close to the ear of William Pitt, who came back into power as Prime Minister in May 1804. Melville, born Henry Dundas, was not only Pitt's First Lord of the Admiralty, he was the Prime Minister's lieutenant and close friend. Evidently he had had something to do with Williamson's recent South American assignment. When Williamson arrived in England, however, Melville was both close to Pitt and close to impeachment.

Dundas had risen in Scotland as a rough political power. Such was his strength that he was called "King Harry the Ninth." He was tough also in his mounting position in the United Kingdom. Under what was called "the Dundas despotism" he had implacably persecuted some of the radicals and reformers whom Jefferson, in a variety extending from Priestley to Callender, had welcomed to America. He did not seem a man who would be interested in South American or any other sort of freedom. His liberal opponents had apparently found a crack in his crusty armor. A commission had been named to scrutinize his accounts as Treasurer of the Navy from 1782 to 1800. The commission, in 1805, was piling up its reports. It was doubtful that even Pitt could protect him. He listened to Williamson. Perhaps Pitt listened to him. But when Burr returned from the West to meet Miranda, it was clear that there would be little British aid for either.

The two unsuccessful supplicants for aid from His Majesty's purse did not hit it off well. Apparently Burr met Miranda's ardor with coldness on the only occasion on which they met "at the house of a common friend." Certainly Miranda came from their encounter with enduring resentment. Burr told his friend Biddle that "Miranda was a fool, totally unqualified for such an expedition." Later he modified this expression saying that he was greatly pleased by Miranda's "social talents and colloquial eloquence." But: "The bare suspicion of any connection between him and me would have been injurious to my project and fatal to his."

There was basis for suspicion of such a connection. Indeed, the supporters of the two men in America could almost be described as an interlocking directorate. One of the chief supporters of both was William S. Smith, at this time Surveyor of the Port of New York. He was Jefferson's old Paris friend who, a dozen years before, had brought him the first news of Genet's adventurous Western plans. Smith had toured Europe with Miranda before he came back to America to plunge heavily into land speculations and politics. He was one of the officials from previous administrations who remained in office under Jefferson.

Smith's partner, Samuel Ogden, while supporting Miranda, was closer to Burr. From childhood Burr had had close ties with the Ogden family. His boyhood chum and a companion on the Quebec campaign was Matthias Ogden. The son of Matthias was to be one of the Colonel's confidential messengers to Wilkinson. Also backing Miranda was Burr's chief partner, Senator Dayton, who was married to the sister of Matthias. Some evidence of the prestige of the Ogdens is indicated by the marriage of Samuel Ogden to a sister of the "high flying Federalist" Gouverneur Morris.

Behind Miranda too were the Swartwout brothers, who had been Burr's ardent aides in New York politics. They apparently had no connections with Miranda save possibly through Burr or via Burr through Williamson. Some less well-known friends of Burr were also active in Miranda's preparations. There is no evidence that he sought to hold them back. Possibly, as has been said, he was jealous of the South American. Undoubtedly support of Miranda divided the funds available to Burr in the all too evident event that no British aid would be forthcoming. In any event, backed by Burr's friends and some of Jefferson's officials, the "precursor" of South American liberty sailed away in confidence. Like other Americans then, Burr was ignorant of the letter which in farewell Miranda had written Secretary of State Madison. The matters he had communicated to Madison, the South American wrote, "will remain, I doubt not, in the deepest secret until the final result of this delicate affair. I have acted here on that supposition, conforming myself in everything to the intentions of the government which I hope I have seized and observed with exactitude and discretion."

Madison was later to deny that the government had any "intentions" or involvement in the whole business. Such disavowal of complicity came only after Yrujo, who had suspected Burr's intentions, came loudly complaining of this enterprise against his country conducted under the very nose of the Jefferson administration with indeed its Surveyor of the Port of New York actively involved in the plot.

The crisscrosses and complications in this matter were compounded by an astounding episode at the time of Miranda's preparations for departure. Possibly it indicated that without support Burr and his first civilian aide Dayton were ready to become mere picaresque rogues ready to pick up any scraps that they could from the collapse of their planning. At any rate, pretending to be a traitor to Burr, Dayton, who stuck with Burr to the last, went to see Yrujo. The Spanish Minister wrote Don Pedro Cevallos, Spanish Minister of Foreign Affairs, that Dayton with a great show of candor came and offered to betray Burr for thirty or forty thousand dollars. Without committing himself on the price Yrujo said he encouraged him to proceed. Dayton, he said, told him of Burr's dealings with Merry, of his plans for taking the Floridas and Mexico and joining them to the West. Moreover, according to the diplomat, Dayton said that the British Cabinet was favorable to the scheme and Pitt was considering it seriously.

Walter Flavius McCaleb, as great student of the Burr "conspiracy," regarded Dayton's proposal to Yrujo as a "palpably fictitious fabric." With it, he believed, Burr and Dayton hoped to terrify the Spanish into paying the expenses of an enterprise against their own possessions. Schachner wrote that this was Burr's own scheme after learning from Jefferson that there would be no war with Spain. At this point he believed that the possibility of heroic participation in a war with Spain had passed. Only the Ouachita settlement was possible. There was no harm in exposing an extinct plot and some profit might be gained from Spanish fears. Yrujo, whose government had Wilkinson on its payroll, was not alarmed at what must have been old news to him. But like throwing a bone to a possibly useful dog, the Minister gave Dayton fifteen hundred dollars and ultimately a thousand more.

Not all were ready to believe that Burr's proposed move toward Mexico was a lost cause. Evidently in England Williamson still had some hopes. Dayton in his talk with Yrujo had told the Minister that the British agent was expected back in the United States "within a month or six weeks." That would be just before the sailing of Miranda. Indeed, Williamson himself had hoped to join Miranda. But the impeachment of Melville and the military situation in Europe made that impossible. The British Colonel, however, had not given up his hopes for Burr.

On January 3, 1806, and again on January 6, he repeated his importunities to Melville. Evidently at this time Melville was too preoccupied to discuss the matter with his protégé personally. Williamson, with a new view of Burr's plans, sent his memorandums to one of Melville's associates requesting that he show them to him, who "will take, I dare say, Measures to give his Opinions to the only Man in the Nation [Pitt] that can, after all, act on them." He held up again the glittering promise of a triumphant march into Spain's American jewel, Mexico City.

When Williamson wrote his second letter this January, Pitt's colleagues were already desperately worried about his health. By January 15 they were determined to force him to resign as the only means of saving his life. Eight days later, on January 23, 1806, Pitt was dead. The new ministry was dominated by Charles James Fox as Secretary of State for Foreign Affairs. He had opposed much of Pitt's foreign policy as a crusade against freedom in the interest of despotism. He scorned much of the underground diplomacy of this period. When a French adventurer, whom Fox at first "did the honor to take for a spy," came to him with a plan for the assassination of Napoleon, the British Minister sent a warning, on February 20, to Talleyrand. The incident provided a momentary hope for peace. Apparently Fox took a similar though less contemptuous attitude toward Merry's eagerness for machinations in America. That gentleman who was more dupe than devil received, to his astonishment, a polite communiqué that His Majesty's government consented to his request for recall. Merry protested in surprise that he never expressed any such wish. Fox disregarded the plaintive protests of the diplomat whose dinner-table distaste for America had evidently disappeared.

With his great friend Pitt gone, Lord Melville was brought to trial. He was acquitted, but he never again held office. His protégé Williamson had no longer an ear close to power into which at least he could pour his plans. He returned to America and during the next two years was an articulate, if unheeded, advocate of the overthrow of the "Frenchified" Jefferson regime and now of American separation. He still regarded Burr, according to Cox, as "a dependable agent."

The situation had swiftly changed. Soon after Merry's "request for recall" had been graciously granted, Yrujo's turn came. His public quarreling with Madison had reached such proportions that he was asked not to show his face in Washington even before his status as Minister was terminated at American request. Other changes were not so easily seen. Burr's friend and biographer Davis wrote of the news of Pitt's demise: "Wilkinson must have heard of the death of the premier late in the spring of 1806. From that moment, in Mr. Burr's opinion, Wilkinson became alarmed, and resolved on an abandonment of the enterprise at the sacrifice of his associates."

Even earlier, Burr in Washington showed his readiness for a change —even if temporary—in his plans.

2.

Rope or Dagger

"Aaron Burr has been several times in this city this session," diarist Senator Plumer wrote on February 22, 1806, in Washington. "He came here a few days since from Charleston. He dined this day with the President of the United States."

Evidently the Colonel had gone South to see Theo and "little Burr" about whom he was so much concerned. He had written his son-in-law, who was then Speaker of the House in the South Carolina legislature, that he knew Alston would be involved in his South Carolina ties and engagements. So the father and grandfather would come and bring them to a climate he believed more salubrious.

"I determine, at any sacrifice," he wrote, "to rescue Theodosia and son."

Little information is available about this visit to Theo in Charleston or at The Oaks near Georgetown, South Carolina. Alston undoubtedly was much involved in the politics of this year. William Loughton Smith and other anti-Jeffersonians were endeavoring to raise to new heat old party differences. When Burr was in the state the news about the President's messages seemed to provide an issue for the Congressional elections ahead. Federalists were preparing to campaign under the now ironic old slogan "Millions for Defense but not one cent for Tribute." There was furious talk that Jefferson preferred a bribe to France to appropriations for the repair of American defenses. Smith undertook—unsuccessfully as it turned out—to defeat a Democratic Congressman who had voted for the President's preference.

There is no information that Burr took part in this debate beginning while he was in South Carolina. Certainly he was not taking a loud part in it. He made the return journey over the rough roads to Washington ready to make his peace with the President, with whom he dined on Washington's birthday—ironically the second anniversary of that day when, among Federalists, he had lifted his glass "To the Union of All Honest Men."

Some historians have assumed, possibly on the basis of Plumer's diary entry, that February 22, 1806, was the date of the last recorded confrontation between the two men. In his *Anas* entry for April 15, 1806, Jefferson vaguely fixed the date as "about a month ago." Certainly other significant dates, all in one way or another relating to Burr, had preceded it.

On January 10, 1806, the President had received the first of a series of letters charging Burr and Wilkinson with treasonous purposes in the West. They came from one of the Federalists Jefferson had left in office, U. S. Attorney Joseph Hamilton Daveiss of Kentucky. Daveiss, who had adopted his middle name because of his adoration of Hamilton, was a brother-in-law of another Kentuckian, Humphrey Marshall, first cousin of Chief Justice Marshall. Jefferson had good reason to be wary of these Federalists.

Humphrey Marshall particularly recalled an earlier episode Jefferson always remembered with unease. This arrogant Federalist, who was said to measure his money by the peck, had, in 1793, exposed and opposed the plot of Genet and George Rogers Clark to attack Spanish and English territories in the West. He had accused Jefferson's friend, Governor Isaac Shelby, of complicity. In the resulting furor he had defeated for the United States Senate John Breckinridge, now Jefferson's Attorney General, who had been ready to back Genet. Happily for Democrats, Marshall overplayed his role as ardent Federalist and was subjected to mob violence before he was displaced in the Democratic sweep of 1800. His arrogant Federalism, which he shared with Daveiss, was not shaken. The warning letters which Daveiss began sending, in January 1806, cried treason not only at Wilkinson and Burr but at Breckinridge and other good Democrats too. The President declined to be disturbed by Daveiss' charges.

He was more disturbed about another recent event. Unpleasant as Yrujo had become, his cries of protest about Miranda's expedition against Spanish possessions could not be disregarded. So shortly after the South American was safely out of the harbor, Jefferson, on February 6, 1806, had ordered the District Attorney in New York to investigate the sailing as a violation of neutrality. Smith and Ogden, who, as partners in various speculations, had provided the *Leander* for Miranda, were indicted. As a defense they undertook to prove that the expedition had sailed with government approval. Jefferson in his *Anas* said of the case that his old friend Smith and Smith's partner Ogden "contrived to make it a government question, in which they mean to have the administration and the judge tried as the culprits instead of themselves." Certainly this case was going to give Jefferson and Madison some squirming moments.

When the defendants tried to call high government officials as witnesses, apparently to prove government complicity, they refused to appear. They sent instead a statement that the President "has specifically signified to us that our official duties cannot . . . be at this juncture dispensed with." Denied such witnesses as they felt they required, Ogden and Smith were nevertheless acquitted and, some felt, the administration was convicted. Jefferson confided to his private journal that Burr's friend U. S. Marshal John Swartwout packed the jury with the "bitterest federalists." It was high time to get rid of this Swartwout who had so recently circulated with approval Van Ness's *Aristides* pamphlet.

The third matter much on Jefferson's mind before he saw Burr was related to affairs discussed in this same pamphlet. Indeed, Jefferson said he only wrote this *Anas* passage about his meeting with Burr because of old "falsehoods" in it which long troubled him. His report of this meeting, prompted by his resentment, is the only record of it which exists:

"I did not commit these things to writing at the time," he wrote of his conversation with Burr, "but I do it now, because in a suit between him [Burr] and Cheetham, he has had a deposition of Mr. Bayard taken, which seems to have no relation to the suit, nor to any other object than to calumniate me."

This was, of course, reference to an affidavit about the 1801 tie fight which Congressman Bayard made at the request of some of Burr's friends —not Burr. In it Bayard swore that it was Jefferson who made the deal for the Presidency in the election contest—not Burr.

"Bayard pretends to have addressed to me," the *Anas* entry went on, "during the pending of the Presidential election in February, 1801, through General Samuel Smith, certain conditions on which my election might be obtained, and that General Smith, after conversing with me, gave answers from me. This is absolutely false. No proposition of any kind was ever made to me on that occasion by General Smith, nor any answers authorized by me. And this fact General Smith affirms at this moment."

This *Anas* passage was never published until 1830, after Jefferson's death. Then the matter was opened again by Bayard's sons in an effort to prove that not their father but Jefferson lied. The truth may never be known. Jefferson's sensitiveness about the affair and his bitterness to those who charged him with making a bargain are certain facts. It is also certain that the Daveiss charges, the Miranda business, and the Bayard affidavit were items which shaped his feeling in the long bitter passage about this meeting with Colonel Burr.

Jefferson wrote that on this occasion Burr made his second request for some mark of favor. As he had a year before, the ex-Vice-President referred to that letter which Jefferson had written him in December 1800, when the possibility dawned that they might be tied for the Presidency. The words were there in Jefferson's hand. Burr so recently, according to them, had been one of those "whose talents, integrity, names, and dispositions should at once inspire unbounded confidence in the public mind and ensure a perfect harmony in the public affairs." Two years before at their meeting in January 1804, the President had given Burr an involved, almost convoluted explanation of his meaning in that letter. Now, he wrote that he spoke bluntly.

As Jefferson described him, Burr had come to this meeting with at least a small chip on his shoulder. He was quoted as saying that he "could walk on his own two legs and take care of himself." But he thought he was entitled to more than cold politeness from Jefferson. He "could do me much harm" but did not wish to do so. Jefferson wrote that he replied that he had never done a single act that he "feared to have fully laid open." Indeed, he [Jefferson] had "never done a single thing with a view to my personal interest, or that of any friend, or with any other view than that of the greatest public good." He could give Burr no position, because he had "lost the public confidence."

Then Jefferson wrote a remarkable thing. By loss of confidence, he told his caller, he did not refer to newspaper charges, but: "to the late Presidential election, when, though in possession of the office of Vice-President, there was not a single voice heard for his retaining it."

Jefferson's report to his private records did not indicate that Burr made any answer to this. It would be incredible, however, to believe that Burr made no reply unless he was shocked into silence by a Presidential

distortion of the facts which history has much silently accepted. It is difficult to think that Jefferson would have made this statement knowing
that both he and Burr knew better. It is certain that Burr would not have
silently accepted this declaration that the lack of votes for him in the
nominating caucus of 1804 was an indication of a feeling of universal
obloquy about him.

Burr had had friends in that caucus. And nobody knew better than
Jefferson that he was not even a candidate for the nomination when it
met. Beginning at least as early as September 1801, Jefferson had managed
to array enough of his party's votes to beat Burr in the caucus. Burr understood that when, on January 26, 1804, he expressed to Jefferson his willingness to retire to prevent a party schism. On February 18, 1804, Burr
removed himself from the contest for the Vice-Presidential nomination
by accepting nomination for Governor of New York. The caucus in which
he received no votes, not being a candidate, was not held until February
25, 1804. As a credulous man, Jefferson in writing this entry counted on
the credulity of history and he was not much mistaken about that. If the
exchange took place as Jefferson described it, it seems incredible that, as
was the case, after this meeting Jefferson gave and Burr accepted an invitation to dine soon again at the Executive Mansion where presumably
pêle-mêle protocol still prevailed.

Soon after Burr talked with Jefferson at this meeting in the spring
of 1806, he wrote to Andrew Jackson the conviction he had come to after
conferring with the President and others. The Tennessean, he wrote,
had "doubtless before this time been convinced that we are to have no
war if it can be avoided with honor, or even without." So Burr was, as
Jefferson said he told him, "disengaged from all particular business—willing to engage in something." His story at this time suffers much from
a lapse of Davis as his biographer and editor of his letters. During the
rest of the spring and summer, which he spent principally in Washington and Philadelphia, wrote this amateur archivist, "his correspondence
is voluminous, but in no manner develops any other views than such as
relate to land speculations." So Davis apparently passed them around as
souvenirs or threw them away. Space made it "absolutely necessary to
exclude them from the work." Yet land speculation, in which so many
Americans were engaged, formed a main theme in Burr's whole story
and related to the principal purposes in which he said he was engaged
now. Some doubted that. The letters would have helped historians.

General Wilkinson was a land speculator, though he assured Jefferson he was not. He was dealing in lands for Daniel Clark before Burr first went West. Still a letter to him from Burr soon after he saw the President does not sound like a communication between real estate dealers. On April 16, 1806, the Colonel wrote: "The execution of our project is postponed till December; want of water in Ohio, rendered movement impractical; other reasons rendered delay expedient."

"Want of water in Ohio" was probably a way of saying lack of money for the West. Burr and Dayton were energetically seeking it. Burr had secured the support of Alston through the enthusiasm of his daughter. Burr and Dayton turned to the filibuster financiers Smith and Ogden, smarting under the treatment of themselves in the Miranda case. Their efforts, Jefferson suggested later, extended from Maine to Mississippi and New Orleans. Money from the Kentucky insurance company was secured through William Morton of Lexington, called Lord Morton because of his lavish living and the fact that he was a younger son of a titled English family. Earlier Burr had been in correspondence with the supposedly very rich Irishman Blennerhassett whose island he had visited the year before and who was eager to join Burr in "any contemplated enterprise." Blennerhassett's letter indicated he understood the one which he was invited to join would be action against Spanish territories in the event of war.

The one man essential to such an event was Wilkinson, and evidently Burr and Dayton had some doubts about him. The General had been uneasy about his status under Jefferson. Before his election, but in anticipation of it, he had sent Jefferson two Italian busts by one of his agents, Philip Nolan. This Nolan, whose name has been used in fiction as a man without a country, was actually a bold operator on the Spanish frontier. Indeed, he ranged far into the territories of the Dons to round up wild horses on the plains and, some said, useful information as well. Protégé of the General and brother-in-law of Stephen Minor, when he was killed later there were speculations that his death had been arranged because he knew too much.

Wilkinson made another move designed to please Jefferson. Less than a month after the Virginian's inauguration the General issued an order requiring all his officers and men to cut off their queues of hair, which had come to seem a symbol of Federalism. Still it was suggested that his place under Jefferson was far from secure.

In a letter dated July 24, 1806, Dayton played on Wilkinson's fears as to Jefferson. He wrote: "It is now well ascertained that you are to be displaced in the next session. Jefferson will affect to yield reluctantly to the public sentiment, but yield he will. Prepare yourself, therefore, for it. You know the rest. You are not a man to despair, or even despond, especially when such prospects offer in another quarter. Are you ready? Are your numerous associates ready? Wealth and glory! Louisiana and Mexico! I shall have time to receive a letter from you before I set out for Ohio —OHIO."

A letter in cipher from Burr to Wilkinson, dated five days later, cannot be quoted with complete confidence. Wilkinson later claimed he had difficulties in deciphering it. Also, he admitted he made erasures and alterations to suit his own safety. The generally accepted version, however, reads:

Your letter postmarked 13th May, is received. At length I have obtained funds, and have actually commenced. The Eastern detachments, from different points and under different pretences, will rendezvous on the Ohio 1st of November. Everything internal and external favors our views. Naval protection of England is secured. Truxton is going to Jamaica to arrange with the admiral on that station. It will meet us at the Mississippi. England, a navy of the United States, are ready to join, and final orders are given to my friends and followers. It will be a host of choice spirits. Wilkinson shall be second to Burr only; Wilkinson shall dictate the rank and promotion of his officers. Burr will proceed westward 1st August, never to return. With him goes his daughter; the husband will follow in October, with a corps of worthies. Send forthwith an intelligent and confidential friend with whom Burr may confer; he shall return immediately with further interesting details; this is essential to concert and harmony of movement. Send a list of all persons known to Wilkinson west of the mountains who could be useful, with a note delineating their characters. By your messenger send me four or five commissions of your officers, which you can borrow under any pretence you please; they shall be returned faithfully. Already are orders given to the contractor to forward six months' provisions to points Wilkinson may name; this shall not be used until the last moment, and then under proper injunctions. Our object, my dear friend, is brought to a point so long desired. Burr guarantees the result with his life and honor, with the lives and honor and the fortunes of hundreds, the best blood of our country. Burr's plan of operation is to move down rapidly from the Falls, on the 15th of November, with the first five hundred or a thousand men, in light boats now constructing for that purpose; to be at Natchez between the 5th and 15th of December, there to meet you; there to determine whether it will be expedient to seize on or pass by Baton Rouge. On receipt of this, send Burr an answer. Draw on Burr for all expenses, etc. The people of the country to which we are going are prepared to receive us; their agents, now with Burr, say that if we will protect their religion, and will not subject them to a foreign Power, that in three weeks all will be settled. The gods invite us to glory and fortune; it remains to be seen whether we deserve the boon. The bearer of this goes express to you. He is a man of inviolable honor and perfect discretion, formed to execute rather than project, capable of relating facts with fidelity, and incapable of relating them otherwise; he is thoroughly informed of the plans and intentions of Burr, and will disclose to you as far as you require, and no further. He had imbibed a reverence for your character, and may be embarrassed in your presence; put him at ease, and he will satisfy you.

Obviously Burr was going some lengths with the truth to bolster Wilkinson's courage. England had not agreed to supply naval protection. Commodore Truxtun had not agreed to join in the enterprise which Burr told the Commodore was one against Spain but without governmental approval. Neither the seizure of New Orleans nor Western separation were mentioned in this letter of Burr's. Baton Rouge was then a city of Spanish West Florida. The agents of the "country" who wished Burr to protect their religion were obviously Mexican Catholics.

The two letters were sent on the long way westward by two young men destined to have prominent connections in American life. Peter Ogden's uncle was to be a Governor of New Jersey; his brother was to serve in the Battle of New Orleans in 1815 as aide-de-camp under General Jackson. Samuel Swartwout, youngest of the three brothers ever faithful to Burr, was to become, according to Jackson biographer Parton, the man outside his Tennessee circle to whom Jackson would be most "affectionately devoted." They started promptly on a long overland journey to Wilkinson which would require two months.

These young men were typical of the recruits Burr was seeking. In reference to the Colonel's project, Yrujo had written that "it is beyond question that there exists in this country an infinite number of adventurers, without property, full of ambition, and ready to unite at once under the standard of a revolution which promises to better their lot." An impression was to be made that this was the sort of revolutionary gang

Burr recruited. Jefferson was to describe Burr's companions as desperadoes, Wilkinson as "an undisciplined rabble in a bad cause." Perhaps Comfort Tyler, who was to be a sort of top sergeant of Burr's company, was such a man. Apparently he had fallen on evil days and had been arrested for vagrancy in New York. But Burr rescued him from this situation as a stalwart citizen he had known earlier as a member of the New York Assembly. Tyler was no ordinary vagrant, and no adventurous boy. He had been conspicuous in the early development of western New York. Schoolteacher and surveyor, Tyler was given by the Indians who respected him the name To-whan-ta-gua, or one who could be a gentleman and a laboring man at the same time. He had aided Burr in recruiting other men from western New York, some whom Burr was to say he would "choose to lead armies, or engage in any high achievement that required talents and energy of character." Orsamus Turner, in his history of this region, footnoted what he called "a curious historical fact" that "the maps and charts, by which the British fleet approached New Orleans in the War of 1812, were those prepared in western New York, by a then resident here, for the south-western expedition of Col. Burr." He added: "The circumstance was accidental; the facts in no way implicating the author or maker of the maps." The fact does remain curious.

Burr's adherents were by no means only those he had known on the New York frontier. Some European gentlemen adventurers joined him. Notable among them was Dr. Justus Erich Bollman, who had won the acclaim of Americans, including Jefferson, for his heroic attempt to rescue Lafayette from an Austrian prison. This summer Burr was reported recruiting adventurous young men of the best families in Philadelphia. Jackson wrote that Burr wanted "none but young men of talents to go with him" who would help to draw to his settlement "wealth and character." Among his small group of followers were such young men as Presley Neville, son of the Chief Justice of Pennsylvania; and Thomas Butler, son of a brave Colonel who had resisted to his death Wilkinson's order that he cut off his queue. One who saw a group of Burr's adherents assembled on Blennerhassett Island said that they "looked like gentlemen, such as live upon their own property."

Having dispatched his cipher letter to Wilkinson, the Colonel was ready to move westward again. He seemed oblivious of the mounting tide of rumor and wild report about his plans. Some of it was built up by a flamboyant and dissolute character around Washington then, William

Eaton, who wore the self-assumed title of General. In 1797 Eaton had served as an undercover agent for the government in the Blount conspiracy. Then, as U. S. Consul in Tunis, he engaged in a series of remarkable adventures, the more remarkable as he told them time and time again. His story was that he was about to overthrow the piratical government of that North African country, then preying on American shipping, in daring fashion. Suddenly he received orders to return home since a treaty satisfactory to the United States had been made. In Washington he wore some of the florid costume he had assumed in Africa, including a brilliant colored sash. His demands for the sums and honors which he claimed were due him became tedious. He was garrulous in the lobbies of Congress and in the taverns frequented by officials. He was regarded more as a pest than a hero. Jefferson, however, in his message to Congress, on December 3, 1805, had praised his gallantry in Tripoli. The President did not pay equal tribute to his discretion.

It is difficult to fix the exact time when Eaton made a call on the President with regard to Burr. Jefferson only mentioned Eaton's story in the *Anas* late in October 1806. Eaton himself said that he called on Jefferson in the late winter or early spring, probably before Burr's visit. He may have seemed to the President a Burr emissary since he came to propose that Burr be sent as ambassador at London, Paris, or Madrid. He did this, he said, on the patriotic ground that "Colonel Burr ought to be removed from the country, because I considered him dangerous in it. . . ." However, he "perceived the subject was disagreeable to the President," so he did not, he said, amplify his reasons for believing Burr dangerous.

Outside the Presidential office, nothing deterred him from telling an amazing tale to members of Congress who, to his amazement, "did not seem much alarmed." Nobody seemed interested in his story—or even believed it—until later. And Eaton temporarily did no more about it.

Eaton said the usually reserved Burr, undertaking to enlist him in his plan, told him as a notoriously instable man an amazing tale. His project, he declared Burr disclosed, was one of "revolutionizing the territory west of the Allegheny; establishing an independent empire there; New Orleans to be the capital, and he himself to be the chief; organizing a military force on the waters of the Mississippi, and carry conquest to Mexico." He quoted the Colonel as talking more wildly still. He planned "overthrowing the present Government" and "would turn Congress neck and heels out of doors, assassinate the President, seize the treasury and Navy; and declare himself the protector of an energetic government."

This would, indeed, have been the action of a Catalinarian Burr or a madman. Burr looked like neither as he started westward in August behind his messengers to Wilkinson. In addition to a few associates, including a German secretary and a former French army officer, on this trip he was accompanied by Theodosia.

Her depression of the summer before had apparently been a swiftly passing delusion. She appeared as the perfect daughter-consort of a man who might be Emperor of Mexico. Floating down the rivers to Blennerhassett Island with her father on an ark like that upon which he had traveled the year before, she must have seemed like a young Cleopatra on a new Nile to the romantic Blennerhassetts. On the island she moved like a young woman who might grace a throne.

Now Burr, with Blennerhassett and his island, had both an aide and a base. He also had a fool in his train. Witnesses later described the master of the island as a man with "every kind of sense except common sense." He had come to this retreat so far from his homeland with books, musical implements, and scientific apparatus not merely because of his poetic preference for solitude. In a sense he was a fugitive from disapproval in Ireland where it seemed incestuous that his wife was his niece. A description drawn of him later was of a nearsighted man armed with "one brace of horse pistols, a brace of pocket pistols and a dirk." It was uncertain what such an armament would avail him because he could not distinguish a man from a horse at ten steps. Unfortunately he was also armed with a romantic pen.

If, as Jefferson was to say in one of his more charitable moments, Burr's activities were "the most extravagant since Don Quixote," Blennerhassett was a Sancho Panza lacking entirely in rustic cunning, wit, and sense. His chief appeared like no tilter at windmills. Neither did Burr seem, as he was pictured later in poetic prosecution oratory, a "destroyer" at whose approach the flowers in the Blennerhassett gardens should have withered. Decorating him to damn him, prosecutor William Wirt was to describe him beside those gardens as a man who found his way into hearts "by the dignity and elegance of his demeanor, the light and beauty of his conversation, and the seductive and fascinating power of his address." Certainly he looked like a commander on the boats upon which his few followers arrived on the island. The crafts were built on "the Schenectady model, such as are used on the Mohawk River."

Burr and Theodosia were joined on Blennerhassett Island by Joseph Alston, who was advancing funds for the expedition. Soon the Colonel seemed to be everywhere seeking recruits, having boats built, buying supplies. Blennerhassett, with dreams of imperial titles like sugarplums dancing in his head, took up his pen. He wrote a series of articles published in the *Ohio Gazette* under the pseudonym of Querist. In these pieces he wrote of separation of the West from the Union. Though he long denied their authorship, Blennerhassett was immediately suspect—and with him Burr.

Another journalistic explosion was being set off farther south in Lexington, Kentucky. There Daveiss, as impatient Federalist, had been joined by his brother-in-law Humphrey Marshall in publishing a newspaper, the *Western World*, which was printing and refurbishing the charges Daveiss had made to the President and which Marshall had made at the time of Genet's proposed Western adventure. One of the paper's ostensible editors was the same Wood, the suppression of whose book by Burr had served as a beginning for Cheetham's accusations of the political infidelity of the Vice-President.

Jefferson was still disregarding Daveiss and would soon discharge him. But as the fall came on in 1806, he was listening with mounting interest to every other suspicion about Burr's purposes. It is easier to follow the Colonel's journeys in the West than to date the steps in Washington in Jefferson's increasing conviction of his guilt—or, as Isaac Jenkinson put it, the steps he took in "hunting a conspiracy" which he could hang on Burr. Jenkinson, in his *Aaron Burr*, published in 1902, wrote that from the moment Jefferson learned of the Bayard affidavit procured by Burr's friends, his mind was "filled with venom and vengeance against Burr, and he determined to pursue him to the death." This, of course, amounts to reading the mind of a President long dead. In his evident antipathy Jefferson might more easily have convinced himself of Burr's guilt. Still, as a man often charged with gullibility, he should not be denied possible credit for unmalicious credulity in this matter.

In the same month in which Burr and Dayton dispatched their messengers with letters for Wilkinson, the President was writing home that "all public matters are in a state of tranquility, and seem as if they will continue so." That was not quite correct. In June 1806, orders had been

sent to Wilkinson at St. Louis to "descend with all practical dispatch" to
the South where the Spanish seemed threatening. In July the President
was only waiting for the Ogden and Smith case to be finally settled before firing Burr's friend John Swartwout. But of Burr he made no mention in his *Anas* from April until October 22, 1806, when he recorded
not only suspicions but convictions of Burr's guilt of treason.

He noted reports he had had from Eaton and others, not mentioning the early reports he had had from Daveiss and from some writers of
anonymous letters. Burr was "a Catalinarian character." But the President also noted that "suspicions of infidelity in Wilkinson" had become
very general. Also, that commander had disobeyed his June orders to
quickly move South, improve defenses, and take command at Natchitoches.
On October 22 the cabinet decided on the basis of reports to send confidential letters of warning to governors and district attorneys in the West.
Jefferson wanted them to have the Colonel strictly watched and "on his
committing any overt act unequivocally, to have him arrested and tried
for treason, misdemeanor, or whatever other offense the act may amount
to. . . ."

Two days later the President was moving at an accelerated pace to
warn and alarm the West with his suspicions about Burr. He dispatched
John Graham, on his way to become secretary of the territory of Orleans,
to follow Burr's path, warn governors of danger, and "to arrest Burr if he
made himself liable." On October 25 the President indicated a lapse or
a letdown. Mails from the West brought no news of Burr. Jefferson concluded, "The total silence of the officers of the Government, of the members of Congress, of the newspapers, proves he is committing no overt act
against the law."

During these days Burr was moving far down the mid-American
country. On September 27, at a public dinner given Burr in Nashville,
General Jackson offered the old toast, "Millions for Defense; not one cent
for Tribute." His eye was on Mexico, too. On October 4 Jackson publicly
called upon the militia to be on the alert because of the menacing attitude of the Spanish forces, "already encamped within the limits of our
government," who had taken up an "unjustifiable and insulting position east of the river Sabine, in the territory of Orleans."

Though Burr had no way of knowing it, soon after this occasion,
on October 8, young Swartwout arrived at the camp of Wilkinson at
Natchitoches, where, despite orders in the early summer, the General had

arrived only on September 22. From there, on September 28, the General was writing boldly about war against Mexico to John Adair and Senator John Brown of Kentucky. Adair was a famous Indian fighter and Revolutionary soldier who would later lead Kentucky riflemen in the Battle of New Orleans and become the Governor of his state. He regarded Burr as a patriotic advance agent of the national government sent to arouse the West in the prospect of war with Spain. Brown also was a Revolutionary soldier. Moreover, after the war he studied law under the supervision of Jefferson. Like many other Kentuckians, however, he had had dealings, back in 1787, with the Spaniards which men like Humphrey Marshall and Daveiss elaborated now. He was Burr's friend and host in Frankfort but always a staunch Jeffersonian.

Wilkinson had moved boldly in accordance with plan on September 23, notifying the Spaniards that if they did not leave the east bank of the Sabine immediately, he would march against them. They did evacuate the area almost at exactly the time of Wilkinson's bold letters. Suddenly Wilkinson had won a bloodless victory but he—and Burr—were deprived of a glorious war.

This whole border incident is clouded with confusion and suspicion. It was suspected by some of Wilkinson's enemies that the Spanish commander was bribed to move back. McCaleb doubted that. He thought that the Spanish move prompted a quick shift on the part of the devious General. It put him in a position to acquire in the United States that "honorable fame" about which he talked much, and to prove the value to the Spaniards of his pension. There would be no glory or cash for him for being only a man on a scene from which the Spanish had withdrawn. There might be none of either if it were disclosed that he had been plotting with Burr both to strike his purchasers and to involve the United States in war. The villainy of Burr was essential to him and that required the betrayal of Burr and the ruin of Burr and others. The General did not hesitate. Ponderous as he was, he moved into perfidy as on a parade with flags flying and bugles blowing.

With slight revisions, the cipher letter Swartwout brought him provided him with the proof he needed that Burr had dared to offer him fortune and rank if he would join in his illegal enterprise. This the General, as Jefferson later put it, promptly reported to his government "with the honor of a soldier and the fidelity of a good citizen." To the Spanish he sent a messenger asking reward for saving Mexico. He began to write

Jefferson crying warning of a Western separation movement which he had or would prevent. The Spanish with some cynicism declined to pay, but Jefferson, despite his doubts as to the General's fidelity written on October 22, two days before Wilkinson began to write him in alarm about the conspiracy, welcomed and accepted the General's report that he had confounded horrid conspiracy. The President even promptly paid a bill the General sent him to cover the expenses of the messenger he had sent to his Spanish employers in Mexico City asking for more money.

On October 20 Wilkinson first wrote his "suspicions" to Jefferson about a plot he had just discovered to capture New Orleans and move from there an invasion force to Vera Cruz. He was staggered at what he was hearing. He named no names. But he shaped the charge of treason against Burr and figuratively tied the knot in the noose for his neck: "Should this association be formed, in opposition to the Laws and in defiance of Government, then I have no doubt the revolt of this Territory will be made an auxiliary Step to the main design of attacking Mexico, to give it a new Master in the place of promised Liberty." He saw the "Horrors of a civil contest" and a little later was suggesting that it might include "an insurrection of blacks as well as whites."

In another of his several messages to Jefferson, and with less declamation, he disclosed possibly a basic reason for his outbursts and his betrayal of Burr. He mentioned in indignation the charges of the *Western World* involving him as a conspirator with Burr. He was, he told the President, suing for libel. No such suit was ever filed. The paper's backers were energetically trying to arouse the West. In their efforts they were stupidly aided by Blennerhassett's communications to the *Ohio Gazette*, in which he spoke melodramatically of Mexican empire and, implicitly, of separation of the Western states from the Union. These articles helped a writer using the signature "An Observer" (probably Marshall) in the *Western World*. On October 15 this anonymous agitator called upon Kentucky to move against the man in its midst who, he cried, was working for disunion as the resurrector of the old Spanish conspiracy. Like Jefferson's warning letters to officials this did help to arouse alarms. Already in the country in which Blennerhassett Island was located, citizens who had long distrusted such an exotic stranger as Blennerhassett had passed resolutions denouncing the "apparently hostile movements" going on on the island and calling for the mustering of the militia to deal with "the designs of a certain character," evidently Burr.

Disturbed by the ominous mutterings around her, Mrs. Blennerhassett sent a warning to Burr in Lexington. The Colonel was not alarmed. The Alstons had left him to return to South Carolina, but he had many friends. He moved in his preparations. He was in Nashville again arranging with Jackson about boats and provisions when he heard that Daveiss had risen in the U. S. District Court at Frankfort asking for his arrest and the summons of witnesses against him. On the bench sat Judge Innes, with whom Jefferson had corresponded about Indian artifacts and Western politics. The Judge himself had been subjected to Daveiss' charges. He denied the Daveiss motion. Burr, however, went posthaste to Frankfort and asked that he be examined despite the quashing of Daveiss' motion. At a hearing on November 11 the District Attorney announced that he was not prepared to proceed because of the absence of a witness. Burr was cheered and Daveiss ridiculed. Undeterred, Daveiss moved again on November 25. Once again Burr, this time with Henry Clay as his lawyer, announced himself ready to meet the issue. This time all the evidence Daveiss could find was presented. The Grand Jury in reporting "not a true bill" added that no evidence had been presented which in the "smallest degree" indicated any guilt. Once again there was laughter and cheers. A ball was given in the Colonel's honor.

Daveiss was to be subjected to more than ridicule. He was to be discharged and publicly rebuked by Jefferson for "premature" action in the case. Jefferson had reason to suspect that Daveiss and Marshall, as furious Federalists, were moving to embarrass him as well as strike Burr who had killed Daveiss' idol. Others suspected that Jefferson had been winking in the case of Burr as they believed he had in the case of Miranda. Jefferson was to insist that Burr had subtly tried to give the impression of Presidential involvement in his plans. Still it was ironical that when Daveiss was being laughed at in Kentucky for his pursuit of Burr, Jefferson, who rejected Daveiss, was in Washington in great solemnity issuing his proclamation calling for a manhunt of traitors.

Not naming Burr, the President proclaimed to the nation and particularly to the West, on November 27, 1806, that "information has been received that sundry persons, citizens of the United States or residents within the same, are conspiring and confederating together to begin and set on foot, provide, and prepare the means for a military expedition or enterprise against the dominions of Spain; that for this purpose they are fitting out and arming vessels in the western waters of the United States, collecting provisions, arms, military stores, and means; are deceiving and seducing honest and well-meaning citizens, under various pretenses, to engage in their criminal enterprises; are organizing, officering, and arming themselves for the same, contrary to the laws in such cases made and provided. . . ."

There was no mention of treason in the proclamation, only of such a filibustering expedition as that upon which Miranda had embarked. But as the damning document was brought by couriers with their long hair flying in the wind behind them, the West quickly understood that the chief of the "sundry citizens" was Burr and that Jefferson was warning of threatened treason. The West stiffened in alarm and fury. Militia was organized. Even the suspicions of General Jackson had momentarily been aroused. While Burr was triumphantly confronting Daveiss in Kentucky, an unnamed friend was convincing Jackson in Nashville that Burr was probably connected with a "gigantic scheme of iniquity" involving the dismemberment of the United States. Quickly, on November 12, Jackson had dispatched a warning to his friend Governor Claiborne in New Orleans.

"Put your town in a state of defense. Organize your militia, and defend your city as well against internal enemies as external. . . . I fear you will meet with an attack from quarters you do not at present expect. Be upon the alert; keep a watchful eye upon our General [Wilkinson] and beware of an attack as well from our own country as Spain."

Then he spoke the sentiment of the West: "I hate the Dons; I would delight to see Mexico reduced; but I will die in the last ditch before I yield a foot to the Dons, or see the Union disunited."

After his acquittal, Burr came again to Nashville and this time was confronted by a Jackson of ice and iron. Burr convinced the General of his innocence of treasonable intent to such an extent that Jackson, while keeping his fingers crossed and the militia assembled, let his wife's nephew join the Colonel's company.

Certainly by this time Burr was aware that he was the subject of fierce suspicions. He did not know that, on December 10, his small company of recruits on Blennerhassett Island learned that the muttering around the island had reached mob-spirit proportions. So warned, Burr's men slipped down the river in the darkness. And the next day the undisciplined militia invaded the once serene scene of solitude in a combined mood of patriotism and plunder. First it invaded Blennerhassett's wine cellar and got drunk. Then with inebriated deliberation the outraged patriots smashed the pictures and china, tore down drapes, ruined furniture, and left even the shrubbery trampled and destroyed.

Burr had, however, no more knowledge that such fury awaited him than he did that his friend Wilkinson had betrayed him. Apparently, though there is some doubt about the exact date, the President's proclamation did not reach Nashville until December 23, the day after Burr departed. So Burr escaped a delirium of patriotic fury there though Jackson was keeping his head and keeping his hand on a better disciplined militia. Burr probably received his first news of the proclamation when the fleeing Blennerhassett met him at the conjunction of the Ohio and Cumberland rivers on December 27. Realizing that he was pursued—and possibly by the kind of undisciplined militia which had ruined Blennerhassett Island—he moved down the Mississippi toward Natchez where he had friends and to meet somewhere beyond another on whose friendship he still counted—General Wilkinson. Certainly his boats made no formidable appearance on the river.

Actually Wilkinson had not only betrayed Burr to the President, he had also written the Chief Executive that as a soldier he was in danger of being overwhelmed by Burr and his armed myrmidons of treason. In great show of alarm he informed Claiborne that he was surrounded by spies in a plot which "implicates thousands and among them some of your particular friends as well as my own." He added, "The storm will probably burst on New Orleans, when I shall meet it & triumph or perish."

To Jackson, who had made inquiries, the commanding officer at Fort Massac on the Ohio gave a different report about the supposed armada of destruction. This officer reported to Jackson that, on December 31, 1806, "Colonel Burr, late Vice-President of the United States, passed this with about ten boats, of different descriptions, navigated with about six men each, having nothing on board that would even suffer a conjecture more than a man bound to market."

On January 13, 1807, Burr's little armada arrived at Bayou Pierre near Natchez. There Burr learned the full extent of the charges against him and the zeal for his capture which Wilkinson had added to betrayal. He realized quickly that if he was to receive any justice or save his life he must not let himself fall into the hands of the General who, in the panic he was creating, was ruthlessly dominating civil as well as military authority in New Orleans. On January 17 Burr surrendered for trial in

Mississippi. Nobody knew better than he his danger from Wilkinson down
the river. This marching savior of his country there had good reason to
fear that Burr might be able to implicate him in the maneuvers in which
they had been engaged together. The disclosure of these maneuvers, innocent or treasonous, would mark the General as a false friend or national Double-Dealer No. 1, as well as Spanish agent No. 13. Knowing
Wilkinson, he knew, too, that the General would not want him to live
to tell the tale. This danger to Burr was far from incredible. Indeed, at
Washington the almost radar-eared Senator Plumer wrote in his diary a
month after Burr's surrender—a short time as news traveled then.

He noted: "John Randolph says within a few days he has seen a
letter from Genl. Wilkinson written to a friend in this city that contains
this idea. That altho' Aaron Burr's treasonable plans are supprest—he will
soon revive them—To prevent which, its best *to take him off*—& that he
had provided 2 or 3 men who are well qualified to effect that laudable
service for their country.

"The plain English of which is That Wilkinson has men in pay to
assassinate Burr."

The Colonel in custody had true friends in the Natchez region. Also
the public seemed recovering from its fevers. Reports of the search of
Burr's boats were reassuring. The count of his company only varied from
some fifty-five men, a few women and children, and some Negro servants
to "one hundred men and the major part boys just from school." They
did not look like "desperadoes." Skepticism about Wilkinson's furious reports was already growing in Mississippi before Burr was arraigned.
There were, however, no doubts about Burr's treason in the Executive
Mansion in Washington—and there never would be any admitted.

From the "tranquil happiness and prosperity of a nation," the President wrote to his friend, former Democratic Senator from New Hampshire John Langdon, even before Burr surrendered:

"Our prospects are great if we can preserve external and internal
peace. With England I firmly expect a friendly arrangement. With Spain
we shall possibly have blows; but they will hasten, instead of preventing
a peaceful settlement."

Then his mind and his pen turned darkly westward.

"The most instant pressure is now from among ourselves, our Cataline is at the head of an armed body (we know not its strength), and his
object is to seize New Orleans, from thence attack Mexico, place himself

on the throne of Montezuma, add Louisiana to his empire, and the Western States from the Allegheny if he can. I do not believe he will attain the crown; but neither am I certain that the halter will get its due."

Burr maintained every air of dignity in what seemed a too evident descent to doom. Received as a gentleman in the company of gentlemen, in Natchez he did not look like a man facing the prospect of the dagger or the rope.

3.

Road to Exile

Mr. Jefferson had not been very comfortable in Washington in the late fall or early winter of 1806. This should have been a time of special triumph for him. He was then waiting to welcome as returning heroes, Meriwether Lewis and William Clark, from the exploration of the Far West which he had been planning since he talked much of it with travelers and philosophers over the wine at his Paris table. As he waited expectantly, he suffered an accident in which the whole nail of a finger was torn off. At the same time he was painfully concerned about what he said was the plan of Aaron Burr to tear a whole region from the Union. His proclamation had pointed an accusing finger at Burr though not naming him.

The two matters coincided strangely. Lewis and Clark promised to be the forerunners of a more stable movement of settlers who would fill and hold the West. Burr's purported adventure involved—as Jefferson, under the bombardment of Wilkinson's reports, was coming to believe—a threat of conflict, confusion, possibly secession, in the already settled trans-Appalachian areas of the Union.

Lewis, with Clark and his other companions, had returned to St. Louis from the great and hazardous journey on September 23, 1806. They had not found the giant Indians or the mountain of salt Jefferson had anticipated. Still they came loaded with specimens for the President, many of which would line the halls of Monticello. Also they brought, as walking specimens, an Indian King and Queen. They had a great story to tell of their survival over the dangers of weather, beasts, deserts, Indians.

Apparently they never knew that they had also escaped Spaniards to whom Wilkinson had suggested their arrest as spies.

As still not yet replaced Governor of Louisiana Territory, that military personage was not in St. Louis on their arrival. He had, however, left behind angry divisions between his friends and his foes. Indeed, on the day the explorers returned, he had just arrived at his post at Natchitoches, opposite the Spaniards on the southern border. Apparently he had remained in St. Louis until after he sent out young Lieutenant Zebulon Pike on a similar exploration, on July 15, 1806. Pike was arrested by the Spanish, though in reconnoitering the Spanish settlements of New Mexico he had been warned to "move with great circumspection . . . and to prevent any alarm or offense." Some thought Pike had been sent off by Wilkinson in connection with his and Burr's plans. Dr. Thomas Maitland Marshall, secretary of the Missouri Historical Society, wrote that "apparently the war department was aware of the projected expedition but did not openly approve it."

Lewis and Clark had been out of touch with civilization for approximately twenty-six months. Great events had happened in their absence. The first news poured into the vacuum of their information was that Aaron Burr had killed Alexander Hamilton in a duel over two years before. Soon, as they moved slowly toward Washington and national acclaim, they heard the fresher and more exciting news about Burr. As reported in the West, in advance of Jefferson's accusations, this did not seem necessarily bad news.

One revealing report, certainly not expressing alarm, was written from Pittsburgh, on December 3, 1806, by Frederick Bates. He was an ambitious young Virginian seeking his political fortune on the frontier. He had changed his politics from republican to Federalist and now back to republican again. He had first gone West, in 1797, to Detroit to serve in the Quartermaster Department of the Army of the West under the command of General Wilkinson. Now he had been named secretary (or second in command) of the Louisiana Territory of which St. Louis was the capital. There he was replacing Burr's brother-in-law, Dr. Joseph Browne. His appointment, according to Dr. Marshall, "was due to the fact that the Burr Conspiracy was then developing and Jefferson wanted an official in the trans-Mississippi region on whom he could rely." If so, in Pittsburgh, Bates did not seem concerned about it. He wrote from Pittsburgh six days after the President's proclamation. That document could hardly have arrived in so short a time. Lewis had taken ten days to go from Washington to Pittsburgh on his way West in 1804. So Bates presented an evidently admiring picture of Burr's upriver confederates on the eve of national hue and cry. Bates wrote:

> All Pittsburgh is in commotion. Col. Burr's enterprise appears to be matured for execution, and large stores of provisions are daily loading on board the boats for the supply of his troops in the lower countries. Natchez will be the rendezvous, but their object and destination are altogether unknown, except to those in whom the leaders have thought proper to confide. The most intelligent with whom I have conversed appear to imagine that the army will be composed of about ten thousand chosen men, who will remain in the neighborhood of the Spanish settlements, until a declaration of war, or other political events shall authorize our government to justify the preparations, and avow them as their own. Most of the young men in this vicinity, respectable by birth, education and property are descending the river.

Obviously Bates was not appalled but impressed. And evidently he was one of many watching these operations who expected Washington officials at the proper time to "avow them as their own." Apparently he saw with very big eyes, however. The most careful combing of the country was never to disclose that Burr's mobilization anywhere reached such proportions. Such an impression of Burr's moves as an inevitable tide was needed if he was to attract the followers he required. Yet, that impression was now best to serve Wilkinson, who in New Orleans was as busily exaggerating danger as Burr's friends in Pittsburgh were evidently able to exaggerate momentum. What in Pittsburgh was made to look like an invincible army composed of young "chosen men" of lineage, education, and property could, in New Orleans, be made to look like an unholy horde of desperadoes before whom neither money nor maidens, not even the republic would be secure. Wilkinson was working frantically at the southern end of the line. And in Washington, given credit for even a part of the credulity attributed to him, Mr. Jefferson may have felt that parts of the republic were as beset as Virginia had been when his flight as Governor before the British provided lasting material for his enemies.

Triumphant as the occasion was for himself as well as for Lewis and Clark, Jefferson was preoccupied when they finally came with their stories and their trophies and the King and the Queen of Mandans. After Lewis appeared at the President's House on January 10, 1807, Jefferson gave

GENERAL JAMES WILKINSON
By C.B.J. Fevret de Saint-Mémin.

JOHN MARSHALL
By J. W. Jarvis.

THOMAS JEFFERSON AS PRESIDENT

THEODOSIA BURR ALSTON
By John Vanderlyn.

DAVID MEADE RANDOLPH
By C.B.J. Fevret de Saint-Mémin.

MRS. DAVID MEADE RANDOLPH
By C.B.J. Fevret de Saint-Mémin.

21

ANDREW JACKSON

THOMAS JEFFERSON IN OLD AGE
By Thomas Sully.

AARON BURR
After a painting by J. Vandyke.

him a reception and welcomed the Indian King and Queen with attention
to protocol which Merry and Yrujo felt was denied them. He took strange
seeds Lewis had brought him to try in the gardens at Monticello. It was
but justice to say that the explorers had "by their arduous service deserved
well of their country." Soon he would name thirty-three-year-old Lewis,
whose only administrative experience had been in the wilderness, to succeed Wilkinson as Governor of Louisiana Territory, a post deemed equal
to the prestige of Monroe, to whom it was first offered.

It was a position which the President told Monroe was "the 2nd office
in the US in importance." Indeed, Jefferson had twice urged the office on
Monroe, who was in London trying to negotiate a treaty to put an end to
British injuries to American commerce and the impressment of American
sailors claimed to be British deserters. Jefferson's importunities also
related to his eagerness to prevent Monroe from allowing the bitter Randolph of Roanoke from pushing him for President against Jefferson's already chosen Madison. The position in St. Louis, he said, offered "the
finest field in the United States for acquiring property." Wilkinson, who
had left suspicions and animosities behind in St. Louis, certainly had
been aware of that.

The President, who used Lewis on delicate as well as daring missions
despite his awareness of the young man's mental instability, knew as he
listened to the explorer that the bitter Randolph was preparing to
strike at him in Congress. The alleged sexual impotency of this gaunt personage made him seem a sort of emaciated eunuch to his enemies. They
never doubted the potency of his tongue. Now in increasing scorn of the
President, he was ready to use the Burr case as a cudgel with which
to point what he regarded as Jefferson's pusillanimity. Randolph was no
friend of Burr's. Nearly two years before, the caustic Congressman had
written from the Bizarre plantation that a rendezvous in the West of
Burr and Senators Dayton and Smith was "a conjunction of malign plan-
ets [which] bodes no good." But Jefferson, whom he called "St. Thomas
of Cantingbury," was his chosen target. On January 16, looking like a
skeleton in parchment, he rose in the House.

"If the Government," he said in his high piercing voice, ". . . had
taken a manly and decisive attitude towards Spain, and instead of pen,
ink and paper, had given men and arms—is there a man who believes that
not only Spain would have been overawed, but that those domestic traitors

would have been intimidated and overawed, whose plans threaten to be so dangerous?"

In a resolution he demanded that the President lay before Congress any information he possessed concerning the conspiracies he had mentioned in his proclamation and in his December message to Congress. The President replied on January 22, for the first time naming Burr, "whose guilt is placed beyond question," and also, for the first time, adding the charge that the aim of the expedition was to separate the Union as well as attack Spain. To support all this, however, the President said he had "little . . . to constitute legal and formal evidence."

Such evidence seemed all that was lacking, too, in Natchez and the nearby capital of Mississippi Territory at the village of Washington, where Burr appeared before Judge Thomas Rodney on January 18. He was bound over for the Grand Jury under five-thousand-dollar bond. He was free but surrounded by all the elements of melodrama. Burr's portfolio containing papers, which he said would prove Wilkinson's perfidy, was broken into, its contents "tumbled and abused." This was done, Blennerhassett thought, by "servants." Others suspected spies, not slaves. Wilkinson had agents in Natchez. He sent three officers in civilian clothes up from New Orleans apparently to kidnap the Colonel. There was to be a story—fabricated, McCaleb thought—of a secret, menacing message which Burr sent, sewed up in his cloak, by a slave boy to his companions on the boats. There was an element of romance. Mississippi historian John Francis Hamtramck Claiborne wrote, like a gentleman with a magnolia in one hand and a julep in the other, a story of Burr's declared love for Madeline Price, a widow's daughter who was "a miracle of beauty." Apparently in the three weeks Burr spent in the Natchez district, he won her heart but not her favors. Also, in this Natchez interlude, there was a combination of the comic and the sinister.

Colonel Silas Dinsmore, a well-known frontier character, had written as Burr's flotilla was approaching to Colonel McKee, who like himself was an Indian agent. Dinsmore beckoned McKee as to a frolic: "We are in a flurry here hourly expecting Colonel Burr & all Kentucky & half of Tennessee at his [back] to punish General Wilkinson, set the negroes free, Rob the banks & take Mexico. Come and help me laugh at the fun."

There was nothing funny in a letter Dinsmore received at approximately the same time from Wilkinson, who was crying havoc in New Orleans. There the General had disregarded the courts and the guarantees of liberties which Jefferson had insisted be added to the Constitution. He had arrested Burr's friends Swartwout, Ogden, and Bollman and shipped them off to Washington without a chance to be heard. He had also sent soldiers to arrest an editor who had criticized the denial of hearings under habeas corpus writs to these and other men. A lawyer who sought the writs was jailed. The dangers Wilkinson cried in New Orleans were so terrifying that word of them in Washington had brought Jefferson to the panic point. Then he had contemplated the possible need to send twenty thousand soldiers down the river "to retake New Orleans." Indignation against Wilkinson's military dictatorship in New Orleans, however, began to alter to ridicule. But Wilkinson was deadly, possibly desperately serious.

He wrote Dinsmore: "To cut off the two principal leaders [Burr and Blennerhassett] would in my opinion be to discomfit the sinister design, and gain time for preparation to resist successfully the baneful plot . . . If you fail your expenses will be paid. If you succeed I pledge the government to you for five thousand dollars."

McCaleb interpreted this letter as an offer of five thousand dollars for Burr's life. Certainly it could have been connected with the report Randolph received in Washington and passed on to Plumer that Wilkinson had arranged for assassination. Burr's friends in Natchez—notably Lyman Harding who had been U. S. District Attorney under President Adams, Colonel Benijah Osmun, a rich farmer planter, and Dr. John Cummins, wealthy physician who had studied under Dr. Benjamin Rush —feared Wilkinson might grab the Colonel. What they did not understand was the long arm of Thomas Jefferson.

So great was the crowd which wanted to hear the trial on February 2 that there was no hall big enough to hold it in the little town of Washington. In weather only ten degrees above zero, the hearing was held outdoors under spreading trees which were to be known as the "Burr Oaks." In full command on the bench was Judge Thomas Rodney. Some have assumed since that Burr must have known that he could expect little consideration in Rodney's Court. Yet, he had had friendly relations with the Rodney family in Delaware. The Judge's son, Caesar Augustus Rodney, had been a friend Burr particularly wanted Theo and her husband to see as they passed through Wilmington on their wedding journey southward. The younger Rodney had then written of the "noble part" Burr had played in the Presidential contest in the House in 1801.

How many lines in the Jefferson-Burr story run back to that contest! In 1802 Jefferson had chosen Caesar Rodney to do a job which he very much wanted to be done. According to Rodney's biographer, Jefferson had "prevailed" upon Rodney to run against the President's bête noire Bayard and with "Jefferson's backing" he defeated that Federalist. The punishment of Bayard was not permanent. Within two years Bayard was promoted to the Senate to begin a long service there. And at the end of one term Rodney was replaced in the House by a Federalist.

The Rodneys did not lose Jefferson's gratitude. In August 1803, Caesar's father, Thomas, was named U. S. Judge for Mississippi Territory. On January 20, 1807, while Burr was waiting for trial in Mississippi and Jefferson was preparing the statement of his crimes for Congress, the President named Caesar his Attorney General. He succeeded John Breckinridge who died on December 14, 1806, and who had personally known a lot more about charges of conspiracy in the West. Nearly two months before his appointment Rodney had been going to see members of Congress in their lodgings to give them ominous word about Burr's plot. One on whom he called, late in November just after the issue of the President's proclamation, was Senator Plumer. It seems safe to assume that in the weeks before Burr appeared in court in Mississippi, Caesar Rodney passed on the President's views to his father on the frontier, possibly at the President's own suggestion.

Except for threat from Wilkinson in New Orleans, Burr's situation in the Natchez district seemed good. He appeared urbanely confident by his lawyers. And the U. S. District Attorney rose to say that he had no case and that he doubted that the court had jurisdiction. Rodney turned down his motion to dismiss. He sent the case to the Grand Jury. Afterwards, in an almost standard charge, it was said that this jury was packed with Federalists. It not only found no guilt. Its verdict went on to give in this case some real justification for Jefferson's complaint in the Miranda case that his enemies made an effort to try the government instead of the culprit.

The Grand Jury presented as "a grievance, destructive of personal liberty, the late military arrests, made without warrant, and, as they conceive, without lawful authority; and they do sincerely regret that so much cause has been given to the enemies of our glorious Constitution, to rejoice at such measures being adopted, in a neighboring Territory, as, sanctioned by the Executive of our country, must sap the vitals of our political existence, and crumble this glorious fabric in the dust."

Such a reference to the "Executive of our country" was an obvious slap at Judge Rodney's great friend and patron. It was calculated to make silly the efforts of his son. He was not pleased by the applause which greeted this third finding that no cause existed for the trial of Burr. In an unheard-of procedure, he declined to release the Colonel and continued him under bond to appear in court from day to day.

Burr and his friendly hosts became apprehensive. To them he did seem threatened now between the President in Washington, writing of the hangman's halter, and the frantic military kidnaper in New Orleans. On advice of friends he decided to go into hiding and await developments. He did not appear in court on February 5. And on February 6, his fifty-first birthday, he was proclaimed a fugitive by Governor Robert Williams, another Jefferson appointee and ex-Congressman from North Carolina. On this occasion Williams certainly seemed to Burr and his friends, as Historian Claiborne described him, a man "too repulsive and peremptory to please the country and refined people among whom he resided." The Governor also posted a two-thousand-dollar reward for Burr's arrest. He ordered a roundup of his young companions, many of whom, Claiborne afterwards wrote, were to remain to supply the territory with "school masters, singing masters, dancing masters, clerks, tavern keepers, and doctors."

After writing an indignant letter to Governor Williams, charging both him and Judge Rodney with acting in bad faith, Burr tarried in the neighborhood no longer. On one of Colonel Osmun's swiftest horses and accompanied by a dependable guide, he fled southeastward. Wilkinson told Jefferson his destination was "France beyond all doubt." Some thought he hoped to find sanctuary in a British ship in the Gulf. As he left, according to Historian Claiborne, he took a last leave of Madeline, who promised to wait for his return.

In winter weather, across swollen streams, the two horsemen reached Washington County, Alabama, above Mobile on the Tombigbee River. The polished Burr was transformed if not adequately disguised in "an old blanket coat begirt with a leathern strap, to which a tin cup was suspended on the left and a scalping knife on the right." On February 18, making inquiries as to directions, he was recognized by Nicholas Perkins, an impecunious lawyer and registrar of the local land office, who had heard of the reward. He called the Sheriff, then notified Lieutenant Edmund Pendleton Gaines of nearby Fort Stoddert. Gaines, then at the beginning of a tempestuous military career, put Burr under arrest. The Lieutenant found that he as well as Burr was in a predicament. The surrounding community hoped that Burr had come to lead an attack on Spanish Mobile. Many of its citizens were ready to follow him. There was resentment about his arrest. Inside the fort, however, Burr took his imprisonment with grace. Apparently he was well treated. He played chess with Mrs. Gaines, whose father, Judge Harry Toulmin, a protégé of Jefferson, was giving rough Rodney-like treatment to some of Burr's associates.

In the resentful community the Colonel seemed too hot to hold. So on March 6 Gaines sent the vigilant Perkins as commander of a guard of eight men to carry the prisoner to the national capital. The journey across Alabama and Georgia to South Carolina was a rough one for the young guards as well as the middle-aged prisoner. Parts of it were like Burr's trip across the Natchez Trace as a free man two years before. Then he had been plagued by the miasmas and the flies, swamp and rain. Now he moved in the cold, wet from the crossing of unbridged rivers. He was sternly guarded but not harshly treated by the young soldiers. To Perkins he had cash value. He was given the best of the scant provisions the company carried and allowed to sleep in the one tent it possessed.

Perkins hurried his squad and prisoner along as they reached the more settled country in South Carolina. In Chester the lawyer almost lost the small fortune of $3331 in reward he would collect. This was a country Burr had traversed before. Chester was midway between the Alston upcountry retreat at Clifton and the home of Nathalie at Stateburg. Suddenly in the town Burr jumped from his horse and climbed a rocky eminence. From it he shouted to a nearby group of citizens. Identifying himself, he demanded the protection of civil authorities. At pistol point now he was ordered to remount. He refused. Whereupon Perkins, a powerful fellow, flung him back into his saddle. They drove on, leaving behind the citizens who apparently only gaped at the spectacle.

The rest of the trip at the rapid pace of forty miles a day was uneventful. Surrounded by his more vigilant young guards, the discomforted Burr was never once "heard to complain that he was sick, or even fatigued." He could hardly, however, have looked debonair in the homespun pantaloons and flopping wide-brimmed beaver hat he wore. The little cavalcade moved on through North Carolina into Virginia. It passed close to the Bizarre Plantation of Randolph of Roanoke who two years before had expressed his foreboding about Burr. On March 25, 1807, he wrote a friend: "Col. Burr (quantum mutatus ab illo!) passed by my door the day before yesterday under a strong guard."

Randolph added a passage indicative of a sort of wonder which Burr seemed to evoke. He wrote: "His very manner of traveling, although under arrest, was characteristic of the man—enveloped in mystery—and, should he be hanged for treason, I dare say he will 'feel the ruling passion strong in death,' and contrive to make posterity doubt whether he was actually executed, or whether (as was alleged in the case of the Duke of Monmouth) some counterfeit did not suffer in his place." No such notions troubled Burr's guards. Soon afterwards, under new orders from Washington, the prisoner was delivered in Richmond. He was placed in the Eagle Tavern under strong guard.

Mr. Jefferson was more jubilant than consistent in his comments on Burr as he was brought to Richmond. On March 24 he wrote to Chancellor Livingston that the imprisoned ex-Vice President had "made a most inglorious exhibition of his much over rated talents." But on the following day to an unknown correspondent he said that "no man's history proves better the value of honesty. With that, what might he not have been!" He was confident that "if the judges do not discharge him before it is possible to collect the testimony from Maine to New Orleans, there can be no doubt where his history will end." Evidently on the gallows.

Possibly, however, the President's doubts about the judges had something to do with the incapacitating headaches he was suffering at the time. He had certainly gone about the business of collecting the evidence. On February 27, when the guarded Burr was being held in Alabama, Jefferson had instructed Attorney General Rodney to "appoint good men" to investigate and take affidavits from New York to New Orleans and "particularly" at Pittsburgh, Marietta, Wood County, Cincinnati, Louisville, Nashville, Washington, D.C., Vincennes, St. Louis, Natchez, upstate New York, Newark and Trenton in New Jersey, Newport in Kentucky, and, strangely, in Stateburg, South Carolina, where Nathalie with three little daughters had no testimony to offer but her devotion.

In addition to this corps of investigators, the President, who had felt so strongly about the rights of man, was ready for Congress to strictly curb them. On the day after his January message declaring Burr guilty, his old, pugnacious aide Giles rose in a secret session of the Senate to propose the suspension of the Constitutional right of habeas corpus. The obvious purpose of this was to hold in custody Samuel Swartwout, Justus Erich Bollman, and others whom Wilkinson had shipped East from New Orleans in defiance of their legal rights. The proposal swept through the Senate with only Bayard of Delaware opposing what might amount to military dictatorship for the country. Possibly time for thought explained the entirely different attitude toward the resolution in the House. Secrecy was dispensed with there by a vote of 123 to 3. And the resolution itself was defeated 113 to 19. Not even Jefferson's two sons-in-law in the House seemed sympathetic to the drastic proposal. Eppes led opposition to the suspension of the right of habeas corpus. Thomas Mann Randolph, sick and jealous of the greater attention he thought Jefferson was giving to Eppes, muttered his doubts. He told Senator Plumer, in the boardinghouse to which he had moved from the unhappy President's House, that he thought Wilkinson should be removed or "his father-in-law's administration would fail."

Doubts were arising about the alarums Jefferson had loosed. Earlier in the year, old John Adams, in retirement at Quincy, had testily declared that "I have never believed him [Burr] to be a fool. But he must be an Idiot or a Lunatick if he has really planned and attempted to execute such a Project as imputed to him." He added that politicians have "no more respect to Truth than the Devil . . . I suspect that this Lying Spirit has been at work concerning Burr." Moreover, "if his guilt is as clear as the Noon day Sun, the first Magistrate ought not to have pronounced it so before a jury had tryed him."

Similar comments closer at hand made Jefferson feel that now again, as he had said in the Miranda outfitting case, efforts were being made to make the administration the defendant instead of Burr. He wrote on the day of Burr's arrival in Richmond, "the federalists appear to make Burr's cause their own, and to spare no efforts to screen his adherents. Their great mortification is at the failure of his plans. Had a little success dawned on him, their openly joining him might have produced some danger."

Jefferson saw that danger panoplied in Chief Justice Marshall, seated on the bench since Richmond was in his circuit, in this day when the Supreme Court Justices held courts away from Washington. Marshall not only represented the President's concern about judicial usurpation, though he embodied that. Moreover, this year the Chief Justice published the final chapters of his *Life of Washington,* which the President regarded as a "five-volume libel" against republicans. And from the Marshall clan in Kentucky came a furious pamphlet by Daveiss which damned Jefferson with Wilkinson and Burr.

Still, at the outset of the Burr trial, the President had some reason to believe that the Chief Justice had entrapped himself. In freeing under writs of habeas corpus some of Burr's associates whom Wilkinson had clapped into irons and sent East, Marshall had added to his decision an obiter dictum. He stated a doctrine of "constructive treason" under which a defendant need not have been shown to have been present at a treasonous assemblage if he had performed any part, "however minute, or however remote," in the treasonous enterprise. This was exactly the ruling that the government required since it had chosen as the scene and time of treason an occasion on Blennerhassett Island when Burr was far away.

The proceedings against Burr, which extended from his first appearance before the Chief Justice, on March 30 to October 19, 1807, have been minutely described by historians and legal scholars. Throughout, it has seemed to many a great and high, though secretly sometimes petty and vindictive, contest between the President in Washington and the Chief Justice on the bench in Richmond. But only Burr's neck was at hazard. If, as Jefferson said, the Federalists had made Burr's cause their own and the greatest one of them was on the bench, the Jeffersonians were thick around him and in strategic places, too. There would be no danger of such jury packing against the administration as the President had suspected in the Miranda case. The Grand Jury, carefully picked by U. S. Marshal Scott, seemed actually packed with many of the state's ablest republicans and most fanatic Jeffersonians. Burr wrote Theo that, as called, it was composed of twenty Democrats and four Federalists. Even his known personal enemies, Giles and W. C. Nicholas, were reluctant to get off, but did. Randolph of Roanoke, whom Marshall named foreman, was no Burr friend if he had become a Jefferson enemy. The situation was even more adverse to Burr when the selection of the petit jury took place. Such a procession of men announced that they had already formed a conviction of Burr's guilt that at last he agreed not to insist upon his right to be tried by men with unfixed minds about his case.

For those more interested in the drama than the dialectics of history, the personalities surrounding the trial seem almost more significant than the interminable arguments of the lawyers and the wary rulings of the Chief Justice in the crowded, sweltering courtroom. The opposing counsel dramatized not only the contest in the courthouse but the fierce division in Richmond—and in America. Bankrupt and abandoned as Burr had seemed on his enforced journey from Alabama, his was the most imposing array of lawyers.

First in position among them was Edmund Randolph, who, as Attorney General under Washington, Jefferson had described as a "trimmer" playing both sides against the middle in the Hamilton-Jefferson feud. By Burr's side also was Charles Lee. He had been President Adams' Attorney General and had been one of the late-named Federalist judges with whom Jefferson believed Adams improperly packed the courts. He had been deprived of his place on the bench by the Jeffersonian repeal of the Judiciary Act. His brother, Light-Horse Harry Lee, the President's bitter enemy, had been a principal in stirring up the story about young Jefferson's improper approaches to Mrs. Walker which Callender had printed.

To Burr's assistance had also come John Wickham, whose eminence at the bar was equaled by the social position he occupied. Indeed, the poet Tom Moore, who may have picked up some of his material for his anti-Jefferson verses at his table, praised Wickham in amazing hyperbole as the only gentleman he found in America. Certainly Wickham's hospitality was never made more prominent than in this summer when Jeffersonians were outraged that he had as dinner guests at the same time his close friend Justice Marshall and his client Burr.

No one was more passionate in Burr's cause than rough, brilliant, steadily drinking Luther Martin of Maryland. A violent Federalist, he had hated Jefferson at least as early as 1797 when he had reviled and ridiculed Jefferson's *Notes on Virginia*. His antagonism to the President had been indicated again in his appearance as one of the attorneys for Judge Chase. In this Richmond summer, at fifty-nine, harsh-voiced, shabbily attired, and with his face crimsoned by brandy, he steadily suggested that the trial was a vindictive persecution by Jefferson. That brought from the President the suggestion that perhaps he should be indicted as *particeps criminis* with Burr. Jefferson thought he had evidence from a respectable flour merchant in Baltimore, named Graybell, that for a year Martin had been privy to Burr's "criminal enterprise." Graybell's evidence, he thought, would "pull down this unprincipled & impudent federal bull-

dog, and add another proof that the most clamorous defenders of Burr are
all his accomplices."

Burr himself was his own effective advocate. Dignified, contained, perfectly tailored again, by his demeanor and skill as a lawyer, he drew admiration even from those who regarded him as almost a devil. Young
Winfield Scott, later to become the nation's most revered soldier, described
Burr at the bar: "There he stood in the hands of power, on the brink of
danger, as composed, as immoveable, as one of Canova's living marbles."

Beside these defenders, the prosecuting lawyers were unimpressive.
U. S. Attorney General Rodney did not appear in the case, perhaps, as
Schachner concluded, because "he saw no profit for himself in the proceedings, and wisely foresaw a considerable lessening of prestige." Possibly his father had sent him word that he had a very doubtful case. He
may have been too busy collecting evidence on a continental scale from
New York to Stateburg, South Carolina. Chief of the prosecutors was
thirty-six-year-old George Hay, Monroe's son-in-law, whom Jefferson had
appointed U. S. District Attorney. Opinions differ as to his abilities as a
lawyer; he had been effective as a fierce anti-Federalist pamphleteer. Associated with him was the greater William Wirt who brought the gifts of
a literary man to his orations for the prosecution. His flowery speech,
in description of Burr's descent like the "destroyer" on the West in general
and Blennerhassett Island in particular, was to become a classic in the
repertoire of reciting schoolboys. The third figure in the prosecution,
Alexander McRae, Lieutenant Governor of Virginia, has been described
as "a definitely inferior lawyer, brought into the case for political reasons."
Minnigerode and Wandell described him as "a little inadequate for his
task . . . sour, belligerent and sarcastic." Rewarded after the trial with a
diplomatic assignment, he was to become the agent of lasting and vindictive enmity to Burr in his exile.

Chief attorney for the prosecution, however, was Jefferson himself.
In Washington or Monticello his mind was steadily on the Richmond
scene. He directed the moves of the prosecution. He incited his lawyers.
Before proceedings were well under way the President had written his
man Giles about Burr in words almost echoing those Hamilton had used in
his letter written before the duel. He had never had a "hostile sentiment"
against Burr.

Nothing, however, could be more clear than his determination to
convict Burr and his willingness to depend upon any and all kinds of evi-

dence to bring that about. He disregarded all evidence which did not serve his aim. While he was spreading a net of agents to secure evidence against Burr, he was offered evidence discrediting Wilkinson.

A Major who had served under Wilkinson in the West told Attorney General Rodney he could give evidence to Wilkinson's treasonable complicity in Burr's plans. Rodney shrugged: "What would be the result if all this should be proven?—why just what the federalists and the enemies of the present administration wish—it would turn the indignation of the people from Burr on Wilkinson; Burr would escape, and Wilkinson take his place." And with Wilkinson would stand Jefferson. The President himself regarded all charges against Wilkinson as "malicious insinuation." He excused his infringements of civil liberties in New Orleans. Even after suspicions of Wilkinson's loyalty had mounted to conviction in the minds of many thoughtful men in Richmond, Jefferson told the General that "the virulence of those whose treasons you have defeated only place you on higher ground in the opinion of the nation."

Jefferson's participation in the case was not limited to his expressions of faith in the General. He sent Hay constant suggestions along with maledictions toward both Burr and Marshall. He gave Hay blank pardons to be given any lesser "conspirators" who could be induced to turn state's evidence against Burr. The most remarkable of such cases was that involving Dr. Bollman. Soon after he was released in Washington, this highly educated German went to see Jefferson to assure him that Burr had no plans involving the separation of the nation, only under certain eventualities action against Mexico. The President listened and called in Madison to listen too. On the following day the President asked Dr. Bollman to write down the substance of what he said, promising that the paper would never go out of his hand. Nevertheless, Jefferson promptly sent the document to Hay. So anxious was he to get Bollman to turn state's witness that he sent to the District Attorney in Richmond a pardon so that the German could testify without danger of incriminating himself. Amazingly, before Bollman testified, Hay offered the pardon to him in open court. The adventurous German indignantly declined it. The whole government was put behind the effort to convict. Army officers were made U. S. Marshals in rounding up witnesses and securing answers to elaborate, widely distributed questionnaires.

Jefferson moved in all these operations not only with dispatch but with a high tone of righteousness. His conscience was not disturbed in the Bollman case. Indeed, soon after the German scorned his overtures, the President wrote Lafayette for whom Bollman had risked his life. The German had been, Jefferson told his great French friend, "Burr's right hand man in all his guilty schemes." His "tergivesations" have proved him "conspicuously base. . . . Be assured he is unworthy of ever occupying again the care of any honest man." This damnation was delivered well before the conclusion of the trial.

Perhaps the situation surrounding the trial seemed to Jefferson to justify such moves on his part. It gave the President reason for his suspicion that the Federalists, under the greatest one of them on the bench, were trying to make him and Wilkinson the defendants instead of Burr. Richmond was packed with witnesses, V.I.P. spectators, reporters including Washington Irving, roughly dressed men from the frontier and gentlemen and ladies from Northern cities, the concerned and the curious. Moreover, it was a town sharply divided in sentiment. Commodore Truxtun, who seemed the most intelligent and dignified witness at the trial, described the city as indulging in a sort of special social season. The observing mass of Jeffersonians was mutteringly ready with the halter for Burr. But those whom Truxtun described as the "Worthies" made Burr the social hero of the occasion.

The District Court had convened for trial in the Chamber of the House of Delegates on May 22, 1807, but postponement was necessary pending the arrival of the government's chief witness, Wilkinson. Hay, for the government now, suggested that during the delay Burr might slip away and moved that the Colonel be committed to jail for treason, an unbailable offense. Compromise was reached by raising the bail to twenty-thousand dollars. Then as the proceedings still waited the arrival of Wilkinson, Burr rose dramatically and moved that papers in the possession of the President were essential to his defense. He asked that a *subpoena duces tecum* be issued to the President, requiring him to appear personally in court with the papers.

Burr's motion set off sharp debate. Marshall was embarrassed by this proposed bold challenge to the Executive. Some remembered that Jefferson had interdicted the appearance of his Cabinet officers subpoenaed by the defense in the trial following the Miranda expedition. Marshall issued the writ but carefully modified it with a statement that the papers would be adequate without the "personal attendance" of the President or members of his Cabinet. Thus contrary to persisting belief Marshall did not issue a direct challenge to the President, nor did Jefferson defy the Chief Justice.

In a long argument to Hay with regard to any summons to the President to come and bring the papers with him, Jefferson was clearly not only the lawyer but an irritated man on the defensive. He was particularly stung by a statement Marshall made evidently intended to sting him. In obvious reference to the much time Jefferson spent at Monticello, the Chief Justice said, "It is apparent that the President's duties as chief magistrate do not demand his whole time, and are not unremitting."

Almost querulously Jefferson commented on that to Hay: "If he alludes to our annual retirement from the seat of government, during the sickly season, he should be told that such arrangements are made for carrying on the public business, at and between the several stations we take, that it goes on as unremittingly there, as if it were at the seat of government. I pass more hours in public business at Monticello than I do here, every day; and it is much more laborious, because all must be done in writing."

Wilkinson arrived strutting and bemedaled on Saturday, June 13. And on Monday, a dramatic confrontation took place between the General and the defendant. Its different descriptions matched the many contradictions in the case. Wilkinson described their meeting in the courtroom to the President. He wrote: "In spite of myself my eyes darted a flash of indignation at the little traitor, on whom they continued fixed until I was called to the Book;—here, sir, I found my expectations verified—this lion-hearted, eagle-eyed Hero, jerking under the weight of conscious guilt, with haggard eyes in an effort to meet the indignant salutation of outraged honor; but it was in vain, his audacity failed him. He averted his face, grew pale, and affected passion to conceal his perturbation."

That was not what Washington Irving saw and reported. Wilkinson, he wrote, "strutted into court . . . swelling like a turkey-cock." But Burr "did not take notice of him until the judge directed the clerk to swear General Wilkinson; at the mention of the name Burr turned his head, looked him full in the face with one of his piercing regards, swept his eye over his whole person from head to foot, as if to scan its dimensions, and then coolly resumed his former position, and went on conversing with his counsel as tranquilly as ever. The whole look was over in an instant; but it was an admirable one. There was no appearance of study or constraint in it; no affectation of disdain or defiance; a slight expression of contempt played over his countenance."

Wilkinson was kept on the stand for four days and forced to admit that his version of Burr's cipher letter was an altered one. A motion was then made in the Grand Jury room to indict the General for misprision of treason. It was defeated by the narrow margin of seven to nine. Randolph of Roanoke wrote in disgust: "The Mammouth of iniquity escaped—not that any man pretended to think him innocent, but upon certain wire-drawn distinctions. . . . Wilkinson is the only man that I ever saw who was from the bark to the very core a villain. . . . Perhaps you never saw human nature in so degraded a situation as in the person of Wilkinson before the grand jury, and yet this man stands on the very summit and pinnacle of executive favor. . . ." Loudly the General complained to the President of his treatment. Jefferson wrote to encourage the General: "Your enemies have filled the public ear with slanders and your mind with trouble on that account. The establishment of their guilt will let the world see what they ought to think of their clamors. . . ."

Regardless of the impression made by the General, on June 24 the Grand Jury brought in indictments against Burr and Blennerhassett for treason and misdemeanor. At this time the passions of men around the courtroom and America had been heightened by an incident having nothing to do with the trial. It made loud patriotism the fashion, however, which boded no good for persons charged with lacking it. Two days before, off Norfolk the British frigate *Leopard* had demanded the right to search the American frigate *Chesapeake*. The demand was refused. Whereupon the English warship poured a full broadside into the American ship from a distance of only one hundred fifty to two hundred feet. More blasts came until the *Chesapeake*, which had been able to fire only one countering shot, was helpless. The British came aboard and carried off four men who, they claimed, were British deserters. As hardly ever before, the nation was inflamed and united. The promised war now was with England, not Spain.

In the aroused country the trial in Richmond went imperturbably on. Indicted for the non-bailable offense of treason, Burr spent one night in jail, but on June 26 Marshall agreed to let him be confined in a room in Luther Martin's house behind padlocked doors, barred windows, and a guard of eight men. This did not please the prosecution and arrangements were made to remove the illustrious prisoner to commodious quarters in the state penitentiary on the last day of June.

Perhaps undertaking to reassure the approaching Theodosia, he wrote her how comfortable he was there in rooms having "an extent of one hundred feet." Moreover: "My jailer is quite a polite and civil man —altogether unlike the idea one would form of a jailer. You would have laughed to have heard our compliments the first evening. . . . While I have been writing different servants have arrived with messages, notes, and inquiries, bringing oranges, lemons, pineapples, raspberries, apricots, cream, butter, ice, and some ordinary articles."

Visitors poured in. Fortunately he had an antechamber in which to receive them. He could even provide suitable quarters for Theodosia and Alston who were approaching. He wanted her presence, but: "Remember, no agitations, no complaints, no fears or anxieties on the road, or I renounce thee." The Alstons arrived on August 4 and settled in the rooms the Colonel had vacated at Martin's house. Theo appeared in the Spartan role her father required of her. Alston had earlier been much disturbed by his connection with the case. Even before Burr surrendered in Mississippi, Jefferson had written Governor Charles Pinckney of South Carolina that Alston, at this time Speaker of the House in that state's legislature, was involved in Burr's unlawful enterprise. Alston in a hasty letter had disassociated himself from his father-in-law. But now he stood by Theo in a family solidarity.

Theodosia was given the social world's embrace as Burr had been. Also, she became the recipient of places in multiplying legends. Possibly the aging, slovenly Martin did regard her with "idolatrous admiration." Also a fiction was afterward made to the effect that on this visit to Richmond, Theo was involved in a love affair with Meriwether Lewis. None of Burr's major biographers even mention the presence of Lewis at the trial. Yet the story persists that he was present as a secret observer, perhaps message bearer for the President. Beckley, who often performed such functions, who, indeed, the President had planned to send on a "flying trip to London" to Monroe the year before, was dying in 1807. Lewis was living at the President's House when Burr was being brought to Richmond. He was not to leave for his post in St. Louis until after the Burr trial.

Two biographers of Lewis, John Bakeless and Richard Dillon, wrote that he was present at the trial as a Jefferson agent. Bowers, in his almost ecstatic *Jefferson in Power*, wrote of him as sitting "quietly in the courtroom" at Richmond. Bowers accepted as fact a story that their romantic attachment had begun in Washington while Theo's father was Vice-President. There was then, he wrote, "chatter over the card tables about the infatuation of young Meriwether Lewis, the brilliant and elegant, young secretary of Jefferson! They dance together, dine together, and together they canter over the Virginia hills on horseback. And she a married woman! How the country town would have rocked had it then known that he had declared his passion, and the wise Theodosia, unshocked, had dismissed it as 'romantic idiocy' and remained his friend!"

This was better material for novelists than for a Jeffersonian historian replete with exclamation points. When Theodosia visited in Washington at the inauguration in 1801, Lewis had not arrived to be Jefferson's secretary. When she visited the city again in October 1803, the explorer was already on his way to the West. But there was gossip aplenty in Richmond in this summer in which it was both the judicial and social center of America.

The bewildered Blennerhassett heard some from Mrs. David Randolph. She was, according to the nearsighted Irishman, "a middle-aged lady and very accomplished; of charming manners, and possessing a masculine mind." She needed a disciplined mind. She had come through hard times since Rochefoucauld described her as "young and amiable" at Presqu'ile. Apparently her husband had been able to get his money out of that well-farmed plantation. With that and his salary as marshal, David and Molly Randolph had, in 1798, built a two-story dwelling house with attached offices located in "a square of four lots" on the south side of Main Street in Richmond. After their combined names it had been called Moldavia. Their tenure became precarious after David was dismissed from his position. In 1804 he advertised Moldavia for sale and in 1805 it was sold to Joseph Gallego. Where David and Molly were living in 1807 is uncertain, but there is no question about Molly's bitterness which surprised Blennerhassett. She poured out to him "more pungent strictures upon Jefferson's head and heart, because they were better founded than any I had ever heard before."

A man did not have to be long in Richmond to hear such tales as Callender had printed and wilder ones. It was revealing of Molly Randolph's tattling that she also "ridiculed the experiment of a republic in this country. . . . And as for treason, she cordially hoped whenever Burr, or any one else, again attempted to do anything, the Atlantic States would be comprised in the plan."

Blennerhassett himself may have been manufacturing some gossip. In a journal kept only for the eyes of his wife, he wrote that Duane, the Jeffersonian journalist, came to him and suggested that if he would make certain admissions, the editor would intercede for him in Washington "where nothing he should ask would be refused him." He also reported that other witnesses were similarly approached. Colonel Julien DePestre, French soldier of fortune who had appeared as something like Burr's Chief of Staff, was said to have been approached with an offer of handsome treatment in the American army "if his principles or engagements were not adverse to the administration." Furthermore, Blennerhassett reported that while playing chess during the trial, the Chief Justice had said to Wickham, "Don't you think . . . you will be able to check-mate these fellows, and relieve us from being kept here three more weeks?"

More and more beset District Attorney Hay was hearing things, too. He wrote Jefferson that the Chief Justice was obviously biased against the prosecution. He had heard that the rule of constructive treason set up in the earlier trials of minor figures might not be deemed binding by the Chief Justice in the case of the supposed major malefactor. That turned out to be true. In a laboriously argued long decision the Chief Justice now rejected the theory of "constructive treason." On September 1 the jury, after an absence of only twenty-five minutes, returned to report: "We of the jury say that Aaron Burr is not proved to be guilty by any evidence submitted to us. We therefore find him not guilty." Burr's lawyers rose protesting that the verdict should be the simple and regular "Not guilty." Marshall ruled that the verdict should stand on the bill as the jury wished it but that the entry of "Not guilty" be made on the record.

The cases against most of Burr's associates fell with this verdict. But he was not a free man. Quickly the government began to try him for misdemeanor for having set on foot an invasion of Spanish territory from another scene than Blennerhassett Island. After presenting fifty witnesses, however, Hay moved to drop the case. Burr insisted on a verdict. This time the jury brought in a straight verdict of "Not guilty." This meant that the Colonel had been found guiltless twice in Kentucky, once in Mississippi, and twice in Richmond. But Jefferson was not content. His verdict was that "the criminal is Preserved to become the rallying point of all the disaffected and the worthless of the United States, and to be the pivot on which all the intrigues and the conspiracies which foreign governments may wish to disturb us with are to turn."

Jefferson had Hay commit Burr on another filibuster charge which could bring him to trial in Ohio, Kentucky, or Mississippi. Marshall, evidently fearful Jefferson might bring about his impeachment, as he had that of Chase, opened the doors to any and all testimony. Obviously Jefferson was presenting his tatterdemalion evidence to the country and the Congress and not merely to the Court, and Marshall did not mean to be accused of letting anything be covered up. The result of this, however, was an opportunity for Burr's attorneys to discredit—even disgrace—the chief witnesses upon whom the government depended from a perjured sergeant to perfidious Wilkinson. Even Jefferson's credulity must have been strained by the admissions and the performance of his General on the witness stand. Hay at last had to tell Jefferson that his faith in his chief witness was gone.

Wilkinson was subjected to public condemnation on the streets of Richmond. Andrew Jackson harangued crowds with his proclamation of Wilkinson's guilt. Old Hickory was "wild with delight" when young Sam Swartwout shouldered the portly General from the sidewalk into the gutter. When Wilkinson swallowed the insult Swartwout challenged him. The General declined to fight. Swartwout then publicly posted him as a traitor, a forger, a perjurer, and a coward. This was the basis of an enduring devotion of the great Tennessean for the young New Yorker.

Wilkinson was reviled not only at fashionable dinner tables but in crowded taverns as well. But Jefferson never publicly wavered in his faith in his witness. After the trial he sent him on a diplomatic mission to Spanish officials in Havana and Pensacola. Soon Daniel Clark, angered at the General, would publish a book, *Proofs of the Corruption of Gen. James Wilkinson*. Yet, incontestable proof of his guilt as Spanish spy in the American service was only provided when archives in Havana were opened to American scrutiny many decades later.

Still, with Jefferson's aid he had destroyed his old friend Burr, and Jefferson even now was unwilling to accept the Richmond acquittals as a final act. Marshall granted Hay's motion and committed Burr and two associates for trial at Chillicothe, Ohio, on the misdemeanor charge. Bonds of three thousand dollars each were required of Burr and Blennerhassett. The nearsighted Irishman was frantically worried about his losses and growing glum with his chief. He could not comprehend how Burr could

be "as gay as usual, and as busy in speculations on reorganizing his projects for action as if he had never suffered the least interruption."

It is doubtful that Burr was truly gay, though he helped build legends
about himself as a man who often celebrated disaster with gallantry. His
euphoria may have been a sort of hallucination about his invincibility.
Still some stories of his behavior in disaster were produced by persons
more romantic than he. Perhaps the most preposterous of all such tales
was dated at this time. "According to tradition," was the label put on
this one by *Washington—City and Capital,* an exhaustive guide to the
place, published by the Government Printing Office. It was that after his
trial Burr climbed the ten-foot wall at the famous old Octagon House in
Washington to tell Dolley Madison good-bye. Unfortunately for "tradition," the Madisons were not then living in the Octagon House. Burr was
not dallying in Washington.

There was little room for romance in Burr's story now. Repeatedly
acquitted in the courts, he was still under indictment. As a free man he
was also one hunted by creditors and by vindictive mobs ready to apply
tar and feathers, sticks and stones to the man Jefferson had taught them to
hate. In Baltimore, to which he traveled with "bull-dog" Martin, a threatening crowd surrounded the lawyer's house. They brought fifes and drums
to play the "Rogue's March." Incendiary handbills were circulated damning the Chief Justice, Burr, Blennerhassett, and Martin together. So
serious became the threats that Burr had to be spirited away to Philadelphia.

There he found hiding place and friends. One, who probably alone
in America at the time found excuses for both Burr and Wilkinson, was
Charles Biddle, who had sheltered the Colonel after the duel. "Colonel
Burr at this time kept himself concealed in a French boarding house,"
Biddle wrote. "When I used to call of an evening, he was generally alone
with little light in his room. He was very pale and dejected; how different
from what he had been a short time before when few persons in the city
were not gratified at seeing him at their tables, where he was always one
of the most lively and entertaining of the company. It would not have
surprised me on going there to have found he had ended his sufferings
with a pistol. If ever man could be justified in committing such an act it
was Colonel Burr. To have found he had could hardly have given me
more pain than I have sometimes felt on seeing him in this melancholy
situation."

His situation was not only melancholy but also a harassed one. Some of his remaining friends were as bad off as he was. On his way to England with laudatory letters but little money, David Randolph dined with Burr on November 18, 1807. The Colonel received most attention, however, from creditors. The whining Blennerhassett found his hiding place. So did one Luckett and a Wilkins from Pittsburgh. They brought suits. A lawyer named Hollowell furnished bail. So did George Pollock, described by Biddle as Burr's friend and relative. Young Nicholas Biddle, not yet the great financier he was to become, found him completely "broken in fortune & character, & . . . pursued by his creditors." Young Biddle gave him aid. However, this gifted Biddle, who had recently served as secretary to Minister Monroe in London, felt it necessary to explain his kindness to Burr to this patron in Jefferson's triumvirate.

Still Jefferson did not see the end of the trajectory of this Lucifer he had brought down. It was difficult, he wrote, to "see what shape Burr's machinations will take next. If we have war with Spain, he will become a Spanish General. If with England, he will go to Canada and be employed there. Internal convulsion may be attempted if no game more hopeful offers. But it will be a difficult one, and the more so as having once failed."

Strangely, however, while the trial was in process, Jefferson had written to Madison almost proposing just such an operation against Mexico as that in which Burr had hoped to participate. Troubled now by both England and Spain, he told his Secretary of State, "I had rather have war against Spain than not, if we go to war against England. Our southern defensive force can take the Floridas, volunteers for a Mexican army will flock to our standard, and rich pablum will be offered to our privateers in the plunder of their commerce and coasts."

During Burr's first days in Richmond, Mr. Jefferson had been engaged in laying out and planting the oval and round flower beds around the house at Monticello. During the summer he wrote his granddaughter that he found little poetry in the newspapers to send her perhaps because writers, preoccupied with the Burr trial and the *Chesapeake* incident, were prevented from making their weekly visits to Parnassus. In the fall of the Colonel's acquittal, the President in Washington was inquiring how his tuberoses were doing. An explorer had made him a present of two grisly bears which were too dangerous and troublesome to keep. But some flowering peas which Meriwether Lewis had brought him from the West were flourishing in Virginia.

His reaction to the news which Martha brought him of David Randolph's bankruptcy was a comment on his own troubled financial problems and a homily for Martha: ". . . I know nothing more important to inculcate into the minds of young people than the wisdom, the honor, and the blessed comfort of living within their income, to calculate in good time how much less pain will cost them the plainest stile of living which keeps them out of debt, than after a few years of splendor above their income, to have their property taken away for debt when they have a family growing up to maintain and provide for."

Jefferson made no comment on Martha's report that David Randolph in middle age had gone to England "upon some mercantile scheme with barely money to defray his expenses." Molly, left behind, had "opened a boarding house in Richmond, but she has not a single boarder yet." Among Randolph relatives ruin was spreading. The slaves of one had to hide "to save themselves from the sheriff." Another depended upon charity for shelter. And a cousin was going about constantly armed "to keep the sheriff off." Only Nancy, whose trial for Bizarre crime in 1793 had scandalized Virginia, seemed on the way to security. A year later she would marry the rich, aging Gouverneur Morris, whom earlier the President had described as "a high-flying Federalist."

Hard times in Virginia would be worsened by the Jeffersonian embargo imposed in December 1807, soon after the Burr trial. It interdicted all foreign commerce and confined all U.S. vessels to port. More Virginians and others looked for hope in the West. Early in 1808, Jefferson's sister Lucy, married to her cousin Charles Lilburn Lewis, made what was described as "a dreadful journey" to Kentucky to join there her sons, Lilburn and Isham, who had gone ahead with their slaves.

For Burr the West now meant the possible trial in Chillicothe which Jefferson kept hanging over his head. Even in the East he seemed pursued. Living incognito now, he spent some time at the country seat of Peter Kemble, near Belleville, New Jersey. This must have been pleasant sanctuary though the bluffs of Weehawken were nearby. As a friend of the Kemble family, Washington Irving described the antique elegance of the place in his *Salmagundi,* calling it Cockloft Hall. But before he had left Richmond the Colonel had told Blennerhassett that he was preparing to go to England, "that the time was now auspicious for him."

He made his plans in understanding that the times were ominous for him in America. Theodosia joined him in New York, this time as no lady of fashion holding her head high among Richmond aristocrats. This time, though "with dignity and fortitude," as her father said, she came almost furtively, too. He evidently was hiding in New York and they only made secret visits to each other. They met by arrangement at different places, and at night. The Swartwouts were active in aiding them. So was Gouverneur Kemble, member of the brilliant coterie of young New Yorkers who gathered around Irving. He could be trusted with Burr's papers. Burr himself had written to his friend Williamson in London. At one point he was using the name George Melville, obviously borrowed from Williamson's great friend Lord Melville. As he sailed he wanted Theodosia to get an article in the papers to the effect that Aaron Burr had been seen passing on his way "to Canada, accompanied by one Frenchman and two Americans or Englishmen. On the same day Mrs. Alston passed through on her way for Saratoga, for her health (or some such thing)."

In her communications, Theo was no longer Mrs. Alston but Mary Ann Edwards, sister of a gentleman named H. E. Edwards. "Mr. Edwards" seemed almost deviously moving, from the house of young Kemble, to that of Robert Swartwout in New York, to the home of "Mrs. Pollock" where he had his last interview with Theo, though neither expected then that they would never see each other again.

On the packet *Clarissa Ann* was a gentleman named W. E. Hosack of whom he would see much in England and on the Continent. This young man indicated complicated relationships. He was the younger brother of Dr. Hosack who had attended the first Theodosia in her last illness, and, also, Alexander Hamilton after the duel. He was attending Theodosia Alston now. Moreover, he was one of those providing funds to Burr at this dark point in his career. On June 8 the air was breathless between the Narrows and Sandy Hook. But on June 9, 1808, at 7 P.M., the *Clarissa Ann* set sail.

Burr or Edwards sent back to Theo or Mary Ann a journal in which he made an entry: "Fair Winds."

IX.
DARK JOURNEY

1.

Man Without a Country

Aaron Burr, who had given "so much trouble," had become "absolutely invisible," Jefferson wrote his prosecutor Hay four months before "H. E. Edwards" sailed secretly for England. That was not quite correct. The President evidently knew Burr had been in Philadelphia. His eyes or his agents followed the exile across the Atlantic. He arranged to receive reports about Burr in London where the President charged the acquitted conspirator was giving it out that the British government "offers him two million dollars the moment he can raise an emblem of rebellion as big as a handkerchief." He pooh poohed the possibility. For himself, Jefferson wrote, even at Burr's most threatening periods, "I never entertained one moment's fear."

The West was secure, if it had ever been menaced. So was the Virginia Presidential succession which, though absurd to recall now, Burr once had seemed to threaten. Madison's advent was assured. Monroe, his impatience curbed, waited his turn. This had been accomplished despite a futile, almost comic, episode involving Vice-President George Clinton whose chief merit as a replacement for Burr had seemed that he was too old to hope to follow Jefferson in the Presidency. He suddenly didn't think he was too old. He sought Federalist votes to put him forward as Burr had been charged with doing when he ran for Governor in 1804. Easily the Virginians kept the old man in his Vice-Presidential place from which he hoped to be promoted.

Without perturbation Jefferson had seen his sister Lucy, Mrs. Charles Lilburn Lewis, move to the no longer alarming West. The plantation of her sons, Lilburn and Isham, was at a point near the conjunction of the

Cumberland, Tennessee, and Ohio rivers where Burr had recently made rendezvous with companions. Her "dreadful journey" led to a replica of plantation Virginia which Jefferson found near to perfection. Also, confidently westward went Meriwether Lewis to take his place as successor to Wilkinson at St. Louis, where he would arrive a full year after his appointment. There were no reports that on this trip Meriwether met with dangers. He was to meet at its end, however, enemies and complaints that he had been so spoiled "by so many flattering caresses of the high & mighty, that, like an overgrown baby, he began to think everybody about the House must regulate their conduct by his caprices." This came from Acting-Governor Bates who had reported an exaggerated Burr mobilization at Pittsburgh two years before. There were no suggestions that Lewis was still suffering from "hypochondriac affections."

Jefferson followed the journeys of his sister and his protégé with interest. He was not looking westward only. In the month in which he spoke of Burr's efforts to "raise an emblem of rebellion," he was thinking of Europe in terms of his garden as well as his troubles. He wrote home that his old friend André Thouin, head gardener at the *Jardin du Roi*—now of the Emperor—had sent him seven hundred species of seeds. He was also thinking of Europe in terms of the dragon's teeth he insisted that Burr still meant to plant in the United States. He declined to quash the indictments which he had hung over Burr's head. He did not press them. But if Burr had escaped the halter, Jefferson did not mean to free him from harassment. All this the President may have done in righteous wrath. Virtuous or vindictive, Jefferson helped make Burr's a "dreadful journey." For whatever reason, he moved through his agents—or his agents moved in the hard spirit he had aroused—to make "descent with dignity" impossible for Aaron Burr.

Certainly Burr, as he arrived in London on July 16, 1808, did not seem bereft of dignity or friends. The voyage had been pleasant. Neptune, he once wrote, was always good to him. At sea, along with Hosack, he enjoyed the youthful companionship of Charles Alexander Williamson, relative of his old friend in speculation and high adventure. But he was distressed and embarrassed in London to find Williamson himself gone on one of his secret missions. From off Cádiz, then serving as the capital of all Spain under the control of Napoleon, Williamson wrote his great regret at his absence. He had, however, he told Burr, made arrangements for important persons in the government to see the Colonel as the best informed man in the world on how "to prevent the French in the present crisis from having the command of the Floridas and Mexico."

Williamson had, indeed, prepared the way for Burr. Within the week of his arrival in London he received word that George Canning, Secretary of State for Foreign Affairs, and Lord Mulgrave, First Lord of the Admiralty, would be glad to see him. What came of these meetings is not known. Less than a month later, however, when Burr filled out a document as an alien for John Reeves, official of the British Alien Office, who was to become his friend in need, he stated that he was personally known to Canning and Mulgrave "to whom the motives to my visit here have been declared."

He wore no alias now. Amusingly, as a man of fifty-two he gave his age as "forty and upward." More seriously he added to this document a line which was later to bring much American criticism on his head. By his signature, he stated that "the undersigned was born within the king's allegiance and his parents British subjects." His respectable address was Craven-street, No. 30.

Burr biographers have universally failed to note that Burr's most frequent companion in his English exile was that other subject of Jefferson's antagonism, David Meade Randolph. He had already gone to England, Martha Jefferson reported, before January 2, 1808. Howard N. Eavenson in *The Virginia Magazine of History and Biography* wrote that he was sent abroad to study the coal business there and soon sent back the suggestion that low-grade Virginia coals be turned into coke. Burr was in touch with him immediately after his arrival in England when Randolph reported to him on July 18, 1808, "my hopes having vanished, I am left without any other resource than your own superior view of things." Burr, whose own hopes were not justifiably high, regarded Randolph as a little mad "on poetry and politics." Such interests must have been an avocation with Randolph whom Burr described as a "tall, eager, pale, white-haired man." He was about sixty, Burr said, though he was actually only fifty-two. Broke as he was in Virginia, Randolph had come to England with very good letters and the "United States Bedford's patent for making shoes." This enterprise did not turn out well and he put his limited finances into "a new project for impelling boats by steam." Finally he failed with an invention of his own for an improvement in "wheel-carriages" with which many were "delighted" but in which none were ready to invest. Burr himself, who made some gentle fun of Randolph, was looking for lesser projects than his imperial "X."

Much has been written of the awe and admiration which the Colonel gave to the great reformer and philosopher Jeremy Bentham and the friendship Bentham gave him in return. Burr enjoyed the philosopher's hospitality but he never turned to him for help even when his pockets were most empty. The Colonel had admired this British savant's work long before he came to England. The probability, however, is that their immediate acquaintance in London related to Bentham's interest in South American independence as a part of his universal love of liberty. The English economist and utilitarian had earlier been concerned about Miranda's hopes and plans. The philosopher's brother, Sir Samuel Bentham, naval architect and inspector general of naval works, had known the Venezuelan in Russia. Jeremy had shared their friendship. He had at first been prejudiced against Burr both on account of his duel with Hamilton and his antagonism to Miranda. Burr's charm, however, soon overcame that. He was invited to visit Bentham on August 11, 1808. And, on August 22, he was lodged in Bentham's town house in Queen's Square Place. There he received an invitation to call on the powerful Lord Liverpool, then Home Secretary.

Through Bentham probably he met personages more important to his mind than his projects. Chief among them was the radical writer William Godwin. Earlier in America one of Hamilton's charges against Burr was that he talked "perfect Godwinism." Now he enjoyed talk in the household of Godwin. His first wife, now dead, had been the famous Mary Wollstonecraft, whose views on the emancipation and education of women had long before buttressed Burr's own. Through Godwin he became acquainted with Charles and Mary Lamb. He undertook to help Godwin with his American literary rights. Also, in the British author's house he commented on the "two daughters of Mary Wolstoncraft[sic] . . . very fine children (the eldest being no longer a child, being now fifteen)." Godwin had more than two daughters in his household at this time. Three would be involved in complicated love relationships with Percy Bysshe Shelley and Lord Byron.

Burr had other close English friends. He was welcomed by his wife's relatives, the Prevosts. Also, his relationship with Williamson's distinguished family was much closer than one based on their association in land speculation and Mexican adventure. Such ties explain the warm wel-

come he received on a visit to Scotland where Williamson's brother David
was a Lord of Sessions and in consequence assumed the title of Lord
Balgray. Colonel Williamson's daughter Ann, soon to marry a very rich
young man, regarded Burr almost as a father. The ties were tightened
but Burr's hopes were further reduced when sad news came of Williamson.
On what was euphemistically called his "mission of trade and good will"
to Spanish America, he contracted yellow fever in Havana and, on September 4, 1808, died on his homeward voyage. His death, Burr wrote
Lord Balgray, "inflicted a wound on my peace and happiness which no
time can heal or assuage. You knew something of the intimacy which
subsisted between us, but its whole extent could be known only to him
and to me. It is such as had I with no other man living, and such as it is
utterly improbable I should ever have with anyone again."

Williamson's death was a loss to his hopes as well as his heart. Signs
of trouble were mounting. Erich Bollman wrote him from Philadelphia of
his ostracism in New Orleans and of the problems of the embargo which
Jefferson had imposed on American commerce with England and France.
He realized that Burr could not safely communicate with him. Charles
Smith, a friend of Williamson's, wrote the Colonel, on August 25, suggesting that "the political and personal enemies of Col. Burr might not
look on the Atlantic as an obstacle to their persecution." Samuel Swartwout was in London at this time, still interested in the Mexican project—
always designated by "X" in Burr's correspondence. Apparently, however,
he was now willing to settle for an adventure in shipping cotton bagging
through Jefferson's embargo. At this time also, Burr indicated to Theo
discouragement about "X," even its possible abandonment, something
she sadly said has "so long lain near my heart." Though she wrote him
that the "world begins to cool terribly around me," she had friends in the
North where she had remained for her health's sake for months after his
departure. She felt very much alone, lacking his "counsel and tenderness."
She would not "yield to infantine lamentations or impatience." Still,
"when my tongue and hands trembled with disease, have I besought
Heaven either to reunite us, or let me die at once!"

She was obviously very ill. Her dosage with mercury suggested that
she suffered from the malignant disease of which her mother died. And
Burr's imperious injunction against the use of mercury indicated that this
was ground over which he had been before. He consulted famous English
physicians. All agreed, he wrote, that what she needed was a sea voyage

to join him in England. Apparently the cost of that did not trouble him. "As your strength and life are fast ebbing," she should come quickly to England; "bring Sam and your black woman."

Trips to England were not so simple. Theo might have come but at this time Burr was hearing from Bollman about his travel difficulties. Sick and impoverished, the physician-adventurer would have sailed on a ship "lately dispatched by government to France, if Mr. Jefferson, hearing of my intention, had not ordered the collector of this port to prevent my going in that vessel." He added, "This pitiful resentment could not forego this opportunity of thwarting my pursuits."

Though Balgray and others were still trying to convince the British government of Burr's usefulness to it, evidently Burr felt in the late fall that there was little he could do in London. He set out on a sight-seeing tour which he described to Theo as "The Adventures of Gil Blas Moheagungk de Manhattan." At Stratford a barmaid gave him a detailed account of a recent jubilee honoring the memory of Shakespeare. On Christmas Eve in Birmingham, his celebration caused him "contrition and remorse." He had "lost or spent" twenty-eight shillings. Such incidents, some more scandalous, reported with little reticence were to enliven his *Journal* and help smirch his character. Davis, in the first publication of this diary, "suppressed certain parts." Other such Americans as Benjamin Franklin and Gouverneur Morris followed less than Puritan paths abroad and at home as well. Burr, who dreamed of great conquests, often required the possession of women—not all of them Helens or Queens. This necessity he shared with Miranda, probably most other Casanovas. He constantly made note of pretty faces and well-turned ankles. Particularly, in his anatomical comments, he noticed lovely wrists and forearms. But in Scotland not all his exchanges with women were in gallantry. Solemnly with great ladies of good works he discussed hospitals, poor laws, libraries, and lunatic asylums. Certainly he was no mere roué. He was a man equal to the company of Walter Scott. Francis Jeffrey, then making literary and political history as the editor of the *Edinburgh Review*, was particularly attentive to him.

Back in England, William Cobbett, who as "Peter Porcupine" had pricked Jefferson in Philadelphia, wanted the American exile to somehow enter Parliament. This would, of course, have involved the acceptance of British citizenship, something Burr said he never contemplated but a discussion of which he could not quite explain. Bentham continued his hospitality and friendship. One item of their friendship, amusing in the light of later events, was Burr's mention of Bentham*ana*. To which he added to Theo, "Don't you hate anas?" Certainly he had no idea then that a famous personage was preparing one.

Burr's prospects were not improved by Balgray's report to him of dreadful news from Spain where Napoleon had driven a British army into desperate retreat. He had begun to count his shillings, even his pence, though when he was most hard up he reported giving two shillings to beggar girls. Theo was writing him in anxiety, in January 1909, about her failure to secure funds due him.

In his *Journal*, on January 30, he noted a matter which apparently did not concern him: "Of the Duke of York's mistresses." Frederick Augustus, Duke of York, was in trouble. His latest mistress, one Mary Ann Clark, had used her connection with the noble lord to collect fees from those who wanted civil or military promotions. Burr did not amplify this to support the statement of Davis that he had prepared for profligacy an earlier mistress of the Duke, the Margaret Moncrieffe, later Mrs. Coghlan, who wrote a book about giving her virgin love to an "American colonel" on General Putnam's staff. Burr described the Royal Duke's conduct as "disgraceful."

One other item must have touched his pride, or pique. In February his old rival Miranda was in London dining with General Bentham. Even then the South American must have been planning his next campaign which the following year would land him in brief triumph in Venezuela. But an event more important to Burr's pocket than his pride occurred early in February 1809. Then a London bookseller threatened his arrest unless he paid a debt for books he had ordered four years before for Alston. Lacking ability to pay, Burr saw visions of arrest. Coincidentally he wrote David Williamson that he found himself becoming "an object of suspicion and alarm." Though the book debt was explained and adjusted, he feared that his presence in Bentham's house might involve that great friend in his humiliation. Coincidentally there were signs that as a controversial character he was increasingly regarded as *persona non grata* in England. So, on February 10, 1809, he moved to obscure quarters, in the house of a huckster on St. James-street, under another assumed name. (A little later he wrote to a friend that letters might come to him addressed "to Edwards, Melville, Kirby, Dunbar &c. You see I have as many names as any thief or nobleman in England.")

Needing protection, he got it in superabundant measure from the St. James-street housekeeper or landlady, whose name was oddly Prevost though she was certainly no connection of his relatives by marriage. The suppression by Davis of much of this episode made his landlady and a cousin of his wife seem one and the same. William K. Bixby, in his full publication of the *Journal* in 1903, was less sensitive and less confusing. In Burr's unexpurgated *Journal,* Burr described the woman of St. James-street as "extremely attentive." She had *"un air d'elegance et d'abbatement. Peutetre 28."* She was, he protested, sent by the Devil to seduce him. Evidently, however, she tried to be his guardian angel.

At this juncture, if the lady needed him, he needed her shelter. He wrote that "foreseeing that we might go the round of sentiment, though I think we shall go rapidly through it, thought it necessary to coo dow [kowtow]." He described the progress in fractured French. "An hour with Mdame P. *La 2 lecon car. et souprs."* (The second lesson consists of ca-resses and sighs.) Then: *"Des progres; ça je finira en deux jours."* (He would get through this in two days.) He underestimated himself. That same night he noted: *"Couche at ½ p 10 . . . Des. progr. rapides."*

Suddenly his whereabouts and his identity seemed discovered. Mad-ame Prevost warned him that she had heard "not pleasant" talk about her guest. He felt he must instantly move. He went to bed thinking much and concluding nothing. In the morning Madame Prevost "made the fire and got the breakfast as usual." But: *"Regard triste, sombre, pas maligne.* A sort of explanation ensued. Madame said that one of her acquaintances had met us walking the evening of the second, and knowing lui, on Friday had made the remarks by description and not by any name." Burr began to pack.

He slipped off to stay with friends in Hertfordshire, but apparently soon returned. The situation confronting him seemed not only mysterious but confused. On April 4, 1809, though Mrs. Prevost tried to reassure him about prying persons, he had "a confused presentiment that something was wrong." He packed up his papers and clothes, planning to go out and seek other lodgings. Then suddenly at one o'clock in the morning, without knocking, four "coarse-looking men" came in with the announcement that they had a state warrant for his arrest and the seizure of his papers. On his demand he was shown a warrant signed "Liverpool," but he was not allowed to read it. No reasons were given for the arrest. The officers seized his trunks, searched the room for papers, threw all loose articles into a sack and carried him off to the Alien Office. There Burr refused to go in but sent in a note to his friend Reeves, who came out saying that Burr must be patient. He was taken for the night to the house of one of the officers who had arrested him. Though kept there incommunicado, he characteristically made himself at home. He played cards and chess with his "host" and his wife, "a very pretty young Welsh girl." Then came orders that he was to be deported to Heligoland. Burr put an exclamation point after the name of that barren, almost inaccessible island. Then pending deportation he was released and his papers restored with apologies from Lord Liverpool. It was at this time, apparently for purposes of delay, that Reeves drafted a document, on April 16, arguing that once a British subject, a man was always a British subject.

Out of custody he returned to St. James-street. Madame Prevost was not there. He needed her "zeal and firmness." Moreover, going to the quarters of his friend Hosack on Palace-street, he found that his papers and effects had also been seized. In the face of what Burr called the "pressing invitation" of Lord Liverpool, he gave up any idea of resistance to the "intimation that his presence was embarrassing" to His Majesty's government. He only proposed that he be allowed to go direct to Sweden, since there was no prospect of early passage from barren Heligoland to Scandinavia. Also, he proposed that he be permitted to take one or two companions with him. There were then in London, he wrote, "a number of young Americans who would be glad to accompany me."

Still, if he bowed inevitably to Britain, he expressed his resentment toward those to whom he felt his deportation was due. He wrote to an unnamed lady in New York that "Mr. Jefferson, or the Spanish Juntas, or probably both, have had enough influence to drive me out of this country." To a British friend, however, he narrowed the blame to "the unrelenting persecution of the American government."

Though Liverpool had first "expressed his expectations" that Burr be out of the country by April 14, his departure from London was delayed until the twenty-fourth. During this time he wrote a batch of letters of thanks and farewell to many who had been kind to him in England. On the last day Hosack, who was to follow him, helped him pack. He spent an hour with Bentham, then called at William Godwin's house. On the twenty-seventh he sailed from Harwich Bay on board His Majesty's packet *Diana*. On the voyage he made a lounging place in a lifeboat where an amiable fellow passenger, a Mrs. Daily, read aloud to him from Mary Wollstonecraft's book about Sweden.

In the northern spring he had at least the consolation that Theo had written him she was much better. However, he regarded her return to South Carolina as summer approached as "the most unaccountable instance of inconsiderate folly that ever was practiced by one out of bedlam." He damned again "those South Carolina swamps."

Possibly nobody, not even Burr himself, considered that this harassed spring had once promised to be the time of his ultimate ascension, in an almost formed tradition by which Vice-Presidents rose in their turn to the chief magistracy. He was counting his pennies as exile and outcast when transition in the Presidency came again in March 1809.

Certainly he must have been far from the thoughts of all who gathered in Washington to see the inauguration of Madison which Mrs. Smith, the diarist, described on Saturday, March 4, 1809. In scenes of greatness, gaiety, and exultation, she wrote she was melancholy. She had driven through streets full of carriages and people to the inauguration of James Madison, then back to the reception where the new President and his wife stood to receive their company. Dolley, once the Philadelphia Quakeress to whom Burr had brought the "great little Madison" now "looked extremely beautiful, was drest in a plain cambric dress with a very long train, plain around the neck without any handkerchief, and beautiful bonnet of purple velvet, and white satin with white plumes. She was all dignity, grace and affability. . . . It would be *absolutely impossible* for anyone to behave with more perfect propriety than she did." But then Mrs. Smith added mysteriously, "Ah, why does she not in all things act with the same propriety? She would be too much beloved if she added all the virtues to all the graces." Beside the queenly Dolley, Mrs. Smith wrote that Madison was extremely pale. She remembered that he had "trembled excessively" when he began his inaugural address. At the reception, he seemed "spiritless and exhausted . . . looking as if he could hardly stand."

Others echoed Mrs. Smith's admiration of Dolley. Some were less kind than Mrs. Smith was to Madison. Soon Francis Jeffrey, who had entertained Burr in Scotland, made his note about Madison looking like a schoolmaster dressed up for a funeral. Washington Irving drew his contrast between the buxom Dolley and her "withered little apple-john" of a husband. These could have been prejudiced remarks from friends of Burr's who not even disaster could wither.

Mrs. Smith, despite her continuing intimacy with her Bayard relatives, was almost panegyrical on this occasion and on others about Jefferson. She could not help but note the contrast between him and Madison. The retiring President removed himself early from the Madisons' party. He seemed "in high spirits and his countenance beamed with a benevolent joy. I do believe father never loved son more than he loves Mr. Madison, and I believe too that every demonstration of respect to Mr. M. gave Mr. J. more pleasure than if paid to himself."

Apparently the pêle-mêle system of official etiquette had been abandoned. Mrs. Madison was escorted into dinner by the French Minister Turreau and another lady was given the arm of the new young English Minister who had succeeded the unhappy Merry. At a time when the United States seemed in the dangerous middle between England and France, it was evidently deemed proper that the ministers of the two countries occupy the places beside Dolley at supper.

In the summer following these official festivities Mrs. Smith went on invitation to visit at both Monticello and Montpelier. She and her editor husband ascended to Jefferson's great house up the steep road upon which his happy slaves had propelled his carriage with jubilant cries long ago. Now Mrs. Smith noted "the outhouses for the slaves and workmen. They are all much better than I have seen on any other plantation, but to an eye unaccustomed to such sights, they appear poor and their cabins form a most unpleasant contrast with the palace that rises so near them."

On the hilltop Jefferson showed the Smiths his great house from its pavilions to its dome, the devices he had designed for his convenience, the alcoved library, the closet in which he kept a vast variety of seeds in labeled vials. And as she regarded him and listened to him, Margaret Smith kept returning to the metaphor of his mountain. He was beyond all calumny, all the irksome burdens of politics and power. "I looked upon him as he walked, the top of this mountain, as a being elevated above the mass of mankind . . . simple and majestic . . . meek, humble, gentle and kind. . . ."

All seemed more hearty and less philosophic at Montpelier. When the Smiths arrived in the dining room there, some gentlemen were still smoking cigars and drinking wine. Everything "bespoke comfort . . . No restraint, no ceremony. . . . Wine, ice, punch and delightful pine-apples were immediately brought . . . Hospitality is the presiding genius of this house, and Mrs. M. is kindness personified."

These pleasant Virginia visits were made in August 1809. And in this month in a primitive spa at Rocky River Springs, South Carolina, Theodosia was still hoping for an answer to a letter she had written Mrs. Madison on June 24, 1809. Indeed, in May, the month of her father's arrival in Sweden, she wrote him from The Oaks: "I have written the draught of a letter to Mad. M. It does not quite please yet. You shall have an exact copy of that which is sent. For my soul I cannot bring myself to say a civil thing, even the good I really think of her, because I need her assistance, and might incur an imputation of flattery. It is not yet time to send it. The tide has turned, but not strong as it will be."

Her letter to Mrs. Madison as finally shaped was a desperate appeal: "Why . . . is my father banished from a country for which he has encountered wounds & dangers & fatigue for Years? . . . Why is he driven from his friends, from an only child, to pass an unlimited time in exile, and that too at an age when others are reaping the harvest of past toils?" Then in conclusion she said, "To whatever fate Mr. Madison may doom this application, I trust it will be treated with delicacy; of this I am more desirous as Mr. Alston is ignorant of the step I have taken in writing to you." Mrs. Madison must understand the zeal of a daughter for a "Father almost adored."

She was particularly sensitive about Mr. Alston's feelings because shortly before Blennerhassett had written him threatening that unless his losses were covered by Alston to the extent of thirty-five thousand dollars he would publish a pamphlet which would ruin him. On August 1, Theo wrote her father again, "My letter to Mrs. M. has been sent; but no answer has reached me, and this delay strengthens my apprehensions as to success. The gazettes . . . continue every now and then to propagate calumnies and make use of expressions calculated to enliven every spark of animosity which exists in the country. This looks ill. Our best and most numerous collection of friends is in New York. There are many there who wish to see you once more established at home."

It was in this letter that she told him that the Sumters had set off to Philadelphia, thence to Brazil. "N.," she wrote, "in very ill health."

Here, too, were the far more important lines in the story of her love for her father, whom so many around her reviled. She told him of the failure of one who had promised funds, later to be bitterly described by her as Judas.

"His conduct," she said, "is a serious addition to all the accumulated difficulties which already pour in upon us, and which would absolutely overwhelm any other being than yourself. Indeed, I witness your extraordinary fortitude with new wonder at every misfortune. Often, after reflecting on this subject, you appear to me so superior, so elevated above all other men; I contemplate you with such a strange mixture of humility, admiration, reverence, love, and pride, that very little superstition would be necessary to make me worship you as a superior being: such enthusiasm does your character invite in me. When I afterward revert to myself, how insignificant do my best qualities appear. My vanity would be greater if I had not been placed so near you; and yet my pride is our relationship. I had rather not live than not be the daughter of such a man."

When she so wrote, Burr in Sweden was contemplating a French chevalier, "who lives on forty dollars per annum, and is always gay."

He made a note in his *Journal:* "I must take some lessons from him."

There was fortitude and brave show in both Sweden and South Carolina. Theo wrote of the progress of her boy, "little Gampy." Now at seven he was reading and speaking French with facility. She would set him to reading history as her father proposed. She mentioned discussions with her husband about a tutor. Alston preferred a European to a Cuban exile. Yet there were at least rumors of unhappiness in the Alston household. Alston had remained in the Low Country "busily engaged in political affairs," while Theo guarded her health at the springs. Already Alston, at thirty-two, was engaged in a campaign for governor which he would win in a bitterly contested election the following year. Her health and his ambition kept them much apart.

Nathalie Sumter heard the rumors about them in Washington. Sumter, evidently in favor with the Madison administration, was on his way to his post as Minister to Brazil. Theo hoped that Nathalie could perform a more delicate diplomatic mission in the capital by speaking to important persons in the interest of Burr whom they both loved. Undoubtedly Nathalie did. Evidently she failed. Certainly she was distressed by what she heard in conversations about her almost sister and almost father.

On August 2, 1809, when Burr in Stockholm was once again damning the South Carolina climate, Nathalie wrote from Washington to her

friend Mrs. Mary Hooper in Stateburg. In a letter almost breathlessly devoid of pauses or punctuation, she told her fears:

"I told you yesterday how distressed I was about Mrs. Alston—she has
been very sick as well as Burr ["little Gampy"] since she was with us she
wrote to me she could not see but from one eye she has such inflamation
in her face she said her soul was harrowed from what she heard of her
father—her husband was not with her—nor did she know when he was
coming or if he was coming at all—I am going to tell Mrs. Huger as much
as I want the family to know by Mrs. Huger, that is how much she is
respected here—that the report here is that they have separated & that she
inspires more respect & interest than him & that for his own importance he
ought to be with her—I can hardly believe though that he means to discard
her & has lost his affection for her it cannot be, I am sure I never was more
mistaken in a man if it is—do tell me what is said with you. I have not
written yet to Bartow Prevost he can do no good at present, if it is true her
father is deranged I hope she will be able to have him with her & nurse
him it will be her only consolation—the only thing I am afraid of is if she
hears this when she is at the springs by herself sick is that she will die,
sometimes I think of writing to Mr. Alston but I don't know what to do I
write often to her & try to keep up her courage."

2.

Stranger's Sojourn

Burr in Sweden was an impecunious but much sought-after celebrity tourist. Due in part to the good offices of his friend Henry Gahn, Swedish Consul at New York, he was entertained by royalty, statesmen, literary men, and scientists. Certainly no international intrigue concerned him in this country of honest men and women who seemed to have no faults except a habit of opening doors without knocking. In Denmark he was similarly entertained. And there, like any gentleman making the grand tour, by moonlight he visited the tomb of Hamlet at Elsinore late in October. Burr at this time was engaged in a soliloquy of his own.

"It is no easy matter, ma Min. [my Minerva], to determine how to dispose of myself. Why stay here? To be sure, I am unmolested, and live at no great expense, but tem. fug. [tempus fugit] and nothing done. When I came here it was with intent to stay till answers should be received to my letters written to the United States at the moment of leaving London."

No satisfactory answers had come. So he moved at first without aim through the principalities and states of Germany, attending dinners and levees, meeting the powerful and the beautiful. Accompanied part of the time by young Hosack and Thomas Robinson, a young Scotch merchant of New York, he was also joined as he traveled from Stockholm to "Gottenburg" [Göteborg] by Diedric Luning, a rich young man who was on impulse to lend Burr money when he most needed it. The Colonel took notes about governments and laws for a possible book. He visited museums. There were episodes of gallantry. Yet in a world tormented, as he said, by England and France, he moved and wrote with care. To an unknown lady he insisted: "Be careful what you write. Every letter is liable to inspection. One indiscreet expression might expose your letters to be burned, and perhaps me with them. Avoid everything having reference to politics, and there is no danger."

Hardly any passage in the *Journal* is more fascinating and mysterious than the danger in the gay, cultured Weimar of the enlightened Duke Charles Augustus which Burr described to Theodosia. There Burr seemed almost a pet of the colorful court of potentates and poets. One scene seemed properly set "chez Goethe." The great poet had published the first part of *Faust* the year before. His house was crowded with characters who might have been in his plays. At a midday musicial party the guests were baronesses, princesses, duchesses, and a very special lady, "la belle de Reizenstein."

Evidently she had been in America, possibly Burr had known her there. When he met her he wrote: "M'lle has lost no ground today. We ran over the United States. Her recollections charmed and astonished me." After the party at Goethe's house, they walked together. At another party he could hardly listen to the conversation of Goethe's friend, the poet Johann Daniel Falk, for preoccupation with La Reizenstein.

Then suddenly, on January 8, 1810, he wrote: "Felicitate me, my dear Theodosia, on my escape from the most critical danger of my life." He had ordered post horses for six in the morning, not choosing to hazard the lapse of two or three hours for the regular diligence. He put fifteen English miles between himself and the lady, leaving a number of broken engagements behind him, and still did not feel quite safe.

"But I have escaped. That is my consolation. I do really believe that De Reizenstein is a sorceress. Indeed, I have no doubt of it; and, if I were president of the Secret Tribunal, she should be burned alive tomorrow. Another interview, and I might have been lost; my hopes and projects blasted."

In this passage, possibly designed only to amuse Theodosia, Burr did seem like a Faust flying from temptation, which certainly was not generally characteristic of him. Perhaps had he declared himself to the lady his poverty might have been exposed. Or rescued from poverty, he might have been only a lady's ornament in a world in which he hoped for eminence.

The grand tour had its delights as well as its dangers, sometimes together. But he was not forgetting his hopes and projects. And hostility was not forgetting him. While in Sweden he had sought a passport to

Russia, where Miranda had found caresses, but John Quincy Adams, apostate Federalist and Madison's Minister there, stopped that. Burr met hostility as well as hospitality. He found the American colony in such a city as Hamburg decidedly cool to him. He also learned that he was spoken of in Paris newspapers "in a manner no way auspicious." The French Minister in Hamburg had received word from Paris that Burr was a dangerous man who needed to be watched. Apparently, however, Burr's charm and behavior overcame the Frenchman's fears and he gave him a passport, which he must pick up in Frankfurt, to a French border town. And there with friends and relatives at work he was finally permitted to move into France. Now "X" or Mexico was much back in his mind.

When Burr had written from Hamburg, on December 8, 1809, to the Minister of Police in Paris asking for a passport, he said that he desired to visit France "from motives of curiosity and amusement only." But as he approached Paris, on February 16, 1810, he noted in his *Journal* that he was "very bad company and unsocial, my head being so full of Mexican affairs." He arrived also counting his sous but keeping a valet. He went quickly to work trying to secure an audience with the Duc de Cadore, Minister of Foreign Relations. He did not neglect, however, his amusement and his curiosity. Though he counted the cost of every drink and ticket, he enjoyed the cafes and went much to the theater. He strolled in and about the Palais Royal, "where the ear and the eye may be always amused, and the other senses, if you please." At the Théâtre François he made a "very pleasant acquaintance" in the adjoining box.

"She invited me to sup, which I declined. How wonderfully discreet; but then I engaged to call on her tomorrow. How wonderfully silly."

Quickly, however, he sought the comfort and companionship of friends. He inquired in vain about the whereabouts of Madame Sénat and Nathalie's kin, the Delages. Happily he found his old friend and protégé, the painter Vanderlyn. More important to his hopes and projects he met and embraced the Comte de Volney, the savant and traveler, whom he had known when the Count was traveling in America in the decade before. Volney could be expected to be much interested in Mexican plans. In America in 1797, he had been accused of being a French spy sent to prepare for the reoccupation of Louisiana by France. He had been forced to leave the United States but there he had enjoyed the hospitality of Richmond Hill. Another whom Burr sought out early was Monsieur Adet, who had succeeded Genet as French Minister in Philadelphia.

Also interested in the American West, Adet had said that "Success was so near that if [Genet's] orders had been obeyed this brilliant revolution would undoubtedly have been achieved." He also had been entertained by Burr at whose suggestion the Frenchman had had his portrait done by Vanderlyn.

Burr's hospitality had been shared by other Frenchmen in Paris—notably Talleyrand. This great triple turncoat later told George Ticknor, proper Bostonian who wrote of visits to both Europe and Monticello, that during Burr's stay in Paris he "would have nothing to do with him. I hated the man who had murdered Hamilton." His word for Burr, according to Ticknor, was "Assassiné." Actually, however, before Burr arrived in Paris, Talleyrand was out as Foreign Minister, Napoleon having received many complaints of his venality and doubtful loyalty. Certainly, nevertheless, Talleyrand could have helped create Burr's difficulties.

What the Colonel chiefly faced, however, was not merely some French suspicions, preoccupations with other matters, and the maze of bureaucratic red tape. He met in Paris an almost mobilized American hostility in important places. In June 1804, soon after Burr's defeat for Governor by the Jefferson-Hamilton-Clinton-Livingston combine, Jefferson had named John Armstrong as Minister to France to succeed his brother-in-law Robert R. Livingston. Armstrong had been Burr's friend, but he had become the better friend of DeWitt Clinton. Now he was Jefferson's diplomat retained by Madison. Burr described him as "my personal and political enemy" who "was indefatigable in his exertions to prejudice the French government against me."

Burr had intended, he said, to stay in France only a month, but the weeks and months dragged on. Not only were the doors of French ministries closed to him and silence greeting his proposals to Napoleon. More and more he also faced, he wrote, "the machinations of our worthy minister, General Armstrong, who has been, and still is, indefatigable in his exertions to my prejudice; goaded on by personal hatred, by political rancour, and by the natural malevolence of his temper."

Burr wrote this in August 1810, after a year of exile in England and on the Continent. Armstrong left France in September, but left behind as chargé d'affaires, Jonathan Russell, who had gladly accepted Burr's hospitality in years before. Now Russell was ready to treat the exiled former Vice-President with cruelty and arrogance like a fugitive criminal. And behind and beside Russell as U. S. Consul in Paris was Alexander McRae, who had been the least able but most vindictive of Burr's prosecutors at his trial in Richmond.

To give Burr's American devils in Paris their due, however, they may have regarded themselves as vigilant rather than vindictive. Much report current then and history written afterward seemed to justify their behavior. An anonymous correspondent, who signed himself only as "Citizen of the United States," wrote Madison on December 11, 1811, that Burr had presented an elaborate plan to the French government proposing that the bitter enemies, England and France, combine in secret to back Burr in operations against the United States from both Canada and the Spanish territories in the South and West. Before his death the Colonel's friend Williamson had dreamed of a Northern secession against the "Frenchified" Jefferson government like that to which New England Federalists had proposed to Burr in 1804. Those who believed Burr had been improperly found not guilty of treason at Richmond found it easy to believe that his purposes were treasonous now. Minnigerode and Wandell regarded documents, not by Burr but by minor functionaries in the French government, about such a plan, as proof "incontestable that Colonel Burr was, on paper at least, contemplating treason." They concluded that the fantastic quality of the plan made Burr's behavior not a case for the courts but "for the alienist."

As Nathalie Sumter indicated in August 1810, reports that Burr was "deranged" were going around in Washington. Burr's own fantasies about enrichment by a variety of schemes, inventions, speculations seem almost mad as he set them down in his *Journal*. There was the taint of irrationality in his Edwards ancestry. At the time of the "conspiracy," Senator Plumer, John Adams, acting Governor Meade of Mississippi, and others had written that if he were guilty he must be insane. If there was a cracking point in his brilliant mind, hue and cry, exile, hardship, ostracism certainly could have brought him to it—and to treason.

The best evidence, however, even in the secondhand reports in the French archives is that Burr's proposals now were revisions of his plans in the Southwest—now adding England to Spain in war *from*, not war *against*, the United States. As war with Spain had threatened in 1806, now the involvement of the United States in war with England was not only possible but actually in prospect. Now there were not only restless settlers on the Mississippi, habituated to hatred of Spain, there were in the New England towns thousands of sailors idle because of the embargo brought on by England's predatory arrogance against American commerce on the seas. A bold leader aided by France, in desperate grapple with Britain, might attract to his standard thousands ready to strike at England as well as Spain in America. The vision of Mexico set free remained, evidently only altered by the new situation created by the ambitious adventures of Napoleon who so few years before had himself been only an obscure Corsican artillery officer.

Whatever were Burr's plans—and the debate about them may never end—there can be no doubt about his condition of hardship and humiliation in France where he was both disregarded and imprisoned. Certainly also, he described himself in his *Journal* as dissolute. The copy of the *Journal*, which he sent to Theo and which was lost with her papers, could not have been the one he saved. This was a man's confessions for himself. The sexual passages in it were not pornographic but statistical. He drew the warts on his own portrait. He was extravagant and penurious by turns and sometimes together. He piled up gifts and possessions for Theo and little Burr and then had to sell the ribbons and coins he bought for them for necessities. And necessities, even when he was poorest, included women and wine. He got books when he lacked bread. He shivered for lack of fuel in draughty attic rooms. He was sick for lack of tobacco. He suffered with his teeth and from hemorrhoids. Yet, to the last of his days in Paris, he maintained an appearance, a charm, and a dignity which brought him the admiration of such men as Hugues-Bernard Maret, Duc de Bassano, who became Napoleon's Foreign Minister in 1811, and Dominique Vivant Denon, Baron de Denon, Director General of Museums. Both these gentlemen were close friends of Napoleon.

Three of his associations with women in Paris indicate both his kindness and his charm. Only one of these involved any sexual relationship. One was the maid or slavey at his humble pension, Jul (or Jeannet). She was deaf. He listened to her troubles. But she faithfully cared for him when he was ill. Sometimes he was late in paying her, even borrowed sous from her pitiful store. Once with her own money she bought wood to make a fire in his chill room. He wrote, "Certainly no person in Paris deserves from me as much as does Jul."

There was a Mrs. Robertson, a rich widow, "amazingly well preserved," who often invited him to dinner when he needed a good meal. He served her as adviser, occasional attorney. Obviously, however, she bored him and he resented his dependence on her table. He was evidently in love with Madame Paschaud, a Swiss whose husband was a bookseller. She was, he wrote, a "beautiful, sensible, well-bred woman . . . about the size and form of Mrs. Madison, though some ten years younger . . . very black hair and eyes. A fine, clear, fair brunette, with the complexion of full health." She helped him prepare in excellent French his communications to the ministries. He added: "Her husband is at Geneva."

He was often at her house. Indeed, as a better address than his own, he had mail sent him at her residence on the Rue des Petites Augustines. Then in August there was a quarrel, and afterwards "we were very civil but no more." This came at a time when he needed much more than civility. Hopes for his "X" project had collapsed. He had determined to go back to America and face both indictment and debtors. Indeed, by this time his debts were pursuing him to France. One significantly was due to Stephen Jumel, who had married the beautiful Eliza Brown and purchased for her the Roger Morris mansion which Burr had once considered as an alternative to Richmond Hill. At the same time Bollman, still detained in America, wrote that the *Aurora*, "the organ of Mr. Jefferson," had published that "you are employed by the emperor." Burr wrote in his *Journal* "no passport; no money."

Fortunately, as it seemed, he received word in the late summer that Napoleon had consented to a request for a passport. That was the beginning of a full year's run-around involving French bureaucracy but in greater measure American hostility. Indeed, this was stiffening. Burr noted that a combination of Americans was forming to shun every man who spoke to him. Much more certain was the attitude of American officials. Police had ruled that he must apply for his passport to American diplomats. Without much hope Burr applied to Consul McRae. McRae bristled in reply that "his knowledge of the circumstances under which Mr. Burr left the United States renders it his duty to decline giving Mr. Burr either a passport or a permis de séjour." Burr appealed to Chargé Russell and was told: "The man who evades the offended laws of his country, abandons, for the time, the right to their protection. This fugitive from justice, during his voluntary exile, has a claim to no other passport than one which shall enable him to surrender himself for trial for the offenses with which he stands charged. Such a passport Mr. Russell will furnish to Mr. Burr, but no other."

This stiff note came on November 4, 1810, when the winds were chilling along the banks of the Seine. Two days before, he had had to pawn a watch which he had bought for Theo. With winter coming on the Colonel grew speculatively desperate. The shares of the old Holland Land Company were down because of the stagnation of world commerce. Burr knew as much about their true value as anyone in Europe. With Edward Griswold, from whom he had borrowed money, he saw a chance of profit, even riches. The gain was there but Burr didn't get it. Another "friend" to whom he had confided his plan cheated him even of his small investment. He had dreams of riches from vinegar made out of tree sap, from other inventions and ventures which glittered before they faded. Winter came on. He shivered and starved. His foot was run over by a hack.

Somehow he survived the winter. Griswold lent him more money. Spring warmed but did not feed him. Then at last came a break. Denon, realizing Burr's plight, took up with Bassano the matter of the passport. The Foreign Minister thought Russell should issue it. Burr told him of that official's refusal. Bassano moved in a Gallic way, not through diplomatic channels. He told Denon: "The *person* through whom I have communicated to Mr. Russell that he should *not* have refused a new passport to Mr. Burr, was in the country. I wrote to HER yesterday to return. She arrived at the moment that your note was received. I shall have the passport in the course of the day. . . . I am convinced that you will receive it tomorrow, to transmit to Mr. Burr." Davis, in footnoting this letter, suggested that a little benevolent blackmail was used in connection with the unnamed "her" and the "pure patriot" Mr. Russell.

There was kindness in the world. Bassano not only got the passport but lent Burr money for his passage home. The Colonel's difficulties were not over. He was cheated by a ship captain. The ship on which he first left France was seized as a prize by a British frigate. On October 16, 1811, he was in London with two shillings in his pocket. He saw Bentham, to whom neither then or ever did he mention his poverty. They discussed Miranda. And Burr wrote of his old frayed purpose, "There is a possibility, perhaps something more, that I may mingle, personally, in the affairs of Spanish-America." He would like very much to help Miranda. Neither Burr nor Bentham looked forward then to Miranda's impending doom in a Spanish dungeon.

Actually Burr's prospects did not seem much better. In London he was as poor as the melancholy David Randolph who again was appearing

regularly with reports of his disappointments. Indeed, now Burr feared
that Randolph might hang himself or blow out his brains. Still, Randolph, "having four three shilling pieces, lent me two of them, but one
proved a counterfeit." All hopes seemed spurious. Yet there was a little
light. The Colonel was happy and could be candid about his situation in
the household of the William Godwins who were themselves deep in debt
to friends. His visits to that house were only half a year before the better-
remembered first visits to it of Percy Bysshe Shelley.

In February 1812, Burr made notes in his *Journal*: "Called at Godwin's to leave the newspapers which I borrowed, and to get them of today. *Les goddesses* kept me by acclamation to tea with *La Peintresse* Hopwood. I agreed to go with the girls to call on her on Friday." Again:
"Called and passed an hour at Godwin's. That family really does love me.
Fanny, Mary and Jane, also little William, and you must not forget
either, Fanny Hopwood, *la peintresse*." Then in March he wrote: "Mr.
and Mrs. Godwin would not give me their account, which must be five
or six pounds; a very serious sum to them; they say that, when I succeed
in the world, they will call on me for help."

No success for Burr appeared likely then. He seemed imprisoned in
England. Jonathan Russell had moved from his place as Chargé d'affaires
in Paris to the same position in London. He arranged that Burr could
secure passage on no American ship. Finally, Burr found a sea captain
ready to take the chance of having him as a cargo. Then kindness again—
or perhaps the softer side of diplomacy. Reeves of the British Alien Office,
who had been his friend on his earlier stay, provided the passage money
and provided the Colonel a passport in the name of Monsieur Adolphus
Arnot. Possibly Reeves acted less from benevolence than from desire to
get the embarrassing personage off his and His Majesty's hands. Something of the sort is suggested by his obliging statement on his issue of
the passport that "if you are tired of the name Arnot, and wish any other,
you may have it."

At the last Burr almost failed to reach the ship, ominously named
the *Aurora*, on time. But not the least amazing fact about his homeward
passage at last was that his baggage consisted of eighteen pieces, "trunks,
boxes, portmanteaus, bundles, rolls, &c."

He landed in Boston bearded and wearing a wig for disguise on May
5, 1812, almost four years since he had left New York. He was just in
time. On June 18, 1812, after a seven-month debate during which little

had been done to strengthen the army or the navy, the United States declared war on Britain. But M. Arnot, now Colonel Burr, was safely home, still wary about his position there.

Even Mr. Jefferson was rather relieved when war had come after ten years, as he said, of insults and injuries. England, he thought, would "have the sea to itself, while we shall be equally dominant at land, and shall strip her of all her possessions on this continent." He was ready for extreme measures: "She may burn New York, indeed, by her ships and congreve rockets, in which case we must burn the city of London by hired incendiaries, of which her starving manufacturers will furnish abundance." The acquisition of Canada this year, as far as the neighborhood of Quebec, "will be a mere matter of marching," he wrote.

He had watched the war come as philosopher on his hilltop, much interested in a fine wheat crop and the prices it would bring. He was changing his ideas about the virtues of agriculture over industry, seeing the necessity for both in America and on his own plantation. He kept up a wide correspondence—some of it troublesome. On March 21, 1812, a day on which Burr, with Mrs. Godwin's help, had spent the whole day running around London trying to sell a watch, Jefferson at Monticello wrote a polite but firm note to a gentleman in New York. He had been asked to make a contribution to a fund being raised for the support of the family of Editor Cheetham. That hatter turned editor, who had mounted the attack on Burr with Jefferson's approval, had died shortly before of "a congestion of the brain by walking hatless in the sun."

Jefferson was embarrassed, he wrote, by the many such requests made to him as President and continuing now. He had had to make a rule against them. "Nor," he went on, "was there anything in the case of the late Mr. Cheetham, which could claim with me to be taken out of the general rule. On these considerations I must decline the contribution you propose, not doubting that the efforts of the family, aided by those who stand in the relation to them of neighbors and friends, in so great a mart for industry, as they are placed in, will save them from all danger of want or suffering."

Another letter to Monroe, on January 11, when Burr was still in London, seemed more troublesome. His old friend had written him to inquire about a matter connected with one of the numerous court-martials of General Wilkinson. It concerned the Spanish closing of the port of New Orleans to American traffic in October 1802. Mr. Jefferson's answer to Monroe seems convoluted and complex but finally clear in answer to the amazing suggestion that he had been willing to keep the West bottled up by Spain.

He wrote: "The question indeed whether I knew or approved of General Wilkinson's endeavor to prevent the restoration of the right of deposit at New Orleans, could never require a second of time to answer. But it requires some time for the mind to recover from the astonishment excited by the boldness of the suggestion. Indeed, it is with difficulty I can believe he has really made such an appeal; and the rather as the expression in your letter is that you have 'casually heard it,' without stating the degree of reliance which you have in the source of information. I think his understanding is above an expedient so momentary and so finally overwhelming. Were Dearborn [Secretary of War] and myself dead, it might find credit with some. But the world at large, even then, would weigh for themselves the dilemma, whether it was more probable that, in the situation I then was, clothed with the confidence and power of my country, I should descend to so unmeaning an act of treason, or that he, in the wreck now threatening him, should wildly lay hold of any plank. They would weigh his motives and views against those of Dearborn and myself, the tenor of his life against that of ours, his Spanish mysteries against my own cherishment of the western interests; and, living as we are, and ready to purge ourselves by any ordeal, they must now weigh, in addition, our testimony against his. All this makes me believe he will never seek this refuge. I have ever and carefully restrained myself from the expression of any opinion respecting General Wilkinson, except in the case of Burr's conspiracy, wherein, after he had got over his first agitations, we believed his decision firm, and his conduct zealous for the defeat of the conspiracy, and although injudicious, yet meriting, from sound intentions, the support of the nation. As to the rest of his life, I have left it to his friends and his enemies, to whom it furnishes matter enough for disputation. I classed myself with neither, and least of all in these times of his distresses, should I be disposed to add to their pressure."

The former President closed with a devout wish: "I hope, therefore, he has not been so imprudent as to write our names in the panel of his witnesses." Certainly it was now clear that neither Jefferson nor his successors would bring forward Wilkinson as a witness against Burr at Chillicothe, Ohio, or anywhere else.

Exiles were ending. Even David Randolph, who had seemed ready to hang himself when Burr saw him last in London, somehow got home. In a list of the Federal Patent Office in 1815 his name appeared as patentee of devices used in "making candles" and "in ship building" and "an improvement in drawing liquor." Possibly he found them no more profitable than the inventions he had desperately tried to peddle in London. But now Molly Randolph's boardinghouse was apparently flourishing. She advertised her establishment in Cary Street "for the accommodation of ladies and gentlemen. She has comfortable chambers, and a stable well supplied for a few horses." She was proclaimed the "Queen" by a Virginia gentleman who "aided in enlisting subjects for her new realm" where "wit, humor and good fellowship prevailed, but excess rarely." She justified the title by a much reprinted cookbook, *The Virginia Housewife, or Methodical Cook,* which was first published in Washington in 1824. David, who was one of the Revolutionary officers assembled to welcome Lafayette to Richmond in 1824, died by God's will and not his own hand six years later.

3.

Again, The Last Word

Aaron Burr could hardly have been a man with "no memory for injuries," on June 7, 1812, when he arrived in New York as stealthily as he had left it four years before. He was as much a stranger to the scene as Jefferson said he felt himself to be when he came back from happier years in France in 1789. Moreover, while Jefferson had moved to his place in Washington's Cabinet as a reluctant aristocrat, Burr felt it necessary at first to move with the furtiveness of an outcast. Though friends had written him many carefully worded letters and he had avidly read American newspapers whenever he could get them, he was as ignorant about many happenings as Lewis and Clark had been when they emerged from the encompassing West to learn first of a two-year-old duel. The one thing Burr was eager to learn at first hand, and with his own eyes, was the truth about the health of Theodosia and his grandson. He could give them no Richmond Hill welcome in New York. It was at Theo's insistence that he had returned to New York to show himself and his powers. But now though safely on the same shore they were a many-day voyage apart. The gap was closed like thunder from heaven. The very gods seemed against him now.

Three weeks after he arrived in New York the grandson for whom he had collected gifts during his European poverty died in South Carolina. Theo shared her broken heart with him in a note from Seashore, South Carolina, near those swamps which Burr had cursed so long. Though he wished it, she could not come quickly to New York. Her husband as Governor also commanded a brigade. Furthermore, although Alston's Governorship was "distinguished by its vigorous measures in support of the War of 1812," at this time he was awaiting the sitting of "a military court of inquiry which he demanded." She hoped to come soon though she could not "go alone by land, for our coachman is a great drunkard, and requires the presence of a master."

Alston was less reticent in his grief. Before the boy's death and since Burr had gone away, he had faced embarrassments, troubles, and disappointments. They were nothing. Now: "One dreadful blow has destroyed us. . . . That boy, on whom all rested; our companion, our friend—he who was to have transmitted down the mingled blood of Theodosia and myself—he who was to have redeemed all your glory, and shed new lustre upon our families—that boy, at once our happiness and our pride, is taken from us—*is dead.*"

But heaven seemed not content. Alston was rather hurt when in December Burr sent Timothy Green, a man with some medical talents, to Charleston to escort Theo northward. The Governor, or one of his brothers, would have attended her. At Georgetown, Green engaged passage for Theodosia and himself on "a pilot boat that has been out privateering." He was afraid that Alston "might think this mode of conveyance too undignified, and object to it; but Mrs. Alston is fully bent on going. You must not be surprised to see her very low, feeble and emaciated. Her complaint is an almost incessant nervous fever."

The *Patriot* sailed from Georgetown on December 30. Sometime thereafter, off Hatteras, a vessel in the British blockading fleet stopped the privateer whose guns were hid under a supposed cargo of rice. The British Captain read a letter Alston had written requesting the safe conduct of his sick wife and waved her northward. Theo, then not quite thirty, was never heard from again except in a multitude of legends about pirates, mutiny, coastal looters who on the North Carolina shore lured the vessel to wreck and robbery. Political malignancy even tried to put together the wild tales of Burr's philandering with his daughter's death. Without knowing that Theo would sail on her, he had arranged, so this malicious melodrama went, a mutiny to get rid of the ship's Captain whose wife Burr had ruined. In relating this odious story a newspaper, called the *Carolina Spartan*, solemnly concluded that "her fate was an awful retribution upon her abandoned father." Actually, there seems little or no doubt that the *Patriot* sailed into the storm which at this time battered and dispersed a British squadron. On the tombstone over Alston and the boy in the family burying ground at The Oaks is engraved the home faith that the disconsolate wife and mother "perished . . . at sea."

Evidently, when at last hope could only be a delusion clung to without reason, Burr wrote Alston that he felt severed from the human species. Alston, almost in hysteria, wrote of his tortured mind. Far off in Brazil, months later, Nathalie had not heard of Theodosia's death but before news of it came she was filled with forebodings. She wrote to a friend in Stateburg crying for news about Theo and what seemed an ominous silence: "some time I fear she is crazy, thus I think she'll die." Then as her letter lengthened she put it bluntly, "I think she must be dead." More lonely now than he had ever been in exile, Burr seemed caught in an emotional catalepsy which showed the world no hurt.

Mental derangement seemed much closer to Jefferson, dramatically shown in two dark episodes in the West where some had suspected Burr was mad. They had occurred while Burr was writing his eccentric *Journal* in cold dark rooms abroad. He must have learned the confused stories about each only after he returned. Some aspects of both are still lost in mystery and horror.

As Jefferson awaited what he regarded as release from his Presidential burdens and Burr was arranging escape from the United States, the President had written his sister Lucy in Kentucky. She was apparently happily settled there with her sons Lilburn and Isham. These young men were not only Jefferson's nephews as his sister's sons. Also, their father was his cousin.

"I have never ceased," he wrote Lucy on April 19, 1808, "to wish to descend the Ohio & Mississippi to New Orleans, and when I shall have put my home in order, I shall have the leisure, and so far I have health also, to amuse myself in seeing what I have not yet seen."

Westward, in addition, he wrote to his much-honored and well-loved Meriwether Lewis, who had belatedly arrived at his post in St. Louis. With much enthusiasm he told Meriwether about plans for larger fur-buying operations to be centered there by "a most excellent man, a Mr. Astor," which he thought would be so effective that the British Mackinac Company "will probably withdraw from competition." This was, of course, John Jacob Astor, whose interests also included the onetime Burr property at Richmond Hill.

Lewis seemed a dilatory correspondent after he reached St. Louis. Apparently the first word in months Jefferson received about him was from Lucy's son Isham, who arrived in Monticello on August 23, 1808, after visiting Meriwether at his territorial capital. The relationship of Isham to Meriwether is not clear but as both were from Albemarle County and were often welcome members of Jefferson's household, their kinship was close enough for intimacy on the frontier. Both were to reflect a sort of Albemarle madness from which Monticello was not immune.

In St. Louis, where Meriwether succeeded Wilkinson, Jefferson wrote, his protégé "found the territory distracted by feuds and contentions among the officers of the government, and the people themselves divided by these into factions and parties." Also he found a bitter enemy in the furiously ambitious Bates who had ruled in his absence. Soon after Jefferson left the Presidency, the security of Lewis as both Governor and man was threatened by what appeared to be pettifogging bureaucracy in Washington. A draft he had drawn was disallowed. More such actions might follow. Lewis' health was not good. He was reported to be drinking heavily. He was overextended in that acquisition of property which Jefferson had mentioned as an incentive to Monroe when he offered him the post. But most angrily Lewis evidently believed that representations had been made to Washington that as Jefferson's man he was suspect of just such action as had brought Burr to the dock on charges of treason. It stemmed from the expedition to return the Mandan Chief to his village which Jefferson thought essential to national honor whatever the cost.

Possibly, as Lewis wrote at this time, the territory was in "the most perfect state of Tranquility which I believe, it has ever experienced." Lewis was not in any such state when he set out to Washington to defend himself. Before he left St. Louis for the long journey eastward, he wrote a long and still startling letter, on August 18, 1809, to the Secretary of War. Expressing pain and calling God as his witness, he denied any misuse of funds. With more emotion, he addressed himself to another charge which he believed had secretly been made against him.

"I do most solemnly aver," he scrawled, "that the expedition sent up the Misoury under the command of Mr. Pierre Chouteau, as a military Command, has no other object than that of conveying the Mandane [sic] Chief and his Family to their Village—and in a commercial point of view, that they intend only, to hunt and trade on the waters of the Misoury and Columbia Rivers within the Rockey-Mountains and the Planes bordering those Mountains on the east side—and that they have no intention with which I am acquainted, to enter the Dominions, or do injury to any foreign Power."

Then he added a mystifying sentence:

"Be assured, Sir, that my Country can never make 'A Burr' of me—She may reduce me to Poverty; but she can never sever my Attachment from her."

He had been much with Jefferson, serving as his agent, in the summer and fall of the Burr trial. Could his letter suggest that his observations then made him feel that his country had made "A Burr" out of Burr? Hastening eastward less than two months later, on October 11, 1809, he came to violent death from bullet wounds and a cut throat at one of the stands, or crude hostels, on the Natchez Trace. The debate has continued since as to whether his death was suicide or murder. Jefferson apparently had no doubt. On his receipt of the news, he wrote, on November 26, 1809, from Monticello to Madison, indicating no such indignation as murder would have merited, of "the unfortunate Governor Lewis." Eight days later he spoke of "the catastrophe of poor Lewis." But this was in a letter largely devoted to a conversation with the sulking Monroe to whom he had offered the territorial governorship before. He was hopeful he and Madison could put Monroe in some civil or military post which would placate him. He mentioned that in the conversation Monroe had said that "he would sooner be shot than take a command under Wilkinson."

Jefferson waited four years to write his formal verdict of suicide. Lewis himself, Jefferson wrote, "did the deed," at a time when those about him were "alarmed at the symptoms of derangement." He indicated that he was not surprised, having known his family background and seen symptoms of mental depression in his behavior before he entrusted him with important enterprises. The President put emphasis on hereditary disposition to mental derangement.

Less attention has been paid to the second episode. Isham Lewis went back from Monticello to Kentucky. Not long afterward his and Lilburn's mother, Lucy Jefferson, died. Possibly while she lived she had restrained her sons who were known far and wide for the cruel treatment of their numerous slaves, whom they "drove constantly, fed sparingly and lashed severely." As a result the brothers had a runaway problem over which they brooded in heavy drinking. One seventeen-year-old boy named George had recently been retrieved after a skulking spell in the woods. Weak and sick he had little worth as a slave but, to deranged and drunken minds, value as an example. Soon after his return, or apprehension, he broke a glass pitcher which had belonged to Lucy Jefferson. The Lewis brothers herded all their slaves into the hog-killing house. There they butchered the boy, hand after hand, foot after foot, then flung his body into the fire. Let other slaves take warning.

In spite of terror, slaves whispered. One day a neighbor, as he passed the Lewis place, saw a human bone a dog had dug up. Infuriated plain white country folks found other remains of the hacked-up slave boy. There were threats of lynching. Then, on March 18, 1812, "Lilburn Lewis, gentleman, and Isham Lewis, yeoman" were indicted for murder. Before they were arrested, the brothers made a suicide pact to kill each other in the family burial ground. At this arranged mutual murder, however, Lilburn accidentally shot himself fatally. Isham decided not to go through with the agreement. He fled to the woods but was apprehended and sentenced to be hanged. He escaped, and tradition says that he was killed at the Battle of New Orleans.

Jefferson rendered no verdict in this case. Indeed, apparently he left no comment about this dreadful mark on his house and his blood. Word of the crime certainly came back to Monticello—and whispers about it probably to the slave quarters there. There was no outcry in Virginia about it as there had been in the case of Nancy Randolph. Two years after this time Randolph of Roanoke would accuse this sister-in-law of Jefferson's Martha of infanticide, the poisoning of his brother, fornication with a slave. He ranted on that Nancy was now married to Gouverneur Morris so that she could strike "her harpy fangs into an infirm old man." On this occasion the eccentric Randolph of Roanoke would meet in Nancy of Bizarre his equal in vituperation and scorn. Generally Virginia quietly buried its dead and its damned. Lilburn and Isham were Kentucky murderers. News came slowly, sometimes softened by distance. Possibly this crime was as irrelevant to Monticello as it was reticently treated there. On his hill Jefferson kept his philosopher's poise, maintained his magnificent correspondence, and labored earnestly in the building of the University of Virginia. It would be some time before he received other news related to the West which he could not disregard.

Before and after the death of Theodosia there seemed nothing deranged about Burr unless it was his almost manic need for sex, for appreciation, and for admiration. He needed beggars to thank him as well as women to love. He had to have young people to whom in the purest fashion he gave tenderness, teaching, and care like that he had given Theodosia and Nathalie. He preferred to be lavish in charity rather than prompt in the payment of his debts. Certainly there was no aberration shown in his practice as a lawyer. In all the buffeting he had met and misfortune, he had lost none of his perspicacity as a politician.

Certainly his hopes for political advancement were gone. There were those who stonily passed him by. Still the constant suggestion that he was treated as a pariah on his return to New York deserves some reconsideration. Some of the socially erect and some of the politically insecure avoided association with him. His friend Van Ness is said to have fallen away. There was no welcome for him in the homes of the Hamiltonians. He had friends and acquaintances new and old who looked upon him with expectation in the courts as well as curiosity on the streets.

Samuel Swartwout was happy to welcome and shelter him. So were the other two loyal Swartwout brothers. A good deal of confidence in his great prosecutor Jefferson had abated in the hard times under the Embargo. One evidence that there had been softening of resentment against Burr was given by Robert Troup. He could look back over the death of his friend Hamilton and remember that he had been devoted to Burr in their youth. Troup had built his fortune as manager of the Poultency properties from which position Burr's friend Williamson had been removed for his expansive extravagance. Now rich in real estate in western New York, Troup had retired from the law. He offered the returning Burr the use of his law library, until his son should come to the bar. Such books and evidence of esteem aided Burr in the remarkable fact that clients coming to him paid him fees of several thousand dollars in the first weeks after he returned to the bar.

Nothing so much indicates that Burr was not regarded as an untouchable as the conduct to him of Martin Van Buren. Possibly, as Wandell and Minnigerode strongly suggest, Van Buren was Burr's son. They pointed to the statement of John Quincy Adams in comparing Burr and Van Buren that "there is much resemblance of character, manners and even person between the two men." The younger Adams, however, in antagonism to Van Buren, might have liked in Puritan fashion to call him a bastard. Minnigerode and Wandell wrote that in Burr's lifetime many thought it was unquestionable that Van Buren was Burr's son. They noted that this ostensible son of a small tavern keeper had been placed in the law office of Burr's friend Van Ness, probably at the instance of Burr. One flaw in the supposition, however, is that when Burr, in 1804, was beset by so many enemies, young Van Buren declined to support him, clinging instead to the Clinton-Jefferson-Livingston-Hamilton alliance.

Certainly if Burr was a subject of universal obloquy in 1812, Van Buren as a very careful rising politician would hardly, as he did, have taken him into his house as a guest and into his company as a friend. Van Buren understood the political situation in New York at this time better than some who have described Burr as a man outside the pale. Jefferson had left the White House unpopular in an unhappy land. Now in 1812, when Madison was coming up for re-election at the outset of an unpopular war, politics in New York was mightily shifting. As early as 1809, DeWitt Clinton had made overtures to the Burrites but drew back when he was greeted by jeers from the "Martling" or "Bucktail" faction which recalled his utterances about Burr in 1804.

Now in the summer of Burr's return, Clinton was drawing away from the Virginians. And in a fashion for which he and his Cheetham had condemned Burr in 1804, he secured the attention of some Federalists. Indeed, at a meeting in New York on September 15, 1812, Clinton was proposed as candidate for President by Harrison Gray Otis, elegant Boston Federalist, who opposed the war and the Embargo. Many of his associates were still talking of a New England withdrawal from the Union like that to which Jefferson had thought Burr hearkened. Clinton ran a strange race. He was recommended to New England Federalists as a man who would stop war with England, to republicans as one who would fight it more vigorously. The Virginia dynasty was no longer riding high. Clinton was defeated by an electoral vote of one hundred twenty-eight to eighty-nine, but he got all of the Northern states except Vermont and Pennsylvania as well as five of Maryland's eleven votes. Had Pennsylvania voted with its Northern neighbors, Clinton would have been President.

So soon after his return Burr was not taking part in national politics. Indeed, he never played a leading role again. Biding his time he looked West, and early saw a chance to strike at the Virginia power. Many things happened which must have angered him. He saw his enemy John Armstrong put forward as Secretary of War in January 1813. And a month later Armstrong, evidently at the behest of Wilkinson, ordered Jackson, who had brought impatient Tennessee militia to Natchez, to dismiss his forces, go home and turn over all articles of public property to Wilkinson.

In a fury Jackson led his men home over the rough Natchez Trace. It was on this march that Jackson won his name "Old Hickory." Also, as a result of it, the bitterness of Burr toward Armstrong *et al.* was increased with his admiration for Jackson.

In New York, Colonel Burr cried to Van Buren, "I'll tell you why they don't employ Jackson. It's because he's a friend of mine."

One better reason might have been that, at the trial of Burr, Jackson on the Richmond streets had proclaimed that not only was Wilkinson a traitor but that Jefferson was a man afflicted with the demons of persecution.

In the generally disastrous war, the Colonel was delighted when the old friends Wilkinson and Armstrong fell to quarreling over Wilkinson's supposed incapacity in the fighting on the Canadian border. This led to another military inquiry and acquittal for the General. Despite acquittal he was never reinstated in the service. He lived, however, to write a confused and turgid defense or apology. Finally, he moved to Mexico, seeking land and serving at the last as a representative of the American Bible Society. He died, reputedly after an overdose of opium on December 28, 1825, to be remembered as perhaps America's most disreputable soldier, Benedict Arnold not excepted.

In addition to Wilkinson's troubles, Burr had the pleasure also of witnessing Armstrong's disgrace in the collapse of the defense of Washington and its burning by the British. With other Americans Burr was outraged at the burning of the capital, from which Dolley Madison emerged as a heroine while her husband, his Secretary of War, and his generals were humiliated. Certainly, Burr felt more gratification than regret when Armstrong, sputtering defense for his incompetence, was gently pushed out of office by Madison, whose own behavior had been less than heroic. Like many others, Burr was appalled at the gall of Armstrong in criticizing Jackson's role in the defense of New Orleans. Burr was ecstatic at the victory Jackson achieved there over Wellington's veterans. The tall Tennessean led, he knew, in his forces of Kentucky and Tennessee riflemen, coonskin-capped pioneers and the Baratarian pirates of Jean Lafitte, such men as he had hoped would flock to his standards in an invasion of Mexico.

General Jackson won his great victory early in January 1815. Actually the peace had already been made before the battle was won, but as news of his triumph spread across America, it was hailed by a nation the pride of which had been battered. Burr looked early beyond the cheers to a political prospect. He hoped the nation would follow Jackson, not Virginia.

How early Burr began to back Jackson for the Presidency is not clear. His admiration of "Old Hickory," based much on his gratitude to him, was evident soon after his return to New York. He gave strong expression of it in the house of Van Buren, who had scarcely heard Jackson's name. To Congressman John Sage, of New York, just after Sage had voted for the war declaration, he had talked about the generals Madison was appointing. Madison had told Sage that he thought it best, and in fact indispensable, to select those with some military experience in the Revolution. Jackson had been little more than a boy then. Burr told the Congressman: "I know that my word is not worth much with Madison; but you may tell him from me that there is an unknown man in the West, named Andrew Jackson, who will do credit to a commission if conferred on him."

Parton suggested that Burr, or one of his agents, may have been the "very intelligent gentleman from the Northeast" who, in August 1815, was making inquiries in Tennessee as to potential support in the West for Jackson for President. The certain fact is that Burr was pushing Jackson for President on November 20, 1815, fourteen years before the Tennessean reached the White House. Then he wrote a very serious letter on the subject to his son-in-law Alston. Even if a man with "no memory for injuries," he wished not only to put the hero of New Orleans forward but to use him as an instrument with which to strike his Virginia enemies.

He spoke balefully of the probable nomination of Monroe in the Virginia succession as "odious," and of the Congressional Caucus system of candidate selection as "hostile to all freedom and independence of suffrage." He described the Virginia Jeffersonian organization which he believed had systematically undertaken to destroy him as: "A certain junto of actual and factitious Virginians, having had possession of the government for twenty-four years, consider the United States as their property, and, by bawling 'support the Administration' have so long succeeded in duping the Republican public. One of their principal arts, and which has been systematically taught by Jefferson, is that of promoting State dissentions, not between Republican and Federal—that would do them no good—but schisms in the Republican party. . . . Let not this disgraceful domination continue." He could remember that well in his own case.

Then he gave his furious attention to Monroe, who, though once calling upon him as his friend in a threatened duel with Hamilton, had supplanted him as proposed Minister to France, and secretly opposed his nomination as Vice-President. It was for Monroe as well as Madison, he believed, that his removal as a possible threat to the Virginia dynasty had been arranged. Burr may have remembered best and with most bitterness that Monroe's much-trusted son-in-law, George Hay, had been his chief prosecutor in Richmond. Now he described Monroe with fury and contempt: "Naturally dull and stupid; extremely illiterate; indecisive to a degree that would be incredible to one who did not know him; pusillanimous, and, of course, hypocritical; has no opinion on any subject, and will be always under the government of the worst men; pretends, as I am told, to some knowledge of military matters, but never commanded a platoon, nor was ever fit to command one. *He served in the Revolutionary War!*' that is, he acted a short time as aide-de-camp to Lord Stirling, who was regularly [drunk]. Monroe's whole duty was to fill his lordship's tankard, and hear, with indications of admiration, his lordship's long stories about himself. Such is Monroe's military experience. I was with my regiment at the time. As a lawyer, Monroe was far below mediocrity. He never rose to the honor of trying a cause of the value of a hundred pounds. This is a character exactly suited to the Virginia junto.

"To this junto," he told Alston, "you have twice sacrificed yourself, and what have you got by it? Their hatred and abhorrence. Did you ever know them to countenance a man of talents and independence? Never, nor ever will.

"It is time that you manifested that you had some individual character, some opinion of your own, some influence to support that opinion. Make them fear you, and they will be at your feet. Thus far they have reason to believe that you fear them.

"The moment is extremely auspicious for breaking down this degrading system. . . . If, then, there be a man in the United States of firmness and decision, and having standing enough to afford even a hope of success, it is your duty to hold him up to public view: that man is *Andrew Jackson*. Nothing is wanting but a respectable nomination, made before the proclamation of the Virginia caucus, and Jackson's success is inevitable. . . .

"Exhibit yourself then, and emerge from this state of nullity. You owe it to yourself, you owe it to me, you owe it to your country, you owe it to the memory of the dead."

He urged Alston to advise Jackson to "be passive for the moment he shall be announced as a candidate he will be assailed by the Virginia junto, with menaces, and with insidious promises of boons and favors."

Alston did not receive Burr's letter until the middle of January 1816. He was already in a last illness which would bring him to death in September. Though only thirty-seven, he had not been able to muster courage in grief. He wrote Burr that he agreed with his sentiment "but the spirit, the energy, the health necessary to give practical effect to sentiment, are all gone. I feel too much alone, too entirely disconnected with the world, to take much interest in anything." The one interest he did express in this letter was securing from Vanderlyn the portrait of Theodosia and a copy of a small one which the artist had done of Nathalie.

Jefferson seemed almost as eager to be withdrawn from struggle as Alston did. He was beset not by grief but debt. Though he had come from Washington still loaded with debt in 1809, he was encouraged by good crops and good prices in the fall of 1812 when he counted an income of over ten thousand dollars a year. He looked forward to the extinguishment of his debts. He was overoptimistic. He was so pressed in 1813 that he took a doubtfully honorable course in handling funds he held in trust for his old friend Mazzei. Instead of putting this $6342 which he had received for the sale of his friend's lands into banks, which he distrusted, he put it to his own uses. He paid the interest regularly but when Mazzei's heirs wanted the principal Jefferson could not pay.

In 1815 his debts, as well as his patriotism, prompted the sale of his long-accumulated library to Congress to replace its library which had been burned by the British. Of the $23,950 which he received for his 6487 volumes, however, all but $8580 went directly to creditors. Then strangely and suddenly his final financial disaster came from the West in the third of the blows which struck him from that region.

Jefferson had not engaged in land speculation. His debts grew from elegant living and an almost mania for the constant remodeling of houses, particularly his beloved Monticello. He had been concerned with the West only as philosopher, politician, and protector. Indeed, as late as 1814, he expressed his feeling of ignorance about that region to a prospective settler who asked his advice.

"You could not have applied for counsel to one less personally acquainted with the Western country than myself, having never been fifty miles westward of my own house."

Many of his friends had long been westering. Among them were the Nicholas brothers, his neighbors and close friends. George Nicholas, who helped Jefferson with the Kentucky resolutions, was a heavy speculator in Western lands. He had, according to Thomas Abernethy, student of Western conspiracies, been involved in the Spanish Conspiracy in 1797. George's associations in Kentucky with Wilkinson and Harry Innes were, Abernethy said, "certainly devious." More important to Jefferson, his closer friend, Wilson Cary Nicholas, had joined George in Western investments. Wilson Cary's daughter had married Jefferson's grandson. Wilson Cary's ador as Jefferson supporter had something to do with Burr's description of him at the Richmond trial as "my vindictive and avowed personal enemy."

As Jefferson's personal friend, in 1818, he had gone on a note of Jefferson's for three thousand dollars which the Monticello sage greatly needed. And Jefferson was hardly in a position soon afterwards to refuse to sign a twenty-thousand-dollar note for him, related to Nicholas' overextension in Western land speculations. Nicholas went backrupt, died and left Jefferson caught with twenty thousand dollars more debt. He buried Nicholas in his own Monticello burial ground and buried his own hopes of escape from bankruptcy with him.

Monticello still maintained its impeccable and apparently impregnable façade. Behind it Jefferson resumed a beautiful correspondence with John Adams whom Beckley and Callender had helped him alienate. In eagerness but with irritation at the parsimony of the legislature and the suspicions of some clergymen, he pressed the building of the University of Virginia at the foot of his mountain. An endless stream of visitors, not all of them reverent pilgrims, came to see the patriarch at Monticello. Some only wanted a convenient and free stopping place on their way to the springs. Beggars, Overseer Bakon recalled, came in crowds and Jefferson could no more refuse them than could Burr. Some who filled the great house's halls and beds were friends of the philosopher's growing grandchildren. They danced in the south pavilion until midnight. "Famous kick-up dancing," one such said.

Despite the dancing and the music of violin and harpsichord, all was not gay around the master of Monticello. The immaculate palace on the hill was, as the years passed, beset by more than debt. Charles L. Bankhead, living at Monticello as the husband of Jefferson's grandchild Anne Randolph, was a drunkard. He once lunged at his father-in-law

Thomas Mann Randolph with a knife. And Randolph, who was becoming increasingly eccentric as his own financial affairs grew worse, soon would be beating his grown son Jefferson Randolph with a cane, and knocking down his son-in-law Bankhead with an iron poker. Before Jefferson died, Randolph, bitterly resentful of his father-in-law for not coming to his financial aid, and of his son, who handled Jefferson's precarious affairs, would be living apart from his family. Reluctantly Jefferson had to sell more slaves—or put them up as collateral with his richer son-in-law Eppes. The great Virginian hated slavery but he was fearful about Northern efforts to eradicate it. Evidently he feared that if he died bankrupt, his slaves might be sold for his debts. He was more afraid that what property he was able to save from the wreckage of his fortune for Martha and her children might be grabbed and wasted by the now evidently aberrant Thomas Mann Randolph. He drew a will to try to protect her and the best loved of his slaves, including members of the Hemings family.

In the midst of such harassment he remained the apparently imperturbable philosopher. On January 6, 1821, at the age of seventy-seven, he began to write his autobiography which only covered his life to his arrival in New York as Secretary of State in 1790. It is less easy to determine when he began to give the "calm revisal" to his *Anas*. This, he wrote, was done "after the lapse of twenty-five years, or more." It is not quite clear whether this refers to the section of the *Anas* ending with his retirement as Secretary of State in 1794, or from the last entry in later sections of the journal which ran to February 25, 1809. If from the first date, the revisions would have begun in 1819. There were not twenty-five years left to him after the last date. He was certainly, however, an old man scribbling for immortality. He was entitled to it. But he was sensitive about his reputation in these last years. As early as 1813, he did not welcome the publication of the papers of his late friend Tom Paine. "Retired from the world, and anxious for tranquility," he wrote, "it is my wish that they should not be published during my life, as they might draw on me renewed molestations from the irreconcilable enemies of republican government."

As he looked back to the past with concern for his story, he looked forward with an uncomfortable sense about his country. His own troubles must have been thick about him, in 1824, when Daniel Webster, already famed as orator, came to see him on his hill. Afterwards Webster wrote a long description of Jefferson and his visit to him. Some of Jefferson's friends felt that the New England statesman made the octogenarian Virginian more ill-looking than they relished, though all agreed that his account was written in "no unfair or unfriendly spirit."

The two great Americans talked of the past in terms of Patrick Henry, and of the present in contemplation of Andrew Jackson. Jackson had recently received the largest, though not the necessary majority, vote in the electoral college. Webster quoted Jefferson's comments on the Tennessean:

"I feel much alarmed at the prospect of seeing Jackson President. He is one of the most unfit men I know of for such a place. He has had very little respect for laws or constitutions, and is, in fact, an able military chief. His passions are terrible. When I was President of the Senate he was a senator; and he could never speak on account of the rashness of his feelings. I have seen him attempt it repeatedly, and as often choke with rage. His passions are, no doubt, cooler now; he has been much tried since I knew him, but he is a dangerous man."

That last was the same phrase which, used by Hamilton about Burr, had brought about their duel and his death. Certainly Burr did not share Jefferson's phrase about Jackson any more than he was willing to let pass Hamilton's remark about him when he was beset by the powerful combination which included Jefferson in 1804. As Burr had feared in his letter to Alston after 1815, Jackson had received caresses—notably from Monroe. Jackson did not share Burr's contempt for Monroe. He only entered the fight for the Presidency after Monroe's terms were ending. It is clear, however, that Burr did not give up his hope to see Jackson President. As he had wanted Alston to take the front place, he acted behind others later.

What Jefferson had feared when he talked to Daniel Webster did not take place then. Once more the Presidential decision went to the House of Representatives as it had in 1801. The vote of the country by electoral votes was: Jackson, 99; John Quincy Adams, 84; W. H. Crawford, 41; and Henry Clay, 37. However, in what the Jacksonians described as "bargain and corruption," Adams was chosen by the House. This time, watching, Burr knew there had been a deal. John Quincy Adams named Clay Secretary of State, but a fury had been built among the people for Jackson.

As the tumult grew far from Jefferson's hill, Burr was not visible in the campaign for Jackson which began immediately after the younger Adams was put in sedate possession of the President's House, which his father had left in dismay as Jefferson entered in triumph. Burr was among those present and pushing. His long loyal lieutenant Samuel Swartwout was one of those closest to Jackson. And with much greater visibility so also was now Van Buren. In the 1828 election, when Jackson swamped Adams, 178 to 83, Burr at seventy-two expected and required no other reward than the triumph itself. Possibly he deserved little credit for the victory. Burr's friends, Van Buren in honor as Secretary of State, and Swartwout in pay as Collector of the Port of New York, received the highest gifts Jackson had to give. And Jackson's election put together the city masses whom Burr had first mobilized and the Western settlers he had hoped to lead to glory. The combination seemed disastrous to the elegant.

Many of the revolutionaries of Jefferson's victory in 1800 had become definitely the respectables. Far from there being any pêle-mêle policy in the President's House now, Dolley Madison was addressed as "Her Majesty" without rebuke. The days of Jefferson's ostentatiously democratic dress were completely gone. Under Dolley's plumes, elegance in dress was absolutely required in the Madison administration. On one occasion President Monroe refused admission to a public function to a near relative who happened not to have a suit of small-clothes and silk hose. Such dignity attended the administration of John Quincy Adams that at its end one close to him described the change in Presidents as the arrival of King Mob.

Perhaps the fates were kind to Jefferson in ending his long and fruitful life before the "dangerous man" came into the house he himself and his friends had occupied so long. Indeed, the fates seemed almost melodramatic in terminating his time in the history of the republic. By a coincidence in history which would be scorned as corny in fiction, he and old John Adams, who had helped put the republic together, died on the same day in 1826—the day of the fiftieth anniversary of the first glorious Fourth of July. Then Jefferson had put his last words neatly together in his *Anas* for a timed explosion later.

The effulgence from this coincidence did not warm the house Jefferson left behind. Indeed, there is hardly a more chilling passage in American reminiscence than that of Margaret Smith about her second visit to Monticello a year and a half after Jefferson's death. The road up the great hill was so rugged and broken that the carriage could hardly move upon it. The place was startlingly silent. There was no train of domestics hastening with "smiling alacrity to show us forward," on the way "to the summit of the mountain, on which his now desolate mansion stands." Ruin had already commenced its ravages. At the house a poorly dressed little Negro girl cracked the door.

"We entered the hall once filled with busts and statues and natural curiosities to crowding, now empty! Bare walls and defaced floor, from thence into the drawing room, once so gay and splendid, where walls were literally covered with pictures like the Hall, bare and comfortless. The furniture, pictures, statues, servants, all gone, sold, yes sold. . . . Scarcely chairs to sit on!"

Jefferson had explained this progress to poverty to Madison in February 1826. He wrote, "of the long succession of years of stunted crops, of reduced prices, the general prostration of the farming business under levies for the support of manufacturers &c., with the calamitous fluctuations of value of our paper medium, have kept agriculture in a state of depression, which has peopled the Western states by silently breaking up those on the Atlantic; and glutted the land market, while it draws off its bidders."

There was much in this diagnosis. Yet this had happened to Virginia in the twenty-four of the twenty-six years of the century in which the Virginia dynasty had ruled in the nation. Also, not all Virginians had come to disaster as Jefferson did. Down the mountain Mrs. Smith found opulence and plenty still at Montpelier where Dolley was gracious and spry little Madison gay. As philosopher, Jefferson had served the sciences but especially applied his wisdom to agriculture. Yet his fields were worn. The Merino sheep he had brought to improve the flocks of Virginia had turned out not to be pure bred stock but something less and different. Few men in his or any other generation kept such a careful record of pennies as they ran through his fingers in extravagant living and building. Few men left more preachments about the wisdom of keeping outgo within income as he who never could. Few great philosophers have profited less from their own wisdom. Though he wrung his hands about the evils of slavery in his last years this greatest advocate of human rights feared that those who would be called Abolitionists would give the Negro freedom and a dagger at the same time. His Monticello when he died seemed a magnificent façade before debt and decadence, proximity to madness and the promise of disaster.

Aaron Burr presented no such façade. History has provided him with none. The story of his last years has been steadily written as a frayed, even disreputable one. The portrait James Vandyck did of him in his late seventies showed a cynical old man, with spectacles pushed up on his receding hairline, looking steadily at the world with cold eyes under arched brows. His arms were folded in a sort of posture of bored resignation. Certainly pictures of him drawn by biographers, including his own chosen Davis, were those of a financially irresponsible old goat. Even his generous, parental care and instruction of young people like that he had given Theodosia and Nathalie was sometimes ascribed to his propensity to bastardy.

Two relationships especially marked this period of his life. One related to the "conspiracy" in which he was both acquitted and destroyed. In his old age Luther Martin, that bulldog of Federalism, had come upon evil times as a result of misfortunes, drunkenness, extravagance, and illness. In 1821 the legislature of Maryland had passed a resolution compelling every lawyer to pay an annual license fee of five dollars to be turned over to trustees to care for the ruined old lawyer. But in 1823 it was repealed before its constitutionality could be tested, though only one protest had been made against it. Then Burr had gratitude enough and establishment enough to take the seventy-three-year-old man into his household for care until his death in 1826. Then Martin was buried in Trinity Churchyard where Alexander Hamilton lay.

Burr himself was seventy years old at that time. Four years later, in 1830, he suffered a stroke which temporarily paralyzed his right side. Yet, on Wednesday, July 23, 1833, the famous New York diarist Philip Hone made an entry: "The celebrated Colonel Burr was married on Monday evening to the equally celebrated Mrs. Jumel, widow of Stephen Jumel. It is benevolent in her to keep the old man in his later days. One good turn deserves another."

Hone's comment has been described as ironical. What good turn deserved another is certainly not clear. Neither is it clear as to whether the initiative in this marriage was taken by the seventy-seven-year-old Burr or the fifty-seven-year-old ex-beauty. Much mythology has been made about the earlier relationship of both Burr and Hamilton with this once delicious creature of easy virtue. Little notice has been given to the fact that one of the creditors who pursued Burr in Paris, in September 1810, was an agent of this woman's husband, Stephen Jumel. He was an immensely rich wine merchant who was said to have offered to bring Napoleon to America after Waterloo. Madame Jumel had come to America alone in 1826, but with a power of attorney by which she gained control over most of her husband's property. That gentleman had died in "re-duced circumstances" a little over a year before she married Burr. He died, it was said, from a fall from a wagon. No suggestion was made that he had been pushed.

Certainly Burr's marriage to her crowned in almost disreputable comedy Burr's last years. The marriage did not last long. She accused him of seizing and squandering her money. Three months after his marriage he was ill again. A second stroke partially paralyzed his legs. A third stroke crippled him. In the July which marked the first anniversary of their marriage Madame Burr, née Betsy Bowen or Eliza Brown, instituted suit in chancery for an absolute divorce alleging that Aaron Burr, aged seventy-eight, had recently committed matrimonial offenses "at divers times with divers females."

Amazingly perhaps, there were still those who loved Burr, including women of good character and great charity. Old friends were faithful. Like Jefferson he tried to arrange his papers. But his most significant last words were spoken rather than written. In his last days he made the statement that he would have as readily undertaken to invade the moon as to separate the Union. But when, in the year of his death, the same sort of Ameri-cans, whom he had hoped to lead, declared the independence of Texas, he cried his old purpose.

"There!" he exclaimed. "You see? I was right! I was only thirty years too soon! What was treason in me thirty years ago, is patriotism now!"

Possibly more significant was a quieter thing he said in his declining days. He had been reading in *Tristram Shandy* the passage in which Uncle Toby cupped an offending fly in his hand and released it out-side the window with the remark that there was room enough in God's world for both him and the fly. Burr closed the book and looked long be-fore him.

"Had I read Voltaire less, and Sterne more," he said, "I might have thought the world wide enough for Hamilton and me."

There could never have been enough room in American politics for Aaron Burr and Thomas Jefferson. Possibly there is not room enough in heaven. As Burr lay dying, he was addressed, as was the custom in those days, by a minister who spoke of "this solemn hour of your apparent dis-solution."

Do you, the preacher asked, have "good hope, through grace, that all of your sins will be pardoned?"

Burr declined to commit himself. "On that subject," he said, "I am coy."

Before he died Jefferson had written in precaution that the stone over his grave be so simple that "no one might be tempted hereafter to destroy it for the value of the materials." Burr left no such directions. Indeed, after he was buried with honor at Princeton beside his father and his grandfather, no stone was placed over his grave for twenty years. Then a relative provided a simple marker. It was mutilated by someone described as a patriotic vandal. The stone over Jefferson was overthrown and broken, too. Sometimes only enmity seems immortal.

SOURCES AND ACKNOWLEDGMENTS

I was reared in the worship of Thomas Jefferson. A bronze statuette of this great American, which stands in my house now, was the only idol before which my father, strict Methodist and staunch Democrat, bowed in all his days. In my instruction Burr and even Hamilton were villains in the American story chiefly useful to demonstrate the Jeffersonian triumph of good over evil. Certainly in terms of the principles of our heritage, we owe much to Jefferson, less to Hamilton, little to Burr. But all three deserve remembrance as the very human men they were once and together. There is no attempt here to write a biography of any of them. All have been sufficiently scrutinized as separate figures, but it seems to me inadequately in their companionship and conflict. This is especially true of Burr's place in the triangle. He was certainly more than Hamilton's murderer. His conflict with Jefferson has been much studied in connection with the "Burr Conspiracy." Too little attention has been given to the long interlocking enmity of the three men before Hamilton fell and Burr took the road westward to his doom.

What I have tried to do is to intermesh the lives of these three certainly formidable—and fallible—figures. In the process I have been surprised to discover much neglected material. I have followed some little-noticed rabbit paths into Burr's early adventures, foreshadowing his last great one, as land speculator in Western lands. They led me to his relationships in the first West with the great Revolutionary financier Robert Morris and the American land speculator and British secret agent Charles Williamson.

Strangely, I have found fresher aid from the biographers of natural-

ists than those of politicians. It was incredible to me to find how much
neglected has been John Beckley, a chief aide and informer of Jefferson.
Fortunately, two able writers in the field of botany, Edmund and Dorothy
Smith Berkeley, came across Beckley in writing a biography of John Clayton, the early Virginia botanist. They gave me the privilege of reading
their then unpublished study of this remarkable man. Similarly, I found
most about that cliché villain, the journalist James Thomson Callender, in
the biography of Alexander Wilson, the ornithologist, by Robert Cantwell.
As one of the most frequently kicked dead dogs in history, Callender
still may have been, as Abigail Adams said, the serpent which Jefferson
warmed before he himself was stung by it.

So much more needs to be known about other ladies, less articulate
than Abigail. Both the Theodosias of Burr are too little remembered. And
Nathalie de Delage (whose first and last names were spelled in various
ways), the lovely French refugee child whom Burr raised as his own, is
almost entirely forgotten. Did Alexander Hamilton build an elaborate
and imaginative lie about his affair with Mrs. Reynolds? Was Mrs.
Merry, the British Minister's wife, the virago Jefferson considered her, or
the charming woman of the world Burr admired? What did Jefferson's
much-loved friend, the letter writer Margaret Bayard Smith, mean when
she wrote her wish that Dolley Madison's virtue matched her grace? Was
Sally Hemings only a plantation creature shaped by slander to serve
Federalist politicians and such poets as Thomas Moore and William Cullen Bryant? Fortunately not all these ladies were silent while they lived.
Some whispered. Some screamed.

The two prime sources which put Burr and Jefferson together are, of
course, Jefferson's own *Anas* and the *Memoirs* and the *Private Journal*
of Aaron Burr, edited by Matthew L. Davis. Scholars, says the *Dictionary
of American Biography*, have shown Davis "a good deal of scorn." Also
they have rewritten him extensively. True, he was, from Burr's point of
view, in much "an unwise biographer." But almost all the material related
to Burr lies in the four volumes he edited. Fortunately some of the materials Davis suppressed were rescued by William K. Bixby in a later and
complete version of the *Private Journal*.

I am conscious of two great but unavoidable gaps in my sources.
Dumas Malone has not yet brought the volumes of his great life of Jefferson beyond the end of his first term as President, so short of the days
of the "Burr Conspiracy." In his tremendous task of editing *The Papers*

of Thomas Jefferson, Julian P. Boyd has only come to the period at which the Burr-Jefferson acquaintance began. Also, in a less comprehensive way I regret that Boynton Merrill, Jr., has not yet completed his study of the fantastic Kentucky murder committed by Jefferson's nephews. Strange as it may seem, despite the mountains of books about this period, much research still needs to be done about the early life of the republic and about the people who moved in it with ambition and devotion, and deviousness and enmity, too.

Mr. Jefferson is safe on his pedestal. Hamilton's picture properly graces the American ten-dollar bill. Colonel Burr, like Lucifer, will never be lifted to the heavens from which he fell, or was "hurled headlong." Any attempt to alter their allotted places now would be a pretentious folly. Yet, it should be possible to examine the anatomy of their antagonism. That is what I have tried to do.

As in all my writing, this book has actually been a work done in collaboration with my wife, Lucy. And we have rejoiced to have had as consultant and companion, sometimes professor in residence, Lodwick Hartley, sworn enemy of the dangling participle and the split infinitive. Many others have given me creative and sometimes admonishing (Hi, Julian) assistance. Particularly I name with thanks: William T. Alderson, John Bakeless, James A. Bear, Jr., John Broderick, Samuel Engle Burr, Jr., Carl Carmer, Thomas D. Clark, Elizabeth Boatwright Coker, Richard Dillon, Peggy Duke, Lloyd A. Dunlap, Vardis Fisher, William H. Gaines, Jr., Frank Graham, Pearl M. Graham, Patricia Gregory, John Melville Jennings, Mrs. A. Waldo Jones, Mrs. John Law, Helen G. McCormack, Marjorie P. Meares, David C. Mearns, Maria Leiper Miller, J. W. Muir, Fillmore Norfleet, Mrs. Henry C. Patterson, Margaret Price, Edward Roberts, Jr., George C. Rogers, Jr., Dorothy Valentine Smith, Louis L. Tucker.

BIBLIOGRAPHY

Abernethy, Thomas Perkins. *The Burr Conspiracy*, New York, 1954.

Adams, Charles Francis, editor. *Letters of Mrs. Adams, the Wife of John Adams*, 2 vols., Boston, 1841.

Adams, Henry. *The Life of Albert Gallatin*, reprint, New York, 1943.

————. *History of the United States During the Administration of Thomas Jefferson* and *History of the United States During the Administration of James Madison*, 4 vols., edited by Henry Steele Commager, New York, 1930.

————. edited and abridged by Herbert Agar. *The Formative Years*, 2 vols., Boston, 1947.

Adams, James Truslow. *The Living Jefferson*, New York, 1936.

Agar, Herbert. *The People's Choice*, Boston, 1933.

American Guide Series of the WPA.

Anderson, Dice Robbins. *William Branch Giles*, Menasha, Wisc., 1914.

Annals, 10th Congress, 1st Session.

Atherton, Gertrude. *The Conqueror*, New York, 1902.

Austin, Mary S. *Philip Freneau—The Poet of the Revolution*, New York, 1901.

Axelrad, Jacob. *Patrick Henry—The Voice of Freedom*, New York, 1947.

Bakeless, John. *Background to Glory—The Life of George Rogers Clark*, New York, 1957.

————. *Lewis and Clark—Partners in Discovery*, New York, 1947.

Bear, James A., Jr., editor. *Jefferson at Monticello*, Charlottesville, Va., 1967. (paperback)

Beard, W. E. "Colonel Burr's First Brush with the Law," *Tennessee Historical Quarterly*, vol. I, no. 1, March 1915.

Bemis, Samuel Flagg. *Pinckney's Treaty—America's Advantage from Europe's Distress 1783–1800*, New Haven, Conn., revised edition, 1960.

Bergh, Albert Ellery, editor. *The Writings of Thomas Jefferson*, Definitive Edition, Thomas Jefferson Memorial Association, 20 vols. in 10, Washington, D.C., 1907.

Berkeley, Edmund and Dorothy Smith. *John Beckley,* unpublished manuscript.

————. "John Beckley," *The Virginia Magazine of History and Biography,* October 1962.

Betts, Edwin Morris. *Thomas Jefferson's Garden Book,* Philadelphia, 1944.

———— and Bear, James Adam, Jr., editors. *The Family Letters of Thomas Jefferson,* Columbia, Mo., 1966.

Beveridge, Albert J. *The Life of John Marshall,* 4 vols., Boston, 1916.

Bicentennial Commission pamphlet, *Thomas Jefferson.*

Biddle, Charles. *Autobiography of Charles Biddle, 1745–1821,* Philadelphia, 1883.

Biddle, Francis. "Scandal at Bizarre," *American Heritage,* XII, 5, August 1961.

Biographical Dictionary of the American Congress 1774–1949, Washington, D.C., 1950.

Bobbé, Dorothie. *DeWitt Clinton,* New York, 1933.

Bowers, Claude G. *Jefferson in Power—The Death Struggle of the Federalists,* Boston, 1936.

————. *Jefferson and Hamilton—The Struggle for Democracy in America,* Boston, 1925.

————. *The Party Battles of the Jackson Period,* Boston, 1922.

————. *Pierre Vergniaud,* New York, 1950.

Boyd, Julian. *Number 7,* Princeton, N.J., 1964.

————. *The Spirit of Christmas at Monticello,* New York, 1964.

Bradford, Gamaliel. *Damaged Souls,* Boston, 1923.

Brady, Joseph P. *The Trial of Aaron Burr,* New York, 1913.

Brant, Irving. *James Madison—*
Vol. I, *The Virginia Revolutionist 1751–1780,* Indianapolis, 1941.
Vol. II, *The Nationalist 1780–1787,* Indianapolis, 1948.
Vol. III, *Father of the Constitution, 1787–1800,* Indianapolis, 1950.
Vol. IV, *Secretary of State 1800–1809,* Indianapolis, 1953.
Vol. V, *The President 1809–1812,* Indianapolis, 1956.
Vol. VI, *Commander in Chief 1812–1836,* Indianapolis, 1961.

Bridenbaugh, Carl. *The Seat of Empire,* Williamsburg, Va., 1950.

Brinton, Crane. *The Lives of Talleyrand,* New York, 1936.

Brooks, Van Wyck. *The World of Washington Irving,* New York, 1944.

Brown, Everett Somerville, editor. *William Plumer's Memorandum of Proceedings in the United States Senate, 1803–1807,* New York, 1923.

Brown, Ray. *Madame Jumel,* Jamestown, Va., 1965.

Bruce, Philip Alexander. *The Virginia Plutarch,* 2 vols., Chapel Hill, N.C., 1929.

Bruce, William Cabell. *John Randolph of Roanoke 1773–1833,* 2 vols., New York, 1922.

Bruckberger, R. L. *Image of America,* New York, 1959.

Burr, Aaron, *The Private Journal of,* reprinted in full from the Original Manuscript in the Library of Mr. William K. Bixby, 2 vols., Rochester, N.Y., 1903.

Burr, Samuel Engle, Jr. *Colonel Aaron Burr*, New York, 1964.

————. *Colonel Aaron Burr—The Misunderstood Man*, San Antonio, Texas, 1967.

————. *Napoleon's Dossier on Aaron Burr*, San Antonio, Texas, 1969.

Campbell, Tom W. *Two Fighters and Two Fines*, Little Rock, Ark., 1941.

Cantwell, Robert. *Alexander Wilson—Naturalist and Pioneer*, Philadelphia, 1961.

Carmer, Carl. *Genesee Fever*, New York, 1941.

Carter, Clarence E. "The Burr-Wilkinson Intrigue in St. Louis," *Bulletin Missouri Historical Society*, vol. X, no. 4, part 1, July 1954.

Carter, Hodding. *Doomed Road of Empire*, New York, 1963.

Catchings, Benjamin S., editor. *Master Thoughts of Thomas Jefferson*, New York, 1907.

Chase Manhattan Bank. *News*, September 1961.

————. Pamphlet, "The Church Pistols."

————. Pamphlet, "Water for Old New York."

————. Reprint from *Journal of American Pictorial Living*, "The Guns of Weehawken," by Doug Storer.

Chase Manhattan Bank N.A. "What it is and What it does," mimeographed article, May 1968.

Chinard, Gilbert. *Thomas Jefferson—The Apostle of Americanism*, Boston, 1929.

Claiborne, J. F. H. *Mississippi as a Province, Territory and State*, Jackson, Miss., 1880.

Clark, A. C. *Life and Letters of Dolly Madison*, Washington, D.C., 1914.

Clark, Thomas D. *Frontier America: The Story of the Westward Movement*, New York, 1959.

Coleman, J. Winston, Jr. *Slavery Times in Kentucky*, Chapel Hill, N.C., 1940.

Coues, Elliott, editor. *The History of the Lewis and Clark Expedition*, "Memoir of Meriwether Lewis" and "Supplement to Jefferson's Memoir of Meriwether Lewis," 4 vols., 1893.

Cox, Isaac J. *The West Florida Controversy*, Baltimore, 1918.

Cresson, W. P. *James Monroe*, Chapel Hill, N.C., 1946.

Curtis, William Eleroy. *The True Thomas Jefferson*, Philadelphia, 1901.

Dabney, Richard Heath. *John Randolph*, Chicago, 1898.

Daniels, Jonathan. *The Devil's Backbone*, New York, 1962.

————. *They Will Be Heard*, New York, 1965.

Davis, Matthew L., editor. *The Private Journal of Aaron Burr*, 2 vols., New York, 1838.

————. *Memoirs of Aaron Burr*, 2 vols., New York, 1838.

de Delage, Madame. "Memoirs of the French Revolution," *Forum*, vol. LXXIV, nos. 2 & 3, August, September 1925.

DeVoto, Bernard. *The Course of Empire*, Boston, 1952.

————. *The Journals of Lewis and Clark*, Boston, 1953.

Dictionary of American Biography.

Dillon, Richard. *Meriwether Lewis—A Biography*, New York, 1965.

Dumbauld, Edward. *Thomas Jefferson—American Tourist*, Norman, Okla., 1946.

Eaton, Clement, editor. *The Leaven of Democracy*, New York, 1963.

Eavenson, Howard N. "Some Side-Lights on Early Virginia Coal Mining," *The Virginia Magazine of History & Biography*, vol. L, 1942.

Eckenrode, H. J. *The Randolphs: The Story of a Virginia Family*, Indianapolis, 1946.

Encyclopaedia Britannica, 11th and 1967 editions.

Every, Dale Van. *A Company of Heroes*, New York, 1963. (paperback)

————. *Ark of Empire*, New York, 1964. (paperback)

————. *Forth to the Wilderness*, New York, 1962. (paperback)

————. *The Final Challenge*, New York, 1965. (paperback)

Falkner, Leonard. *Painted Lady*, New York, 1962.

Faulkner, Robert K. "John Marshall and the Burr Trial," *The Journal of American History*, 1966.

Fisher, Vardis. *Suicide or Murder*, Denver, 1962.

Fiske, John. *Old Virginia and Her Neighbors*, 2 vols., Boston, 1897.

Fleming, Thomas. *The Man from Monticello*, New York, 1969.

Foley, John P., editor. *The Jeffersonian Cyclopedia*, New York, 1900.

Furman, Kate. "General Sumter and His Neighbors," *The Southern Historical Association*, vol. VI, nos. 5 & 6, September, November 1902.

Gaines, William H., Jr. *Thomas Mann Randolph—Jefferson's Son-in-Law*, Baton Rouge, La., 1966.

Garland, Hugh A. *The Life of John Randolph of Roanoke*, 2 vols., New York, 1860.

Gayarré, Charles. *History of Louisiana*, vols. I–IV, 3d ed., New Orleans, 1846–1847.

Graham, Pearl M. "Thomas Jefferson and Sally Hemings," *The Journal of Negro History*, April 1961.

Gregorie, Anne King. *Thomas Sumter*, Columbia, S.C., 1931.

Hamilton, Allan McLane. *The Intimate Life of Alexander Hamilton*, New York, 1911.

Hamilton, J. G. deRoulhac, editor. *The Best Letters of Thomas Jefferson*, Boston, 1926.

Hillard, George S., editor. *Life, Letters, and Journals of George Ticknor*, 2 vols., Boston, 1876.

Hirst, Francis W. *Life and Letters of Thomas Jefferson*, New York, 1926.

Hunt, Charles Haven. *Life of Edward Livingston*, New York, 1864.

Jackson, Donald, editor. *The Letters of the Lewis & Clark Expedition*, Urbana, Ill., 1962.

James, Marquis. *Andrew Jackson—The Border Captain*, New York, 1933.

————. *Andrew Jackson—Portrait of a President*, Indianapolis, 1937.

Jefferson, Thomas. *The Life and Morals of Jesus of Nazareth*, New York, 1902.

Jellison, Charles A. "That Scoundrel Callender," *Virginia Magazine of History and Biography*, vol. 67, 1959.

Jenkinson, Isaac. *Aaron Burr*, Richmond, Va., 1902.

Kane, Harnett. *Natchez on the Mississippi*, New York, 1947.

Karsner, David. *Andrew Jackson—The Gentle Savage*, New York, 1929.

Kimball, Marie. *Jefferson War and Peace 1776–1784*, New York, 1947.

————. *Thomas Jefferson's Cook Book*, Richmond, Va., 1938.

————. "William Short, Jefferson's Only Son," *The North American Review*, September, October, November 1926.

Kirschten, Ernest. *Catfish and Crystals*, New York, 1960.

Letter from Aaron Burr to Edward Livingston, February 16, 1805.

Letter from Henrietta Maria Colden to Thomas Jefferson, February 5, 1791.

Letter from Thomas Jefferson to Wilson C. Nicholas, October 19, 1795.

Library of Congress. *The Jefferson Bicentennial*, Washington, D.C., 1943.

————. *The Story Up to Now*, Washington, D.C., 1947.

————. Photostat, "Subscription for the Author of the Declaration of Independence."

Logan, Deborah Norris. *Memoir of Dr. George Logan of Stenton*, Philadelphia, Historical Society of Pennsylvania, 1899.

Lord, Russell. *Behold Our Land*, Boston, 1938.

Loth, David. *Alexander Hamilton—Portrait of a Prodigy*, New York, 1939.

Lutz, Francis Earle. *Chesterfield, An Old Virginia County*, Richmond, Va., 1954.

MacAnear, Beverly. *Politics in Provincial New York*, unpublished doctoral dissertation, Stanford, Calif., 1935.

McCaleb, Walter F. *New Light on Aaron Burr*, Texas Quarterly Studies, Austin, 1963.

————. *The Aaron Burr Conspiracy and a New Light on Aaron Burr*, New York, 1966.

Malone, Dumas. *Jefferson and His Time—*
　　Vol. One, *Jefferson The Virginian*, Boston, 1948.
　　Vol. Two, *Jefferson and The Rights of Man*, Boston, 1951.
　　Vol. Three, *Jefferson and the Ordeal of Liberty*, Boston, 1962.
　　Vol. Four, *Jefferson the President—First Term 1801–1805*, Boston, 1970.

———— and Ranch, Basil. *Empire for Liberty*, 2 vols., New York, 1962.

Marryat, Frederick. *A Diary in America*, 1st Series, vol. 3, London, 1839.

Marshall, Thomas Maitland, editor. *The Life and Papers of Frederick Bates*, 2 vols., St. Louis, Missouri Historical Society, 1926.

Mayo, Bernard. *Thomas Jefferson and his Unknown Brother Randolph*, Charlottesville, Va., 1942.

Minnigerode, Meade. *Jefferson Friend of France*, New York, 1928.

Mitchell, Broadus. *Alexander Hamilton—The Revolutionary Years*, New York, 1970.

Moore, J. H. "The Death of Meriwether Lewis," *The American Historical Magazine*, vol. IX, no. 3, July 1904.

Morgan, George. *The True Patrick Henry*, Philadelphia, 1907.

Morrison, A. J. "Virginia Patents," *William and Mary College Quarterly Historical Magazine*, vol. II, no. 3, July 1922.

Mott, Frank Luther. *American Journalism*, New York, 1956.

————. *Jefferson and the Press*, Baton Rouge, La., 1943.

Myers, Gustavus. *The History of Tammany Hall*, New York, 1901.

Nevins, Allan. *The Evening Post—A Century of Journalism*, New York, 1922.

New England Paladium, January 18, 1805. (photostat)

Nicolay, Helen. *Our Capital on the Potomac*, New York, 1924.

Nock, Albert J. *Jefferson*, New York, 1926.

Norfleet, Fillmore. *Saint-Memin in Virginia: Portraits and Biographies*, Richmond, Va., 1942.

Oberholtzer, Ellis Paxson. *Robert Morris—Patriot and Financier*, New York, 1903.

Padover, Saul K., editor. *Thomas Jefferson and the National Capital*, Washington, D.C., 1946.

Parker, Arthur C. "Charles Williamson Builder of the Genesee Country," *The Rochester Historical Society*, vol. VI, Rochester, N.Y., 1927.

Parton, James. *The Life and Times of Aaron Burr*, 2 vols., Boston, 1890.

————. *The Life of Andrew Jackson in Three Volumes*, New York, 1860.

————. *The Life of Thomas Jefferson*, Boston, 1899.

Peterson, Merrill D. *The Jefferson Image in the American Mind*, New York, 1960.

————. *Thomas Jefferson and the New Nation*, New York, 1970.

Pettengill, Samuel B. *Jefferson—The Forgotten Man*, New York, 1938.

Phelps, Dawson A. "The Tragic Death of Meriwether Lewis," *The William and Mary Quarterly*, third series, vol. XIII, no. 3, 1956.

Pidgin, Charles Felton. *Blennerhassett or The Decrees of Fate*, Boston, 1901.

Pollard, James E. *The Presidents and the Press*, New York, 1947.

Randall, Henry S. *Life of Thomas Jefferson*, 3 vols., New York, 1858.

Randolph, Robert Isham. *The Randolphs of Virginia*, Chicago, 1936.

Randolph, Thomas Jefferson, editor. *Memoir, Correspondence and Miscellanies from the papers of Thomas Jefferson*, 4 vols., Boston, 1830.

Reinach-Foussemagne, La Comtesse H. de. *Une Fidèle—La Marquise de Lage de Volude 1764–1842*, Paris, 1908.

Renwick, James. *Life of DeWitt Clinton*, New York, 1840.

Reports of the Trials of Colonel Aaron Burr for Treason and for A Misdemeaner, taken in short hand by David Robertson, 2 vols., Philadelphia, 1808.

Rivers of America Series.

Rochefoucauld-Liancourt, Duc de la. *Travels through the United States of North America*, London, 1799.

Rogers, George C., Jr. *Charleston in the Age of the Pinckneys*, Norman, Okla., 1969.

––––––. *Evolution of a Federalist*, Chapel Hill, N.C., 1962.

––––––. "The Letters of William Loughton Smith to Edward Rutledge," *South Carolina Historical Magazine*, 4 articles, vol. 69, nos. 1, 2, 4, & vol. 70, no. 1, January, April, October 1968 & January 1969.

Rothert, Otto A. "The Tragedy of the Lewis Brothers," *The Filson Club Historical Quarterly*, vol. 10, no. 4, Louisville, Ky., October 1936.

Ruffin, Edmund. *Sketches of Lower North Carolina*, Raleigh, N.C., 1861.

Safford, William H. *The Blennerhassett Papers*, Cincinnati, 1864.

Saxon, Lyle. *Fabulous New Orleans*, New York, 1928.

Schachner, Nathan. *Aaron Burr*, New York, 1961. (paperback)

––––––. *Alexander Hamilton*, New York, 1961. (paperback)

––––––. *Thomas Jefferson*, 2 vols. in 1, New York, 1964.

Seaton, William Winston. *A Biographical Sketch*, Boston, 1871.

Seitz, Don C. *Famous American Duels*, New York, 1929.

Seton, Anya. *My Theodosia*, Boston, 1941.

Shreve, Royal Ornan. *The Finished Scoundrel*, Indianapolis, 1933.

Sloane, Eric and Anthony, Edward. *Mr. Daniels and The Grange*, New York, 1968.

Smith, Margaret Bayard. *The First Forty Years of Washington Society*, New York, 1965.

Sorley, Merrow Egerton. *Lewis of Warner Hall—The History of a Family*, Columbia, Mo., 1935.

Stone, William L. *Life of Joseph Brant—Thayendanegea*, New York, 1838.

Thomas, Elbert D. *Thomas Jefferson—World Citizen*, New York, 1942.

Todd, Charles Burr. *A General History of the Burr Family in America*, New York, 1878.

Turner, Orsamus. *History of the Pioneer Settlement of Phelps and Gorham's Purchase and Morris' Reserve*, Rochester, N.Y., 1851.

Turner, Orsamus. *History of Pioneer Settlement of Phelps and Gorham's Purchase and Morris' Reserve*, Rochester, N.Y., 1851.

––––––. *Pioneer History of the Holland Purchase*, Buffalo, N.Y., 1850.

Wandell, Samuel H. and Minnigerode, Meade. *Aaron Burr*, 2 vols., New York, 1925.

Warren, Robert Penn. *Brothers to Dragons*, New York, 1953.

White, Mary Virginia Saunders. *Fifteen Letters of Nathalie Sumter*, Columbia, S.C., 1941.

White, Newman Ivey. *Shelley*, 2 vols., New York, 1940.

Wilkinson, James. *Memories of My Own Times*, Philadelphia, 1816.

Wiltse, Charles Maurice. *The Jeffersonian Tradition in American Democracy*, Chapel Hill, N.C., 1935.

Wise, James Waterman. *Thomas Jefferson Then and Now, 1743–1943*, New York, 1943.

Index